The Left's Dirty Job

Pitt Series in Policy and Institutional Studies
Bert A. Rockman, Editor

Studies in Comparative Political Economy and Public Policy
Michael Howlett, David Laycock, Stephen McBride, Editors

The Left's Dirty Job

The Politics of Industrial Restructuring in France and Spain

W. RAND SMITH

University of Pittsburgh Press
University of Toronto Press

Parts of chapter 2 appeared, in slightly different form, in "'We Can Make the Ariane, But We Can't Make Washing Machines': The State and Industrial Performance in Postwar France," in *Contemporary France,* ed. G. Ross and J. Howarth (London: Frances Pinter, 1989). Parts of chapter 7 appeared in "Nationalizations for What? Capitalist Power and Public Enterprise in Mitterrand's France," *Politics and Society* 18 (March 1990), 75–99. Parts of chapters 8 and 9 appeared in "Industrial Crisis and the Left: Adjustment Strategies in Socialist France and Spain," *Comparative Politics* 28 (October 1995), 1–24; and "The Left's Response to Industrial Crisis: Restructuring in the Steel and Automobile Industries," in *The Mitterrand Era: Policy Alternatives and Political Mobilization in France,* ed. Anthony Daley (New York: New York University Press, 1996). I am grateful to St. Martin's Press, Macmillan Press Ltd, New York Unversity Press, *Comparative Politics,* Sage Publications, and Cassell Academic for permission to use this material.

Published by the University of Pittsburgh Press, Pittsburgh, Pa. 15261
Manufactured in the United States of America
Printed on acid-free paper

Published in Canada in 1998 by University of Toronto Press Incorporated, Toronto

Canadian Cataloguing in Publication Data
Smith, W. Rand, 1947–
    The left's diry job
    ISBN 0-8020-8231-9
    1. Industrial policy—France.   2.   Economic stabilization—France.
    3.   Industrial policy—Spain.   4.   Economic stabilization—Spain.   I.   Title.

    HD3616.F82S6 1998   338.944   C98-930812-X

10   9   8   7   6   5   4   3   2   1

Smith, W. Rand, 1947–
    The left's dirty job : the politics of industrial restructuring in France and Spain / W. Rand Smith.
          p.   cm.—(Pitt series in policy and institutional studies)
    Includes index.
    ISBN 0-8229-4053-1 (alk. paper). — ISBN 0-8229-5658-6 (pbk. : alk. paper)
    1. Industrial policy—France.   2. Economic stabilization—France.
    3. Industrial policy—Spain.   4. Economic stabilization—Spain.
    I. Title.   II. Series.
    HD 3616.F82S6   1998
    338.944—dc21   97-45319
                                                        CIP

A CIP catalog record for this book is available from the British Library.

For Caleb and Ellie

CONTENTS

FIGURES
AND
TABLES

Figures

Tables

ACKNOWLEDGMENTS

This is one of those rare occasions when one finds pleasure in acknowledging heavy debts. Through years and byways too numerous to recount, I have relied on friends and colleagues for advice, material resources, and contacts. Without their help, I would still be toiling away or would have given up long ago. Before giving individual credit, I must first salute another group collectively: the 108 public officials, business executives, and labor representatives in France and Spain who consented to interviews. During twenty-six months of fieldwork between 1987 and 1994, these respondents—ranging from former prime ministers to CEOs to local union activists—made my documentary material come alive by providing personal perspective and context. Though I have pledged in all but a few cases to protect their anonymity, I have liberally deployed their own words so as to make for livelier reading and to infuse the historical record with a sense of proximity and immediacy. Without these respondents' willingness to open themselves to my ceaseless, often naive questions, this study would be far drier and more abstract. It would also have been much less interesting and (dare I say it?) less fun to do. I only hope that this nameless means of public recognition can express, however partially, my gratitude to all of them.

In France, I had immense help from several sources. First, I am thankful to the directors of several *labos de recherches* for providing office space, library access, stimulating colleagues, and that most crucial of research resources: a telephone with message capability. I especially want to acknowledge the support and counsel, going back over two decades, of Jean-Daniel Reynaud, long-time director of the Laboratoire de Sociologie du Travail et des Relations Professionelles (later LERPSO). I am also grateful to Renaud Sainseaulieu of the Laboratoire de Sociologie de Changements Institutionnels and to Pierre-Eric Tixier of GIP-Mutations Industrielles. Second, I know I speak for scores of Americans researching in France when I praise the librarians at the Salle de Documentation de Presse at the Institut d'Etudes Politiques. Tirelessly cutting and filing newspaper articles, these librarians provide "one-stop shopping" for anyone seeking to piece together the chronology of events on virtually any issue. How could one even begin without those mountains of clippings, encased in crumbling blue folders and trussed in kite string?

Third, journalists not only write the news, they know everyone and make great sources for contacts. Experience has taught me that the first research stop in any European capital is the local office of the *Financial Times*. In Paris, successive FT bureau chiefs David Housego and David Buchan generously shared views and contacts. I also thank Eric Le Boucher of *Le Monde* for several long conversations and useful suggestions. Fourth, for aid in my analyses of the French steel and automobile industries, I am grateful to Bernard Espel and Daniel Richter of the CFDT and to Raphael Garcia, formerly of the CGT. In the Lorraine region, Gérard Sautré was a hospitable host during my stay. I owe special thanks to Anthony Daley, who freely shared his extensive knowledge of the steel industry and his Lorraine contacts and who provided several helpful critiques of earlier drafts.

Finally, several people in Paris helped me in various ways: Genevieve Acker of the Franco-American Commission has wisely counseled me through three Fulbright grants during the past twenty years; J. Paul Horne of Smith Barney shared his considerable knowledge of French political economy and gave me several invaluable contacts; Roland Cayrol, Guy Groux, and René Mouriaux— all of the *Centre d'Etude de la Vie Politique Française* (FNSP, CNRS)—gave me their insights into French politics and much encouragement; and Vincent Blocker, now of the Carter Center in Atlanta, generously proffered contacts, suggestions, and moral support.

In Spain as in France, an array of institutions and people made my task possible. Most notably, in Madrid the *Centro de Estudios Avanzados en Ciencias Sociales*, a unit of the *Instituto Juan March de Estudios e Investigaciones*, provided a welcoming, efficient base of operations. Thanks go especially to three staff members at the *Centro:* former director Victor Pérez-Díaz, general secretary Leopoldo Calvo-Sotelo, and library director Martha Peach, all of whom made my stay enjoyable as well as productive. I am also grateful to José María Maravall, professor at the *Instituto* and former Socialist minister of education and science (1982–88), for several essential contacts. In Madrid as in Paris, the *Financial Times* bureau proved a gold mine, as Peter Bruce, Tom Burns, and David White gave generous advice and access to their own press files. Patricia Zahniser of the Madrid Fulbright office also helped with arrangements, especially a lecture trip to the Universidad de Málaga. For my research forays into the steel regions of Asturias and the Basque Country, I received much assistance from Antonio López Pina, Miguel Angel García Herrera, and Jaime del

Castillo. For my study of the SEAT operations in Barcelona, Robert Fishman paved the way with many contacts and suggestions.

As all writers know, critiques, despite their occasional sting, make analysis deeper, meaning clearer, and writing stronger. I thank Chris Howell for giving me not one but two extremely detailed, insightful readings of earlier drafts. So, too, have others given valuable feedback on earlier versions or portions of this material, notably Nancy Bermeo, Anthony Daley, and Vincent Wright.

Finally, I gratefully acknowledge financial support from the following: the German Marshall Fund of the United States, the American Political Science Association, and the Fulbright European Regional Research Program. My home institution, Lake Forest College, supported me through several summer research grants and a sabbatical leave. As is customary in such acknowledgments, I exculpate, *d'avance*, all of the preceding institutions and individuals from any responsibility for whatever errors and misinterpretations remain.

My deepest thanks, of course, go to my "base camp," my family. In the implicit *pacto social* made within every writer's family, the other members invariably settle for less in the exchange: less of the writer's presence and attention to the essentials of daily life. My wife, Janet Kelsey, bore with grace and indulgence my hours before the keyboard and days away in the field. Beyond any reasonable call of duty, she insured that bills were paid and children were clothed and fed while I pursued research abroad on several extended trips. She also provided an essential goad for completing this book: a $100 bet that I would never finish. While I am relieved to prove her wrong, I cannot in good conscience demand payment; we both know who owes whom. Finally, my children, Caleb and Ellie, to whom I dedicate this book, have grown up—and put up—with this project for too much of their young lives. Without their patience I would never have summoned the concentration to finish; without their entreaties and distractions, I fear this project would have crossed the line between work and obsession. For pulling me back and keeping me "real," thanks, kids.

ABBREVIATIONS

AHM	Altos Hornos del Mediteraneo
AHV	Altos Hornos de Vizcaya
CCOO	Comisiones Obreras
CEOE	Confederación Española de Organizaciones Empresariales
CERES	Centre d'Études, de Recherches et d'Éducation Socialistes
CFDT	Confédération Française Démocratique du Travail
CNPF	Conseil National du Patronat Français
CSI	Corporación de la Siderurgia Integral
EC	European Community
ECSC	European Coal and Steel Community
EMS	European Monetary System
ERM	Exchange Rate Mechanism
FO	Force Ouvrière
Fr	Franc
INI	Instituto Nacional de Industria
PCE	Partido Comunista de España
PCF	Parti Communiste Français
PS	Parti Socialiste
PSOE	Partido Socialista Obrero Español
PSU	Partido Socialiste Unifié
PTA	Peseta
SFIO	Section Française de l'International Ouvrière
UCD	Unión de Centro Democrático
UGT	Unión General de Trabajadores

The Left's Dirty Job

INTRODUCTION

> When a Left government makes an industrial decision that has human costs,
> it does so because if it does not make that decision, the costs will be even
> greater. This is what I once called the Left's "dirty job."
>
> —Laurent Fabius, Socialist prime minister of France, 1984–1986,
>   in an interview with the author, 9 December 1987

Personal experience inevitably informs any scholarly work, and this book is no
exception. Of the myriad influences that shaped my interest in the politics of
industrial change, two experiences stand out. The first was a day in June 1977 in
the western French city of Nantes. Spending a Fulbright year in Paris, I had been
sent by a now-defunct English-language newspaper, the *Paris Métro,* to report on
the Socialist Party's biannual congress. During the morning of the last day, as
delegates were settling into another routine round of speeches, a speaker announced: "Felipe's coming—he left Bilbao early this morning." The effect was
electric. "Felipe," of course, was Felipe González, the thirty-five-year-old leader of
the Spanish Socialist Party, who only days before had led his party to a stunning
second-place finish in his nation's first democratic parliamentary elections in over
forty years. Overnight, his party, which only two years earlier had been hounded by
Franco's police, had become a strong contender for power.

Throughout the day, delegates were kept abreast of González's progress as he
made his way north by car. After lunch another speaker reported: "Felipe and his
party have crossed into France and are between Pau and Bordeaux." Like radio
flashes from the Lindbergh flight, frequent updates built expectations of the grand
arrival. At around 5:00 P.M. the delegates were told, "They've left La Rochelle and
are making good time." Just before 7:00 P.M. word went out that "Felipe's only an
hour away—he'll be here soon." Finally, the moment—and the charismatic hero—
arrived. Entering from the back of the hall, the road-weary emissary made his way
up the center aisle, shaking hands like a candidate, enveloped in thunderous
applause.

Waiting on the podium was a French *camarade* old enough to be his father:
François Mitterrand, head of the French Socialist Party. In the midst of his own
march to power, Mitterrand had reunited the disparate elements of the non-
Communist Left, taken over the "new" Socialist Party, and only narrowly lost the

1974 presidential election. Just three months before this congress, the Socialists had outperformed all other parties in local elections. Now Mitterrand stood poised to lead his party and the Left coalition to victory in the 1978 legislative elections. Such a triumph would signal the Left's first turn in power since the 1958 founding of the Fifth Republic.

As the two men, arms clasped aloft, saluted the exultant throng, the prospects for "Latin" socialism, indeed for European social democracy in general, seemed as bright as the leaders' smiles. Having witnessed this symbolic fraternal embrace, I became interested in what would become of the two surging political movements. If the French and Spanish Socialist parties, so long consigned to the political desert, came to power, what reforms would they attempt? My initial interest was heightened in the early 1980s when the two parties finally gained power—the first time Left parties had governed either nation in over a generation. In May and June 1981, Mitterrand and his party won both the presidency and parliamentary control; then, a year and a half later, in October 1982, González became prime minister with his own Socialist majority. Throughout the following decade, I continued to pay close attention to political events in France and Spain, knowing that the experiences of the two Socialist parties would be important not only for domestic politics in each country but for the fate of the European Left in general.

A second formative experience began on my return to the United States from that year abroad. Taking up a teaching position at Lake Forest College on Chicago's North Shore, I learned that the main plant of the American Motors Corporation was located in Kenosha, Wisconsin, twenty-five miles north of my office. Soon I was teaching a course on labor processes, and I began taking students to visit the plant. During the next few years my students and I observed a transformation. In the late 1970s the company was losing money, operating only one of its two assembly lines, and producing boxy, unreliable Gremlins and Pacers. The factory floor recalled the 1930s: dirty, dark, noisy, and cold. As workers glumly carried out their tasks, a sense of doom pervaded the grimy environs.

A change in ownership, however, brought hope in the early 1980s. Renault, the flagship of France's state-owned firms, bought a controlling share in AMC, dismantled one of the old lines, and replaced it with state-of-the-art equipment. Soon new Alliances were rolling off the line and winning kudos as "Car of the Year." While one old line was left standing like a darkened, silent memorial (or perhaps warning), the brightly lit working line, with its baby blue Unimate welders and other automated devices, hummed with quiet efficiency.

Alas, AMC's adventure with its French savior proved short lived. Not only did the Alliance quickly lose favor with American buyers, but changes occurring well beyond southeastern Wisconsin—in particular, shifting demand and supply trends in the world auto industry, coupled with Renault's own strategic errors—caused the company, beginning in 1985, to scale back investment, reduce production, and lay off workers. In early 1987, Renault finally gave up, selling its AMC stake to Chrysler. A year later Lee Iacocca announced his intention to close the plant. The denouement came two days before Christmas 1988, with the rollout of the last cars to be built in Kenosha. By this time, city officials were already planning to demolish the plant and convert the site to a lakeside marina.[1]

Within a decade my students and I had witnessed not only the end of a company whose roots stretched back nearly ninety years, but also the travails of a French "national champion" buffeted by shifting world markets. In the Kenosha microcosm we saw the rippling effects of profound changes in a global industry. We observed firsthand that massive investments, new managerial practices, union concessions, and the introduction of innovative models—all in the name of increasing competitiveness—were no guarantee of market success. In an environment of rapidly shifting technologies, production processes, and consumer tastes, corporate "adjustment," while imperative, remained fraught with risk.

The confluence of these strands of experience—the observation of the symbolic promise of socialism and the perils of global market competition—have led, circuitously but inevitably, to this study: an analysis of how recent Socialist governments in Spain and France grappled with industrial change. Specifically, this book compares how these governments confronted the "dirty job" of restructuring or adjustment in core industries experiencing long-term market decline.[2] Restructuring was indeed dirty in several senses. In both countries, adjustment constituted an essential task that prior governments had downplayed and even avoided, thereby making the Socialists' challenge all the more daunting. Ironically, Left governments had to confront the problem of reversing the failure of their conservative predecessors to strengthen private industry. Moreover, restructuring proved enormously costly and controversial, evoking widespread collective protests and imposing difficult policy choices on top policy makers. Restructuring, it is no exaggeration to claim, was the most wrenching, preoccupying issue faced by both governments during the 1980s and early 1990s.

In analyzing the cases of Spain and France, this study raises broader questions concerning economic governance in industrialized democracies. Most generally, this book asks: What choices do governments in industrialized democracies have as they confront transformations in their nations' economic and industrial structures? As today's headlines make clear, corporate "downsizing" is only one manifestation of a global reshuffling of economic assets and liabilities that is remaking not only markets but the political structures and practices that govern those markets. Contemporary industrial change places governments in the crossfire between conflicting pressures: on the one hand, (voting) citizens demanding economic stability and job protection, and on the other, capitalist firms and international financial markets advocating efficiency and "flexibility."

Although all governments must cope with these tensions, the issues are especially acute for governments dominated by parties of the Left. The electoral and organizational structures of these parties rest to a large extent on the support of workers affected by industrial change, who naturally expect Left governments to "help their own." At the same time, owners and managers, ranging from domestic manufacturers to international financiers, naturally tend to view Left governments skeptically, and often brandish the threat of capital strikes if Left governments become too labor friendly. The political space for maneuver by Left governments thus appears particularly restricted. The French and Spanish cases, then, exemplify a policy dilemma that confronts all governments in liberal capitalist societies.

Chapter 1 sets the stage for this book's analysis by assessing the nature and political implications of contemporary industrial change. This chapter also introduces the French and Spanish cases, summarizes the book's main conclusions, and sets forth a framework for explaining the French and Spanish governments' industrial-adjustment responses.

Part II analyzes the economic and political legacies that initially shaped Socialist rule. Chapter 2 weighs the long-term economic impact of Gaullism and Francoism, while chapter 3 examines the influence of leadership strategies, specifically attempts by Mitterrand and González to build governing coalitions. Part III then investigates how these governments approached the general issue of macroeconomic adjustment, with chapter 4 tracing the fate of the Mitterrand government's initial *relance* or stimulus plan and chapter 5 evaluating the González government's more orthodox strategy.

Part IV considers the problem of industrial restructuring. Chapter 6 analyzes the González government's effort at public-sector reform and industrial "reconversion," and chapter 7 assesses the nature and fate of the Mitterrand government's sweeping nationalization program. Chapters 8 and 9 compare how French and Spanish Socialists carried out adjustment in two key industries, steel (chapter 8) and automobiles (chapter 9). Chapter 10 concludes the book by reframing the central arguments and explanations.

1

Dilemmas of Industrial Restructuring

Profound changes have transformed the world economy during the past two decades. Within the advanced industrial nations, these changes can be characterized as declining performance amid shifts in the nature of economic activity itself.[1] During the two decades following the 1973 oil shock, growth in these nations declined roughly by half while inflation and unemployment doubled, as compared with the two decades prior to that year. Although inflation has slowed significantly since the mid-1980s, growth has remained highly cyclical—robust in the late 1980s but followed by a sharp recession, then modest recovery, in the 1990s. Meanwhile, unemployment has stayed consistently higher than in the pre-1973 years. Among nations belonging to the Organisation for Economic Co-operation and Development, declining performance on all three indicators—growth, inflation and employment—has been especially steep for the members of the European Union (EU).[2]

Accompanying this weakening performance has been a series of broad shifts in the nature of global economic activity, including trade expansion, the emergence of the newly industrializing countries (NICs) as export competitors, and the internationalization of capital markets and corporate operations. Other trends include the formation of global corporate alliances, the consolidation of regional trading and monetary blocs such as the EU, and changes in technology, industrial production, and management organization.[3]

Of these shifts, one of the most controversial, both conceptually and politically, has been a transformation in basic economic structures. According to popular belief, advanced industrialized economies are undergoing a triple transition. First, in the emerging "postindustrial" society, information-based services are replacing industrial manufacturing as the motor of economic growth and job creation.[4] Second, within manufacturing itself, high-technology "sunrise" industries such as microprocessing, biotechnology, and telecommunications are displacing "sunset" industries such as steel and textiles, because the latter have succumbed to rising energy prices, falling demand, new sources of supply (especially in the export-led NICs), and technological obsolescence.[5] Finally, these broad changes are affecting operations within firms, as Fordist work methods featuring long, standardized production runs and specialized, repetitive tasks, all taking place within large, centralized units, give way to post-Fordist practices embodying rapid innovation, lean production, flexible specialization of workers and machines, and smaller, decentralized structures.[6] The nature of this triple transition remains subject to debate.[7] There is little dispute, however, that the *political* implications of these changes are far reaching. At the broadest level, these structural shifts have reinforced the power of business interests—in manufacturing and in service industries such as finance— in relation to other sectoral interests such as labor or agriculture.[8] In the case of labor, the growing stress on capitalist flexibility—in terms of both general mobility and discretion over work place and labor market practices—has tended to undermine organized labor's role as an agent of work place representation.[9]

At the same time, changes in class structure, economic organization, and mass attitudes have eroded the electoral appeal of social-democratic parties that historically have relied on working-class voters.[10] Accompanying these trends has been an ideological shift among major political parties, including those on the Left, toward such neoclassical precepts as free enterprise, competition, self-reliance, "less government" (deregulation, privatization, budgetary restraint), and tolerance of economic inequality and insecurity.[11] Finally, there is evidence that such tolerance has been born of necessity created by rising unemployment (especially long-term unemployment), the expansion of various kinds of "precarious" labor such as part-time and temporary work, general wage stagnation, and income polarization.[12]

These economic changes and power shifts have created new challenges for governments of the industrialized democracies, which have faced growing pressures, from both business and labor, to guide economic change and cope with the consequences. Paradoxically, these pressures have increased at the same time as growing interdependence among economic actors across national borders has diminished the ability of individual states to regulate economic activity.[13] Governments are increasingly caught in a triple bind of rising demands for action, declining efficacy, and challenged legitimacy.

How have governments responded to these economic and political challenges? Broadly speaking, their responses have taken two forms: industrial promotion and industrial restructuring. First, most governments have sought to promote development of targeted industries and technologies, especially high-technology industries in rapidly expanding markets. These efforts have taken many forms, including government-supplied infrastructure, tax breaks, capital grants and loans, protective trade measures, and guaranteed public markets. Promotion is not merely a question of governments helping private enterprise; just as often, especially in Western Europe, publicly owned firms have assumed the role of developing and disseminating innovative technologies. Even in nations such as the United States, which claims to leave the initiative for industrial innovation in private hands, government agencies such as the Department of Defense and NASA have been central to promotion efforts. Increasingly, governments are viewing such promotion as essential for preserving and enhancing national security.[14]

In addition to promotion, governments have also encouraged restructuring or adjustment in older, contracting industries. Economically, the process appears straightforward: the alignment of supply (capital and labor) with structural changes in demand. Adjustment thus encompasses measures taken by both private and public actors to improve economic performance, notably productivity and profitability, in industries experiencing medium- or long-term market decline. Politically, however, restructuring has proved problematic because its effects tend to be sudden, massive, and dislocating. By its very nature, industrial restructuring undermines individual and collective stability, often producing immediate unemployment for workers and long-term economic distress for communities and regions. Adjustment has often provoked domestic resistance and violence, and even trade tensions between nations.

Predictably, workers facing job loss have demanded that their jobs and factories be maintained, while local owners and managers, confronting foreign competitors who are taking away customers, also clamor for government help. These and other groups have often pressured public officials to shelter vulnerable domestic markets while boosting exports. Industrial adjustment, therefore, has frequently taken the form of increased tariffs, negotiation of "voluntary" import quotas, stringent import regulations, export subsidies, and government-to-government agreements to increase foreign market access or win public works contracts. By raising the specter of economic nationalism, adjustment has often been at odds with countertrends of international integration and trade liberalization. Cases in point include the fractious, politically charged trade in automobiles and steel among the United States, Europe, and Japan. Far from constituting a smooth, market-led transition to a postindustrial order, restructuring in basic industries has taken place on contested political terrain, evoking grassroots mobilization and requiring government mediation between business and labor.

This book focuses on the politics surrounding industrial restructuring, a process that forces governments to promote economic growth while trying to preserve social peace and political support—goals that clash, at least in the short term. Put starkly, democracies face the dilemma of "how to encourage (or at least not hinder) the continual resource reallocation process that is crucial to economic growth while reconciling the dictates of economic efficiency with other widely held values including redistributive justice, job stability, and community preservation."[15] Although coping with this tension has challenged all governments regardless of partisan makeup, the problem has been especially difficult for those dominated by parties of the Left.[16] For such governments industrial adjustment forces a possible trade-off between an ideological commitment to social solidarity and the capitalist imperative of efficiency. Doctrinally committed to defending working-class interests—and in some cases even pledged to break with capitalism and launch a transition to socialism—Left governments also face market pressures that contradict such aims.

One would naturally expect Left governments to seek to protect the jobs of workers in distressed industries, and thus to be more likely than Center or Right governments to adopt such measures as subsidies, protectionist trade policies, and ownership changes (such as worker-owned cooperatives or even nationalization).[17] If "shedding" workers became imperative, Left governments, one would predict, would be more likely to soften the blow through income-support programs, worker retraining, and investment incentives for distressed regions. Yet for both structural and political reasons, Left governments are pressured to follow orthodox adjustment strategies that favor market efficiency. These governments, whatever their ideological goals, depend on private capital to generate investment, growth, employment, and tax revenues, and thus must promote capitalist interests to ensure their own political survival.[18] In the case of industrial adjustment, this dependence often requires job cuts in inefficient or unprofitable industries.

Moreover, for electoral reasons such governments cannot base their program on the interests and preferences of any single class such as industrial workers. Not only are such interests and preferences far from uniform, but industrial workers, as mentioned above, form a diminishing segment of the electorate. To amass a majority of votes, Left parties must appeal to nonworkers as well, but in so doing they "erode exactly that ideology which is the source of their strength among workers."[19] As a result, the prospects for a distinctive Left approach to economic policy in general and industrial adjustment in particular do not appear bright.

What choices, then, do Left governments have as they confront industrial-adjustment crises? If economic policy concerns the "relationship between structural constraints and political choice,"[20] must Left governments accede to the former, or can they exercise a margin of autonomy in order to realize their ideological goals? The relevant literature, which focuses on whether and how the partisan composition of government affects economic policy, gives no clear answer.[21] Research indicates that during the 1970s social-democratic governments, especially those allied with strong, centralized labor unions, did adjust fairly successfully to the initial global downturn. Compared with governments dominated by Center and Right parties, social democrats promoted higher growth and employment along with less labor strife and lower inflation.[22] This tendency, however, largely evaporated during the 1980s.[23] Left governments still tend to favor certain macroeconomic strategies, in particular supply side strategies focusing on public investment, wealth redistribution, and human capital development, as opposed to traditional monetary and fiscal policies.[24] To date, however, there has been little examination of Left versus Right and Center approaches to the problem of industrial adjustment.[25]

TWO CASES: FRANCE AND SPAIN

This book addresses the policy dilemmas faced by Left governments by comparing industrial-restructuring strategies in France and Spain from the early 1980s to the mid-1990s, a period during which both nations were governed largely by parties and leaders of the Left.[26] This period also witnessed two major recessions (1980–1983 and 1990–1993) that produced rising unemployment and financial losses for several basic industries. For Spain, this era brought entry into the European Community (EC) in 1986, followed by membership in the European Monetary System (EMS) in 1989. In both France and Spain, rule by Socialist governments coincided with mounting international pressures to enact adjustment programs to improve industrial competitiveness.

These governments, of course, came to power within a broader historical context marked by the long-term shifts in productive activity discussed above. Despite differences in overall output, level of industrial development, and per capita income, France and Spain have both experienced a decline in manufacturing accompanied by a strong increase in the service sector.[27] These shifts have had important political and policy consequences, influencing not only labor market policies but also policies concerning regional development, transportation infrastructure, housing, and education. Industrial shifts have raised questions about the state's role in seeking to retard or accelerate industrial change—questions that became especially acute after Socialists took power in the early 1980s.

In the context of industrial adjustment, the French and Spanish cases are important for three reasons. First, since the second oil shock of 1979 these governments have been in power longer than any other Left government in Europe and thus have had the time and the political strength to carry out their economic strategies. Second, both governments, coming to power after long periods of conservative rule, took office in an atmosphere of heightened public expectations that created a window for reform.[28] Finally, both Socialist parties rose to prominence vowing to reshape domestic economic priorities and structures. The French Parti Socialiste (PS), pulled leftward during the 1970s by its alliance with the Parti Communiste Français (PCF), went so far as to promise that it would "changer la vie," change the way people lived. Its Spanish counterpart, the Partido Socialista Obrero Español (PSOE), although rejecting both a Communist alliance and a PS-style program of sweeping reforms, advocated such measures as a massive job creation program and selective nationalizations. All three factors—political longevity, initial public expectations, and party program—favored a distinctive Left approach to industrial adjustment. Thus the French and Spanish cases are critical in the sense of providing relatively robust examples of whether such an approach is possible.

THE CENTRAL ARGUMENT

How did Socialist governments in France and Spain respond to the challenge of industrial adjustment? To address this question, we must first ask what choices they had. Generally speaking, any restructuring strategy consists of both *capital* and *labor* adjustment. The former refers to efforts made by companies to restructure their capital stock or supply—including such aspects as technology, product lines, productive capacity, and relations with suppliers—in order to respond to changes in market demand. Labor adjustment encompasses the (usually simultaneous) adjustment of labor supply, including such aspects as total manning levels, work force composition and qualification, pay levels, and work organization.

Given this basic distinction, table 1.1 presents four ideal types of adjustment approaches potentially available to *any* government. These are distinguished by the degree and nature of government intervention and proceed roughly from lesser to greater market regulation by public authorities.[29] For each type, table 1.1 notes the core goal along with the main capital and labor adjustment measures.

The first approach, Type A (market-embracing), stresses rapid market-driven adjustment that, far from avoiding or delaying adjustment, welcomes it. Inspired by a neoliberal belief in the market as an efficient allocation mechanism, this approach eschews government intervention that would mitigate or cushion labor displacement and thus rejects government subsidies to maintain production or postpone labor adjustment. This approach does, however, permit government intervention in order to create more flexible labor markets that would enable employers to respond more quickly and fully to market shifts. Given its stress on market exposure, this approach encourages privatization of public-sector firms and economic deregulation in general.

Like the Type A approach, the Type B (market-adapting) approach accepts the market as the final arbiter of restructuring strategy. It differs from the Type A approach, however, in permitting government intervention to effect an "orderly exit" of workers whose jobs must be eliminated. It thus allows more time for adjustment than the Type A approach, because the goal is to restructure without causing widespread economic distress or community upheaval. The Type B approach is also more labor friendly than the Type A approach in that it seeks to absorb (though not eliminate) the shocks of labor displacement. It is therefore willing to provide temporary and even long-term subsidies to labor. Under a Type B approach, labor measures can be of two types, active and passive. Active measures encourage redeployment through retraining, relocation incentives, and so forth, whereas passive measures provide income maintenance through such means as severance and early retirement benefits.

The Type C (market-modifying) approach is a qualitative variant of the Type B approach, in that it accepts the need for labor adjustment—and thus accepts market equilibrium outcomes in the long term—but offers a different kind of quid pro quo to labor than the Type B approach. Whereas the latter approach provides mainly quantitative trade-offs to labor—for example, income support and job retraining—the Type C approach extends to labor the prospect of enhanced institutional power. In exchange for labor's compliance with restructuring measures, this approach also seeks to restructure the institutions that govern capital and labor markets. Labor representation is extended to new sites, at the firm level (as in labor-management codetermination arrangements) and within policy-determining bodies at the national level (as in wage earner funds).

Finally, the Type D (market-resisting) approach seeks labor and social stability over other goals and thus seeks to protect threatened industries. Adjust-

Table 1.1   Government Approaches to Industrial Adjustment: Four Ideal Types

A. Market-Embracing

Core goal:	to promote rapid market-driven adjustment in response to international and domestic market forces (with minimal government intervention)
Capital adjustment measures:	deregulation of "inefficient" capital markets while adjusting supply (especially productive capacity) to prevailing market trends
Labor adjustment measures:	use of deregulation to create more flexible and "efficient" labor markets. No special measures for dislocated workers— labor market clears through market processes

B. Market-Adapting

Core goal:	to gradually adjust capital and labor to market forces (with government measures to cushion economic shocks)
Capital adjustment measures:	gradual exposure of firms to market competition in order to avoid sudden crisis or collapse
Labor adjustment measures:	promotion of "orderly exit" of labor. Active measures include job retraining, incentives for establishing small businesses, systems for better matching labor supply and demand, and relocation incentives. Passive measures emphasize income support such as severance payments and preretirement systems

C. Market-Modifying

Core goal:	as in B
Capital adjustment measures:	as in B
Labor adjustment measures:	as in B, promotion of "orderly exit" of labor, but on the basis of an explicit exchange with organized labor designed to reinforce labor's institutional power. In exchange for labor's compliance with adjustment measures, the government seeks to strengthen labor representation in economic decision making at the micro (firm) level and the macro (national) level

D. Market-Resisting

Core goal:	to avoid or delay adjustment of productive capacity and labor
Capital adjustment measures:	price controls, subsidies to cover firms' operating losses, discriminatory trade policies to protect the domestic market, use of public contracts and projects to favor domestic firms and sectors
Labor adjustment measures:	subsidies to preserve jobs

ment is delayed for as long as possible or avoided altogether. In the process, governments employ protectionist measures such as operating subsidies and discriminatory trade practices in order to favor domestic firms. With its emphasis on maintaining labor stability, the Type D approach tends to favor nationalization of lame-duck businesses as an alternative to outright collapse.

Can any of these adjustment approaches be considered characteristically "Left"? To the extent that the Type A approach favors market deregulation, thereby leaving dislocated workers to fend for themselves, it has little in common with such classic Left themes as full employment, job security, and income maintenance and redistribution. The Type D approach, however, embodies such goals, and thus can be considered a Left adjustment strategy.

The Type B and Type C approaches, by rejecting protectionism in favor of long-term adjustment to market shifts, depart from traditional Left intransigence in the face of capitalism's "creative destruction." Yet the Type C approach retains the Left's emphasis on resource redistribution, notably redistribution of power resources. Recognizing the inefficiency and futility of trying to stave off the inevitable (namely, exposure to market competition), the Type C approach seeks to control the process, at least partially, by strengthening labor's voice in institutions that regulate competition. By contrast, the Type B approach does not challenge either the primacy of the market or existing regulatory mechanisms, but seeks only to soften the economic disruption wrought by capitalist competition.

With this range of possible approaches, how did Left governments in France and Spain respond? This book will argue that both governments ultimately adopted variants of the Type B approach. Faced with market failures in older industries such as steel and automobiles, the Mitterrand and González governments took measures that, directly or indirectly, eliminated the jobs of thousands of workers who constituted an important base of Socialist support. What was striking was not the fact of job loss—after all, employment had declined in virtually all such industries in advanced industrial nations during the previous two decades—but the scale and vigor of the cuts, a result that was all the more unexpected (and, indeed, ironic) in light of both governments' preelection pledges to defend employment while transforming capitalism. At the same time, these governments accompanied their drive to facilitate labor reductions with generous programs to soften unemployment shocks for affected workers. Most notably, both relied heavily on passive measures that would maintain the purchasing power of laid-off workers. By contrast, active labor policies such as worker retraining, while present, were of only secondary importance and effect.

It is worth emphasizing what these adjustment strategies were not. The two governments clearly rejected a neoliberal Type A approach. Although both have been accused of "betraying" their own workers,[30] the evidence does not support the claim that affected workers were abandoned to the vicissitudes of unregulated labor markets. The Socialist leaders of France and Spain also rejected the once-favored Type D strategies of the Left that sought to avoid or delay adjustment; in both countries, market "discipline" was accepted as the guiding logic of adjustment. Despite the early Mitterrand government's flirtations with economic nationalism, by the mid-1980s France and Spain had firmly rejected that ideology.[31] Finally, neither government showed interest in pursuing a Type C approach that would empower organized labor in exchange for labor's support for adjustment. As we will see, such an approach held little appeal for either the governments or the main unions.

Neither neoliberal, protectionist, nor socialist (in the sense of empowering worker vis-à-vis owners), industrial adjustment in France and Spain resembled other restructuring efforts throughout Western Europe during the 1980s and 1990s. Why the two countries' Socialist governments failed to implement distinctive industrial-adjustment programs remains a key question, especially given their longevity, initial public support for reform, and electoral promises. A central goal of this book is to explain this failure.

This study also argues that despite a general similarity in the restructuring strategies employed by France and Spain, the processes followed by the two countries differed in important respects. Although both governments ultimately pursued parallel goals, the patterns of implementation diverged in three major ways.

First, the trajectory of industrial adjustment in Spain was more coherent and consistent than in France. Beginning with a 1983 white paper establishing a basis for industrial "reconversion," the González government approached restructuring methodically and holistically. Throughout the next decade, adjustment remained a central, consistent element of macroeconomic strategy. In France, by contrast, restructuring strategy underwent a dramatic shift that paralleled the 1982–1983 U-turn in macroeconomic policy. Initially, the Mitterrand government sought to stimulate growth *(relance)* and redistribute income while employing a state-led adjustment approach that nationalized several large industrial firms and nearly all of the banking sector. Conventional adjustment was downplayed or delayed; far from downsizing industries such as steel and coal, political leaders sought to expand production. Abandonment of the *relance* strategy in 1983, however, also forced a shift in restructuring strategy. Thereafter, the goal was to reduce excess capacity and improve productivity, all in the name of restoring international competitiveness. This change brought with it policy measures favoring profitability and lessening the fiscal drag of public firms.

The second major way in which patterns of implementation differed in France and Spain was with respect to the dynamics of industrial adjustment. Restructuring created more conflict in Spain than in France. Spanish workers resisted adjustment more vigorously than did French workers, and Spanish unions were both more mobilized and more influential than their French counterparts. Although neither labor movement was ultimately able to prevent political leaders from undertaking a Type B approach, Spanish labor more strongly shaped industrial decision making as well as the various social measures that were put in place.

Finally, there was a significant contrast between France and Spain in the impact of restructuring. Simply put, in conventional economic terms the Mitterrand government implemented industrial adjustment more successfully than the González government. Despite the French Socialists' relative lack of strategic coherence and consistency, their policies ultimately facilitated a more thorough restructuring of basic industries.

BUILDING BLOCKS: TOWARD AN EXPLANATORY FRAMEWORK

The ultimate aims of this book are twofold: to account for the similar type B approaches adopted by France and Spain and to explain differences between them in terms of the trajectory, dynamics, and impact of industrial adjustment. Explaining these phenomena is important for two reasons. The first concerns the legacy of Socialist rule in France and Spain. Political observers concur that the Socialists in both countries fell far short of keeping their initial promises, but opinion on why this happened remains divided. The search for an explanation is hampered because little has been written about the González government (the literature on the "Mitterrand experiment," however, is voluminous).[32] Although both governments were in power at roughly the same time and influenced each other, no one has published a systematic comparison of their actions in any political or policy domain. Such a comparison can help us understand the space for policy change that each government faced, as well as the decisions made in that space. This comparison can also provide a framework for examining the experiences of other Left governments in Western Europe that have had to confront similar policy dilemmas.

The second reason for creating an explanatory framework for industrial restructuring in France and Spain is that such an analysis contributes to a central debate in comparative political economy, namely why national leaders adopt particular economic strategies.[33] In this debate, scholars focus on two main issues. The first, stemming from what Almond has labeled the "international-national connection," concerns the relative importance of international as opposed to national (domestic) factors in determining economic strategies.[34] Although it is universally admitted that global economic integration has limited the policy latitude of individual countries while encouraging convergence in macroeconomic strategies, it remains unclear how binding "international constraints" really are, especially for middling economies such as those of France and Spain, which lack abundant natural resources, increasingly depend on foreign trade and investment, and actively seek integration within a regional economic bloc.

Although international constraints are a necessary component of any explanation of adjustment strategies, they are insufficient, for they do not explain varying national responses to common (that is, global) economic pressures. For example, during the world economic crisis of the 1930s, governments adopted diverse strategies ranging from laissez-faire to protectionism.[35] Although large-scale changes during the 1980s and 1990s, notably the growing integration and globalization of economic activity, have indeed narrowed the space for national autonomy, the international economy does not constrain all nations similarly or dictate terms to national governments in an unmediated fashion. To rephrase Marx, states cannot choose their international economic conditions, but they do make their own history. Despite the trend toward market liberalization and deregulation throughout the global economy, nations continue to differ in the mix of fiscal and monetary policies chosen, the timing of their adoption, and the dynamics and efficacy of their implementation. These contrasting responses derive in large part from national differences in domestic political and institutional arrangements, and explanations of these responses must also incorporate domestic factors.[36]

This consideration leads to the second issue focused on by scholars in the debate mentioned above, namely the influence of the state (especially its institutional structures) versus the influence of society (especially classes, sectoral coalitions, and organized interests) in determining policy choices.[37] This issue, which originated in pluralist-elitist and neo-Marxian, instrumentalist-structuralist controversies, has generated a massive but ultimately inconclusive literature, with both sides claiming victory on the basis of selective historical evidence.[38]

These two issues inform the present study's conceptual framework for explaining adjustment strategies. This framework incorporates four variables that encompass both international and domestic (national) factors as well as statist and societal ones. The approach taken here does not exclude one side of the international/domestic or statist/societal controversies, but recognizes the potential relevance of each perspective. The theoretical and empirical challenge is to assess how these variables combined in the French and Spanish cases to shape industrial-adjustment responses and outcomes.

The main variables in the conceptual framework are industrial capacity, state capacity, the nature of the governing coalition, and the policy paradigm. The first, industrial capacity, is an economic-structural variable in that it refers to how a domestic economy is structured, especially in relation to the larger regional and global economy with which it interacts. The inclusion of this variable is a response to a recent call that "political economists must (should) either seek to explain economic outcomes or incorporate economic variables into their explanation of policy outcomes."[39] The other three variables are political-institutional in that they refer to the domain of politics and political institutions. It is now time to briefly define these variables and indicate their relevance.

We begin with the evident observation that economic strategies generally, and adjustment strategies specifically, are largely determined by three types of influences: what political leaders *can* do, what they are *pressed* to do, and what they *desire* to do.[40] If adjustment strategy in France and Spain was determined in part by what leaders could do, then it is necessary to weigh the degree to which these leaders were able to intervene effectively in economic affairs. The first two factors, industrial capacity and state capacity, relate directly to this ability. *Industrial capacity* refers to the ability of an industry (or industries in general) to compete in global markets. This ability, which may be gauged by such measures as export-import balances and financial condition (profitability, level of indebtedness, and so on), largely determines the degree of international constraint a nation experiences. All else being equal, the stronger the industrial capacity, the less severe the adjustment needed (for example, in the number of jobs eliminated), and therefore the greater the government's latitude in effecting adjustment.

Another determinant of what political leaders can do is "the ability . . . to extract resources from society, implement . . . policies even in face of societal opposition, and influence social groups."[41] This ability, which we may label *state capacity,* has traditionally served to distinguish strong from weak states— in other words, to distinguish states that give their officials relatively powerful policy instruments to achieve their intended goals (such as mechanisms that insulate them from interest group influence) from states that lack such instruments.[42] As a general rule, the stronger the state's capacity, the more likely it can achieve its adjustment goals.

Possessing relatively strong capacity does not, of course, explain why the French and Spanish governments embarked on their particular adjustment strategies in the first place. For that we must consider a combination of pressure and motivation. If, as mentioned above, public policy results partly from what political leaders are pressed to do, then we must examine possible sources of societal pressure. A main potential source is the *governing coalition:* the set of parties, organized interests, and voters that constitutes the government's base of popular support. In the case of social-democratic parties, the coalition includes all or part of the labor movement. The governing coalition is important because it influences how public officials perceive and define their goals. But this influence is conditional on the coalition's ability to mobilize and press its preferences on the government. Generally speaking, the greater the governing coalition's organizational strength (its internal unity, organizational density, and so forth), the greater the likelihood that government policy will follow the coalition's policy preferences.[43]

Finally, we must consider what political leaders desire to do, for the literature on state autonomy reveals, if nothing else, that leaders do not respond mechanically to incentives created by state institutions and societal pressures. Instead, leaders develop and apply their own conceptions of national interest and the proper domain of state action. Hall, borrowing from Kuhn's classic study, defines these conceptions as the *policy paradigm,* the "framework of ideas and standards that specifies not only the goals of policy and the kind of instruments that can be used to attain them, but also the very nature of the problems they are meant to be addressing."[44] Along with institutional structures and practices, the policy paradigm (the product of a broad process of "social learning")[45] is a main element of the policy legacy that any new government inherits. The policy paradigm is important because it exercises an inertial influence on policy makers at all times, including moments of change of regime or governing party. New leaders may embrace the existing paradigm or seek to effect a paradigm shift (as Thatcher did in Britain), but in either case they must contend with its effects on policy making.

CONCLUSION: THE IMPORTANCE OF GOVERNING COALITIONS

The complexities of national economic strategy resist monocausal explanations, and thus this book's analysis will continually emphasize that industrial adjustment in France and Spain was shaped not by one factor but by the four factors of industrial capacity, state capacity, the governing coalition, and the policy paradigm. Yet it is not enough to conclude that they all mattered. The explanatory challenge is to specify when and how each factor mattered, under what conditions, and to what effect.

In this analysis, one variable emerges as more equal than others, namely the nature of the governing coalition. The emphasis given to the governing coalition underlines the importance of political mobilization in processes of industrial restructuring. As we will see, adjustment in both countries was strongly affected by what political leaders were pressed (or not pressed) to do by their political allies, especially their parties and affiliated labor unions. This book will argue that the governing coalitions were unable to resist pressures to implement market-adapting adjustment programs and were unable to mobilize sufficiently in support of market-modifying or other alternatives.

In both countries, this incapacity stemmed from intracoalition characteristics, notably a party membership structure that favored middle-strata elements at the expense of industrial workers, conflictual party-union relations, and union weakness and division. At the same time, these coalitions were far from inconsequential in affecting the outcome of adjustment. Despite their inability to withstand or modify market pressures, they were able to extract favorable concessions for affected workers from the government and employers.

The governing coalitions were also important in affecting the adjustment process itself. Differences between the French and Spanish coalitions help to account for the contrasts in trajectory, dynamics, and outcome noted above. First, policy trajectory differences—notably, the early Mitterrand government's reformism versus the González government's moderate stance—were attributable largely to coalitional variations (in particular, contrasting party structures and alliance strategies vis-à-vis other Left parties and organized labor).

Moreover, contrasts in the dynamics of restructuring—Spain's higher levels of conflict and contestation—stemmed largely from differences in intracoalitional relations. Structural differences in party-union ties help to explain the Spanish labor movement's stronger mobilization and influence. Spanish labor's relative clout, especially in the crucial 1983–1986 phase, was due in large measure to an inside-outside alignment: the Socialist-leaning Unión General de Trabajadores (UGT) assumed an important inside role in adjustment decision making and implementation, while the Communist-affiliated Comisiones Obreras (CCOO) sparked an effective outside campaign of grassroots resistance. In France, by contrast, organized labor lacked the organizational links and mobilizational capacity of its Spanish counterparts.

Finally, differences in outcome—the Mitterrand government's relatively greater success in carrying out its adjustment programs—-were directly linked to coalitional factors. French labor's relative weakness sapped its capacity to influence the impact of adjustment, which meant that policy makers faced few pressures from within their own support base to depart from orthodox adjustment measures. Spanish labor, by contrast, was able to combine insider influence (through the UGT) and street pressure (mainly from the CCOO) to delay the adjustment process and to extract generous income-support programs for laid-off workers.

In emphasizing the role of the governing coalition, this book follows the lead of scholars who examine the causes and consequences of political resource mobilization.[46] Such mobilization does not explain everything, but it does explain much about the nature and consequences of industrial restructuring in France and Spain. This is not to deny the contribution of other frameworks featuring such factors as external constraints, institutions, and ideas. Rather, this book seeks to be both selective and integrative, to stress the role of a particular explanatory variable while combining it with others in a multicausal framework. Such an approach, it is hoped, will contribute to the comparative analysis of state economic strategies in a transforming global economy.

MIXED LEGACIES
POSTWAR POLITICAL ECONOMY
AND POLITICS

History matters: what French and Spanish Socialists could do, were pressed to do, and desired to do was influenced strongly by the past. The economic and political legacies left by their predecessors helped frame available options, establish routine decision-making processes, determine institutional and organizational resources, and define policy paradigms.

Part II addresses two questions. First, what kind of economy did these governments inherit? Chapter 2 argues that despite differences in the level of industrial development, the French and Spanish economies both suffered from endemic weaknesses that the "thirty glorious years" of postwar modernization had failed to erase. Hidden during the brisk expansion of the 1960s, these vulnerabilities became evident after the first oil shock of 1973. Moreover, policies designed to correct existing problems often created new ones. Efforts by conservative governments to co-opt, or at least neutralize, working-class support led to increased taxes on business as a means of financing income support for unemployed workers. Within the European context, both the French and Spanish economies lost ground during the late 1970s, in large measure because of inadequate or inappropriate economic policies.

Part II also poses the question, what was the nature of the Socialist political coalitions that took power in the early 1980s? Chapter 3 argues that the political strategies pursued by Mitterrand and González produced quite different organizational coalitions. In France the dynamics of party factionalism and alliance building pushed the PS left and led to the construction of a dominant (though not unanimously supported) policy paradigm that envisioned a vigorous contestation of Western capitalism. However ambiguous, the PS's initial policy framework placed it clearly to the left of its Spanish counterpart, the PSOE, whose relative unity behind González's moderate leadership encouraged the party's movement toward the center.

This is not the whole story, however, for despite the differences in their organizational coalitions, the PS and PSOE developed strikingly similar electorates. Far from representing a conversion by the French and Spanish electorates to socialist principles, the Socialists' initial victories in 1981 and 1982 were votes against ineffective incumbents. Voters expected practical solutions to the problems of unemployment and inflation rather any particular policy orientation. In the Spanish case, this electoral realism accorded well with the Gonzalez government's moderation. In France, however, the PS's more ambitious reform program placed the party at risk in its relations with its electorate. French voters were willing to allow the PS to enact its program, but their support was conditional on demonstrable results. Leftward tendencies, while stronger in France, thus remained fragile and reversible.

The lesson is that the actions of both incoming Socialist governments were shaped by both structural conditions and the legacy of strategic political choices. In the domain of economic and industrial policy, French and Spanish Socialists had to contend with unforgiving world markets, as well as the policy errors of their conservative predecessors. In the political sphere, the Socialists' options were defined not only by inherited constitutional structures but also by their leaders' stategies for gaining power. In making their respective long marches to power during the 1970s, the two governing coalitions established distinct patterns of internal operation and mobilization that persisted into the 1980s and the era of Socialist ascendancy.

2

Failing
to
Adjust

Legacies
of
Conservative
Rule

What economic legacy did conservative governments leave their Socialist successors in the early 1980s? Despite robust growth during the 1960s and early 1970s, the Spanish and French economies remained saddled with structural weaknesses, notably a badly adapted structure of foreign trade that eventually undermined each country's industrial strength and international competitiveness. Obscured during the postwar boom, these weaknesses became pressing during the economic crisis of the 1970s. That crisis, punctuated by the oil shocks of 1973 and 1979, produced rising inflation, unemployment, trade deficits, and foreign debt throughout the advanced industrial nations. Yet while most other European governments were taking corrective action through such means as fiscal and monetary austerity and promotion of energy conservation, French and Spanish leaders failed to respond effectively. As a result, during the 1970s the economic performance of both nations deteriorated, not only compared with the pre-1973 period, but also relative to other European nations. By the early 1980s, industrial capacity in both France and Spain had declined sharply compared with a decade earlier.

Why did these conservative governments fail to adjust? This chapter argues that while structural economic weaknesses hindered their efforts, a key factor was politics, specifically Left mobilization. Both the post-Franco Unión de Centro Democrático (UCD) government in Spain and the Giscard government in France were unwilling to enact stringent austerity measures that would risk alienating workers and the labor movement. Fearing destabilizing mobilization by the Left, these governments either delayed adjustment (Spain) or displaced its burden onto employers (France). Left mobilization and labor militancy during the late 1970s and early 1980s thus produced a double-edged outcome. On the one hand, mobilization built electoral support for Left (especially Socialist) parties and thus helped these parties gain power. On the other hand, by dissuading Center-Right governments from undertaking unpopular adjustment policies, Left mobilization also contributed, albeit unwittingly and indirectly, to long-term economic decline. Ironically, the same social forces that bore Left governments to power also served to limit what those governments could accomplish once they assumed office. This chapter develops this argument by examining conservative responses to the 1970s crisis, first in Spain and then in France.

SPAIN

Spanish economic adjustment in the 1970s took place against the looming backdrop of Francoism. To be sure, the Generalissimo could take some credit for reviving one of Europe's most backward economies.[1] After a failed attempt at economic self-sufficiency during his regime's first twenty years (1939–1959), Franco gradually opened the Spanish economy during the 1960s, encouraging tourism, labor emigration, foreign investment, and trade—all with impressive results.[2] By the early 1970s, the nation had modernized its infrastructure, achieved significant industrial growth, witnessed the emergence of a small but crucial entrepreneurial middle class, and enjoyed a dramatic rise in living standards.

Despite these advances, Francoist development failed to eradicate fundamental economic weaknesses, and in some respects created new ones. The most serious problem was the structure of foreign trade. Not only was Spain's trade balance usually negative, the economy was particularly vulnerable to disruptions from the global economy. Although exports grew rapidly during the 1960s and early 1970s, imports advanced even faster, producing a steadily worsening trade deficit.[3] Moreover, the mix of Spain's trade exchanges gave the country a tenuous position in world markets. Most notably, many of Spain's big export industries, such as steel, textiles and automobiles, faced growing foreign competition as well as stagnating demand.[4]

Finally, although foreign capital and technology were key to Spain's economic takeoff, they also spawned a dependency that hampered the nation's long-term prospects. For example, the most common form of foreign direct investment, the installation of branch plants by multinational corporations

(MNCs), usually was accompanied by production under the MNCs' patents and licenses. Because MNCs tended to restrict the use of their patents to the domestic market, such foreign investment tended to limit the plants' export performance.[5] This dependence also discouraged firms and the Spanish government from investing in research and development.[6] Although the trade deficit was usually offset by tourism receipts, emigrants' remittances, and foreign investment, so that the current balance generally remained positive, these sources of net inflow were sensitive to global economic fluctuations.

Spain's economic performance and structure thus suffered from endemic problems. Although growth outpaced the average among European OECD nations, so did inflation.[7] Moreover, growth was highly uneven across regions, with three areas—Madrid, Basque-Navarra, and Catalonia—becoming investment and population magnets, while regions such as Extremadura, Castilla-León, and Castilla-La Mancha declined.[8] Income inequality also increased throughout the 1960s, making Spain's income distribution considerably more unequal than that of nations such as Sweden, the United Kingdom, and the Netherlands.[9] At the same time, the public sector did little to offset these imbalances, for government spending, and social service expenditures in particular, reached only half the EC average.[10] Not surprisingly, persistent structural conditions continued to hinder growth; in particular, Spanish firms remained small and unproductive by European standards. Sheltered from the impact of open markets, Spanish firms could flourish without expanding, while restrictive labor laws made it difficult to lay off workers, thus removing the incentive to hire.[11]

Most seriously for the country's long-term prospects, the Francoist system sprang from a contradiction, namely that the regime sought to transform the economy without reforming itself. Economic change fostered formation of an industrial working class that not only eventually demanded higher wages and better working conditions, but also the right to organize.[12] Yet the regime could not grant this demand without initiating democracy and thus negating its basic character. Lacking institutional channels for negotiation, in 1970 the underground unions and the "workers' commissions" within the official "vertical unions" called for wildcat strikes, which disrupted production. Reacting harshly with police crackdowns on strikers, the regime only polarized class tensions and undermined its own legitimacy.[13]

Spain was thus extremely vulnerable to the first oil shock, an event that coincided with a decline in Franco's health and hold on power. In responding to that shock, Spain's performance was notably weak. Compared with other European OECD nations in 1974–1982, the country's growth and investment rates were lower, while inflation, unemployment, and current balance deficits were higher (see table 2.1). Inflation was consistently at least 25 percent higher than the European average and, for two years (1977–1978), about double the European average. Investment, while declining an average of 1 percent annually, was especially weak in the industrial sector, where it declined an average of 3.9 percent annually (in fact, industrial investment did not increase on an annual basis until 1986.)[14] Finally, the unemployment rate, which had been lower than the European average until 1978, soared to nearly double the European rate by the early 1980s.

Why did Spain adapt so poorly? Part of the explanation lies, of course, in the structural weaknesses just discussed, in particular Spain's reliance on direct foreign investment and workers' remittances, both of which were highly sensitive to the global downturn.[15] Important as well was Spain's reliance on energy imports (especially oil), a dependence that was heavy even by the standards of the energy-importing European Community and OECD.[16]

Structural deficiencies are not the whole story, however. Crucial to the explanation is a political dimension, specifically the dynamics of the post-Franco succession. Simply put, the political management of this tenuous transition took primacy over economic adjustment. Political leaders—including Franco himself in his last two years, as well as the Center-Right politicians who succeeded him—lacked the political resources to impose adjustment measures that became common elsewhere, such as wage controls, industrial restructuring, and tight fiscal and monetary policies. The result was that adjustment was either postponed or only partially realized.

To establish this conclusion, we must consider two distinct political phases: first, the nearly four years between the 1973 oil shock and the first democratic elections in June 1977, and second, the five and a half years between the June 1977 elections and the Socialists' victory in October 1982. During the first phase, political uncertainty consumed the two years between October 1973 and Franco's death in November 1975. Franco himself became virtually incapacitated, while various opposition groups including workers, students, and Basque separatists increasingly challenged the status quo. After the December 1973 assassination of Prime Minister Luis Carrero Blanco by ETA terrorists, the new prime minister, Carlos Arias Navarro, promised liberalizing reforms but failed to deliver, further alienating the growing opposition to the Generalissimo's regime.

After Franco's death the new head of state, King Juan Carlos, initially signaled continuity by retaining Arias as head of government. In mid-1976, however, he forced Arias's resignation and appointed another Franco loyalist, Adolfo Suárez González, as prime minister. Although the Leftist and regionalist opposition opposed Suárez's appointment, the new prime minister, acting

Table 2.1 Spain and France: Economic Performance, 1974–1982 (annual averages)

	Spain	France	OECD-Europe
Real GDP (% change)	1.8	2.5	2.2
Inflation (% change in private consumption deflators)	17.5	11.5	11.8
Unemployment (%)	7.3	5.1	5.4
Gross fixed capital formation (% change)	−1.2	0.3	−0.1
Current balances (% of GDP)	−2.0	−0.1	−0.6

Sources: Organisation for Economic Co-operation and Development, *Economic Outlook* 52 (December 1992) and 53 (June 1993).

in concert with the king, began laying the groundwork for a democratic transition. Within a year of taking office, the Suárez government convinced the Francoist Cortes to vote itself out of existence, won a national referendum creating a new bicameral parliament to be elected by universal suffrage, amnestied most political prisoners, legalized all political parties (including the Partido Comunista Español, or PCE), and held democratic parliamentary elections.[17]

Preoccupied with the political transition and lacking the legitimacy to impose rigorous austerity measures, political leaders failed to fashion a coherent response to the global crisis. Although the government did seek to reduce the budget deficit, restrict credits, and control wages and prices, its measures were applied weakly and inconsistently. Thus government policy tended to curtail growth and investment but failed to slow inflation or stop the rise in unemployment. Wages increased sharply, largely because of a growing militancy among the working class and newly legalized unions; according to one estimate, wages rose four times as rapidly as productivity—a recipe for further inflation and unemployment.[18] One result was that Spanish economic performance diverged from that of other European nations. For example, during the first four years of the economic crisis (1974–1977), Spain maintained a higher growth rate and lower unemployment, but at the cost of greater inflation and larger current account deficits (see table 2.2). This decoupling of the Spanish economy from other European economies would persist into the 1980s.

The second phase of crisis response, which lasted just over five years, began with the June 1977 parliamentary elections, the first free vote since 1931. Suárez, the incumbent, was elected prime minister, at the head of a UCD that was a loose coalition of Center and Right parties. Now able to claim the legitimacy of popular support, Suárez sought to manage the economy and other social problems such as regional issues through negotiations with political

Table 2.2   Spain: De-Coupling from the European Economy—Economic Performance, 1974–1982 (annual averages)

| | 1974–1977 | | 1978–1982 | |
	Spain	OECD-Europe	Spain	OECD-Europe
Real GDP (% change)	3.1	2.5	0.9	2.3
Inflation (% change)	18.4	2.2	16.2	11.2
Unemployment (%)	4.0	4.8	11.1	7.0
Gross fixed capital formation (% change)	0.0	−0.8	−2.0	0.1
Current balance (% of GDP)	−3.1	−0.6	−1.1	−0.4

Source: Organisation for Economic Co-operation and Development, Economic Outlook 52 (December 1992).
Note: All figures based on 1987 GDP weights expressed in 1987 dollars.

parties, unions, and regionalist representatives. But though he had deftly handled the transition to democracy, Suárez proved less adept as an economic manager and coalition leader. After winning reelection in 1979, he became increasingly withdrawn, unpopular, and ineffectual, frustrated with having to placate the five main groups that constituted his coalition and unable to muster a government consensus on how to respond to the 1979 oil shock. Suárez resigned in February 1981 and was replaced by his cabinet vice-president, Leopoldo Calvo Sotelo.

After weathering an abortive military coup just as he was being approved by parliament, Calvo Sotelo was even less successful than Suárez in holding the governing UCD coalition together. With defections and resignations whittling his parliamentary group to only 122 out of 350 seats, the prime minister finally asked the king to call new elections for October 1982. The second phase of crisis response, which had begun in political euphoria, thus ended in governmental drift and division.

Although these UCD governments lacked cohesion and ultimately collapsed, they did launch an innovation in economic management: a process of pact making among parties, unions, and employer organizations, aimed at such problems as inflation and unemployment. This drive to fashion a series of pactos sociales, beginning soon after the June 1977 elections, produced its first agreement in October, the Pacto de la Moncloa (named for the presidential palace, the site of negotiations). The accord, whose thirty-one signatories included representatives of almost all the political parties, including the main Left parties, the PSOE and PCE, sought to define a common position on major problems such as terrorism, inflation, unemployment, and the trade deficit. The economic measures called for tighter fiscal and monetary policies as well as wage and price guidelines.[19] Although unions and employer representatives were excluded from the Moncloa negotiations—indeed, the leading employers' organization, the Confederación Española de Organizaciones Empresariales (CEOE), was not established until two months later—they later joined the pact-making process and were parties to agreements signed in 1980, 1981, and 1982.[20]

The pacts' effects were both political and economic. Politically, the pacts established a framework for compromise and negotiation between employers and unions that helped legitimate democracy and capitalism in the eyes of the working class.[21] Moreover, by containing and channeling labor and regional-separatist demands, the negotiations helped assuage the military's misgivings that democracy would usher in growing political disorder.[22] Economically, the pacts' effects were mixed. On the positive side, by enlisting union support for wage moderation, the pacts helped dampen inflation. The existence of national-level wage agreements from 1978 to 1982 not only reduced wage drift (the difference between contractual wage increases and actual wages), but also brought wage increases below the rate of inflation.[23]

On the other hand, the labor pacts appear to have reinforced two other trends that hampered economic adjustment in the long term: labor rigidity and public spending. First, the pacts were based on an implicit labor-government quid pro quo in which the unions accepted wage moderation in exchange for keeping the laws protecting workers' contractual status unchanged. Because this meant retaining the Francoist framework that sheltered workers from layoffs, the pacts discouraged employers from hiring new workers, especially young, first-time entrants. Thus the pacts aggravated unemployment while reinforcing a dualistic labor market. In particular, the pacts "biased the distribution of the costs of the crisis between the various segments of the working population. They favored the segments with greater voice capacity, such as the unionized work force of the large firms, public and private, and, more generally, the segment of those already employed, while they penalized the workers of the small firms, the unemployed, and those who were at the gates of the labor market—women and the young."[24]

Second, the pacts contributed both directly and indirectly to public spending, which increased markedly during the late 1970s and early 1980s.[25] Although the advent of democracy and the mobilization of long-repressed social interests inevitably spurred the surge, the pacts bolstered public spending directly by committing the government to a policy of boosting pensions and social security benefits and subsidizing failing firms. As we will see in chapter 6, the Instituto Nacional de Industria (INI) became a veritable salvage operation that nationalized bankrupt enterprises in order to keep them afloat. The pacts also stimulated public spending indirectly in the sense that their negative effects on employment required the government to increase its income support for jobless workers.[26] By spurring social spending, the pacts may have helped provide a short-term cushion against recession in the late 1970s, but they also served to postpone the inevitable need for adjustment.

On balance, Spain's economic performance during the 1978–1982 period remained out of phase with its European neighbors (see table 2.2). Whereas most other European nations had rebounded from the first oil shock by 1976, Spain never fully adjusted. From 1978 to 1982, while growth in other European countries was averaging over 2 percent a year, Spain's economy stagnated. Although investment throughout Europe recovered slightly from a negative trend in the 1974–1977 period to a slightly positive one in the 1978–1982 period, Spanish investment declined sharply. Meanwhile, unemployment, which had been lower than the European average from 1974 to 1977, shot well ahead after 1977. Inflation, though moderating by the end of this period—thanks in part, as we have seen, to the social pacts—also remained well above the European mean. Compared with its economic performance before 1973, the Spanish economy after that year experienced, on average, sharper drops in growth and more rapid increases in unemployment and inflation than did other OECD nations, a trend that owed as much to political fragility as to economic weakness.

FRANCE

France's political situation during the 1970s contrasted sharply with Spain's. Despite the upheaval of the events of May-June 1968, by the early 1970s the country was politically stable, due in large measure to the surprising flexibility and growing legitimacy of the 1958 Fifth Republic constitution. French governments thus faced the 1970s economic crisis without the political turmoil and uncertainty that engulfed their Spanish counterparts. France's adjustment, however, shared two traits with its southern neighbor. The first was growing economic and especially industrial weakness; the second was the prominence of political factors in shaping adjustment strategies.

Despite brisk growth that lasted into the 1970s, French industry, paradoxically, became increasingly vulnerable as it became exposed to foreign commerce. As in Spain, this weakness remained largely veiled as long as global growth prevailed, but after 1973 the nation's main industries suffered sharp setbacks in market position at the hands of international competitors. The roots of this vulnerability lay, as in Spain, in the policies of previous governments, namely those of Presidents de Gaulle (1958–1969) and Pompidou (1969–1974). Coming to power not only in the midst of the Algerian crisis but at the dawn of France's membership in the newly created European Economic Community, de Gaulle inherited an economy undergoing rapid modernization and international exposure. Although the reasons for France's postwar growth have been disputed,[27] nearly all observers agree that a key factor was a new relationship between the state and business, in which the state actively promoted business activity and, in some cases, even acted as entrepreneur.[28] Managing this relationship was the Commissariat Général du Plan (General Planning Commission), which employed "indicative" planning to establish guidelines for production, investment, and price levels for individual sectors and the economy in general.[29]

De Gaulle pushed the state's interventionist tendencies even further. Although he promoted France's opening to international competition, he feared that the smaller, more fragmented French companies could not hold their own against West German and American firms. Thus he sought to create one or two "national champion" firms in targeted sectors, mainly by encouraging mergers through tax and research and development policies.[30] In executing this strategy, the government also altered industrial policy-making patterns: top civil servants in the General Planning Commission and Industry Ministry dealt directly with the heads of the largest firms, thus bypassing the trade associations and professional groups that traditionally had spoken for business. This state-corporate symbiosis, based on shared educational, professional, and personal ties, meant that the line between government and big business became increasingly blurred.[31]

Despite certain successes, the national champion strategy ultimately undermined the ability of French firms to adjust to the 1970s global crisis. The strategy did achieve some goals: average firm size increased, a few world-class firms emerged (such as Dassault-Breguet, Saint-Gobain-Pont-à-Mousson, and BSN), and some state-funded projects gave France dominance in certain technological niches (supersonic air travel and nuclear power, among others).

Yet the strategy also produced four important negative effects. First, by fostering collusion between the state and the *grands groupes industriels,* it largely ignored labor, small business, and other interests. This bias, which fed a perception that the regime favored the strong, ultimately helped erode the legitimacy and popular appeal of Gaullism.[32] Second, the tilt toward bigness contributed to domestic unemployment (which doubled from 1.3 percent in 1965 to 2.6 percent in 1974) by encouraging large firms to expand (and thus create new jobs) abroad rather than at home, and by failing to boost small firms, the main creators of new domestic jobs.[33] Third, by focusing almost exclusively on firm size to the neglect of such factors as investment, production, and marketing, the strategy tended to produce industrial groups that were little more than diversified financial conglomerates.[34] By the mid-1970s, with balance sheets deeply in the red, many of these groups came to the state for bailouts.[35] Finally, in those areas where the state took direct control, it often obtained mediocre results: cost overruns (the Concorde); failed attempts to create national champions (the Plan Calcul to build a world-class computer firm); and the creation of firms permanently dependent on the state (as in the case of state-sponsored "rationalization" plans in steel and shipbuilding).[36]

Thanks in part to this improperly balanced strategy, the French economy responded poorly to global conditions in the 1970s, especially in international trade. Although some industries were conquering foreign markets, whole sectors were succumbing to manufactured imports at home.

This market penetration spelled trouble for three reasons. The first was that while imports penetrated all sectors of the French economy, the trend was particularly marked in industry.[37] Industry's ability to defend itself by expanding exports thus became increasingly critical to France's trade balance.

Second, as table 2.3 indicates, import penetration in manufactured goods in the late 1970s occurred across the board, but manufacturing industries failed to counter this penetration with a comparable export effort. Table 2.3 reveals, for example, that from 1975 to 1980 the export/import ratio (a rough measure of general competitiveness) declined in all five main industrial sectors. Moreover, by 1980 France was running a deficit in manufactured goods—an alarming trend for a highly industrialized, energy-poor country that had to rely on exports to pay a rising oil bill. Reflecting on France's troubled trade, a Finance Ministry official remarked: "We know how to make the Ariane [rocket], but we don't know how to make washing machines."[38]

Finally, trade deficits with other industrialized nations were growing, a sure sign that France was falling behind her chief competitors. For example, from 1973 to 1981 France's deficit in industrial goods with the United States, Japan, and West Germany (the "Big Three" nations) more than tripled.[39] The same pattern held for trade relations with France's other European partners, with the exception of the United Kingdom; even here, however, the industrial surplus was more than offset by imports of British oil.[40]

To give a more precise indication of this loss of competitive position, consider the industrial sector statisticians label "consumer and household equipment goods" (which includes washing machines). From 1973 to 1981, the country's trade balance in this sector moved from black to red. A revealing trend was that the steepest declines occurred in trade balances with the industrialized OECD countries, and that France's trade deficits with those nations were partially offset by trade surpluses with the newly rich OPEC nations.[41]

Other sectors, such as intermediate goods, industrial capital goods, and

Table 2.3   France: Foreign Penetration, Weak Counterattack, 1975–1980

	1975	1980
A. Import Penetration of Manufactured Goods[a]		
Intermediate goods[b]	26.0	33.7
Industrial capital goods[c]	31.0	43.6
Household appliances	37.2	43.9
Automobiles and other land transport equipment	24.0	29.1
Consumer nondurables[d]	17.5	25.1
All manufactured goods	27.1	34.1
B. Export/Import Ratio for Manufactured Goods[e]		
Intermediate goods[b]	93.9	89.2
Industrial capital goods[c]	119.0	97.5
Household appliances	57.1	41.1
Automobiles and other land transport equipment	253.8	174.4
Consumer nondurables[d]	107.3	85.3
All manufactured goods	114.2	96.0

Source: Institut National de la Statistique et des Études Économiques, Annuaire Statistique de la France (Paris, 1984).
   a. Estimated by the following formula: value of imports/value (production of sector + imports – exports)
   b. Steel, glass, chemicals, rubber and plastics, etc.
   c. Mechanical engineering products and industrial electronic equipment.
   d. Leatherwear and footwear, textiles, wood products, etc.
   e. Exports calculated on "free-on-board" (FoB) basis (i.e., not including insurance and freight costs); imports calculated on "cost-insurance-freight" (CIF) basis (including insurance and freight costs).

transportation equipment, underwent a similar reorientation of trade during the 1970s.[42] Losing ground to other industrialized nations, France came increasingly to depend on exports to OPEC countries and the Third World to offset its trade deficits and pay its oil bill. For example, the 1981 industrial deficit with the Big Three, which totaled Fr 55 billion, was offset by an industrial surplus of Fr 86 billion with OPEC and Third World countries.[43] Most of these OPEC and Third World exports—infrastructural projects, turnkey plants, and weapons—were heavily subsidized by the government. To maintain the trade balance, French industry thus relied more and more on the two props of state largesse and petrodollar recycling to the Third World. These proved to be shaky pillars for supporting trade, for a persistent trade deficit developed by the late 1970s.

Moreover, France's industrial decline narrowed the economic maneuvering room of the government. The reason was that domestic demand was growing rapidly (by an average of 3.2 percent per year from 1973 to 1981) for products that were the least competitive with foreign producers, whereas demand grew much more slowly (1.2 percent per year) for products in which French manufacturers were most competitive. This divergence in performance between the two sectors meant, as an OECD publication commented in 1984, that "any boost given to domestic demand sucks in imports whereas the only way the [most competitive] product industries can develop is by exporting more."[44] As we will see in chapter 4, this weakness would strongly constrain the Socialists in the 1980s.

As in Spain, France's loss of industrial position had several causes, including inherited structural weaknesses and poor energy supplies. Yet, again as in Spain, an important measure of responsibility lay with political choices, specifically the adjustment policies of the government of President Valéry Giscard d'Estaing (1974–1981). Taking power in the spring of 1974, just as the oil shock was beginning to plunge the global economy into recession, Giscard rejected, at least rhetorically, the Gaullist vision of *grandeur*. France, he argued, was only a medium-sized nation, not a potential superpower, and thus its main hope lay in the international competitiveness of its most dynamic firms rather than in the overall size or strength of its economy. Competitive firms, the new president reasoned, could not be created by designating national champions and showering them with subsidies and investment incentives. The state's role, instead, should be to promote "redeployment" of capital and labor from low- to high-profit activities through a mix of market exposure and selective financial support.[45]

In practice, Giscard's approach succumbed to the realities of domestic political pressure and the second oil shock in 1979. Its consistent discourse notwithstanding, the government's policies shifted constantly and diverged increasingly from the philosophy itself.[46] In the end, the continuities with Gaullist interventionism far outweighed any purported policy innovation. Giscard's strategy eventually employed three incompatible elements: at the outset he tried market competition, then added rescue operations for failing firms, and finally added to the first two a policy of betting on the strong. By 1981 the president's industrial strategy was a contradictory *mélange*—a policy of "decontrolling the price of bread while nationalizing the steel industry."[47]

Although Giscard preached the virtues of competition from the start, his hands remained partially tied for the first four years of his presidency by the electoral threat posed by the Left. As long as Left victory appeared possible, the government, fearing an electoral backlash, could not safely allow the market's impersonal hand to sort out industrial winners and losers. Following the Left's defeat in the March 1978 elections, however, Giscard and his prime minister, Raymond Barre, launched a wide-ranging program designed to stimulate competition and expose firms to market forces. Giscard and Barre abolished many price controls, created a national commission for strengthening competition, introduced "true" pricing for nationalized firms, and encouraged the development of a private capital market meant to break the state's monopoly on investment finance.[48] At the same time, the government supported a strong franc policy to force firms to be competitive, while opening up the domestic market to outsiders. Honeywell, for example, was allowed to invest in the French computer firm Bull, and ITT and Ericsson were given permission to invest in telecommunications.[49]

By the late 1970s it was clear that competition could threaten the health and even the survival of some industries, for foreign competition in textiles, steel, leather goods, and other industries was costing jobs at home. In this respect, France's competitiveness problem, which it shared with most Western European countries, was not related to the size and fragmentation of its production units but to the product structure itself. According to an industrial economist writing in 1988, "The true difficulties of French industry . . . stem from a maladapted specialization to the new configuration of demand: strong presence in declining industries, weak in expanding ones."[50]

The Giscardist prescription was to modernize these threatened industries by making them "defensible segments," while "redeploying" the surplus labor thus created to growing sectors.[51] To oversee these adjustments the government created two interministerial committees, the Comité Interministériel pour l'Adaptation des Structures Industrielles (CIASI) and the Fonds Spécial d'Adaptation Industrielle (FSAI), whose operation reveals much about the Giscardist industrial approach.[52] On one level, these committees sought to make market viability the condition for industrial aid. For example, firms and localities applying for loans—no outright grants were offered—had to justify their proposals on the basis of future profitability; in no instance would the committees consider a state takeover of a failing firm.[53] Despite the good intentions behind the creation of the two committees, they drew the state even deeper into the process of designating industrial winners and losers (the CIASI's caseload mushroomed from 90 firms in 1974 to 649 in 1980).[54] Moreover, the government's method of financial intervention, the "participatory loan," actually made the state a part owner of a growing number of private-sector firms. While extolling private enterprise, the Giscardist government thus extended France's venerable *étatiste* tradition.

It has been claimed that the Giscard government broke with its Gaullist predecessors concerning the goals of market competition and state intervention. Suzanne Berger, for example, argues that under de Gaulle and Pompidou the state intervened to achieve positive ends such as stimulating growth and creating national champions, whereas market competition was allowed to accomplish negative ends such as diminishing the proportion of the population engaged in agriculture, reducing the share of small-scale commerce in distribution networks, and eliminating inefficient industries. Giscard supposedly reversed these goals: state intervention played the negative role of saving lame ducks, while the market's invisible hand was to tap the growth industries of the future.[55]

Although valid for the pre-1979 period, this distinction faded following the second oil shock, for increasingly the government attempted to designate and foster growth industries. In 1979, for instance, the government created two interministerial committees to support fast-growing, high-technology firms, and the following year it announced a "Strategic Reinforcement" policy designed to aid six "priority" sectors.[56] The Giscard-Barre redeployment strategy thus extended state intervention to encompass both the positive goal of promoting growth and the negative goal of managing industrial decline.

Despite a new rhetoric, this strategy strongly resembled the Gaullist approach in its promotion of massive state investment projects (in nuclear energy, telecommunications, and aerospace), promulgation of state-directed industrial rationalization plans (in steel, textiles, and shipbuilding), reliance on protectionism (quotas and tariffs for textiles, "voluntary" automobile import agreements with the Japanese, and huge export subsidies), and designation of national champion sectors.[57] The chief difference was its attempt to establish greater selectivity and coordination in state intervention. In no sense, however, did Giscard's redeployment strategy reverse the *dirigiste* (statist) tendency; if anything, the strategy resulted in even more direct and detailed government involvement in industry.[58]

Measured against basic indicators, France's economic performance during the Giscard presidency compared respectably with other Western European nations: average gross domestic product (GDP) growth, investment, and current balances were slightly higher, while inflation and unemployment were slightly lower (see table 2.1). Moreover, Barre's strong franc policy helped produce a stable currency, a negligible public debt, and a small budget deficit. These achievements were only relative, however, because the economy declined sharply after the 1979 oil shock; by the time of the 1981 elections, France's annual growth rate was just over 1 percent, inflation was at 13 percent, and unemployment was growing rapidly (having increased from 400,000 in 1973 to nearly 2,000,000 in 1981).

In one major respect—the health of the private sector—the Giscard-Barre record was a notable failure. Consider two key indicators, profits and productive investment. First, as table 2.4 shows, the profit margin (gross margin rate) of the private sector declined markedly in 1973–1980, from 27.6 percent to 23.0 percent of total value added. Industry suffered more than other sectors. Commenting on the decline of the late 1970s and early 1980s, the OECD concluded that "the position of manufacturing firms appears to have worsened more steeply in France than in the other major OECD countries, whereas during the previous ten years the movement of profitability indicators had been more favorable to France."[59]

The second indicator, productive investment, also declined markedly. Given the squeeze on corporate profits, it is hardly surprising that industrial investment also declined during the Giscard-Barre period, averaging only 14 percent of value added from 1974 to 1980, compared with nearly 17 percent for the period 1963–1973.[60] Moreover, although the investment rate declined in all industrial sectors, the drop was particularly severe in intermediate goods (steel, chemicals, rubber, and so on), which were the heart of France's basic industries.[61]

These figures do not reveal the full extent of the decline, however, for there was a dramatic difference between private- and public-sector investment. In 1980 private investment declined 14 percent while public investment in-

Table 2.4   France: Profit Squeeze, 1973–1981

A. Distribution of Value Added in Private, Nonagricultural Firms (percentages of value added)

	1973	1974	1975	1979	1980	Change 1973–1980
Gross wages /salaries	49.8	50.9	51.7	50.4	51.4	+1.6
Employers' social security contributions	14.6	15.1	16.8	17.9	18.3	+3.7
Indirect taxes minus subsidies	8.0	6.9	6.8	7.4	7.3	-0.7
Gross margin rate	27.6	27.1	24.7	24.3	23.0	-4.6
Total	100.0	100.0	100.0	100.0	100.0	

B. Gross Margin Rate *(Taux de Marge)* in Various Sectors (gross margin rate as percentage of value added)

	1973	1981	Change 1973–1981
Industry	26.0	19.5	-6.5
Food and agriculture	26.9	29.8	+2.9
Retail	28.7	27.5	-1.2
Services	28.1	25.4	-2.7

Sources: M. Boeda, "Les Comptes de la nation de l'année 1980," *Économie et Statistique* 135 (July–August 1981): 53; Pierre Muller, "La dégradation des comptes des entreprises industrielles depuis le premier choc pétrolier," *Économie et Statistique* 165 (April 1984): 4.

creased 45 percent. Of the ten largest investors in 1981, *only one* (Peugeot) was a private firm; the rest were public firms such as Renault and the nationalized oil, aeronautics, electricity, gas, railroad, and postal and telephone companies.[62] Yet even the state's considerable efforts could not keep France's level of productive investment from trailing far behind that of such major competitors as West Germany, the United States, Japan, and Italy.[63]

How to explain this decline in profits and investment? Although the recession undoubtedly contributed to stagnating sales and investment uncertainty, blame can also be directed toward the Giscard-Barre government's economic policies, in particular the approach to social spending. As table 2.4 suggests, one of the main reasons for declining profit margins was the marked rise in employers' social security costs. Compared with other European Community nations during the 1970s, France's social security taxes on employers rose the most rapidly, making France's *charges sociales* the highest in the European Community.[64] This rise in employers' mandatory costs contributed directly to the fall in profits and investment. As social security costs mounted after 1974, employers were unable to fund them by drawing on other components of their operating budgets, for they had to contend with, among other things, import competition, price controls, soaring energy costs, and wages that were often subject to cost-of-living indexing, all of which limited their ability to pass on social security costs through price rises. The inevitable alternative was to fund the social security costs out of operating surpluses.

But why did employers' mandatory costs rise so sharply? The answer lies in the adjustment policies adopted by the Giscard-Barre government. Sustained consumer demand derived not from a rapidly growing economy but from a macroeconomic policy designed to make private-sector firms, not households (that is, voters), assume the costs of growing unemployment. As one economist remarked, "After the first oil shock, as after the second one, the French government chose a regulation policy that made enterprises bear the burden of the adjustment cost, whereas Germany chose to penalize consumers and working people."[65]

Ironically, Giscard and Barre, the champions of competition, executed a policy that undermined the competitive position of the private sector. The reason for this policy stemmed from a political dilemma. On the one hand, as mentioned above, until 1978 the government feared the electoral fallout of an austerity policy. Because it lacked strong ties to the major trade unions, it could not contemplate any form of incomes policy that would moderate wages. It therefore sought to keep wages and various social welfare payments, including unemployment compensation, at least even with inflation.[66] On the other hand, the government did not want to fund such payments through deficit spending. A balanced budget was needed, Barre argued, to support both a strong franc and the fight against inflation, and the government eventually decided that the way to sustain domestic consumption while avoiding budget deficits was to make employers pay for its generous program of unemployment benefits through higher payroll taxes.[67] The Giscard-Barre strategy thus forced private firms into a vicious circle: declining profits discouraged investment and led businesses to shoulder more debt, while inflation and the strong franc undermined their ability to compete abroad.[68]

CONCLUSION

In response to the post-1973 global economic crisis, the Spanish and French governments adopted policies that not only failed to correct long-standing problems of industrial structure and foreign trade, but in fact aggravated those problems. In both countries industrial capacity and state capacity weakened in the decade prior to the Socialists' arrival in power. Endemic tendencies toward inflation, trade deficits, corporate indebtedness, and low investment hampered the ability of industrial enterprises to hold their own in the face of intensifying trade competition. These tendencies were only compounded by policy measures that increased the tax and financial burdens on firms. Moreover, despite efforts to reverse the slide, political leaders contributed, albeit unwittingly, to an erosion in their states' capacity to cope with industrial decline. To be sure, this weakening of state capacity was not limited to France and Spain. Throughout Europe and elsewhere, the eclipse of American economic hegemony and the breakup of the Bretton Woods system removed the underpinnings of stable monetary management, sapping governmental ability to control the domestic money supply and thus to control inflation.[69]

Yet international constraints, however important, do not fully explain the decline in industrial and state capacity. In both Spain and France, "local" factors also contributed, specifically the economic policies of the post-Franco and post-Gaullist governments. In Spain the challenges of the democratic transition, accompanied by an escalation in popular mobilization and social demands, prompted the government to postpone rigorous adjustment measures while boosting social spending. In France the threat of a Left electoral victory also made the Giscard-Barre government reluctant to take unpopular adjustment steps.

In both countries, therefore, the economic legacy of conservative predecessors placed tight constraints on what incoming Socialist leaders could accomplish. One of the most pressing challenges facing Socialists in the early 1980s was to improve the competitiveness of their nations' main industries, which meant addressing problems of inflation and lack of investment. At the same time, these governments had to confront one of the social consequences of a declining industrial sector, namely growing unemployment. Although these problems limited the options available to incoming Socialist governments, they did not determine the specific mix of policies chosen, for that determination sprang from political as well as economic factors. To consider these, we must examine the nature of Left politics in France and Spain, and in particular the Socialists' governing coalitions.

3
Building Socialist Coalitions

Legacies
of
Leadership
Strategies

However constraining the economic legacy of previous governments, Socialist leaders ultimately made policy choices that reflected the internal politics and shared values of the Socialist movements themselves. Thus to grasp why particular economic policies were chosen over others, we must inquire about the nature of what this book has labeled the governing coalition—the main parties and organizations aligned with the government. In the French case, the governing coalition included not only the PS but also the PCF, as well as the two largest trade union confederations, the Communist-aligned CGT and the independent but Socialist-leaning CFDT. In Spain, the main elements were the PSOE and its affiliated trade union, the UGT. Unlike their French counterparts, both the PCE and its affiliated trade union, the CCOO, declined to support the Socialist government, at least officially.

To a striking degree, these coalitions resulted from organizational strategies launched by their leaders, Mitterrand and González, a decade earlier. This chapter examines those strategies and their consequences for the French and Spanish Socialist governments. It will argue that the two leaders differed sharply in their strategies for structuring the Socialist party, seeking political allies, and defining the party's program. Moreover, these differences largely accounted for the key contrast in economic policy trajectory noted in chapter 1, namely the early Mitterrand government's vigorous reformism compared with the González government's moderation. Divergent strategies for gaining power thus laid the groundwork for very different approaches to governance once the two leaders took office.

LEADERSHIP STRATEGIES AND CONSEQUENCES

Party Structure

Mitterrand sought to build a new socialist party by uniting his own movement, the Convention des Institutions Républicaines, with other non-Communist parties and "clubs," including the traditional socialist party, the Section Française de l'Internationale Ouvrière (SFIO). This process of incorporating existing groups into a new organization, the PS, produced a coalition of factions rather than a highly unified structure. The new party was inherently fractious and depended on Mitterrand, its presidential hopeful, for a unifying focus. González's goal, on the other hand, was to take over the traditional socialist party, the PSOE, from within, rather than create a new structure. In the process, the González team eliminated internal factions and centralized control over the party apparatus. The result was a more unified, centralized organization rooted in a veritable cult of personality.

France

Beginning in the mid-1960s, Mitterrand devised an organizational strategy to fit the new electoral reality of the Fifth Republic. The 1958 constitution, with its emphasis on a strong executive, gave parties an incentive to form coalitions in order to back an electable presidential candidate. Legislative elections, which required a runoff when no candidate won a majority in an electoral district, also favored cooperation among parties. Because runoffs were necessary in the vast majority of districts, parties had reason to form coalitions behind a single candidate in the second round.[1] But whereas the Gaullists adapted quickly to this new system, the Left responded slowly, and by the mid-1960s appeared on its way to becoming a permanent, divided minority.[2]

Mitterrand's strategy was to forge a presidential majority around himself and a broad alliance of Left parties capable of forming a cohesive parliamentary majority. This required, first, that Mitterrand become the Left's standard-bearer in the perpetual contest for the presidency, and second, that the Left build the broadest possible coalition, encompassing major elements of its two main traditional parties, the SFIO and the PCF. To cement this "Union of the Left," the two parties needed to agree on an electoral strategy and the basics of a governing program.

Mitterrand's own political past as a leader of small Center-Left parties and rival of SFIO leader Guy Mollet dictated that he pursue his aims from outside the two established parties, at least initially.[3] His approach was to rebuild the non-Communist Left around a new structure, with himself as fulcrum. Although he never joined the SFIO, Mitterrand sought to co-opt and transform it. This reconstruction of the SFIO passed through three phases.[4] The first was the party's reorganization, following Mollet's retirement as leader in 1969, around Alain Savary. The second was a palace revolt by anti-Savary forces within the new PS, which ended with Mitterrand's 1971 election as party general secretary. The final phase was the 1974 incorporation of Michel Rocard and many members of his small but influential Parti Socialiste Unifié into the PS.[5]

This incremental process strongly marked the party's internal dynamics. As a series of tributaries joining the old SFIO mainstream, the PS was a factionalized coalition of smaller parties and leftist clubs that grouped behind Mitterrand.[6] During the decade 1971–1981, four factions or "currents" (courants), emerged, each seeking to promote its own leaders and viewpoints within the party structure. On the party's left was the Centre d'Études, de Recherche et d'Education Socialistes (CERES), which had been an organized faction within the SFIO since 1965. From its beginning it sought to move the PS to an unambiguously left-wing and unitaire position vis-à-vis the PCF. The CERES shared several positions with the PCF, such as the need for a break with capitalism that would be initiated by mass action. It also shared as the PCF's affinity for a dirigiste state that would direct the new socialist economy. Aware that opposing capitalism with capitalism would likely arouse the hostility of other capitalist powers (especially the United States), the CERES advocated a nationalistic foreign policy that, like Gaullism, often bordered on anti-Americanism.[7]

A second main current, situated on the party's right, was led by Michel Rocard, who emerged in the late 1970s as the only PS figure other than Mitterrand who stood a chance of capturing the presidency. For this reason alone, Rocard and his followers had an uneasy relationship with Mitterrand, despite the two leaders' similar policy positions. Compared with the CERES, the Rocardians were less interventionist, emphasizing the need for decentralization and a more active civil society. Decrying capitalism's tendency to generate inequalities, they advocated a form of democratic planning but rejected the CERES's call for a break with capitalism. They also viewed the CERES's flirtations with the PCF and Marxism as outmoded and authoritarian.[8]

At the party's center were two groups distinguishable less by ideology than by personal loyalty to their leaders. One group comprised the so-called social democrats organized around ex-SFIO leaders Pierre Mauroy (mayor of Lille) and Gaston Defferre (mayor of Marseilles), both of whom led strong party federations within their *départements*. Mauroy and Defferre supported classic social-democratic causes such as government provision of extensive social welfare services and generous public spending on infrastructure projects. They differed on some issues, however. Mauroy, for example, having cooperated locally with the PCF, strongly backed the union of the Left, while Defferre remained cool toward the Communists. The other centrist grouping was, of course, the Mitterrandistes, who were drawn to their leader as much by personal loyalty as by ideological affinity. While sharing with the Rocardians an emphasis on modernization and pragmatic reform, Mitterrand's followers, unlike Rocard's, favored an alliance with the PCF.

A reflection of Mitterrand's long-term strategy, the PS in 1981 was a contentious coalition of these four currents, which were divided by organization, ideology, and loyalty to faction leaders, but united in a quest for power. As the prospects for gaining power rose, as they did during most of the 1970s, internal disputes remained muted. At the top, of course, reigned the great unifier, Mitterrand. Until 1979 he went unchallenged as party leader, and the inclusion of his current was essential to forming a leadership majority within the party.

Spain

González's struggle for party control during the late 1960s and 1970s took place, of course, in a country undergoing political transformation, and thus we must examine how he and other Socialists adapted to this changing context. The period with which we are concerned can be divided into three phases: the Franco regime's last years (1969 to November 1975), the period of democratic transition (November 1975 to December 1978), and the period of democratic consolidation (December 1978 to October 1982). During the first phase, González and other Spanish Socialists sought to wrest control of the PSOE from an aging, exiled leadership living in France and Mexico.[9] This challenge resulted from a growing cultural and ideological gap between younger activists who had grown up under Francoism but wanted to abolish it, and older exiles who generally remained aloof from events at home. Of the various leaders who challenged the exiled *históricos*, the most important was a group of *renovadores* headed by González, a young labor lawyer from Seville. By organizing the party's grass roots and supporting illegal strikes by the PSOE's affiliated trade union, the UGT, the *renovadores* succeeded in 1970 in gaining representation within the party equal to that of the exiled leadership. Subsequent challenges allowed González and his supporters to finally capture party control at the 1974 congress in Suresnes, France.[10]

The dynamics of the second phase—a three-year transition to democracy beginning with Franco's death in November 1975 and culminating in a referendum ratifying a new parliamentary constitution in December 1978—drew the PSOE from obscurity to prominence.[11] The most dramatic changes occurred during the first half of 1977, when the PSOE and most other political parties were legalized and launched their campaigns for the first general elections, which were held in June. With legalization, PSOE membership soared—from 8,000 to over 51,000 in just six months—and the party performed well in the elections, garnering nearly 30 percent of the vote in a close second-place finish to the UCD under Adolfo Suárez, who became the new prime minister.[12] This impressive result stimulated further growth in PSOE membership and even persuaded some smaller parties to affiliate with the PSOE.[13]

After the elections the PSOE and the government entered into consultations, for Suárez viewed the Socialists as useful and even necessary allies in building a stable democracy. In the eighteen months between the June 1977 elections and the December 1978 constitutional referendum, PSOE leaders helped craft the Pactos de la Moncloa and draft the new constitution. Along with this rapid growth in the PSOE's political influence and electoral appeal came a strengthening of González's personal standing within the party. With fellow Andalusian Alfonso Guerra handling organizational details, González and his closest advisers from Seville took firm control of the party.

The third phase—the period of democratic consolidation—followed the end of the transition process in late 1978 and lasted until the October 1982 elections. During this period González tightened his control over the party, despite protests from a *sector crítico* that he was becoming soft on Suárez's Center-Right government, deserting the party's commitment to radical change (which had been reflected in its embrace of Marxism in 1976), rejecting an alliance with the PCE and other leftists, and centralizing party power.[14] In a fierce internal struggle from May to September 1979, González forced a showdown by threatening to resign if the party did not back him fully. Emerging with a resounding victory over the dissidents, he moved the party away from Marxism while extending his hold over party organization.[15]

During the next three years, until the PSOE's 1982 electoral victory, González and his supporters remained fully in control of the party. Their obsession with internal unity, already quite pronounced, increased as party leaders became determined to avoid the kind of breakup that destroyed Suárez's UCD coalition in 1980–1981.[16] Even though periodic rebellions against the leadership's centralism and policy moderation erupted within the party,[17] González was easily able to deflect these attacks. His internal control was further strengthened by the voting-rule changes of 1979 that produced an influx of delegates loyal to him.[18]

By the early 1980s, the PSOE leadership was more unified, centralized, and personalized than that of the PS.[19] González's dominance of the PSOE was due to several factors: the virtual elimination of the *sector crítico*, imposition of a uniformly moderate ideological line (facilitated by an influx of new members with no connection to the party's anti-Francoist days),[20] and rule changes that solidified his circle's hold over delegate and candidate selection. Moreover, González's exceptional media and speaking skills made him the party's sole public voice, and, in the minds of many voters, the embodiment of the party itself.

Although such personalizing tendencies were hardly absent in the PS, especially given Mitterrand's mantle as the party's leading presidential hopeful, the PS remained more internally divided and dependent on fragile factional alliances to maintain unity. Mitterrand's status, at least until his election as president, was thus more precarious and contested, whereas González's preeminence, as the 1979 party crisis revealed, was never seriously threatened. To draw the contrast starkly: Mitterrand governed the PS, but González ruled the PSOE.

Alliances

Mitterrand and González differed not only in their approach to party structure but also in their approach to possible alliances, particularly with Communists and organized labor. Whereas Mitterrand based his electoral strategy on a "common program" alliance with the PCF, González rejected cooperation with other parties, in particular the PCE, and sought instead to rally the rest of the Left to his own party's banner. As for labor, although Mitterrand and the Socialists desired closer ties with the major confederations and with the working class in general, the PS never developed strong links with the union movement. González, by contrast, consolidated the historically close affinity between his party and the UGT, one of Spain's two main labor confederations. Thus the two parties came to power with different alliance patterns: the PS had a working, albeit conflictual, partnership with the PCF but weak labor ties, whereas the PSOE had almost no relationship with the PCE but strong links to a major labor confederation.

France

Mitterrand wagered that an electoral alliance with the PCF would work to the Socialists' advantage in two ways. First, in presidential elections the PCF would be unable to recruit a candidate who could appeal to centrist voters, and thus Mitterrand would be the alliance's natural leader. Second, for the same reason, in parliamentary elections the runoff provision would favor Socialist candidates, who would capture centrist as well as Communist votes, whereas PCF candidates would fail to attract centrist voters.[21] For its part, the PCF hoped that an alliance with the Socialists would revive its electoral appeal, which had slumped from 25 percent in the mid-1950s to 20 percent in the early 1970s and was increasingly concentrated among industrial workers, a shrinking voter group.[22]

These converging interests led to the 1972 Common Program of the Left, which committed the PS and the PCF (and a minuscule third party) to a program stressing nationalization and Keynesian-style social spending, and to a mutual-support agreement that applied to electoral runoffs and other matters. For all the expressions of unity and cooperation, however, the alliance was tenuous because Mitterrand's goal of establishing the PS as the dominant party on the Left (and as the majority party in French politics) clashed with the principle that the PS and the PCF would remain roughly equal partners in Left politics. The strains began to show almost immediately. In elections held from 1972 to 1977, PS candidates fared consistently better than those of the PCF. Not only did the Socialists enjoy a more positive public image, they also gained an advantage because PCF voters supported the electoral pact more faithfully than their PS counterparts.[23] With Communist leaders openly doubting not only the Socialists' loyalty but also the value of an alliance that worked increasingly to their disadvantage, the two parties split in September 1977 following a failed attempt to revise the Common Program of the Left, and thus entered the March 1978 parliamentary elections divided.[24] Despite a last-minute mutual-support agreement that temporarily muted the parties' differences before voting day, the coalition fell well short of a majority, demoralizing militants in both parties.

During the three years from the March 1978 election debacle to Mitterrand's May 1981 election, relations between the two parties failed to improve. The Communists accused the Socialists of abandoning opposition to capitalism and commitment to radical change. In the presidential election itself, the PCF sponsored its own candidate, Georges Marchais, who excoriated Mitterrand at every turn. Yet in the face of these attacks, Mitterrand remained publicly loyal to the alliance and refused to break with the Communists. Once elected, Mitterrand invited the PCF into his government—to control the party rather than risk its opposition—by offering four relatively minor ministerial posts. From the perspective of the summer of 1981, Mitterrand's party-alliance strategy had succeeded brilliantly: he had built up his own party at the PCF's expense, and despite the PCF's growing resistance to its own marginalization, had managed to keep that resistance contained.

Mitterrand's alliance strategy had a second focus: the cementing of strong ties to organized labor and the working class. Here, however, the results failed to meet expectations, for despite the PS's vow that "the first task of a Left government will be to organize the effective power of workers in the firm,"[25] the party was unable to develop solid organizational links to the working class. A major barrier was structural: the French labor movement's numerical weakness and long-standing division into competing confederations hindered the development of fraternal party-labor ties of the kind found in social-democratic movements in Britain, Germany, Austria, the Scandinavian countries, and Spain. Moreover, by the early 1980s the major unions were experiencing sharp drops in membership and militancy, due not only to the decline of blue-collar jobs but also to such factors as the 1979 collapse of "unity of action" between the CGT and the CFDT and new employer personnel strategies that sought to "individualize" the employment contract and thereby exclude unions.[26]

Compounding these problems was the fact that the PS had no organic or even privileged relationship with any of the three major labor confederations. The smallest confederation, the Force Ouvrière, fiercely guarded its political independence and refused to develop special ties with any political party.[27] The CFDT, the second-largest confederation, had the most PS members and was more ideologically sympathetic to the PS than the other confederations.[28] By 1979, however, the CFDT had decided to "recenter" its strategy on work place bargaining and reject party alliances.[29] When the Socialists took power, the CFDT initially backed the government; indeed, the first Mauroy government included several key CFDT leaders as members of the ministerial staff. But this support, conditional at best, gradually dissolved as the confederation distanced itself from the Socialists' economic program.

The largest confederation, the CGT, had long been under the control of the PCF.[30] Although PS supporters were well represented among the CGT membership, and even usually given a position or two on the CGT's sixteen-member Bureau Confédéral, the CGT's major strategic positions were decided by the PCF. During the postwar period, the CGT experienced only rare and brief periods of autonomy in its relations with the PCF, but such autonomy never extended to allowing Socialists to occupy critical union positions. Thus the PS's relationship with the CGT, always mediated by the PCF, varied with shifts in PS-PCF relations. Although there were PS members—and even some party activists—in the CGT, their presence and influence grew weaker and weaker as one ascended the confederation's hierarchy.[31]

The PS's dilemma, then, was that while claiming to be a party of the workers (or at least of the class front that included industrial workers as a main component), it had only loose ties to the labor movement. Although all PS members were expected to join a union, and most did, their memberships were split among the various industrial confederations and the main teachers' federation, the Fédération d'Education Nationale (FEN).[32] Moreover, despite the PS's professed aspiration to speak for the powerless, the party structure itself reflected oligarchy's iron law: the higher the level in the party hierarchy, the higher the socioeconomic status of the leadership.[33] To compensate for its weak working-class links and to compete against the Communists on their own turf, the PS set up over seven hundred "enterprise sections" and "enterprise groups" in various work places,[34] but their impact was slight. Present mainly in large firms, schools, and public-sector bureaucracies, these organizations tended to be dominated by the same highly educated, white-collar individuals who occupied party leadership posts.[35]

Despite its efforts to develop a mass base and links to labor, the PS thus retained a socioeconomic cast and ideological complexion that one author called "socialism without the workers."[36] Although it wished to speak for a shrinking working class that remained largely loyal to the PCF, the PS reflected the interests of growing middle-strata professions concentrated in the public sector: teachers, professors, health and social security providers, engineers, technicians, managers, and other white-collar workers. Sympathetic to the goals of both the old Left (such as nationalization) and the new Left (such as environmentalism), the middle-strata professionals responded to the PS's critique of the capitalist system yet also tended to oppose reforms that would "diminish the division of labor and democratize relations of production and politics,"[37] because such reforms would threaten their relatively favorable class position. The PS's core constituency thus favored leftist reforms that would reinforce state power without undermining capitalist production relations.

Spain

Unlike Mitterrand, González rejected the prospect of a formal alliance with his nation's Communist party. This reluctance stemmed from a history of mutual antagonism between the parties. The PSOE believed that the PCE had acted treacherously by serving Moscow's interests during the era of the Second Republic and the Civil War, and had helped to bring on Franco's rule. After 1945 PSOE leaders continued to view the PCE as Moscow's puppet, a sentiment reinforced by the PCE's 1964 expulsion of dissidents such as Claudín, Semprún, and Vicens. Despite the fact that González and the new leadership did not share the visceral anti-Communism of the older party membership, and despite the PCE's efforts to restyle itself as a "Eurocommunist" party, PSOE leaders looked on the PCE as opportunistic and domineering.[38]

This antipathy remained constant even as the balance of power between the two parties shifted during the 1970s. Before the watershed 1977 elections, the PSOE feared that an alliance with the PCE would risk overwhelming and smothering the PSOE. Not only was the PCE much larger—claiming, for example, 20,000 members at the time of Franco's death, versus the PSOE's 4,000— it also grew faster than any other party in the wake of legalization, reaching 100,000 members by late 1977.[39] Moreover, the PCE dominated the largest trade union confederation, the CCOO.[40] In these circumstances, a PCE alliance would have been risky for the weaker PSOE, which warily kept its distance.[41]

Following the 1977 elections, in which the PSOE outpolled the PCE by 28.9 percent of the popular vote to 9.2 percent, González and other top leaders saw even less reason for an alliance that would likely benefit just the PCE. This continued division had little ideological basis, for the PCE's Eurocommunism and González's desire to project a moderate and responsible public image caused both parties to adopt reformist, Center-Left positions. The continuing division between the two parties owed more to electoral competition, for both occupied the same electoral space and were competing for many of the same voters.[42] In any case, the issue of a PCE alliance became increasingly moot during the early 1980s as the PCE became embroiled in internal conflict and finally broke apart. Its descent to less than 4 percent of the vote in the 1982 elections consigned it to the political margins.

The PSOE maintained much closer relations with the Spanish union movement—particularly the UGT—than the PS did with the French union movement. The PSOE-UGT tie was fraternal in several senses: PSOE leaders had founded the UGT in 1888,[43] the two organizations overlapped considerably in membership, the UGT's executive committee was overwhelmingly (though not exclusively) composed of PSOE members, and PSOE members were required by party statutes to join the UGT.[44] In the early 1980s over three-quarters of UGT members supported the PSOE.[45]

Despite these close ties, the two organizations always insisted on formal independence, and their relationship remained ambiguous. Some PSOE leaders considered the UGT to be the party's extension in the work place,[46] yet the union, even before 1982, staunchly proclaimed its autonomy.[47] But whatever the precise balance of party control versus union autonomy, relations between Socialists and labor were closer in Spain than they were in France.[48]

The PSOE also surpassed the PS in influence within the working class, an advantage that arose from organizational and institutional shifts during the democratic transition. One important shift, which occurred during the period between the 1977 legalization of political and labor organizations and the 1982 elections, saw the UGT overtake the CCOO as the largest Spanish labor confederation. Whereas the CCOO had led the growing worker opposition to Franco in the 1960s and early 1970s, at a time when the UGT was largely a shell organization, the CCOO lost ground to the UGT after legalization, in large part because the PSOE's fortunes were rising while the PCE's were falling. The UGT's growing power led to a strengthening of the PSOE's roots within the working class.[49] A second shift that enhanced the PSOE's influence within the working class was a key institutional innovation of the democratic transition: the pact-making process that brought government, labor, business, and territorial officials together to regulate economic and regional-autonomy issues. Spanish unions, including the UGT, became key actors in this process, which gave them enhanced political access and influence. To the extent that the UGT through its participation gained in stature in the eyes of workers, so did the PSOE.

Although the PSOE enjoyed stronger labor ties than the PS, it is important not to overstate the difference, for those ties were limited in four ways. First, despite rapid membership gains after legalization, by the early 1980s labor union members as a proportion of the Spanish work force had declined to around 20 percent, a level of labor union participation that was one of Western Europe's lowest and only slightly larger than that of France.[50] Thus the PSOE's influence within the working class was curtailed to the extent that the labor movement itself became organizationally fragile. Second, the PSOE's actual presence in the work place—as indicated, for example, by party membership of work place leaders—remained slight, especially in the smaller firms, which still constituted the bulk of Spanish enterprises.[51] Third, PSOE-UGT relations were frequently tumultuous, in large measure because many UGT leaders believed that the PSOE took their union for granted.[52]

Finally, the PSOE displayed the same kind of organizational elitism that characterized the PS. Whereas over two-thirds of the members of top party bodies—including the parliamentary group, the federal committee, and the executive commission—were university educated, less than one-tenth of Socialist voters and rank-and-file members had such an educational background.[53] The same pattern held true for occupational background: whereas manual workers made up about 37 percent of rank-and-file members in the early 1980s, they were only 7 percent of the party's parliamentary group and 8 percent of its executive commission. Liberal professionals (doctors, lawyers, economists, and teachers) accounted for 60 percent of the parliamentary group and 72 percent of the executive commission.[54] Because of its union ties, the PSOE of the late 1970s and early 1980s cannot be called "a socialist party without workers," but most of its leaders above the rank-and-file level fit the same sociological profile as the PS's.

Party Program

PS and PSOE policy proposals grew far apart during the power struggles of the late 1970s and early 1980s. French Socialists vowed to challenge the capitalist system, both globally and in France itself. Although the party had abandoned earlier, more radical versions of worker self-management, the PS still espoused "structural" reforms that included massive nationalizations and new workers' rights. The PSOE, on the other hand, spoke not of challenging world capitalism but of modernizing the Spanish economy. It thus rejected the prospect of enlarging the public industrial sector in favor of investment incentives to private business.

France

To achieve his organizational and electoral goals, Mitterrand needed a party program that could accomplish several things. First, the program had to attract the PCF, which meant a platform embracing classic Left themes such as equality and hostility to monopoly capitalism. The program also had to attract reform-minded voters who were reluctant, out of fear or disillusionment, to vote Communist. Finally, the program had to be palatable to the Socialist Party's various factions, which were, as noted above, ideologically divided. In practice, the Socialists' program tended to reflect the shifting balance of forces among these factions (see table 3.1.) That balance depended on two factors: the party's relations with its principal ally, the PCF, and the party's prospects for electoral victory. Although there were major continuities over time in the positions taken by the PS, the party's ideology was not a package of fixed positions but the product of internal factional conflicts, which assumed their most overt form during the party's biennial congresses.[55]

During the decade between the 1971 party congress in Epinay and the Left's 1981 electoral victory, the PS was guided by three different factional alignments and three corresponding ideological orientations. The first alignment, which lasted from 1971 to 1975, encompassed the Mitterrandistes, the Mauroy/Defferre social democrats, and the CERES. During this period the party sought to engage the PCF in an electoral alliance while challenging it for leadership of the Left. For Mitterrand an alliance with the CERES was useful for two reasons. Most practically, he needed its support, especially during the crucial 1971–1973 period, to safeguard his position as party leader against opponents such as Guy Mollet, Alain Savary, and Jean Poperen. Moreover, the Left-leaning, pro-PCF CERES helped build the party's leftist bona fides among Communists and the public as a whole. With Mitterrand's imprimatur, the CERES grew rapidly in strength and ideological influence within the PS.

Table 3.1   The French Socialist Party: Factional Alignments, 1971–1981 (in percentages)

1971 Congress	
Mollet/Savary	34
Mauroy/Defferre	30
Mitterrand	15
CERES	8.5
Poperen	12
1973 Congress	
Mitterrand/Mauroy/Defferre/Savary	65.5
CERES	21
Mollet	8
Poperen	5
1975 Congress	
Mitterrand/Mauroy/Defferre/Savary/Rocard/Poperen	68
CERES	25.5
Mollet	3
1977 Congress	
Mitterrand/Mauroy/Defferre/Savary/Rocard/Poperen/Mollet	76
CERES	24
1979 Congress	
Mitterrand/Poperen	47
Rocard	21
Mauroy	17
CERES	15

Source: Adapted from Alistair M. Cole, "Factionalism, the French Socialist Party and the Fifth Republic: An Explanation of Intra-Party Divisions," *European Journal of Political Research* 17, no. 1 (January 1989): 81. *Note:* Figures are percentages, rounded up or down to nearest half percent, of Congress delegates supporting the corresponding *courant* or faction.

The Mitterrand-CERES alliance reflected a particular division of labor, with Mitterrand ceding many aspects of domestic policy to the CERES while reserving foreign policy and constitutional reform issues for himself.[56] This alliance mirrored Mitterrand's objective of gaining PCF support while seeking to surpass the Communists. On the one hand, the PS program featured classic Left themes such as nationalization and even the affirmation of Marxism as its "principal theoretical framework." On the other hand, the PS adopted fashionable new themes such as self-management *(autogestion)*, which were designed to attract "New Left" supporters concerned with issues of participation and decentralization. Although such an effort to reaffirm the old Left and embrace the new produced a pastiche-like program,[57] there is little doubt that this factional alignment, and in particular the CERES's presence, pulled the party leftward.

The PS's policy framework obviously was attractive to voters (the Socialists, for example, performed well in the 1973 legislative elections, and Mitterrand lost only narrowly to Giscard in the 1974 presidential election), but that very success ultimately undermined the Mitterrand-CERES alliance and reversed the Socialists' leftward movement. After 1974, with prospects for a Left victory increasing, Mitterrand sought to prepare the way for taking power. This meant limiting the PCF's influence in a future Left government, which in turn meant reducing the CERES's leftward influence within the PS. Mitterrand also had to confront electoral considerations. Having acquired the lion's share of leftist voters, the PS needed to begin courting centrist voters, and in this enterprise the CERES could only hinder PS efforts. Thus at the 1975 congress, Mitterrand formed a new majority with Mauroy, Defferre, and the newly arrived Rocard, and ejected the CERES from the party's ruling bloc.

This second majority alignment, which lasted until 1979, decidedly slowed the party's leftward movement. Content to rely on its 1972 Common Program proposals, the PS declared the program's nationalization plans largely sufficient, and ultimately broke with the PCF in 1977 over the list of firms to be nationalized. In addition, references to *autogestion* began to disappear from party publications and leaders' speeches. Although the PS never renounced this concept, the party's consensus on the meaning of self-management dissolved in a factional struggle, especially between the CERES and the Rocard current.[58]

This anti-CERES alliance ended and the third majority alignment took shape after the March 1978 electoral debacle, in which the breakup of the Union of the Left allowed the Right to retain power. Viewed by many in his own party as responsible for this failure, Mitterrand came under attack, especially from Rocard, who allied with Mauroy to seek Mitterrand's ouster at the 1979 party congress in Metz. To retain his party majority, Mitterrand renewed his alliance with the CERES, which quickly gained influence over the party's program. But although he allowed the CERES to push the PS's program to the left (as had happened in 1971–1975), Mitterrand reserved some maneuvering room for himself. For example, although the CERES drafted the party's new manifesto, the Projet Socialiste, which reaffirmed the party's commitment to radical change, Mitterrand, as the party's 1981 presidential candidate, ran on his own platform, known as the 110 Proposals, which was considerably more moderate in tone and substance. Mitterrand proclaimed himself the candidate of the Left as a whole, not the exclusive candidate of the Socialist Party, a point emphasized in campaign posters that stressed his personal attributes ("the tranquil force"), not his party affiliation.

By the eve of the 1981 elections, the Socialists' program was one of sweeping, yet vaguely defined, reforms whose appeal lay in a promise of change that was comprehensive and consciously designed, and therefore orderly. If Mitterrand was the "tranquil force," then why not a tranquil revolution in which everyone in the class front, meaning just about everyone, would benefit? Such a vision compared favorably with the limited ambitions of the incumbent Giscard-Barre majority, which appeared increasingly ineffectual in coping with France's economic crisis. Yet the Socialists' program hardly constituted a policy paradigm in the sense of a coherent set of values and priorities for governing, especially given that it rested on a series of fragile factional compromises that often entailed the adoption of apparently conflicting goals, as in the Rocardians' emphasis on decentralization versus the CERES's stress on nationalization. Although such conflicts would have to be resolved once the Socialists came to power, in the meantime they were largely deferred in the interest of party unity.

Spain

Unlike Mitterrand, who crafted a strategy for gaining power within a stable constitutional order, González operated within an uncertain, shifting political climate throughout the 1970s, which made adhering to a coherent program difficult and perhaps impossible. Starting in 1972, Mitterrand anchored his party firmly on the left (despite moderating tendencies in the late 1970s), but González displayed considerably more flexibility, and even sheer opportunism. Broadly speaking, the PSOE's program passed through two phases: a move to the left from the late 1960s to 1976, followed by a move to the center.

Before 1977 the PSOE moved consistently leftward, reaching its extreme in a December 1976 congress that, for the first time in the party's history, officially embraced Marxism and put forward a scenario for political change based on class struggle.[59] This scenario envisioned a *ruptura democrática,* a break with the Francoist order, which would come to pass as a result of both mass pressure and elite-level bargaining.[60] The new regime would be modeled not on social democracy, which the party considered "a mere corrector of the most brutal aspects of capitalism," but on principles of self-management *(autogestión).*[61] Other reforms would include nationalization of the ten largest banks and fifty of the largest industrial firms, elimination of private (that is, religious) education, abolition of the monarchy, and self-determination for the regions.[62] In foreign policy, although the party would work within the EC, it would adopt a neutral stance toward NATO and seek the removal of U.S. military bases. More generally, the party pledged to build socialism in Europe "independently of the imperalisms and in co-operation with the Third World."[63]

There were three main reasons for the PSOE's adoption of this maximalist framework: internal party politics, interparty competition within the Left, and the PSOE's legal status. First, from the standpoint of the party's internal politics, González had an incentive to promote a hard Left line. From 1969 to 1974, as was noted earlier, González was an insurgent against an old-line leadership that had largely made its peace with Francoism, albeit from exile. To distinguish himself from this entrenched elite, González campaigned as an agent of change and reform attacking the elite from the left. Even after his 1974 election as party chief, González had reason to push left. From late 1974 to late 1976—a period punctuated by Franco's death—the PSOE doubled in size (from 4,000 to 8,000 members), with most of the new members coming from the burgeoning anti-Francoist movements among workers, students, and others.[64] With the party's ideological center of gravity having moved well to the left, and with his control over the party still tenuous, González would have had little reason to counteract the leftward trend, even if he had wanted to.[65]

Second, González's desire to establish the Socialists as the premier Left party meant, as in France, challenging the Communists on their own ideological and organizational ground, which in turn meant identifying with workers and other exploited groups.[66] Unlike the French case, however, the PSOE's initial weakness made it wary of Communist domination and led the party to wage an insurgent-style campaign against the PCE from the latter's left, in much the same way as González had attacked his own party's leadership in his drive for power.[67]

Finally, the PSOE's illegal status until February 1977 (fourteen months after Franco's death) made a leftist line both a natural reflex and a necessity. Not until Suárez began consultations with elements of the opposition in the latter half of 1976 did the Socialists become convinced that post-Franco leaders were serious about dismantling the old regime. Until then, the PSOE's status as part of the banned opposition precluded abandonment of a leftist program.

By the time of the PSOE's legalization in February 1977, however, González and the leadership had distanced themselves from the radical positions of the party's congress only three months before. Thereafter, the PSOE strongly defended the democratization process within the new constitutional order. The party also tempered its critique of capitalism, including, as we have seen in the case of the 1979 crisis, the earlier Marxian espousal of class struggle and a classless society. (The only exception to the PSOE's moderate line was a muted but definite *tercermundismo,* that is, a Third Worldist, anti-imperialist slant in foreign policy.) Although the PSOE's moderation did not preclude specific and even general opposition to the Suárez government's policies, the party's behavior resembled that of a loyal opposition which believed it could govern more effectively.[68]

This transition within a transition—that is, the PSOE's move toward the center within the Spanish transition to democracy[69]—can largely be explained by four factors: electoral dynamics, public opinion, policy co-optation, and international influences. First, the PSOE's impressive showing in the 1977 elections made it a potential governmental contender, whereas the PCE's disappointing performance removed it as a serious Left rival. Electoral logic thereafter pushed the PSOE toward the center, for that was where new supporters were likely to be found. Thus the party abandoned its focus on the industrial working class and sought to encompass a PS-style class front.[70] Subsequent electoral trends only reinforced the PSOE's efforts to broaden its appeal. In the March 1979 elections (before the PSOE officially repudiated Marxism), Suárez successfully defended his party's hold on power by quoting the PSOE's 1976 resolutions and portraying the PSOE as dangerously radical. The PSOE's mediocre showing in the elections convinced González that the party had to abandon Marxism forthwith.[71] The PCE's continued stagnation and decline (10.8 percent of the popular vote and twenty-three seats in parliament in 1979, followed in 1982 by 3.8 percent of the vote and just four seats), and the UCD's disintegration after 1979, were further reasons for the PSOE to move toward the center.[72]

Second, the decidedly moderate character of Spanish public opinion reinforced the Socialists' centrist tendencies. Although the Left-Right cleavage remained the primary basis of political identification, the traditional link between Left-Right identification and such identities as class and religion was declining.[73] Moreover, the perceived ideological distance between major Left and Right parties was less, for instance, than in France, Italy, Greece, or Portugal.[74] And although the Spanish public was moving left in its political affiliations and favoring more egalitarian social policies, these preferences were accompanied by a strong belief in the legitimacy of Spain's new democracy and a clear preference for a democratic form of government.[75]

Third, the party's own participation in the transition process gave PSOE leaders a personal stake in its eventual success, and this moderated their erstwhile leftist tendencies. We have already seen, for example, the PSOE's active role in negotiating the Pacto de la Moncloa of October 1977 and in helping draft the 1978 constitution. These co-optive processes, and Suárez's willingness to consult González and other PSOE leaders informally, prompted the

Socialists to replace their earlier goal of *ruptura* with that of promoting and protecting Spanish democracy.

Fourth, the PSOE's foreign patrons within the Socialist International, notably the German Social Democratic Party (SPD), exercised a moderating effect on the party's political agenda. The emergence in 1975 of the SPD as the PSOE's chief foreign benefactor came only after Mitterrand and the PS alienated González by striking up friendly relations with the distrusted PCE.[76] Until that time the PS had enjoyed close contacts with, and indeed had exercised considerable influence over, the PSOE.[77] Thereafter, the SPD supported the PSOE through cash payments, the provision of seminars and training sessions, and sponsorship within the International.[78] Given the SPD's own centrist tendencies, it is reasonable to assume that the German party encouraged the PSOE's moderation.

This comparison of PS and PSOE programs highlights the internal party dynamics within each nation, in particular the polarized French political landscape of Left versus Right that persisted into the 1980s, in contrast to Spain's more consensual pattern, which resulted, among other things, from a democratic transition based on formal and informal agreements among elites. As a coda to the present analysis of what propelled the PSOE's leadership toward occupying the political center, we must of course take note of timing. The PSOE victory of October 1982 came eighteen months after the Socialist triumph in France—enough time for González and his team to judge the first fruits of Mitterrand's "experiment." As we will see in part III, their assessment of the outcome of Mitterrand's policies stiffened their resolve to move toward centrism and moderation.

SOCIALIST VOTERS: A MANDATE FOR REFORM?

This chapter's comparison of leadership strategies must consider one more issue: voter response. Who supported the Socialists, and what mandate did French and Spanish voters confer on their Socialist parties in 1981 and 1982? By the late 1970s and early 1980s Socialist voters in both France and Spain closely resembled the larger national electorates in terms of age, occupation, and other categories (see tables 3.2 and 3.3). The PS, unlike the SFIO of the early 1960s, had become a geographically national party, developing new support in the strongly Catholic eastern and western regions as well as in rapidly growing industrial urban centers, while holding on to the old SFIO base in the south.[79] This growth stemmed primarily from the party's successful adaptation to the socioeconomic changes of the 1960s and 1970s, which included urbanization, feminization of the labor force, and expansion of secondary and university education. These changes not only undermined the Right's traditional bases of authority[80] but also generated new social demands for improved education, housing, and transportation, which accorded well with the Left's public welfare emphasis.

In Spain, the PSOE's rise was attributable to the fact that it was the party most in accord with Spanish public opinion.[81] Especially important to the PSOE's widespread appeal was the public image of its leader, whose support cut across such traditional divides as class and religion.[82] González's image, moreover, improved markedly from 1978 to 1982, as the public came to see him as responsible and honorable.[83]

Table 3.2   France: The PS's Broad Demographic Appeal, ca. 1978 (in percentages)

	National Population	PS and MRG[a] Voters
Sex		
Men	48	52
Women	52	48
Age		
18–34	35	39
35–49	26	26
50–64	21	20
65+	18	15
Socioeconomic category		
Liberal professional, high-level business manager, business owner	16	13
Office worker	21	24
Industrial worker	30	31
Retired or unemployed	25	24
Farmer	8	8
Type of community[b]		
Rural	26	28
Urban		
<2,000 residents	16	17
20,000–100,000	13	14
>100,000	27	27
Paris region	17	13

Source: Sondages 40, no. 1 (1978): 26.
 a. Mouvement des Radicaux de Gauche.
 b. Totals do not equal 100 due to rounding.

Table 3.3   Spain: The PSOE's Broad Demographic Appeal, ca. 1982 (in percentages)

	National Electorate	PSOE Voters
Sex		
Men	48	50
Women	52	50
Age		
18–24	15	18
25–34	19	18
35–45	19	23
46–60	25	23
61+	22	18
Work force status		
Active	44	44
Student	7	6
Housewife	32	32
Retired	10	10
Unemployed	7	8
Occupational status		
Corporate director or corporate executive	7	4
Middle-level office worker or technician	20	17
Lower-level office worker	16	15
Skilled worker	28	32
Unskilled worker	28	31
Type of community		
<10,000 residents	32	30
10,000–50,000	17	18
>50,000–200,000	11	10
>200,000	40	42

Source: Han-Jürgen Puhle, "El PSOE: un partido predominante y heterogéneo," in Juan J. Linz and José Ramón Montero, eds., *Crisis y cambio: electores y partidos en la España de los años ochenta* (Madrid: Centro de Estudios Constitucionales, 1986), 300, 302.

In France, the victory by Mitterrand and the PS reflected not only long-term trends favoring the Left but also specific circumstances, notably President Giscard's rising unpopularity and the disunity in the Giscard coalition.[84] Mitterrand's momentum in the May presidential runoff explains much of the Socialists' success in the June legislative elections. For example, many voters believed that Mitterrand needed a National Assembly majority to carry out his program, and thus voted for Socialist candidates. The Socialists also drew support from voters who wanted to avoid a constitutional crisis if the Right retained control of the National Assembly. Yet despite Mitterrand's lengthy coattails, Socialist Party candidates, with only 9.4 million first-round votes, came nowhere close to matching their leader's runoff total of 15.7 million votes.

Mitterrand's presidential majority, therefore, was a fragile one, dependent on exceptional circumstances and the distorting effects of the single-member district electoral system (which, to offer one example, gave the PS 58 percent of the legislative seats in the first-round voting, although it won only 38 percent of the popular vote). In no sense was the 1981 vote a mandate for socialism, much less a partisan realignment. Rather, it represented conditional consent: an affirmation of voters' willingness to try Mitterrand's proposed alternative, given the manifest failure of the incumbent. As one middle-level manager said in explaining his reasons for supporting the Left, "I was enraged to see my factory disappear. I voted against Giscard and for Mitterrand because I was fed up *(ras-le-bol)*, not because of deep conviction. For me, the Socialists are in a precarious position. They must at least stop the hemorrhaging. I expect concrete results which have to be visible here, and I give them two to three years. After that, *fini!*"[85]

In Spain, the PSOE's 1982 victory was a result not only of the party's positive image, but of a combination of UCD political mismanagement and weak partnership. As noted in chapter 2, Suárez and his UCD government, once reelected in 1979, became increasingly unpopular and eventually self-destructed. Much of the problem stemmed from Suárez's "Franco-Leninist" style that alienated coalition supporters, external groups, and voters at large. Excluding several key party notables from cabinet positions in his second government and engaging in bitter confrontations with the church, the military, business, and labor, Suárez eventually lost the backing of his coalition and the public at large.[86] Unfortunately for the incumbent majority, his resignation as UCD chief and prime minister in January 1981 failed to reverse the public's perception that the government had become unstable and ineffective.[87] Facilitating this growing popular disaffection were weak partisan attachments on the part of voters. Despite the persistence of Left-Right self-identification, many voters had only a weak allegiance to a particular party, and thus could easily shift their support from one party to another, in this case toward the PSOE.[88] In the 1982 elections, the PSOE gained the support of about one-fifth of former UCD voters.[89]

The PSOE's victory was impressive. The party won 10 million votes, nearly double its 1979 total of 5.5 million. The elections witnessed a large increase in turnout—from 67 percent of eligible voters in 1979 to 78 percent (an increase of nearly 3 million voters)—and the PSOE captured most of the newly mobilized voters. The party, for instance, attracted the votes of 67 percent of those who abstained in 1979 but voted in 1982, and 60 percent of young first-time voters. Moreover, the PSOE drew votes not only from the UCD but from other parties as well, notably the PCE; by one estimate, about half of 1979's Communist voters shifted to the PSOE.[90] Finally, the 1982 elections appear to have contributed to a general increase in partisan identification that especially benefited the PSOE.[91]

Impressive as it was, the PSOE's triumph was not a mandate for socialism. Like the Mitterrand/Socialist surge in France, the 1982 shift in Spanish voting patterns was "more a product of the power vacuum created by a discredited political alternative than of a massive realignment of the electorate toward either the Right or Left."[92] Socialist voters were sending a message that they wanted a more activist approach to persistent economic problems as well as a measure of social protection. In both nations, moreover, voters in general were demonstrating that they endorsed change itself. Beyond these broad messages, however, the signals from the electorate were unclear, which meant that the new governments had "leeway, not a mandate."[93] Although the preelection theme had been "throw the rascals out," the postelection message was "do something about our problems." But what the new governments were expected to do remained largely undefined.

CONCLUSION

Although the present discussion has sought to avoid historical determinism, it has proceeded on the assumption that how the Socialists came to power affected their exercise of power. The values, programmatic preferences, and decision-making processes of the Socialist coalitions in France and Spain, it is reasonable to suppose, must have shaped how Socialist leaders viewed and responded to the challenges of governance. This chapter's examination of the development of Socialist governing coalitions in France and Spain has sought to establish two main points: first, that these coalitions reflected organizational strategies embarked on by Mitterrand and González in the late 1960s and early 1970s, and second, that the Mitterrand and González leadership strategies prescribed different approaches to issues involving the structures, alliances, and programs of their parties.

Mitterrand, for instance, created a party structure that incorporated existing groups into a new organization, the PS, and produced a coalition of factions or currents rather than a highly unified structure. González, by contrast, sought to take control of the traditional Socialist party, the PSOE, from within, and in the process eliminated internal factions and centralized control over the party apparatus.

In the realm of party alliances, Mitterrand cemented an electoral agreement with the PCF but failed to establish close links with organized labor, whereas González rejected an alliance with the PCE but cultivated strong ties with a major labor confederation, the UGT. Thus the two parties came to power with distinctively different alliance patterns—in the PS's case, strong relations with the PCF but weak labor ties, and in the PSOE's case, virtually nonexistent relations with the PCE but strong links of long standing with a major component of the labor movement.

Finally, with respect to party program, the dynamics of coalition building within specific national contexts pushed Mitterrand and González to espouse divergent programs. In the French case, the PS's factionalism and its pursuit of a Communist alliance produced a left-leaning platform that advocated a break with capitalism. In Spain, however, González's strong hold on the PSOE, coupled with the party's independence from other Left organizations, enabled González to respond flexibly to new electoral opportunities presented by an emerging democracy. The result was that the PSOE adopted a centrist program that promoted democratic consolidation and European integration over socialist transformation.

Counterbalancing these strategic differences were three factors that caused the two Socialist governments to resemble each other in structure and outlook. First, both coalitions had elitist organizational structures, with only slight representation of working-class occupations and backgrounds at the higher levels of their party hierarchies. Despite the PSOE's stronger union ties, both Socialist parties were dominated by the same middle-status groups of teachers, lawyers, and civil servants. The political orientations and policy preferences of the leaders of both parties were more or less in tune with the interests of these middle-class supporters.

Second, both the PS and the PSOE developed a broad electoral base. In seeking to build majority coalitions, Mitterrand and González sought to extend their parties' appeal to social groups not traditionally attracted to the Left, especially the growing ranks of middle-level white-collar employees, many of whom saw in socialism a promise of efficiency and honesty and a certain idealism—not radical change. Thus the support of many new Socialist party members and voters was highly conditional, driven by rejection of ineffectual incumbents rather than by an ideological conversion to socialism.

Finally, it is again important to underline the fragility of the PS's commitment to a left-leaning program and thus the potential for policy convergence on the part of the PS and PSOE governments. The PS's strategy of *rupture avec le capitalisme* resulted from struggles among party currents as well as from the PS's alliance strategy toward the PCF. Yet the PS's internal splits and the prickly nature of PS-PCF relations meant that commitment to a *rupture* strategy would depend on precarious balances among factional and party forces. For this reason, although Mitterrand and the PS came to power espousing policies well to the left of González's Socialists, the French Socialists' commitment to reform hinged on the initial success of those reform measures.

III | FRAMEWORK FOR ADJUSTMENT
MACROECONOMIC POLICY IN THE NEW EUROPE

If there was any message in the elections that brought Socialists to power in France and Spain in the early 1980s, it was the need for economic and industrial reform. As we have seen, the Socialists owed much of their electoral rise to the failure of previous governments to cope with problems of slow growth, inflation, and rising unemployment. Although such problems were hardly unique to France and Spain, the economies of those two countries had their own distinctive weaknesses. The most obvious deficiency was at the level of the firm, where businesses, especially in the manufacturing sector, were handicapped by growing debt, inadequate investment, foreign penetration, and weak export performance. Yet however obvious the need for adjustment in industrial structures, there remained the question of what that adjustment should be.

In examining how the Socialists responded to the challenge of industrial adjustment, this part of the book focuses on macroeconomic policy, which provided the framework within which adjustment took place.[1] Macroeconomic policy set the parameters for adjustment by establishing basic policy goals, designating the principal instruments or techniques used to achieve to those goals, and determining the settings of those instruments and techniques.[2] In the broadest sense, it determined what kinds of adjustment strategies were possible and desirable.

The present analysis of macroeconomic policy begins in chapter 4 with the French case. Chapter 5 examines Spanish macroeconomic policy and compares the two national experiences. These chapters argue, first, that French and Spanish Socialists ultimately converged toward a Europe-embracing macroeconomic strategy. By the mid-1980s both governments supported the idea of a mixed-economy society, that is, a policy paradigm which sought to reconcile market competition and government activism. The economic policy that grew out of this paradigm combined a monetarily restrictive exchange rate policy with extensive economic intervention. France and Spain adopted a strong-currency approach that tied exchange rate policy directly to the European Community's Exchange Rate Mechanism (ERM), which meant aligning national monetary policy with that of the restrictive German Bundesbank, the dominant player in the ERM. The result was a strategy of competitive disinflation whereby the French and Spanish governments sought to foster a relative price advantage for domestic goods by lowering factor costs, including labor, rather than by devaluing the currency. But within the constraints imposed by this conservative monetary regime, both governments pursued industrial and social goals. While rhetorically championing deregulation and the notion of "less state," they continued to view public firms as key instruments of economic management. Moreover, despite attempts to limit budget deficits, both governments maintained relatively high levels of social spending, especially for unemployed workers.

The second argument put forward in chapters 4 and 5 is that despite the convergence of French and Spanish macroeconomic policy, the two cases differed with respect to policy trajectory, dynamics, and impact. First, macroeconomic policy in Spain remained consistent in that the González government adhered to a moderate strategy of adjustment and modernization from the outset. Key goals included promotion of foreign investment, Spanish participation in the EC, cooperation within the EC, stimulation of domestic investment and competition, and disinflation, which meant that other "socialist" aims such as job creation and income redistribution had much lower priority. By contrast, the French Socialists' macroeconomic strategy was inconsistent and shifting. Beginning with vows to "reconquer the domestic market," the Mitterrand government quickly increased state spending and carried out large-scale nationalizations. This approach proved unsustainable, however, and within a year the government began moving toward a policy of "rigor," which became French Socialist gospel for a decade. Whereas Spain's Socialists kept to a straight economic path, their French counterparts made a jolting U-turn.

The French and Spanish cases also differed in the dynamics of macroeconomic policy. Simply put, in France public opposition to the Socialists' economic policy declined over time, whereas in Spain it rose. From 1982 to 1984, as the Mitterrand government gradually abandoned reflation in favor of economic orthodoxy, policy formulation and execution in France featured intense struggles over economic strategy, both within the government and between the government and organized interests. By the mid-1980s, however, as economic rigor became the preferred approach, broad support for the mixed-economy paradigm emerged. Although this paradigm never engendered wild enthusiasm among French Leftists, once it was established there was little overt Left opposition to government economic policy. In Spain, by contrast, widespread Left support for the González government's moderate economic policy was apparent from the start, even during the 1982–1985 period of austerity that saw the ranks of the unemployed swell by one-third. Policy formulation and execution in the early González years thus escaped the kind of fractious debate over strategy that wracked the French Left. But whereas in France after 1984 the main elements of the Left either adhered to the strong-franc *(franc fort)* strategy or did not effectively contest it, in Spain organized opposition to the government's policy grew over time.

The final difference between France and Spain concerned policy outcomes. Once it abandoned its *relance* strategy and embraced a strong-franc policy, the Mitterrand government proved more successful than González's in achieving its goals. By the early 1990s, the French economy's performance was clearly superior to Spain's in reducing inflation and trade and budget deficits. French performance on unemployment, though hardly impressive, was much better than Spain's, whose joblessness far exceeded that of any other EC nation. Although Spain's economic growth over the entire 1981–1993 period was greater than France's and surpassed the EC average, the growth rate plummeted during the post-1990 recession. Thus despite the PSOE government's more consistent macroeconomic approach, which favored early adjustment measures and encouragement of foreign investment, Spanish macroeconomic policy was less effective than France's as an antidote against endemic inflation, trade and budget deficits, and unemployment.

4
France

Good Things
First,
Bad Things
After

The progress of French macroeconomic policy under the Socialists can be divided into two five-year periods, 1981–1986 and 1988–1993. The first was the period of Socialist legislative dominance following the electoral triumphs of May–June 1981. During these years, the global economy underwent a deep recession (1981–1982) and then a gradual recovery (1983–1986). In 1986 the economic recovery worked to the Socialists' benefit and allowed them to perform respectably in the legislative elections of that year, but they lost their majority, and for the next two years Mitterrand had to work with a conservative legislature. After winning reelection as president in 1988, Mitterrand called new elections, which returned control of the National Assembly to the Socialists and ushered in the second period. The Socialists, though, lacked an absolute majority and had to rely on independent centrists and occasional Communist abstentions to achieve voting majorities. Socialist political weakness was accentuated, moreover, by the global economy's move from strong growth in 1988–1990 to renewed recession in 1991–1993. Because Socialist macroeconomic policy was shaped by the different social and economic developments of the two periods, this chapter will examine each period separately.

FROM *RELANCE* TO *RIGUEUR*, 1981–1986

French macroeconomic policy in 1981–1986 passed through four phases, each with a distinct configuration of demand and supply strategies. On the demand side, the sequence of policies ran almost full circle, from economic stimulation in 1981, to a gradual turn toward austerity in 1982–1983, to a return to moderate economic stimulation through tax cuts in 1984–1986. On the supply side, the government's policies alternated between two types of approaches, sectoral and environmental. The sectoral approach promoted attempts to reorganize and recapitalize specific firms and industries, whereas the environmental approach sought to establish general business conditions that would encourage private-sector investment. Proceeding on somewhat independent paths, demand and supply approaches combined in four distinct patterns or states as indicated in figure 4.1.

Phase 1: *Relance* and Industrial Intervention, June 1981–June 1982

Taking power at a moment when European governments were increasingly attacking inflation through Reagan- and Thatcher-inspired programs of fiscal reduction and tight monetarism, France's Socialists targeted unemployment instead. Their prescription was to stimulate domestic demand through a Keynesian-style reflation, or *relance,* while also undertaking nationalizations and other "structural" reforms to revive industrial investment. The goal was to "reconquer the domestic market" and create jobs at the same time.

Figure 4.1   France: A Tortuous Path—Macroeconomic Policy, 1981–1986

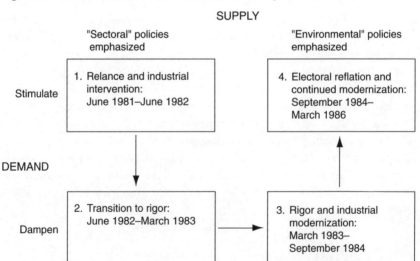

This reflation strategy featured a vast array of measures directed at both aggregate demand and aggregate supply.[1] Demand was to be stimulated in three major ways. First, the government aimed to put more money in people's pockets (especially the pockets of the lowest paid) through substantial (10 percent–50 percent) increases in, among other things, the minimum wage, old age pensions, and family, maternity, and housing allowances. Second, job creation was to be stimulated by shortening the legal work week from forty to thirty-nine hours, increasing legally mandated paid vacation time from four weeks to five, promoting early-retirement "solidarity contracts,"[2] making full retirement possible at age sixty, and similar measures. Finally, the government sought to boost employment by creating 180,000 new public-sector jobs by the end of 1982.

The government's supply side approach, like its demand side approach, exhibited a strongly *dirigiste* or interventionist bias. The approach was two-pronged, with both initiatives aimed primarily at creating, or at least saving, jobs. By nationalizing twelve industrial groups, thirty-six banks, and two finance companies, the government sought to restructure and recapitalize several crucial industrial sectors such as chemicals, electronics, energy, and metallurgy. It hoped that the new public firms would generate new jobs and produce a spillover effect in the private sector. To kick start this process, the government pumped Fr 26 billion in working capital into the nationalized firms from 1981 to 1983, or more than public firms received during the entire period of the Giscard presidency.[3] In the private sector, the government devised sectoral plans for such troubled industries as machine tools, leather goods, textiles, furniture, and toys—all industries that had been hit hard by imports or shrinking markets. A three-year plan for the machine tools industry, for instance, guaranteed new markets (including purchases by nationalized firms), provided research and development funds, and encouraged mergers of small firms. State aid to the machine tools industry under this plan totaled Fr 2.3 billion, for an industry with 1982 sales of Fr 5 billion.[4]

Politically, the government's stimulation strategy made good sense. A majority of the public favored reflation, nationalization, and most of the other economic measures undertaken by the government.[5] Moreover, having promised during the 1981 campaign to bring in a stimulation program, the Socialists did not want to disappoint their supporters. The Left, according to Christian Sautter, Mitterrand's top economic adviser, was euphoric in the wake of Socialist success: "It was, after all, an unexpected Left victory after twenty-three years in opposition. And Mitterrand, who had just been elected, was very attached to certain electoral promises he had made, unlike certain politicians. Normally, one fulfills such promises just before the next election . . . but we played the political cycle exactly in reverse by doing the good things first and the bad things after."[6]

But despite the favorable political climate for *relance,* the strategy was economically flawed because it rested on contradictory policies. It was clearly out of phase with other industrialized capitalist economies, which were experiencing a sharp recession triggered by the second oil shock and the Federal Reserve's strong-dollar policies.[7] To avoid a flood of imports and a burgeoning trade deficit, the government would likely have had to resort to such protectionist steps as a sharp devaluation (which would have required France to leave the EMS indefinitely), severe currency exchange controls, and measures to shelter domestic industry. Yet, for fear of appearing weak and alienating fellow EC members, Mitterrand rejected such an approach and refused to permit an immediate devaluation, even in the face of a massive franc sell-off following his election.[8]

Although reflation initially proved stimulatory,[9] it produced three negative effects. First, by stimulating consumption, reflation fueled an increase in consumer prices; by 1982, France's inflation rate outpaced that of its main European partners.[10] Second, despite the *relance*'s generally favorable impact on employment and investment, both continued to decline.[11] The fall in investment stemmed in part from a contradiction in the strategy itself, namely that a reflationary fiscal policy was coupled with tight monetary measures. With the government forced to intervene to support a sagging franc, interest rates were pushed up from 18 percent to 20 percent in 1981. Corporations' net interest payments, which had already increased 27 percent in 1980, rose another 36 percent in 1981.[12] Investment was also affected by rapidly rising labor costs, a result of higher wages, shorter work weeks (without corresponding wage reductions), and increased social security taxes.[13] With profit margins thus squeezed, firms tended to postpone new investments.[14]

Finally, much of the increased demand was not for domestic products but for imports, especially private consumer goods such as German automobiles and Japanese electronics. As a result, the trade balance deteriorated sharply (see table 4.1). Most alarming was the growing trade deficit with EC nations, in particular West Germany, which caused the franc to plummet in value and led the government to negotiate a devaluation within the EMS in October 1981.[15] Yet this measure offered only temporary respite. With currency speculators circling around a faltering economy and the dollar attracting buyers because of soaring U.S. interest rates, the Banque de France had to intervene on a huge scale to slow the franc's slide.[16]

April 1982, which saw France's overall trade deficit jump to Fr 10.1 billion from the previous month's Fr 4.5 billion, marked the beginning of the

Table 4.1   France: Trade Deficits, 1980–1984 (in billions of U.S. dollars)[a]

	1980	1981	1982	1983	1984
World	23.5	19.2	23.0	13.8	10.3
OECD	12.2	11.3	16.6	11.8	8.8
EC	4.6	5.6	9.8	7.4	6.5
West Germany	4.0	4.2	5.8	3.6	3.2

Source: Calculated from Organisation for Economic Co-operation and Development, *Economic Surveys: France* (Paris: OECD, 1987), 86.

a. Exports calculated on "free-on-board" (FoB) basis (i.e, not including insurance and freight costs); imports calculated on "cost-insurance-freight" (CIF) basis (including insurance and freight costs).

government's policy shift. To encourage investment and boost exports, the government lowered the "professional tax" on employers and froze their social security charges. In an interview with the author, Prime Minister Mauroy recalled his thoughts at the time: "I realized by May that what many experts had predicted, namely an economic pickup in the U.S., wasn't occurring. Therefore, this was a crisis that was going to last. And if this crisis was long-term, then we couldn't continue even our modest reflation, which made everybody happy during the early honeymoon period *(état de grâce)* but which economically profited Germany and which, if it had continued, would have asphyxiated this country."[17]

Mitterrand delayed any dramatic moves until after a G7 summit at Versailles in mid-June, believing, according to Mauroy, that he could persuade Reagan to loosen the Americans' tight monetary policy and thus ease pressure on the franc.[18] Failing to do so, however, Mitterrand suddenly reversed course. Summarily abandoning its stimulative strategy, the government froze wages and prices for four months (until 31 October) and vowed to cut domestic demand, government spending, and taxes on private firms. Accompanying these measures was a second negotiated devaluation of the franc within the EMS.[19] Although government officials refused to state whether this turn toward *rigueur*—as the new policy was euphemistically called—would be a temporary pause or a lasting strategy, it shocked most political observers as well as the public.[20] It also brought to the surface sharp divisions within the government itself over the direction of economic policy.[21]

It has become common wisdom, even on the Left, to treat Mitterrand's experiment with reflation as ill-conceived and even irresponsible. André Gauron, an economic advisor to Economy and Finance Minister Pierre Bérégovoy, remarked to the author in 1987:

> In 1981 there was the idea that we had to move quickly because the Left was legitimated. That the Left would remain in power for the full term was

something a lot of people, even within the Left, doubted; many thought it wouldn't last a year. But we should have taken a more gradual approach. We badly managed the budget. And doing this in an international climate that we also misjudged led to a great budget deficit. If we had held down spending, the deficit would have been managed. As it was, it took us two years to stop the machine.[22]

Even Mitterrand himself later admitted that his government had made several errors, which included failing to devalue the franc, being "carried away" and "intoxicated" by the 1981 electoral victory, and underestimating the severity of the international crisis.[23]

However ill-conceived the policy appears in hindsight, a balanced judgment must consider several facts. First, the Socialists did not initiate reflation. The Giscard-Barre government had begun its own preelectoral *relance* in late 1980, and much of the economic stimulus of 1981 was the result of this.[24] Second, France's budget deficits, and thus the extent of the stimulus, were, in fact, comparatively modest; the Socialists' reflation was hardly a mad dash for growth. In 1982, for example, the budget deficit as a proportion of GDP was well within the range of deficits being incurred throughout the EC.[25] In boosting economic activity less than 2 percent, the 1981–1982 policy was in fact slightly less stimulative than the reflation carried out under Gaullist prime minister Jacques Chirac in 1975–1976.[26]

Finally, the ballooning trade deficit of 1981–1982, which led to an increase in foreign borrowing and greater pressure on the franc, was due as much to external forces—especially the world recession brought on by the doubling of oil prices and the Americans' tight monetary policy—as to the Socialists' reflation.[27] The Socialists inherited a trade deficit of roughly Fr 54 billion, which nearly doubled to roughly Fr 100 billion in 1982. Of the increase of Fr 46 billion, the *relance* accounted for only Fr 18 billion. The rest was due mainly to international conditions (a rising dollar, higher energy prices, and declining world demand in general) and France's two devaluations.[28] To be sure, reflation in the face of a looming world recession and a soaring dollar was, in retrospect, a costly mistake; however, few forecasters (including the OECD) anticipated the full impact of those developments.

Phase 2: The Transition to *Rigueur,* June 1982–March 1983

The ten months following the burial of *relance* were marked by a political struggle within the government over the direction of economic policy. Reluctant to abandon its reformist goals yet determined to bring budget and trade balances under control, the government pursued policies that reflected these contradictory impulses. Thus whereas the newly imposed policy of rigor sought to reduce inflation and restore profit levels among private firms, supply side measures, especially in the public sector, featured extensive intervention in particular sectors and industries. This phase ended with the definitive triumph of the advocates of rigor and a decisive paradigm shift in Socialist policy.

Leading the attack on inflation, Economy and Finance Minister Jacques Delors sounded the new theme: "We want to have wages rise more slowly than prices in order to curb consumer purchasing power and increase profitability."[29] To do so, the government employed three main measures. The first was an explicit incomes policy. Following the 31 October expiration of the wage and price freeze, a new method of wage regulation (called the *système Delors*) sought to break the virtually automatic link between consumer prices and wages, especially in the public sector. Rather than abandon any form of indexation, however, the policy sought to link wages to inflation targets instead of observed price increases. The 1983 target was set at 10 percent (versus a 1982 inflation rate of 11.8 percent). Wages in the government sector and in the nationalized firms, which together encompassed 38 percent of all workers, were required to stay below the 10 percent mark, and private-sector firms were asked to conform to the 10 percent limit as well.[30] A second measure was aimed at limiting public spending in order to reduce fiscal stimulation and the budget deficit. The measure required total spending in fiscal year 1983 to rise less than 12 percent, versus the previous year's 27 percent. Finally, the government sought to stimulate private investment by easing "social charges" on businesses, deferring a tax on "work tools," and accelerating depreciation allowances.[31]

Coexisting awkwardly with this effort to limit state spending and boost private investment was a strongly interventionist industrial policy executed by Research and Industry Minister Jean-Pierre Chevènement. This policy, established by Chevènement's predecessor, Pierre Dreyfuss, was captured in the formula, "There are no condemned sectors, only outmoded technologies."[32] The idea was that in certain industries the government would encourage the development of *filières* (production chains), namely integrated processes beginning with the extraction of raw materials and ending with the production of finished goods.[33] Seeking greater vertical coordination between domestic producers within particular production chains, the *filière* approach was also expected to modernize each segment of a chain, even in older, declining industries.[34] In practice, this approach encouraged the state to reorganize entire sectors and even determine industrial strategies for specific firms.

Chevènement, extending Dreyfuss's sectoral plans for depressed industries such as machine tools, added other industries to the rescue list. To help the steel industry, for example, plans were made to expand production, even though demand had been declining for nearly a decade. Public firms in certain industries, such as telephones, biomedicine, and chemicals, were given no choice in the matter, but simply ordered by Chevènement to pursue his strategies.[35] And in an effort to restructure rapidly growing high-technology industries, Chevènement spearheaded a five-year, Fr 140 billion plan for the electronics sector. To these costly plans, finally, must be added the greatly increased outlays to the nationalized industrial firms, which rose from Fr 5 billion in 1982 to Fr 13 billion in 1983.[36]

Thus an expansive industrial policy was pursued just as the government was trying to limit demand and state spending. The contradictions of this approach quickly became apparent. For instance, while Delors was announcing investment incentives for business, the government was augmenting its subsidies to state-run companies, and while some officials were preaching the virtues of free trade, others were taunting the Japanese by requiring them to import videocassette recorders through Poitiers, a small inland town remote from ports with only a small customs office. Lacking coherent criteria for deciding which sectors should receive aid, the government employed a shotgun approach that was expensive and inefficient, and made worse by the poor financial performance of many public-sector firms.[37] And although the government was beginning to encourage private investment, employers continued to complain about heavy taxes and high interest rates.

Economically, the results of this first attempt at rigor were mediocre. The wage and price freeze of the latter half of 1982 helped bring inflation for the year down to 11.8 percent (versus 13.4 percent in 1981), but this rate was more than double West Germany's (5.3 percent). Largely because of the freeze, industrial production declined 3 percent during the second half of 1982.[38] Most critically, the trade balance continued to worsen. The deficit for all of 1982 was Fr 93 billion, compared with Fr 51 billion in 1981, which led to a substantial rise in foreign borrowing.[39] The only relatively bright spot was unemployment, which actually dropped slightly in late 1982; however, the average unemployment rate for all of 1982 (8.3 percent) was still a full point higher than the 1981 average.

As it became obvious by early 1983 that the wage and price freeze had not brought a quick economic fix, disagreements sharpened within the government over the next step. The debate pitted advocates of continued rigor against those who favored what came to be called "the other policy" (l'autre politique), which entailed maintenance of the relance policy's commitment to expansion and income redistribution, even if this meant leaving the EMS and adopting protectionist measures. The pro-rigor group, headed by Mauroy, Delors, and

Planning Minister Rocard (with outside support from Edmond Maire, head of the CFDT), argued that domestic inflation had to be brought into line with France's main EC partners, especially West Germany, and therefore that considerably more austerity was needed. If not, trade deficits, foreign debt, and a weak currency would sap the country's competitiveness and ultimately undermine political stability (the "lessons of Chile" were frequently cited). The pro-rigor group argued, first, that wages and purchasing power should be restrained until the trade deficits and other economic problems were remedied, and second, that private investment should be fostered by making credit easier to obtain and lowering social security taxes.

Espousing "the other policy" was a collection of strange bedfellows such as Chevènement, his left-wing CERES faction, and several close Mitterrand advisers who otherwise had little in common with the CERES. These included Social Affairs Minister Bérégovoy, Budget Minister (and Mitterrand protégé) Laurent Fabius, National Assembly President Louis Mermaz, and Mitterrand's old friend, industrialist Jean Riboud. The CERES group advocated selective protectionism in order to preserve social reforms and reinforce the state's ability to manage the economy,[40] while the less visible but more influential group of "night visitors," as Mauroy derisively called the Mitterrand confidants, urged that France should leave the EMS, lower interest rates, maintain a tight income policy to hold down wage increases, and raise the value-added tax.[41]

The debate and drift lasted until March 1983, the defining moment in the history of this first Socialist government (indeed, in the history of the entire 1981–1993 period of Socialist politics). Even though economic conditions had been worsening for months, Mitterrand delayed making any policy changes until after the municipal elections in March, for fear of signaling weakness and losing voter support. He also wanted to use the elections as a gauge of public perceptions of his economic program. These perceptions came sharply into focus in the first round of the elections, when the Left as a whole won only 44 percent of the vote and lost control of several large cities.

During the two and a half weeks following the first round, government leaders engaged in a decisive struggle over the future of rigor.[42] The second round, which witnessed an improvement in Socialist electoral performance, apparently convinced Mitterrand of two things: first, that the rigor policy was generally unpopular, and second, that his government still had sufficient public support to return to a voluntarist, *relance* type of policy. Mitterrand thus asked Mauroy to stay on as prime minister but to apply "the other policy." Mauroy at first refused but finally agreed to do so.

In the meantime, however, Budget Minister Fabius, an erstwhile advocate of "the other policy," had a conversion experience. After discussing France's external position with the director of the treasury, Fabius became convinced that the country lacked the resources to pursue "the other policy."[43] Conveying his doubts to the president, he apparently persuaded Mitterrand to opt for the Mauroy-Delors policy. Mitterrand then sent Delors to Brussels to negotiate a realignment of the franc within the EMS, which resulted in an effective devaluation of 8 percent against the mark. It also remained to be decided whether Delors would replace Mauroy as prime minister, but after much vacillation Mitterrand chose to keep the incumbent.[44]

Phase 3: *Rigueur* and Industrial Modernization, March 1983–July 1984

The third phase featured a new combination of demand and supply measures that sought to improve France's ability to compete globally while remaining closely tied to its EMS partners. In distributive terms, this strategy, by restraining demand and funneling resources to business, placed austerity's burden on workers and consumers rather than the corporate sector.[45] On the demand side, the "Delors plan" imposed new taxes and expenditure cuts in order to curb consumer spending, dampen inflation, and balance public accounts.[46] Stressing industrial modernization rather than job creation, supply side policy shifted to "environmental" measures such as financial incentives available to all firms, rather than firm- or sector-specific interventions.

In the private sector, the government sought to increase the pool of savings available for investment.[47] A chief instrument for doing so was a new industrial investment fund, the Fonds Industriel de Modernisation (FIM), which was financed by a new public savings account, the Compte Pour le Développement Industriel. Dispensing low-interest loans for machine and equipment purchases, the FIM sought to facilitate modernization in such sectors as biotechnology, microcomputers, office automation, and energy-saving transportation equipment.[48] From 1983 to 1986 (when it was dissolved by the Chirac government), the FIM lent over Fr 24 billion for such purposes.[49] Other incentives for stimulating investment included tax exemptions for newly created companies, state-funded "creation leaves" for employees starting their own businesses, subsidies for adopting computer-controlled equipment, funds for professional training of engineers and technicians, and research and development aid.[50]

In the public sector, the new approach forced firms to cut costs and become more efficient. As noted above, public firms, especially those nationalized in 1982, had become a fiscal drag requiring huge subsidies.[51] Declaring that these firms would now enjoy almost total freedom from state control, the government also began reducing their subsidies. In September 1983 Industry Minister Fabius announced that subsidies for the following year would be frozen at present levels and that public-sector firms, with the exception of CDF-Chimie and those in the steel industry, would have to break even by the end of 1985. These measures required large-scale layoffs, which began in late 1983 at the public-sector coal producer Charbonnages de France (CDF) and expanded to include shipbuilding and steel in early 1984.

Underlying these policy changes was a dramatic change in official discourse, in which the rhetoric of top Socialist leaders began to ring with terms such as "modernization," "competitiveness," "risk," and "profit." The embodiment of this new-look socialism was Fabius, who stated, "Socialists remained rigid *(sclérosés)* for too long. They continued to view the modern industrial world as that of the nineteenth century. However, business owners have changed; the entrepreneur is no longer an owner thirsty for profit. He is an explorer for whom profit becomes a means rather than an end."[52] Accompanying this new appraisal of capitalists as heroic adventurers rather than heartless exploiters was a new view of the state's proper role. Less *dirigiste* and more modest in its economic ambitions, the state should help foster citizens' initiatives, including private enterprise. According to Mitterand, "We must have a state closer to the people and a market more welcoming toward creators of enterprises and more sensitive to workers' aspirations.[53]

Although the new discourse signaled a paradigm shift on the part of Socialist leaders, it is important to note that theirs was not a pure conversion to Thatcher-style neoliberalism. Retaining vestiges of traditional French *étatisme,* the new paradigm envisioned a mixed-economy society, a symbiotic relationship between the state and the economy. Mauroy later explained this concept to the author as follows:

> We definitively accepted the idea of a market economy; however, this market economy brings problems. It sometimes works badly or stupidly, and therefore you need counterweights. That means you need two things: in the economic sphere, a strong public sector along with a certain amount of planning, and in the social sphere, a solidarity policy that will equitably redistribute the fruits and efforts of economic growth. This is what we call a mixed-economy society, a marriage between the market economy and these counterweights I mentioned.[54]

Economically, rigor showed immediate results, although its impact was mixed. On the positive side, the trade deficit narrowed appreciably, from Fr 93 billion in 1982 to Fr 42 billion in 1983, as a strong dollar and a devalued franc gave a sharp stimulus to exports. Inflation declined markedly, from an annualized rate of just over 10 percent during the first quarter of 1983 to less than 7 percent for the first quarter of 1984.[55] Business performance improved in

Table 4.2   France: Economic Performance of Nonfinancial Corporations, 1979–1984

	1979	1981	1982	1983	1984
Investment ratio[a]	18.3	18.9	18.9	17.2	16.6
Profit ratio[a]	25.3	23.8	24.0	24.4	25.9
Saving[a]	12.9	9.4	9.1	9.7	11.5
Self-financing ratio[b]	65.3	53.7	49.4	60.6	71.2

Source: Organisation for Economic Co-operation and Development, Economic Surveys: France (Paris: OECD, 1985), 21.
  a. As a percentage of value added.
  b. Gross saving and net capital transfers received as a percentage of gross fixed investment.

several respects, as corporate profit ratios, savings rates, and self-financing ratios all climbed in 1983–1984. On the other hand, despite the various measures to promote modernization, the investment ratio declined in 1983–1984 and remained much lower than in the 1970s (see table 4.2). Moreover, rigor indeed shifted the burden to ordinary people. Unemployment, after rising only modestly (from 8.1 percent in 1982 to 8.3 percent in 1983), climbed steeply to 9.7 percent in 1984. Conversely, disposable household income, which rose more than 3 percent in both 1981 and 1982, dropped slightly in 1983 (by 0.7 percent) and 1984 (by 0.4 percent).[56]

Predictably, rigor sparked little public enthusiasm, and both Mitterrand's and the government's popularity sank steadily. By the spring of 1984, only 30 percent of the population gave the president a positive approval rating, one of the lowest ratings in the history of the Fifth Republic.[57] With the decline in public support came a growing willingness on the part of interest groups to manifest their discontents. Farmers, shopkeepers, medical students, butchers, truck drivers, and workers in depressed industries all staged demonstrations against government policy.

Discontent also spread within the government coalition, with the most vocal dissent coming from the PCF and its labor affiliate, the CGT. Since the turn to rigor in 1982 the PCF had been caught in a contradiction, continuing to hold four ministerial posts yet rejecting rigor and blaming the crisis on a capitalist conspiracy. By the spring of 1984 this conflict had become untenable for both the PCF and the Socialists, as massive layoffs in coal, steel, and other heavy industries brought the Communists to the verge of an open break with the government. According to CGT leader Henri Krasucki, the layoffs were "humanly and socially intolerable." He went on to say, "We don't accept the alibi of modernization. Many of these job cuts don't result from technological changes, but from industrial surrender, from reduction of production capacity—for example, in coal, steel, shipbuilding, and textiles. The number one problem is not to reduce capacity, but to increase it."[58]

The other major labor confederation, the CFDT, also criticized the government, although more for its methods than for the content of its policies. For example, the CFDT accused the government of making inportant decisions that affected workers without properly consulting the unions. The head of the CFDT's Economic Sector remarked to the author in 1987, "You can't say there was no consultation *(concertation)* between the government and the unions. The issue is the nature of that consultation. We weren't recognized as an actor. The government didn't comprehend the respective proper roles of unions and the government. The government felt itself to have a double legitimacy. On the one hand it said, 'We were elected by universal suffrage, and now we hold political power.' At the same time it said, 'We are the party of the working class, thus we know what is good for the people.'"[59] Tensions between the CFDT and the government reached a crisis in late 1983 over a government-approved restructuring plan for Peugeot's Talbot division, which, the CFDT claimed, had been negotiated without its participation (see chapter 9). In general, the CFDT became much more combative in late 1983, perhaps concluding (following its loss in the October 1983 union elections for social security board representatives) that its earlier identification with the government's austerity policies had hurt it in workers' eyes.

Finally, disillusionment surfaced within the Socialist Party itself. The CERES labeled Mitterrand's socialism "a kind of moral and ideological surrender,"[60] and many rank-and-file activists complained of feeling cut off from and even betrayed by their leaders. Thus one casualty of Left austerity was the sense of party loyalty and ideological belief that had characterized PS activists since the early 1970s.[61]

In the face of this opposition, the government pushed some social measures designed to reinvigorate Left supporters, including proposals to bring the private (primarily Catholic) education system more fully under public control and to limit "monopoly power" in the press. The main results of this, however, were to stir up even more opposition among the affected groups, such as Catholic teachers and parents, and raise questions about the government's commitment to "personal freedoms."[62] These reactions, coupled with the PS's dismal performance in the June 1984 elections for the European Parliament,[63] forced the government to revise its strategy during the summer of 1984.

Phase 4: Preelection Reflation and Continued Modernization, July 1984–March 1986

With one eye on the economic indicators and one on the electoral calendar, Mitterrand initiated a fourth, final stage of macroeconomic policy in July 1984. From that month until the legislative elections in March 1986, economic and political strategies were tightly intertwined. In the economic sphere the government undertook a mild preelectoral reflation, while in the political sphere it abandoned its alliance with the PCF and sought to reposition itself toward the center of the political spectrum. Both moves were part of a new strategy to regain the votes of pragmatic and moderate middle-class voters who had supported Mitterrand in 1981.

Mitterrand launched the new political strategy by replacing his embattled prime minister, Mauroy, with the much younger Fabius, who sought to embody a new image combining industrial modernization and social justice. Such an image, it was hoped, would appeal especially to centrist voters, including urban professionals, who had swung to the Socialists in 1981 but had deserted them in the 1984 elections. For the Communists, however, Fabius's appointment signaled the government's determination to pursue austerity, and the PCF chose this moment to resign from the government. The Communists' withdrawal met with little resistance, however, because the PCF's electoral decline, capped by its disastrous 11 percent showing in the 1984 elections, made it expendable as a coalition partner.[64]

The economic strategy of the fourth phase reflected the Socialists' awareness of both the bad electoral news and the continued need to stimulate investment by improving supply side conditions. The solution for both problems appeared to be the notion of less is more. On the demand side, Mitterrand, a belated convert to tax cuts, pledged to reduce the tax burden as a percentage of GDP by 1 percent per year for the next three years.[65] At the same time, the government limited state spending, allowing only a 6 percent increase in 1985. These policies were continued into 1986. The tax cuts helped spur an increase in real disposable household income of 1 percent in 1985 and more than 3 percent in 1986, despite only marginal increases in total wages (0.1 percent in 1985, 1.7 percent in 1986).[66] The Socialists, ironically, thus ended their first stint in power with a Reagan-style tax cut that mitigated some of rigor's earlier bite and contributed to their respectable 1986 electoral showing.

On the supply side, the government continued to stress modernization, profitability, and market forces in general through two new "environmental" strategies. The first was the financial liberalization undertaken by Bérégovoy, Fabius's new minister of economy, finances, and budget. By initiating several measures designed to deregulate the nation's financial markets, the government sought to move away from a state-administered financial system to one based on market mechanisms.[67] The second strategy sought to create a more skilled and flexible work force. Having rejected the policy of rescuing failing firms, the government now sought to facilitate worker retraining and to regularize short-term and part-time work conditions.[68]

The Fabius approach proved moderately successful as an instrument for holding on to most of the Socialists' 1981 electoral base. Nonetheless, the Socialists' 1986 electoral performance (32 percent of the popular vote, versus 37 percent in 1981), though respectable, fell well short of garnering a legislative majority. As a result, the Socialists went back into parliamentary opposition, leaving Mitterrand to share power with a conservative majority led by Paris mayor Jacques Chirac. Not until 1988, with Mitterrand's reelection and PS victory in the subsequent legislative elections, did the Socialists again control both of the government's major centers of power.

MANAGING THE CRISIS, 1988–1993

The second period of Socialist dominance contrasted sharply with the first in three main respects. For one thing, whereas the Socialists came to power in 1981 on a wave of euphoric expectations, their return in 1988 was greeted as routine. Thus, unlike 1981, they faced few pressures to embark on a program of ambitious reform. As we have seen, Socialist economic policies after 1983 increasingly resembled those of France's European partners; by 1986, Socialist rule had become, in the words of many observers, "normalized," even "banalized." The Socialists' return to power thus elicited few hopes and few fears. Moreover, the 1986–1988 period of power sharing *(cohabitation)* between Mitterrand and a conservative parliamentary majority, by proving the resiliency of the Fifth Republic's constitution, further reinforced the sense of normalcy that accompanied the Left's return.

Another reality that influenced the political climate in 1988 was the changed character of the governing coalition. Far from having a solid parliamentary majority, as in 1981, Socialists now held only 276 of 577 seats, 13 votes short of a majority. Although still the party with the most seats, the PS had to rely on centrist defections and occasional Communist abstentions to govern. (The Communists themselves, with only 11 percent of the popular vote and 27 seats, were a marginal presence.) Thus the new prime minister, Mitterrand's long-time nemesis Michel Rocard, had little maneuvering room. As for the unions, whereas in 1981 the CGT and the CFDT were part of the governing coalition, by the late 1980s both organizations kept their distance from the Socialists. In any case, the unions' lack of support mattered little, given their continued division and decline. A last difference concerned the relationship between Mitterrand and the Socialist parliamentary group. Whereas in 1981 the president had identified strongly with his party and its program, by 1988 he had progressively distanced himself from the PS. Assuming the Gaullist mantle of "president of all the French people," Mitterrand refused to be identified with any party program. In sum, the Socialists' political position in 1988 was far more precarious than it had been in 1981.

In part because of the differences in the initial conditions under which the Socialists of 1981–1986 and 1988–1993 assumed power, there were also differences in how the political and economic dynamics changed during the two periods of Socialist dominance. Socialist political fortunes had deteriorated steadily from 1982 to 1984, but recovered in 1985 and 1986. Although the PS lost control of the National Assembly in 1986 after winning only 32 percent of the popular vote, the party's performance was still fairly close to the 37 percent it had won in 1981. The Socialists were able to retain most of their popular support because the economy had recovered in 1985–1986 after a recession in 1981–1984. The 1988–1993 period, by contrast, was one of constant political decline marked by ministerial instability, internal scandal, and growing unpopularity. Successive prime ministers—Rocard (1988–1991), Edith Cresson (1991–1992), and Bérégovoy (1992–1993)—proved unable to stop the slide. The Socialists' second term ended in a rout in the 1993 elections, when the party won only 54 of 577 seats. As had happened in 1981–1986, economic conditions paralleled this descent, with the boom of the late 1980s giving way to the deep recession of the early 1990s.

A final contrast between the 1981–1986 and 1988–1993 periods concerns the nature of the Socialists' program. As we have seen, the first period witnessed an internal struggle over economic policy that ended in a definitive paradigm shift in 1983. Thereafter, policy followed a strong-franc path that linked fiscal and monetary measures to those of France's EC partners. The second period, however, was not marked by internal turmoil, and the strong-franc strategy became permanent. All three prime ministers tied exchange rate policy to the ERM in a strategy of "competitive disinflation" whereby external competitiveness was sought not by devaluing the franc but by lowering inflation (and thus costs and ultimately prices). Accordingly, the government's economic measures featured a tight monetary policy, efforts to reduce budget deficits and business taxes, and actions to stimulate labor "flexibility" and general competitiveness (especially in the financial sector).[69]

The strong-franc approach did not represent a complete conversion to neoliberalism, however, for it was accompanied by a second, albeit muted, discourse vaunting the mixed-economy society, in which the state would promote both social justice and industrial dynamism. Responding to persistent unemployment as well as growing criticism within the PS itself over rising social inequality, the government established employment-stimulus plans, retraining schemes, and other measures. Moreover, despite its disengagement from the kind of direct intervention in industrial strategy that had marked the 1981–1983 period, the government strongly supported industrial *volontarisme* at the European level, through participation in EU-sponsored projects. While not even pretending that these policies embodied socialist principles—indeed, the term "socialist" almost disappeared from official pronouncements—PS leaders, in time-honored French tradition, continued to insist on the state's crucial role in economic management.

Despite their general adherence to the policy paradigm just described, each of the three prime ministers developed specific themes and emphases. Rocard, the first prime minister of the period and the one who held power the longest, focused on four goals: fiscal control, business tax cuts, reductions in unemployment and income inequality, and industrial promotion. Following the lead of Finance Minister Bérégovoy, whose goal was to reduce annual inflation to less than 2 percent, the Rocard government sought, first, to minimize fiscal stimuli by reducing the public deficit. Second, in an effort to reduce the tax burden on business, it lowered tax rates on profits and cut employers' mandatory social security charges.[70] Third, once the government came to realize that the resumption of growth during the late 1980s was producing greater income inequality but having little effect on unemployment,[71] it promoted measures to ameliorate the problem.[72] Finally, although seeking to stimulate private-sector investment, the government continued to rely on an active public sector to promote industrial dynamism. Eschewing an ambitious industrial policy as such, the government nevertheless increased spending for research and development while strongly supporting cooperative European high-tech projects such as ESPRIT (information technologies), RACE (telecommunications), and EUREKA (diverse high-technology research).[73]

By the end of its three years the Rocard government could count some definite economic successes, especially in realizing its main goals of limiting inflation and the budget deficit. France's performance in both areas clearly surpassed the European average, although overall growth was about average.[74] Unfortunately, the industrial sector, despite the government's attempts to revive investment and competitiveness, failed to take advantage of the favorable environment of the late 1980s. As in the early 1980s, growth tended to stimulate imports at the expense of domestic products, and the trade deficit in industrial goods increased markedly.[75] Finally, despite a rhetorical emphasis on increasing "social cohesion," the government's efforts to promote job creation and reduce income inequality remained limited by fiscal constraints. Critics charged that these efforts were largely cosmetic because the government was unwilling to move away from the larger goals of fiscal stringency and maintenance of a positive business climate.[76]

With his government wracked by campaign finance scandals, a declining economy, and increasingly fragile legislative support, Rocard was replaced as prime minister by Mitterrand loyalist Cresson in May 1991. In an effort to reposition her government to the left of Rocard's, the new prime minister announced a more nationalist and "voluntarist" industrial policy that attacked Japanese trade practices while seeking to support high-tech "industries of the future." She suspended a plan by the Japanese computer maker NEC to buy into the publicly owned computer firm Bull, and, in classic national champion fashion, planned to create an electronics giant out of the nationalized firms Thomson-Brandt and CEA-Industrie. She also announced aid measures to boost investment and export capacity among small- and medium-sized enterprises.[77] Yet these ambitious plans were to be executed within the framework of the strong-franc policy, which meant that there would be no new major financing to implement them. Moreover, Cresson herself proved politically inept and was immediately unpopular. In April 1992, after less than a year of grand pronouncements, little follow-through, and considerable confusion, Mitterrand again changed prime ministers by appointing Finance Minister Bérégovoy to the post.[78]

With the arrival of the new prime minister, who had been a vigorous advocate of "the other policy" in the 1983 debate but had gone on to spearhead the competitive disinflation strategy, Socialist macroeconomic policy appeared to have traveled full circle since 1981. The Socialists, who at first had emphasized the fight against unemployment through a demand-led reflation, now made zero inflation their Holy Grail. The early Mitterrand-Mauroy government had looked to an interventionist industrial policy as the main way to boost investment and competitiveness, but the Mitterrand-Bérégovoy team sought to achieve these goals through lightening the tax load on business and giving public-firm managers nearly complete autonomy. Finally, whereas the Socialists initially enlarged the public sector and sought to use it to stimulate investment throughout the economy, they now worked to reduce public ownership through partial privatizations.

As the engineer of this policy since his first stint as finance minister in the Fabius government (1984–1986), Bérégovoy held steadily to it throughout his prime ministerial term, keeping the franc pegged tightly to the German mark. This, of course, meant a restrictive monetary stance; at over 7 percent, France's real interest rates remained among the EC's highest. However, Bérégovoy's eleven months in office were plagued by several problems that ultimately helped seal the Socialists' defeat in the March 1993 elections. The first was the debate over the Maastricht Treaty, which was settled by a referendum win for the yes forces but became a phyrric victory for Mitterrand that harmed his prestige and the popularity of his government.[79] A second jolt, triggered by political uncertainty arising out of the Maastricht referendum, was an on-slaught against EC currencies by international currency speculators in the fall of 1992. After speculation forced the pound sterling and the lira to leave the ERM in September, the franc also came under attack, and the Banque de France had to intervene aggressively to maintain the franc within the limits set by the ERM. Although the government managed, with German help, to protect the franc, the September crisis shook investor and public confidence in the long-term benefit of the strong-franc strategy.[80] Finally, after a slight recovery in late 1991 and early 1992, the European recession deepened in mid-1992. In France, the downturn produced sharply higher unemployment and a worsen-ing budget deficit, conditions that helped doom the Socialists in the 1993 elections.

This second Socialist period thus ended with a decidedly mixed record. On the positive side the strong-franc strategy achieved its goal of reducing inflation and budget deficits while producing respectable growth.[81] The most impressive achievement was the mastery of France's inflation, which after being consistently higher than German and EC rates in the early 1980s was running below both a decade later (see figure 4.2). On the negative side, unemploy-

Figure 4.2   France: Reducing the Inflation Gap, 1973–1995

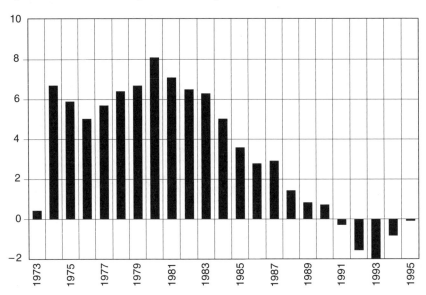

Source: Organisation for Economic Co-operation and Development, *Economic Outlook* (Paris: OECD), various years.
Note: Each bar represents France's consumer price change for the corresponding year minus Germany's consumer price change.

ment—and, more generally, the increasing division of the labor force into a core of secure, well-paid workers on the one hand and a growing number of insecure, low- paid or unemployed workers on the other—stood as an indictment of the strong-franc approach. Despite policies that shifted income from households to firms (see figure 4.3), the latter tended to use their increased resources to invest abroad and reduce debt rather than invest in the French economy and create new jobs at home.[82] One consequence was that by the end of the Socialist era, France's swelling army of unemployed numbered over 3.2 million and constituted 12 percent of the labor force.

Figure 4.3   France: The Income Shift from Households to Firms, 1981–1993
(after-tax income)

Key :
——— Gross disposable household income as a percentage of GDP.
······ Disposable firm income as a percentage of GDP.

Source: L'année politique, économique, et sociale 1993 (Paris: Éditions Évènements et Tendances, 1993), 540.

5
Spain

The Price of European Membership

After nearly three years as prime minister, Felipe González remarked to a visiting journalist, "I am a Socialist, but I am no fool."[1] This comment was one reflection of the consistently pragmatic approach that his PSOE government adopted from the outset and maintained through three terms in office. Whereas French macroeconomic policy underwent a tortuous reversal in 1982–1983, the González government adhered unswervingly to an orthodox adjustment strategy aimed at "joining Europe."

The main reason for the contrast in Spanish and French macroeconomic policy was the decidedly more moderate and less reformist policy orientation of the PSOE at the time it came to power. As we saw in chapter 3, the PS assumed office on the basis of a much more radical set of policy goals. Unlike Mitterrand, González moved his party toward the center during the late 1970s and early 1980s, and after the collapse of the PCE in 1982 the PSOE faced little pressure from elements to its left.

The PSOE's policy moderation arose not only out of internal party dynamics but also out of Spain's economic and political climate in the post-Franco era. In 1982 the new constitution was only four years old, and the elections of that year were only the second to be held under it. Thus the legitimacy of the new democratic order could not be taken for granted, nor could reactionary military elements be ignored, as the February 1981 coup attempt demonstrated. The Socialists had to worry that disruptions caused by drastic political or economic reforms might trigger threats to the democratic system itself. Javier Solana, a top PSOE leader and culture minister, remarked in 1982, "Democracy and its consolidation come first, before our political programs; . . . the Spanish right has shown that it can live very well with both authoritarian and democratic regimes, while the left can only survive within a democratic framework. We have a lot of pain and suffering, and many years behind bars, to prove that."[2]

The economic climate also discouraged radical reforms. As was discussed in chapter 2, from 1939 to 1975 the Spanish economy had remained, along with Portugal's, the most isolated and uncompetitive in Western Europe, despite the economic opening begun by Franco in the late 1950s. By 1982, however, with entry into the European Community less than four years away, the government had to prepare businesses to compete, which meant reforming an outmoded small-scale agricultural sector, an ill-adapted financial system hobbled by undercapitalized banks and securities markets, and an inefficient system of state-run firms. Although membership in the Community promised a brighter long-term future, Spain's archaic economic structures continued to handicap its economic performance. Socialist leaders thus faced strong pressures to encourage modernization along capitalist lines. In an interview a few years later, González asserted, "In Europe, the process of economic adjustment had been going on for seven years, and we were seven years late. . . . In the electoral campaign of 1982 I had the courage to say that rather than have the IMF dictate to us what had to be done with the Spanish economy, we would do it by ourselves."[3]

The timing of the PSOE's victory also mattered, for by October 1982 Mitterrand's *relance* had proved a failure (as had a similar policy undertaken in Greece), and the lessons of this experiment were not lost on Spanish Socialist leaders. According to José Fernando Sánchez-Junco, the Industry Ministry official in charge of industrial restructuring in the steel and metallurgy sectors, "Many people in the Socialist Party believed that we should launch a big nationalization drive—exactly the opposite of what we did. The French Socialists had made this mistake, and the results were becoming obvious by the end of 1982 when Mitterrand began to reverse his policy. [Carlos] Solchaga [the industry and energy minister], along with Felipe González, realized this mistake at the time, and when the Socialists came to power we enacted a policy distinct from that of the Mitterrand government."[4]

All of these influences helped shape a policy paradigm that was strikingly different from that of the early Mitterrand government. Whereas the French Socialists stressed growth and job creation while worrying little about inflation, the PSOE sought to restore a favorable investment climate by drastically cutting inflation and providing incentives for domestic and foreign investors. Compared with their French counterparts, Spanish Socialists considered goals such as income redistribution, job creation, and expansion of the public industrial sector to be of little or no importance.[5]

The lodestar of PSOE strategy was the hope of joining the ranks of the European industrial democracies. This aim, shared by all major elements along the Spanish political spectrum (including the pro-Communist Left), meant accepting and applying the EC's increasingly neoliberal framework. This framework mandated the gradual removal of barriers to domestic competition, including the reduction of state subsidies, deregulation within specific sectors, and the dismantling of regional barriers to trade and finance. After Spain's 1986 entry into the EC and the latter's adoption of the Single Market Act (1986), and then the Maastricht Treaty (1991), the price of European membership meant "convergence," namely bringing inflation, government balances, public debt, interest rates, and other key indicators into line with those of Spain's European partners. Although Spain's embrace of the EC did not entirely eliminate room for autonomous economic reform, it certainly meant that such reform had to be generally compatible with the EC's market-promoting bias.

Once in office, the PSOE never wavered from its plans to modernize the economy by stimulating competition and fostering Spain's continued *apertura* (opening) to Europe and the world. Yet although such an approach was obviously more in tune with extant conditions than was the PS's initial strategy in 1981, we must still account for the PSOE's consistency in carrying out its policy prescriptions. Much of the explanation can be found in domestic political factors. During its crucial first two terms in office (1982–1989), the González government enjoyed a strong parliamentary majority and never had to rely on coalition partners or otherwise dilute its influence within the Cortes. Moreover, as uncontested head of his party, González himself was firmly in control of the government. Unlike Mitterrand, he never had to share power with a prime minister of his own party or work with one from the opposition. Thus he and his economic team had the political leverage to carry out a long-term adjustment strategy. Even though the Socialists' dominance eroded during their third term (1989–1993), when organized labor and other groups sharply opposed the government's economic policies, this opposition did not fundamentally contest the pro-Europe paradigm that shaped government policies. Each of González's three terms in office, however, had its own distinctive policy characteristics, despite the underlying continuity in outlook over the entire 1982–1993 period, and it is to these characteristics that we now turn.

THE FIRST TERM IN OFFICE, 1982–1986

The overriding goal during the first term was to prepare Spain for entry into the EC. This meant, in contrast to the Mitterrand government's approach when it assumed office, doing the bad things first, that is, dampening inflation and promoting industrial modernization. At the same time, the PSOE government sought to honor, at least in part, its electoral pledge to expand social services.

The main focus during the first two years was the fight against inflation. Although prices had moderated during the final years of the preceding UCD regime, Spain's inflation rate remained well above the EC average, and the gap was increasing.[6] Three main initiatives were employed in the battle against inflation: a tight monetary policy, reduction of the fiscal deficit, and wage moderation. First, the government quickly increased short-term interest rates to slow the flow of credit to the private sector. Second, in an attempt to reduce the public deficit, government officials cut back on tax exemptions, modified tax withholding schedules, and raised indirect taxes.[7] Although the authorities sought to limit spending as well—principally by reducing the losses of public-sector firms—they also increased social spending in several areas, including pensions, unemployment compensation (necessary because of the continued rise in job losses), and transfers to businesses.[8]

The third element in the anti-inflation campaign was wage restraint, accomplished principally through the continuation of national-level tripartite negotiations that had begun in 1980 (discussed in chapter 2). Profiting from strong initial support from the Socialists' sister labor confederation, the UGT, as well as conditional tolerance on the part of the CCOO, the government sponsored the February 1983 Interconfederal Accord, an agreement between the two labor confederations and the employers' association, the CEOE, which established a wage-increase band of 9.5 percent to 12.5 percent for 1983—substantially less than the 1982 consumer price index (CPI) increase of 14.4 percent. This process was repeated the following year with the signing of the Economic and Social Accord, an agreement that, among other things, committed the parties to limit wage increases to a range of 5.5 percent to 7.5 percent for 1985 and 4.5 percent to 6.5 percent for 1986.[9]

In addition to these anti-inflationary measures, the government sought to improve the efficiency and competitive position of both public and private firms in four ways. The first was exchange rate policy, in which the government, by devaluing the peseta and relying on the worldwide rise of the dollar, permitted the peseta to decline in value against the mark by nearly 20 percent.[10] A second tactic, and the centerpiece of the government's modernization strategy, was an ambitious program of industrial "reconversion and reindustrialization" that targeted fifteen sectors. Chosen because of their size, international exposure, and failing market performance, they were to be "rationalized" through work force reductions, structural reorganizations, and the infusion of new capital investment. Third, the government sought to improve the efficiency of public firms by ordering the national industrial holding agency, the INI, to cut its losses and even to privatize some firms. Finally, in several instances the government came directly to the aid of ailing private firms, the most notable of which was Rumasa, the country's largest holding company, encompassing over four hundred businesses and eighteen banks. The government nationalized Rumasa, reorganized and recapitalized it, and then, two years later, reprivatized it.[11]

These actions produced solid successes in controlling inflation and improving Spain's trade position. By 1985 the annual rise in consumer prices had been reduced to 8.8 percent (from 14.4 percent in 1982), in large part because of falling unit labor costs.[12] Exports, aided by the peseta's depreciation as well as by slumping domestic demand, increased sharply.[13] Judging that these results had set the stage for an economic expansion, the government shifted emphasis in mid-1985 to stimulating investment and growth. One consequence was that monetary and fiscal policies were relaxed in an effort to revive demand. To help forward its plans for Spanish membership in the EC, the government liberalized regulations affecting foreign investment, which produced immediate and positive results.[14] Finally, to encourage job creation, the government promoted measures to facilitate labor flexibility, including the use of part-time and fixed-duration contracts. A 1986 law, for example, permitted firms to hire workers on provisional six-month contracts for up to three years.[15]

These measures sparked a brisk recovery, and by the end of the Socialists' first term in mid-1986 Spain was poised for rapid growth. Yet for all the obvious success in conventional terms, the Socialists' policies had a human cost, for modernization inevitably entailed massive job losses throughout an industrial sector that had long been protected, inward-looking, and inefficient. Spanish unemployment jumped from 15.6 percent in 1982 to 21.1 percent in 1985, whereas the EC average rose only slightly, from 9.4 percent to 10.9 percent. Rising joblessness, combined with slipping wages and budget pressures on social programs, prompted growing opposition from the major labor organizations, including the UGT. Yet by the 1986 elections, unemployment had begun to fall slightly, and in any case voters did not appear to blame the Socialists for the economy's failings. In those elections the PSOE handily retained its majority, albeit by a reduced margin.

THE SECOND TERM IN OFFICE, 1986–1989

During the PSOE's second term, Spain's annual growth rate averaged 4.7 percent, significantly higher than the EC average of 3.3 percent. This robust expansion was also accompanied by rising profits, declining prices (until 1989), rapid job creation (and a subsequent fall in unemployment), and shrinking public deficits (as a result of growing tax receipts). Fueling this boom was a takeoff in investment, which far outpaced the European average.[16] Especially pronounced was the increase in foreign investment, which resulted from favorable economic conditions (especially declining labor costs), government inducements (investment credits), preferential interest rates, tax exemptions, and other measures), and Spain's new financial and trade opening to the EC.

Spain's entry into the EC on 1 January 1986 had a powerful effect on the nation's foreign trade structure in general and on the flow of foreign investment specifically.[17] Unsurprisingly, EC membership brought a sharp jump in the proportion of trade conducted within the Community.[18] Moreover, as table 5.1 indicates, an increasing proportion of foreign direct investment also came from EC nations. Such investment, devoted mainly to business and portfolio acquisitions, increased in virtually all sectors, but especially in the financial sector. In the manufacturing sector, which despite its decline still remained the largest recipient of foreign direct investment, investment was concentrated in such industries as automobile production, food, paper, and chemicals.[19]

Despite this impressive takeoff, the boom also provoked an increase in social discontent that culminated in a huge general strike on 14 December 1988. For Socialist leaders, the chief challenge of the second term thus became the simultaneous management of growth and its contradictions. The principal opposition came from a new alliance between the two largest labor confederations, the UGT and the CCOO, which accused the government of betraying socialist values and working-class interests. Unlike the French case, in which the major labor confederations, the CGT and the CFDT, remained bitterly divided throughout the 1980s, Spanish labor gradually forged a united front in opposition to government economic policies.

Whereas the CCOO's opposition was not unexpected—the confederation had opposed the Socialists almost from the outset—the UGT's defection was surprising, especially because it had stood by the government during the first two years of austerity and industrial reconversion. Although relations between the PSOE and the UGT were historically close, UGT leaders often resented the PSOE leadership's tendency to view the UGT as the party's extension in the work place. This latent tension between the two organizations came to the surface after 1982, for three reasons: policy differences, competition within

Table 5.1   Spain: Foreign Investment, 1980–1989 (in percentages)

A. Origin of Foreign Direct Investment Projects

	1984–1985	1986–1989
EC Countries	38.4[a]	52.0[b]
United States	18.4	4.9
Other countries	30.3	17.8
Foreign companies in Spain	12.9	25.3
Total	100.0	100.0

B. Sectoral Distribution of Foreign Direct Investment Projects

	1980–1984	1985	1986	1987	1988	1989
Manufacturing and mining	63.6	63.3	61.4	52.6	36.9	41.9
Trade and tourism	16.2	14.0	15.3	18.9	12.4	14.4
Financial	13.7	17.8	19.3	24.4	43.3	37.4
Other sectors	6.5	4.9	4.0	4.1	7.4	6.3
Total	100.0	100.0	100.0	100.0	100.0	100.0

C. Total Foreign Direct Investment

	1980–1984	1985	1986	1987	1988	1989
In billions of U.S. dollars	1.3	1.6	2.9	5.9	7.2	10.5
As a percentage of GDP	0.7	1.0	1.3	2.0	2.1	2.8
As a percentage of business fixed investment	4.3	6.5	8.0	11.7	11.4	14.2

Source: Organisation for Economic Co-operation and Development, Economic Surveys: Spain (Paris: OECD, 1990), 64, 66.
   a. Percentages for selected countries were as follows: Netherlands, 7.3 percent; United Kingdom, 7.5 percent; France, 8.2 percent; West Germany, 10.5 percent.
   b. Percentages for selected countries were as follows: Netherlands, 16.5 percent; United Kingdom, 10.1 percent; France, 9.4 percent; Germany, 8.7 percent..

the union movement, and animosity between González and the UGT leader, Nicolas Redondo.[20]

Policy differences erupted in mid-1985 when the UGT became increasingly critical of PSOE policies that, according to the confederation, hurt workers. Initial opposition focused on the government's attempt to reform the pension system, which, the government claimed, had become a fiscal burden.[21] On this issue the UGT publicly opposed the reform but refused to join the CCOO in calling for a general strike. During the following three years, however, the two confederations increasingly worked together to fight the government's "regressive" policies.

Chief among the government's failures, according to labor, was its poor employment record. The confederations correctly charged that far from stimulating the creation of secure, well-paying jobs, the government's flexibility reforms had mainly fostered various types of part-time or temporary work. As table 5.2 shows, throughout the late 1980s government employment promotion programs created new jobs but few permanent ones. Spain's labor market remained singular throughout Western Europe in its reliance on temporary workers.[22] The unions' disenchantment with labor market policy climaxed in 1988 over the government's three-year plan to create 800,000 jobs for young people by subsidizing employers to offer short-term, minimum wage contracts.

UGT-CCOO competition was a second reason for the strained relations between the government and the UGT. The UGT first drew ahead of the CCOO in the 1982 round of worker-delegate elections, largely on the basis of its close identification with the PSOE. That identification grew even closer during the first two years of austerity, for the UGT generally supported the government's industrial reconversion and other adjustment measures. But unfortunately for

Table 5.2   Spain: Growth of Temporary and Part-Time Labor, 1985–1990 (number of persons, in thousands, hired under government employment promotion programs)

	1985	1987	1990
Without economic incentives[a]			
Fixed-term contracts	432.2	666.6	1,174.9
Part-time contracts	121.9	220.8	410.9
Part-time workers hired to replace partially retired workers	2.9	1.7	3.3
Replacement of workers retired at age 64 (fixed-term contracts)	1.0	0.8	1.0
Subtotal	557.0	887.9	1,589.1
With economic incentives			
Fixed-term contracts	434.7	639.3	715.4
Vocational training[b]	112.7	218.2	303.9
On-the-job training[b]	51.8	128.2	212.9
Public administration–INEM agreements	270.2	292.9	198.6
Indefinite contracts	64.4	132.5	12.8
Subtotal	499.1	771.8	728.2
Total	1,056.1	1,660.9	2,317.3

Source: Organisation for Economic Co-operation and Development, *Economic Surveys: Spain* (Paris: OECD, 1994), 103.

a. Economic incentives included reductions in employers' social security taxes, direct subsidies to cover some wage costs of workers hired, and other measures.

b. Discontinued in April 1992.

the UGT, support for the government was politically costly. In the next round of employee elections for workers' council *(comité de empresa)* representatives, in 1986, the UGT increased its lead over the CCOO, but lost ground to the CCOO in several key sectors and firms, especially the public sector.[23] According to a member of the CCOO executive committee, Julian Ariza, these losses convinced UGT leaders that support for the government's austerity policies had become a handicap. The UGT then began a rapprochement with the CCOO in opposition to PSOE policies.[24]

The third reason for the UGT-government split was the increasingly bitter personal rivalry between González and UGT leader Redondo. A former steelworker from the Basque Country, Redondo had backed González's drive to become PSOE leader in the early 1970s and had remained close to González confidant during the latter's rise to power and first two years as prime minister (Redondo himself sat in parliament as a PSOE representative). By 1985, however, Redondo was claiming that the González government had failed to reward the UGT for its support. The growing UGT-government tension of the following three years not only poisoned their erstwhile fraternalism but also split the UGT when several federation leaders continued to back the government instead of Redondo. One of those leaders was Antonio Puerta, the head of the metalworkers federation, who was sacked by Redondo in 1987 for supporting González. Commenting some years later, Puerta claimed that the Redondo-González split stemmed more from Redondo's drive for power than from policy differences as such: "The conflict between the UGT and the government became, purely and simply, a personal fight between Redondo and González. Until their break, Redondo had supported the government's approach. He gradually saw, however, that the government was displacing him. But the government was doing this because of Redondo's own arrogance. He's the kind of leader who insists on being able to veto a decision if he doesn't like it. He always wants to be on top."[25]

Thus during most of its second term, the government was preoccupied with growing labor protests and strikes. Behind this unrest, which also stimulated protests by secondary-school and university students,[26] was a spreading public perception that the fruits of growth were not being shared equitably. Many people, including PSOE party members, thought the government was betraying its basic principles. Luis de Velasco, a former PSOE leader and high official in the Economy Ministry, even stated, "The values portrayed by the government are nonsocialist values. They are the values of fast money and speculation, values completely different from socialist ones of solidarity and cooperation. Of course, the world in general has been moving in this direction, but I think the Socialist Party has given in to it, and this has helped construct a capitalism of quick profits and speculation, with scandals every day."[27]

This discontent culminated in December 1988 in a forceful display of working-class dissatisfaction when a twenty-four-hour general strike by about 80 percent of the work force paralyzed the country. According to Nicolas Sartorius, leader of the parliamentary group of Izquierda Unida (successor to the defunct PCE), which supported the strike, "On December 14 the unions brought to a head all the bad feelings in Spanish society—about the huge earnings of a rich few, about a majority still struggling for a living, about profits not trickling down."[28]

In response to this depth of opposition, Socialist leaders spent the first half of 1989—the final months of their second term—seeking agreement, albeit unsuccessfully, with the unions on such issues as pensions, wage increases, and unemployment benefits. One reason for their failure was a flagrant contradiction in the government's approach: while seeking to placate the unions with promises of increased social spending, it was also trying to quell an overheated economy by raising interest rates and cutting spending. Whatever its good intentions, the government could not grant the unions' wage or social-spending demands without aggravating persistent inflation or public deficits. The second term thus ended with strong growth accompanied by signs of economic imbalance and weakness.[29] Though the second term produced a boom in investment, construction, and consumer spending, and boosted per capita income 35 percent,[30] it also exacerbated a growing economic split between those profiting from the boom and those left behind.

THE THIRD TERM IN OFFICE, 1989–1993

During the nearly four years of its third term in office, the González government faced political and economic crises that undermined both its popular appeal and its credibility as an economic manager. Committed to a pro-Europe economic policy yet unable to reform basic structural weaknesses, and led by a prime minister who seemed increasingly bored, fatigued, distracted, and aloof, the Socialists vaunted their ability to "manage well," not their aspirations to transform society. In an ironic comment on the decade of PSOE rule, González even admitted that his policies could have been carried out by a government of the "modern Right."[31]

The government's ability to put its economic policies into practice depended, of course, on its political strength. That strength, however, was being sapped in several ways. The first was electoral: in the PSOE's worst performance since 1979, the party emerged from the October 1989 elections with only 40 percent of the vote and a bare majority in the Cortes (175 of 350 seats). Moreover, as the December 1988 strike had shown, economic growth had generated its own discontents. Citizens were increasingly critical of the impact (or lack thereof) of Socialist policies on unemployment and income distribution. As a result, the government faced pressures to deviate from economic orthodoxy in order to placate popular calls for social justice. In addition, the government was plagued by an unending series of internal upheavals, notably corruption scandals, policy and personality splits within the cabinet, and tensions between the government and the PSOE apparatus.

The government's new political vulnerability was reflected in its complicated relations with organized labor. During its first term, as we have seen, the government generally enjoyed the support of the UGT, whereas during the second term relations soured between the government and both the UGT and the CCOO, which joined forces in opposition. Until the successful 1988 general strike, the government had largely ignored the unions, but the strike brought a change in attitude. After their party's narrow reelection less than a year later, Socialist leaders, sensing the need to draw labor back into a more cooperative posture, tried to appease the unions. In 1990 pensions and unemployment benefits were increased and the government passed a law allowing unions to monitor temporary contracts. Attempting to reopen the pact-making process, the government also sought to enlist the unions in an agreement that would link wage increases to productivity.

The government was constrained, however, in its ability to grant labor significant concessions because its commitments within the EC placed a premium on fighting inflation. The principal commitment derived from Spain's June 1989 accession to the ERM. Although the Spanish authorities initially opted for broad band participation, which allowed for slightly greater monetary leeway than the more rigorous narrow band,[32] ERM participation still required a tight monetary policy strongly encouraged by the conservative Bundesbank. The Spanish authorities, however, chose to maintain the peseta at or near the top of the band. This strong-peseta policy required keeping domestic interest rates at historically high levels.

The rationale for the strong-peseta policy arose from the government's decision to couple a tight monetary policy with a relatively lax fiscal approach. Such a mix had both an economic and a political logic. First, high interest rates were imposed primarily to fight inflation. ERM membership thus became the main instrument for narrowing Spain's inflation gap with the EC. High rates, of course, tended to discourage consumer borrowing and spending and reduce import prices. Moreover, high interest rates on corporate borrowing, by raising financial costs and thus squeezing balance sheets, also discouraged employers from allowing generous wage settlements. Accordingly, tight money replaced the earlier incomes policy of the *pactos sociales* as a means of wage moderation. Second, high rates also served to maintain the flow of direct foreign investment, which, as we have seen, was a central pillar of Spain's growth in the late 1980s. Finally, high rates were an instrument for financing the budget deficit in a noninflationary manner.[33]

The years after 1989 saw a sharp increase in the budget deficit, due in part to a fall in tax receipts caused by the recession that began in early 1990, but also to increased social spending, especially income support for the unemployed.[34] This highly permissive fiscal policy flowed directly from the new political equation of government-labor relations. Simply put, the unions' surprisingly potent manifestation of popular support, as evidenced by the December 1988 strike, coupled with the Socialists' mediocre electoral performance, caused the government to relax the public purse strings in an effort to purchase public support. Tight monetary policy thus dovetailed perversely with loose fiscal policy, as the government, for reasons of domestic politics, increased the budget deficit while using high interest rates to finance it.

Ultimately, this policy of slamming on the monetary brakes while pressing down on the fiscal accelerator proved unsustainable. The capacity to maintain such a contradictory strategy hinged, of course, on foreigners' willingness to buy pesetas or invest in the nation's banks and businesses, which in turn depended on the economy's ability to generate the exceptional growth and financial returns of the late 1980s. Unfortunately, the European recession of the early 1990s ended this virtuous cycle. As the downturn hit, growth and investment plummeted, but inflation still remained high by EC standards, partly because of the persistence of generous wage settlements. Investors increasingly lost confidence in the peseta and in the government's ability to bring economic fundamentals—notably inflation and the trade and budget deficits—into line with the performance of the EC's stronger nations.

The financial market's skepticism regarding Spain's economic health continued to grow during late 1992 and early 1993 as prospects for ratification of the Maastricht Treaty (which set forth the principles of European monetary union) appeared doubtful. Testing the viability of a single monetary system, traders attacked the most vulnerable currencies, including the peseta, lira, and pound, and even the French franc. To maintain the peseta within the ERM and to preserve the ERM itself, the Banco de España was forced to spend about two-thirds of its total foreign reserves of $60 billion in a futile attempt to keep the peseta within its established band. Notwithstanding these efforts, the central bank was forced to devalue the peseta three times between September 1992 and May 1993—a total devaluation of 19 percent.[35] Despite a decade of liberalizing reforms, then, the government had not convinced financial markets that the Spanish economy could hold its own with Europe's stronger powers.

The final year of the Socialists' third term raised fundamental questions about the cost of economic modernization within a liberalizing EC. On the one hand, for the unions and even many PSOE members, the cost in terms of lost jobs, diminished buying power, and growing inequality was too high. On the other hand, employers criticized the government for spending too much on social programs, allowing wages and the public deficit to rise, and increasing interest rates and the financial burden on businesses.[36]

Confronted with these growing criticisms from both the Left and the Right, the government's problem was that it lacked the political strength to define a clear policy direction. In April 1992, in an effort to prepare for monetary union, Carlos Solchaga, the economics, finance, and commerce minister, promoted a plan to bring Spain's performance with respect to several key "convergence criteria" into line with EC norms.[37] Because these criteria applied, among other things, to the budget deficit, the government proposed a new and much more stringent fiscal plan that would cut unemployment benefits and other social programs. But the unions, the CEOE, and even major elements within the PSOE rejected the plan as either punitive for workers or harmful to economic growth,[38] and González had to face not only a second—though much less successful—general strike in May 1992, but also a major battle between members of his cabinet and top party officials.[39]

By the time of the June 1993 elections the Spanish government bore more than a passing resemblance to its French counterpart. Both governments were plagued by corruption scandals and internal divisions, while their leaders, Mitterrand and González, increasingly appeared as spent forces, ravaged by illness or fatigue and devoid of their former dynamism and authority. Despite its steadfast commitment to the European partnership, the González government lacked the political strength to implement its convergence plan. The price of membership in the European club now appeared dauntingly high, given Spain's economic condition and the government's frailty. Only the public's residual confidence in González and the opposition's lackluster appeal enabled the PSOE to win a plurality of votes (39 percent) and parliamentary seats (159 of 350) in the June 1993 elections. But having failed to capture a majority, the PSOE was forced to form a coalition with Convergència I Unió, the Catalonian nationalist party headed by Jordi Pujol. Henceforth, the Socialists' power would be mortgaged to the demands of this small regional party.

MACROECONOMIC POLICY IN FRANCE AND SPAIN: A COMPARISON

The analysis of French and Spanish Socialist macroeconomic strategy in chapter 4 and this chapter reveals that the two governments, despite a striking difference in their initial approaches—*relance* in France versus orthodoxy in Spain—were largely following the same path by the mid-1980s. Both were seeking to shift national income from individual workers and consumers to private-sector businesses, which meant, among other things, measures to slow wage increases and inflation, reduce corporate taxes and provide other fiscal incentives for business investment, and induce greater flexibility and deregulation in labor, financial, and other markets. In both France and Spain the strategic keystone was a tight monetary policy tied to participation in the ERM.

Linking the exchange rate, and hence monetary policy, to the EMS represented a new strategy for dealing with inflation and its consequences. As nations with historically high inflation rates, France and Spain had often used currency devaluations to offset the negative impact of high inflation rates on price levels and thus on trade. Such measures had generally achieved their intended effects under the Bretton Woods system of fixed exchange rates, in which the dollar was the linchpin reserve currency, but with the collapse of Bretton Woods in the early 1970s French and Spanish reliance on "competitive devaluation" proved increasingly inadequate as a corrective to inflation. By obliging governments to take monetarist measures to dampen inflationary pressures, participation in the EMS became a new way of responding to inflation.[40]

It is often claimed that the emphasis by French and Spanish Socialists on modernization, liberalization, and deregulation represented a disavowal of state economic intervention in favor of less state. Although true in some respects, this claim glosses over the fact that the state maintained a strong fiscal role. Far from declining, total government spending as a proportion of national output remained about constant (France) or increased steadily (Spain), even taking into account the effects of the business cycle for example, spending's proportion of GDP rose during the recessions of 1981–1985 and 1990–1993 and fell during the expansion of 1986–1989 (see figure 5.1). Especially striking was the Spanish case, where the rise in spending reflected the post-Franco democratization that favored the expression of social and regional

demands.[41] Moreover, social spending in France and Spain was a central element of total government spending, although spending patterns differed in
the two countries. During the 1980s and early 1990s, France's public spending
on social protection programs grew more slowly (in real terms) than Spain's;
nevertheless, France remained one of the OECD's strongest contributors to
social protection spending.[42] Spain, by contrast, devoted a smaller proportion
of its budget to social protection, but the growth rate of its spending in this
area—an annual average of nearly 5 percent in real terms—was among the
highest in Europe.[43]

But though they converged toward the same general economic strategy,
the macroeconomic policies of France and Spain were marked by major differences with respect to trajectory, the dynamics of public support, and impact.
Regarding trajectory, from the outset the Spanish authorities sought to modernize the economy by stimulating competition and fostering Spain's continued *apertura* to Europe and the world. Anticipating Spain's entry into the EC
in 1986, the González government hoped to restore favorable investment conditions, which meant cutting inflation while encouraging both domestic and
foreign investment. As for the public sector, Spanish Socialists sought to limit
its growth while making public firms more market efficient. In the process,
other social measures such as income redistribution and job creation were
downplayed or ignored. In France, by contrast, the Mitterrand government

Figure 5.1   Less State? Government Spending in France and Spain, 1980–1995
              (as a percentage of GDP)

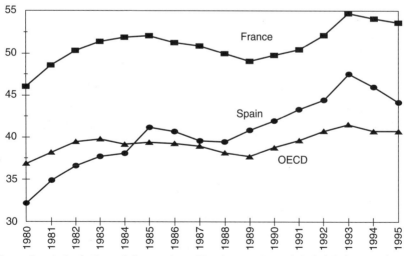

Source: Organisation for Economic Co-operation and Development, *Economic Outlook* 61 (June 1997): A31.

initially adopted a dramatically different strategy. Embracing a policy paradigm emphasizing growth and job creation while downplaying the fight against inflation, this government pursued economic stimulation, income redistribution, and structural changes such as nationalization and industrial relations reform. Its reflation strategy, however, proved unsustainable beyond the first year, and in June 1982 the government began imposing ever-tighter austerity measures, euphemistically labeled *rigueur*. Although there were subsequent periods of mild reflation (1984–1986 and 1988–1990), the essential policy orientation after 1983 stressed monetary and fiscal restraint.

The French and Spanish cases also differed in terms of the dynamics of public support—in particular, labor support—for macroeconomic policy. In Spain labor opposition to the PSOE government's strategy tended to build over time, culminating in the massive December 1988 general strike, whereas in France labor opposition surfaced early but then ebbed away.[44] To consider, first, the Spanish case, public opposition remained generally muted throughout the 1983–1984 adjustment period, notwithstanding fierce protests in particular regions. This was due in part to the nature of public opinion, which was, as mentioned in chapter 2, notable for its realism and moderation. At the outset of González's tenure, the public did not hold unrealistic expectations, but recognized and accepted the need for austerity measures.[45] Once conditions improved in the late 1980s, however, large segments of the public grew increasingly discontented over distributional issues, and many faulted the Socialists for favoring the better-off and failing to resolve the persistent problems of unemployment and underemployment.

Union opposition in Spain also increased over time, especially because of deteriorating relations between the government and the UGT. Initially, the UGT played a key role in providing political support for the government's industrial restructuring and austerity measures. These measures, as we will see in part 4, were highly unpopular in directly affected industries such as steel and shipbuilding, and were a prime cause of the doubling of the strike rate in 1982–1984 (see figure 5.2). With the increase in labor militancy, UGT leaders had to face opposition not only from the CCOO, which opposed the government's policy almost from the start, but also from many of the UGT's own activists and members in the affected industries. Despite this resistance, the UGT signed restructuring agreements for all the targeted industries as well as two major wage-moderation pacts, thus bolstering the González government at a critical time.

In mid-1985, however, cooperation between the UGT and the government broke down. With the government determined, on its own if necessary, to promote labor flexibility, bring monetary targets into line with restrictive

Figure 5.2   Spain: Industrial Conflict, 1980–1995

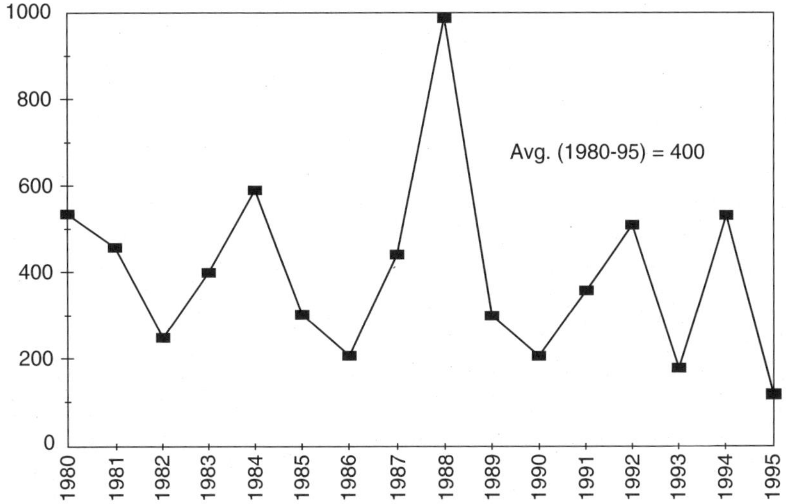

Sources: International Labour Office, *Yearbook of Labour Statistics* (Geneva: ILO), various years; Organisation for Economic Co-operation and Development, *Labor Force Statistics, 1974–1994* (Paris: OECD, 1996); ibid., *Main Economic Indicators* (Paris, OECD), various years.
Note: Figures represent days lost per 1,000 employed workers.

EMS policies, and reduce the fiscal drag of pension programs and some social programs, the UGT-government alliance came to be viewed as either dispensable (in the government's opinion) or harmful (according to the UGT). UGT leaders such as Redondo charged that although their confederation had helped carry out the government's austerity policy, the government itself had not delivered the promised social welfare measures once economic conditions permitted. As a result, the UGT joined with the CCOO in denouncing the government's policies as regressive. This rapprochement, which culminated in the December 1988 general strike, was aided by the economic upswing of the late 1980s. A tightening labor market gave unions the leverage to advance their demands, and the spectacular surge of investments and profits fueled labor's sense of deprivation and injustice. (By the same token, an improving economy no doubt helped convince government leaders, at least until December 1988, that further cooperation with labor was no longer needed.)

As we have seen, the strike produced a temporary shift in government policy. Beginning in early 1989 and continuing into the following year, the government, now considerably more responsive to labor's demands, increased social spending and sought labor's enlistment in a new series of pacts. Although the UGT and the CCOO remained allied against government policy in general, the two confederations maintained at least periodic contact with the government. At the same time, the recession of the early 1990s dampened worker mobilization as unemployment headed upward again. Thus the PSOE government's third term witnessed considerably less worker mobilization than had prevailed in the late 1980s.

In France labor resistance followed an opposite path. French labor's opposition to official policy peaked in the early years of Socialist government (1981–1984) and then dwindled, as figure 5.3 reveals (notice, too, that labor mobilization in France was only about one-tenth the Spanish rate). During the tumultuous years of 1981–1984, strike rates in France remained high, but the character of strikes gradually changed. During the 1981–1982 *relance,* the CGT, seeking to expand its power and audience under the supposed protective umbrella of a sympathetic government, was unusually combative, especially in battling large public enterprises. In its discourse and strike goals, the CGT did not overtly contest the government's economic policies, but instead confronted management and, in firms such as Citroën and Talbot, right-wing "house unions" (see chapter 9). Politically, these strikes were part of the PCF's dual strategy of formally participating in the government while seeking to build up its own organizational capacity by sponsoring worker struggles "at the base."[46]

During 1983 and 1984, however, the focus of PCF-CGT mobilization shifted. As we have seen, the 1983–1984 turn toward austerity, which was accompanied by a restructuring wave in the coal, steel, automobile, shipbuild-

Figure 5.3   France: Industrial Conflict, 1980–1995

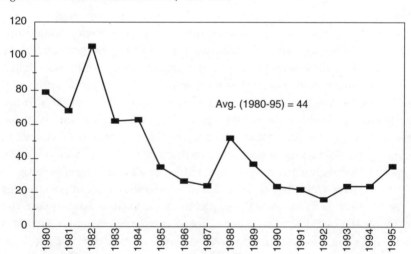

Sources: See figure 5.2.
Note: Figures represent days lost per 1,000 employed workers.

ing, and other industries, prompted a change in PCF-CGT strategy that eventually led to the Communists' withdrawal from the government in July 1984. Increasingly, the PCF and the CGT sought to mobilize workers against government policy.

As for the CFDT, it too distanced itself from the government after the turn toward austerity. Although its leader, Edmond Maire, had been an early advocate of economic rigor, the CFDT accused the government of merely pretending to consult the confederation rather than taking its positions seriously. At the local level, CFDT activists led many strikes protesting the government's restructuring plans. For these reasons, the French strike rate remained high in 1981–1984.

After 1984, however, worker mobilization declined, and throughout the late 1980s and early 1990s France had one of the lowest strike rates in Western Europe.[47] Even the modest increase in strike activity in 1988 demonstrated not a rebirth of union influence but its debility. Many strikes, especially in such public-sector firms as EDF (electricity), SNCR (railroads), PTT (postal and telephone services), and Air France were led by *coordinations,* informal, independent rank-and-file leadership groups.

The reasons for this decline in labor mobilization were related to developments both within and without the labor movement. By far the most important developments arose out of deepening organizational crises within the movement. One crisis was a marked decline in the movement's representativeness as measured by membership tallies, workers' evaluations, and plant-level elections.[48] Another stemmed from persistent divisions between the two major confederations, the CGT and the CFDT. After forging a united front from 1966 to 1979, the two confederations went through a bitter split and thereafter remained locked in a cold war, making concerted action virtually impossible. The two crises, moreover, were related. Even though membership decline was tied, as in most industrialized countries, to structural economic changes—notably the decline of manufacturing employment—it was reinforced by CGT-CFDT bickering.

Another factor contributing to organized labor's increasing weakness as a political force was, ironically, the impact of the government's own labor reforms. The centerpiece of these reforms was the Auroux laws (named after the labor minister), which sought to create a "new citizenship" in the work place by, among other things, giving workers the "direct and collective right of expression" with regard to such issues as work hours and the organization of work, strengthening union rights, expanding the powers and scope of the plant-level works councils *(comités d'entreprise),* making annual collective bargaining mandatory, and establishing new plant-level committees on health, safety, and working conditions. Yet, as Chris Howell convincingly argues, employers were able to turn many of these reforms to their own advantage, in the process reinforcing an emerging "microcorporatism" in labor relations in which the determination of wages and working conditions shifted from national, regional, and federational arenas to the company level.[49] On balance, labor reforms gave employers greater discretion than before in determining wages, working hours, and working conditions, while increasingly weakening union leverage.[50]

A third and final contrast in the macroeconomic policies pursued by France and Spain was in the impact of such policies on economic performance. In this respect, macroeconomic policy was generally more successful in France. Spain had a higher growth rate throughout the period 1981–1993—in fact, one of the highest in Europe—but French Socialists proved more able in dampening inflation and containing unemployment (see table 5.3).[51] With regard to growth, the Spanish economy's performance in 1981–1993 was well above the European average (2.7 percent versus 2.0 percent). However, the early 1990s brought an abrupt end to the strong growth of the late 1980s. As one of the EC's weaker economies, and heavily reliant on foreign investment, Spain was especially vulnerable to swings in the business cycle; growth during expansionary times was brisker than in other countries, yet contraction during downturns was more severe. By contrast, France's growth—throughout the period and within the three phases—was slightly below that of Europe as a whole.[52]

As chapter 4 showed, France made impressive gains in controlling inflation, and by the late 1980s had moved into Europe's low-inflation camp thanks largely to the "Delors system" that linked wage and salary increases to inflation targets rather than to actual inflation. Spain was not as successful, although it did succeed in narrowing its inflation rate gap with the EU during the late 1980s and early 1990s. Nevertheless, Spain continued to exhibit inflationary tendencies, especially in the service sector. A significant contributor to these tendencies was a relatively rigid wage-formation system in which wages responded slowly if at all to changes in employment levels.[53] Wages behaved this way because the Spanish economy was hindered by, among other things, the inertia of a centralized bargaining and wage-setting system, high pay levels at the public companies (a legacy of strong unionism and government bailouts), the widespread use of indexation (upwards of 90 percent of workers were covered by agreements containing indexation clauses), and the rapid escalation of nonwage labor costs.[54]

Analysis of this wage-formation process leads directly to a consideration of unemployment. Despite the creation of nearly 2 million jobs in the late 1980s[55] and a growth rate that was nearly one-third higher than the EU aver-

Table 5.3   Spain and France: Three Economic Performance Measures, 1981–1993

	1981–1985[a]	1986–1990	1991–1993	1981–1993
Growth (average annual percentage change in real GDP)				
Spain	2.0	4.5	0.7	2.7
France	1.5	3.2	0.3	1.9
EC	1.5	3.3	0.8	2.0
OECD-Europe	1.7	3.4	0.9	2.1
Inflation (average annual percentage change in CPI)				
Spain	11.7	6.5	5.5	8.0
France	9.6	3.1	2.6	5.5
EC	9.1	4.3	4.2	6.1
OECD-Europe[b]	8.9	4.3	4.2	6.0
Unemployment (average annual percentage rate)				
Spain	19.1	20.9	19.1	19.9
France	8.8	9.8	10.5	9.6
EC	9.8	10.0	10.2	10.0
OECD-Europe	9.0	9.1	9.6	9.2

Source: Organisation for Economic Co-operation and Development, *Economic Outlook* 56 (December 1994): A4, A18, A23.
   a. Figures for Spain are for 1982–1985 only.
   b. Excluding Turkey.

age, Spain's unemployment rate remained about double the EU's throughout the 1981–1993 period. Although demographics partly explain the persistence of unusually high unemployment,[56] wage rigidity was also important, because employers encountered difficulties in adjusting to recessionary times by reducing wages. To keep wages under control during downturns, employers often resorted to layoffs. But because of Spain's strong tradition of job protection, employers were also restricted in their capacity to lay workers off individually or in small numbers; instead, they often postponed labor adjustment until the point of financial crisis, and then undertook large-scale layoffs.[57]

In attempting to reform this system, the González government, as we have seen, sought to facilitate temporary and part-time work; however, despite the sharp increase in such jobs, the overall effect on wages and employment levels was minor. Thus the wage-formation process, which the Socialists inherited from the Franco era but failed to change fundamentally, tended to maintain and even reinforce a highly segmented labor market. There was a core of about 8 million workers who typically were older, relatively well paid, and secure in their jobs, but also a periphery of about 2 million underemployed part-time or temporary workers along with nearly 3.5 million unemployed, who were disproportionately young and female. Spain's labor market remained distinctive throughout the OECD by combining a high average duration of employment for those with jobs and a high proportion of long-term unemployed among the jobless.[58]

France's employment record was, unsurprisingly, better than Spain's; indeed, over the entire 1981–1993 period France's unemployment rate was slightly lower than the EC average. Yet job creation deteriorated after 1990. Unemployment, after falling below 9 percent that year, climbed back into the double digits, reaching nearly 12 percent in 1993. Moreover, France's labor market evidenced some of the same traits as Spain's, albeit in less extreme fashion, notably a growing gap between holders of secure versus precarious jobs along with a high level of youth unemployment.[59] In the final analysis, the strategy of competitive disinflation proved far more successful in wringing out inflation than in stimulating job growth.

This discussion of macroeconomic strategy has provided a necessary introduction to how French and Spanish Socialists approached the problem of economic adjustment. The next step is to examine how their governments met the need to adapt industrial structures to two kinds of changes in the supranational environment: on the one hand, global shifts in technology, production processes, and trade, and on the other, equally crucial changes in EC institutional frameworks and markets. This is examined in the next part of the book.

IV THE LEFT'S DIRTY JOB

THE LEFT AND INDUSTRIAL RESTRUCTURING

Macroeconomic policy provided a guiding logic for industrial restructuring in France and Spain. The early Mauroy government's emphasis on economic stimulation, for instance, produced industrial adjustment measures that sought to expand production and create employment, especially among crisis-ridden businesses and economic sectors. The main instrument of industrial policy was a sweeping nationalization program that brought several of the largest industrial and financial firms under state control. In Spain, the González government, far from adopting an expansive approach, promoted retrenchment and rationalization for money-losing industries, rejected public-sector expansion, and even advocated selective privatization. And in addition to reforming the public industrial sector, in particular the state holding company, the INI, the Spanish government crafted an ambitious program of "industrial reconversion and reindustrialization" for sixteen sectors in 1984.

As we saw in chapter 4, French Socialists, unable to sustain their *relance* program beyond the first two years, ultimately abandoned their stimulative, redistributionist path. The resulting policy of *rigueur* not only produced restrictive fiscal and monetary measures but also prompted a shift in the government's management of the public economy. After March 1983 public-sector firms were given greater autonomy and a mandate to cut losses, eliminate subsidies, and turn a profit. At the same time, Socialist policy makers fashioned plans for *restructurations industrielles* in ailing sectors where public capital played an important role, notably steel, automobiles, coal, and shipbuilding.

Spain managed to implement most of its 1984 industrial-reconversion program, which reduced the labor force in the targeted sectors by nearly one-third. After 1986, when the program essentially came to an end (and, not coincidentally, Spain joined the EC), Spanish political leaders turned away from comprehensive approaches to industrial adjustment, preferring instead to encourage change on a case-by-case basis. Nonetheless, the broad goals of government policy—slashing the numbers of redundant workers and vigorously reducing capacity in order to lower operating costs and reach the break-even point—remained consistent.

Part IV compares the nature and fate of the French and Spanish industrial-adjustment strategies. It argues that from the mid-1980s on, both countries implemented strategies that, whatever their differences of detail, followed a market-adapting approach (as described in chapter 1). For private firms the strategies brought measures to stimulate new investment, and for public firms the results were greater autonomy and market exposure. In both types of firms, huge job losses accompanied restructuring. To ensure an orderly exit of workers, Socialist governments established income-support and other social programs.

Despite the fact that the French and Spanish policies came to resemble one another, the trajectory, dynamics, and impact of industrial restructuring differed in each country. With respect to trajectory, restructuring mirrored the patterns seen in each country's macroeconomic policies—whereas Spanish Socialists followed a consistent path that stressed market efficiency, their French counterparts displayed little if any consistency, first failing to realize any of the socialist goals they had envisioned for public-sector firms, and ultimately opting for an orthodox approach that included partial privatization. The dynamics of restructuring also differed, notably in government-labor relations, for Spanish labor proved more militant and effective than French labor in pressing its demands. Finally, with respect to impact, in economically orthodox terms France adjusted more successfully, despite Spain's greater consistency of approach. By the mid-1980s most of France's newly national-ized companies had been restructured, recapitalized, and returned to profitability. Adjustment plans for industries such as steel, automobiles, and coal, although engulfed in controversy at the time of their formulation, were in the end carried out relatively smoothly and effectively. In Spain, however, the adjustment process proved lengthier and more expensive. Although the government was eventually able to bring most of its program to fruition, the process was plagued by delays and modifications, and in some sectors was even abandoned.

The analysis that follows begins with an examination of general adjustment strategies in Spain (chapter 6) and France (chapter 7). Chapter 6 focuses on two aspects of the Spanish experience: efforts to reform the public industrial sector, especially the INI, and reconversion and reindustrialization measures. Chapter 7 considers the Mitterrand government's 1982 nationalization program—the heart of the French Socialists' adjustment strategy—as well as the more general issue of public-sector management. The latter half of part IV assesses strategies and results in two key industries: steel (chapter 8) and automobiles (chapter 9).

6
Spain

Public Sector Reform
and Industrial
Reconversion

In the early 1980s, Socialist leaders in both France and Spain viewed the public sector—and public industrial firms in particular—as central to their adjustment strategies. Their judgments on public enterprise differed sharply, however. French Socialists saw the public industrial sector as a grand opportunity and sought to expand it, whereas Spanish Socialists viewed it as a curse and vowed to reduce it. These differences in approach led France and Spain to pursue disparate industrial-adjustment strategies. In France, the heart of industrial-adjustment strategy was the long-promised nationalization of several of the nation's largest industrial firms and nearly all of its banking sector. In Spain, Socialists adopted a two-fold strategy of reducing the fiscal burden of public enterprises by reforming the INI (the main state holding company) while carrying out a comprehensive reconversion and reindustrialization program aimed at both public and private firms.

What explains these different approaches? How did each government put its approach into operation? And what were the results? These are the questions considered in this chapter and chapter 7. The present chapter begins by asking why PSOE leaders wanted to diminish the public sector when PS leaders favored its expansion. The remainder of the chapter analyzes Spanish efforts to reform the public sector and undertake industrial reconversion.

THE PUBLIC INDUSTRIAL SECTOR: CURSE OR OPPORTUNITY?

Three main considerations explain why French and Spanish Socialists viewed public enterprise so differently: the legacy of public industrial performance in each country, the different political configurations of each governing coalition, and the opposing policy paradigms of the PS and the PSOE.

In France, despite two decades of uneven and generally unimpressive industrial policy under Gaullist and Giscardist auspices, the *dirigiste* impulse still retained its allure in the early 1980s. Many of France's most visible international success stories—in air and land transport, aerospace, nuclear technology, weapons systems, and telecommunications—were state-run firms, and their managers and engineers continued to enjoy high prestige, handsome remuneration, and excellent advancement opportunities. The well-trod path from elite schools *(grandes écoles)* to top positions in the civil service, public and private business, and politics continued to attract the nation's best and brightest young people. That the Left sought to dramatically increase the size of the public industrial sector was thus more an extension of past practices and traditions than a sharp break.

Spain, on the other hand, despite a long history of centralized rule, lacked France's tradition of a meritocratically selected, technically trained, and public-spirited civil service. Public companies were popularly associated not with international grandeur but with autarchy, inefficiency, and corruption. The standard-bearer of state enterprise, the INI, was a Franco-era creation designed to foster national self-sufficiency rather than technological prowess. During the economic crisis of the 1970s it became a refuge for lame ducks whose collapse would have meant massive unemployment, and by the early 1980s the number of workers employed by its seventy firms exceeded 215,000. Small wonder, then, that PSOE leaders viewed the INI itself as the ultimate lame duck, a fiscal relic incapable of stimulating economic dynamism. In this light, the PSOE government's move to rationalize and reduce the public sector actually constituted a stronger attack on the status quo than its French counterpart's efforts to expand the public sector.

A second reason for the contrast in Spanish and French government attitudes toward public enterprise had to do with the political configurations of the two countries' governing coalitions, including the organizational cultures of each Socialist party. For French Socialists, nationalizations served several coalitional purposes. First, like *autogestion*, nationalization had been a conceptual magnet for the Left during the 1970s, attracting various constituencies interested in political change. For many leftists, nationalization was a structural reform that could smash capitalist power, boost investment, provide full employment, and even initiate *autogestion* itself. In the early 1980s, nationalization was still popular with many of the party rank-and-file, and indeed with much of the public.[1] Moreover, even though the PS-PCF alliance had splintered in 1977 over the issue of nationalization, Mitterrand's adherence to the Common Program's nationalization pledge, complete with a list of firms to be taken over, was decisive in enlisting Communist support for his government. A nationalization policy thus ensured that the PS, at least at the start of its government tenure, would have no enemies to its left.

Expansion of the public sector was also a notion that fit well into the Socialist subculture, for despite the Left's long exclusion from power before 1981, most high-ranking Socialist leaders were professionally at home in the state. Many of them, especially the younger leaders (Rocard, Fabius, Jospin, Chevènement, and others) were graduates of the Institut d'Études Politiques and the École Nationale d'Administration—the training grounds for the state elite—and members of *grands corps* such as the Finance Inspectorate and Council of State. Imbued with the *haut fonctionnaire's* sense of public mission and confidence in rational, efficacious state intervention, Socialist leaders tended to view enlargement of the public sector as a natural extension of their own field of competence.[2]

All of this was missing in Spain. First, the PSOE's go-it-alone electoral strategy meant that it had no alliance partners pushing it left and creating pressure for the adoption of classic leftist measures such as nationalization. The other major Left party, the PCE, showed no more enthusiasm for an enlarged public sector than did the Socialists, and the negative performance and image of public enterprise meant that nationalization held little appeal for the electorate.[3] Moreover, for the Socialists the INI represented a bureaucratic power center with links to large banks and erstwhile Francoist economic interests, none of which were part of the PSOE's support network.[4] Socialist leaders, accordingly, were wary of augmenting the resources of a governmental entity they could not be sure of controlling.

In addition, whereas the PS's organizational culture encouraged state industrial expansion, the PSOE's discouraged it. To be sure, the government policies of Franco's final two decades had fostered the emergence of a technocratic elite whose members prized rationality, efficiency, and planning. Many of these technocrats, moreover, were sympathetic to PSOE ideology and had become party members and leaders. Yet their collective project did not envision an enhanced economic role for the INI or the public industrial sector. Instead, the technocrats—including government ministers such as Miguel Boyer (Economics, Finance, and Commerce), Carlos Solchaga (Industry and Energy, later Economics, Finance, and Commerce), Luis Croissier (Industry and Energy), and Claudio Aranzadi (Industry and Energy)—leaned more toward an economic policy of international competition, deregulation, and even privatization than toward nationalization.[5]

For the third and final explanation for differences in French and Spanish Socialist government attitudes toward public enterprise we must turn to the policy paradigms of the two Socialist parties. These have already been discussed in chapter 3, so all that is needed here is a restatement of the basic difference. In the early 1980s the PS adhered to the classic French Left (and therefore *dirigiste*) conviction that the market was a faulty mechanism for achieving desirable social ends. In this view, only an interventionist state could guarantee an economy that aided the strong, protected the weak, and defended the nation's global interests (including economic ones). And if a limited amount of state intervention was good, then more—especially public ownership and control of key economic agents—was better. The only unresolved issue was not whether the Left would nationalize, but what purpose its nationalizations would serve.

For the PSOE, by contrast, *dirigismo* was still closely associated with Franco's legacy of economic insularity and inefficiency on the one hand and political repression and arbitrary rule on the other. The path away from Francoism, chosen by all major democratic elements in Spain, led toward "Europe," a symbol embodying progress, especially democracy and economic growth, which in turn meant open borders, competitive domestic markets, and national firms capable of competing internationally. Measured against these imperatives, the INI's track record and prospects appeared dismal, and thus few Socialist voices called for extending its scope and authority. Instead, the party leadership favored a policy that would prepare public and private enterprises for the coming economic battle. To accomplish this task, a simple withdrawal of the state—deregulation—would not do; the government, treading a fine line between being *dirigista* and encouraging market forces, would have to initiate a broad process of rationalization throughout the industrial sector. That process, however, would preclude a dramatic expansion of state ownership.

INI REFORM AND INDUSTRIAL RECONVERSION

The PSOE government's dual goals of reforming the INI and reconverting industry were pursued simultaneously; indeed, the two tasks were related, because several of the larger firms targeted under the July 1984 industrial reconversion and reindustrialization law belonged to the INI. The INI was in such dire need of reform because of its history as an agent of autarchic industrial growth.[6] Founded in 1941, during the early years of the Franco regime, the

INI's mission, which was based on the goal of import substitution, was to develop Spain's capacity in industries deemed important for national defense and economic security. During its first two decades, the INI established public firms in such fields as armaments, electricity, oil refining, motor vehicles, coal mining, metals production (copper, aluminum, iron, and steel), and chemicals.

The INI's autarchic mission changed in the early 1960s in conjunction with Spain's opening to world trade. With the Franco regime—and in particular, the new technocratic elite that guided economic policy—intent on promoting private firms capable of carving out market niches, the INI was given a new mission: to intervene only in situations where the private sector had failed to invest in economic projects necessary for national advancement. This "subsidiarity" policy enjoined the INI from competing directly against private firms.[7] An important result was that when the post-1973 economic crisis hit, the INI became a huge salvage operation for firms teetering on the verge of financial collapse. From 1971 to 1982 the INI nationalized twenty-five firms in the steel, shipbuilding, automobile, chemical, and other industries. With Spain simultaneously undergoing the political pressures of the democratic transition—especially those created by a rapidly mobilizing workers' movement—the INI also served as a social safety valve, saving jobs and staving off mass discontent. Predictably, the INI became a chronic money loser, and from 1977 to 1982 its annual deficits rose steadily from PTA 23 billion to PTA 138 billion (about $1.1 billion).[8] By the time the Socialists came to power, the INI's losses, along with those of other public enterprises, equaled about 1.5 percent of GDP and accounted for almost half of the government's net borrowing requirement.[9]

Given the INI's dire financial condition, Socialist leaders had no intention of extending the list of nationalized companies.[10] Government officials realized that the INI's losses, if persistent, would sap the budget and jeopardize the government's social goals. Industry and Energy Minister Solchaga, for example, declared an "urgent and pressing need to change [the INI's] direction" and framed the problem in terms of opportunity costs, stating, "Each million pesetas that we devote to financing losses represents two unemployed people who don't receive a minimum of social protection, or a lost opportunity to improve education and sanitary levels in this country."[11]

Government attempts to slash the INI's deficits embraced productivity improvements, privatizations, and structural reorganizations. Improving productivity mainly meant lowering operating costs. The most obvious problem—whose solution required a rigorous reduction of excess labor and capital—was the bloated scale of most INI firms vis-à-vis market demand. Whereas the previous UCD government had recognized this problem but had taken only tentative and ineffectual measures, PSOE officials, led by Solchaga and Economics, Finance, and Commerce Minister Boyer, made the INI's rationalization a primary goal, and throughout the period of Socialist government there was a steady effort to cut personnel. The most concerted push came with the 1984 industrial reconversion program, which targeted several sectors in which the INI played a major role. From 1982 to 1993 the number of workers in INI firms dropped from 219,000 to 142,000, a reduction of 35 percent.[12]

Privatization of certain parts of the INI served several purposes. One was to ensure the survival of chronic money-losing firms whose recapitalization would have heavily burdened the budget, as in the cases of the automotive firms Seat (sold to Volkswagen) and Enasa (to Fiat). Another goal, paradoxically, was to strengthen several profitable firms by selling minority interests to private investors, thereby "providing these firms with new financial resouces while subjecting them to the discipline of private financial markets."[13] Two such firms were Ence (paper) and Endesa (electricity). The largest wave of privatizations came during the buoyant late 1980s, when improvements in financial performance made many INI firms more attractive investments. In 1985–1989 partial or full ownership of forty-six companies was sold off.[14]

Although impressive in the aggregate, privatization under the Socialists remained highly selective and circumscribed. Part of the reason for this was related to the nature of the INI itself, a formidable bureaucratic structure that did not participate happily in its own dismembering. According to Oscar Fanjul, head of Spain's largest oil company, Repsol (itself a public firm, though outside the INI's network), the INI's bureaucrats resisted privatization because it would rob the agency of its *raison d'être* and put them out of work.[15] Moreover, the enthusiasm of PSOE officials for privatization was hardly unbridled. Rather than seeing it as a way to loosen the state's suffocating grip, they viewed privatization as a means to resolve structural weaknesses in the public firms themselves. Their aim was to adapt the INI for global competition, not dismantle it.

Whatever their commitment to economic liberalization within the EC, government leaders believed that the public industrial sector would continue to play a strategic role in Spain's economy. Because of the continued weakness of private domestic capital, the INI was needed to maintain investment in core sectors and to ensure some degree of autonomy for the Spanish economy in the face of foreign penetration. As the INI's vice-president said, "If public industrial enterprise disappears or sells off much of its stock, . . . either there will be no large industrial groups in Spain or they will be in the hands of foreign interests. If this country had several large, private industrial groups, I wouldn't be speaking of public or private firms; but such private groups do not exist and thus it is necessary to maintain a strong public group."[16]

A third and final strategy for improving the INI's performance was a structural reorganization in 1992 that divided INI firms into two groups and was driven by EC strictures on state subsidies to public firms.[17] One group consisted of forty-seven profitable (or potentially profitable) firms. These firms, which accounted for 80 percent of the INI's total sales, 70 percent of its foreign sales, and 56 percent of its work force,[18] were brought into a new entity called Teneo, which focused on electrical power, air transport, the manufacturing of industrial equipment, and the processing of aluminum, paper, and chemicals. The other group was made up of nine firms that had consistently lost money, notably in coal mining, shipbuilding, steel, and defense, all of which remained within the traditional INI structure, renamed Grupo INI.

Government officials had different goals for the two groups. For the money-losing Grupo INI the goal was its dissolution. Each of the nine firms in Grupo INI was expected either to close, to divest itself of state control, or to return to profitability, in which case it would join Teneo. Teneo, on the other hand, would continue to privatize its capital and expose its firms to global competition, but privatization would remain selective and limited because perceived strategic national interests were at stake. An INI official remarked, "We want to maintain a hard core of national, Spanish capital. Other European countries do the same; for example, the French and others maintain a 'golden share' that ensures the state ultimate control. It's a way of defending the trade of the world's largest consumer bloc, the European Union, against potential rival blocs like the Asians."[19]

The impact of INI reform was uneven. After reaching a nadir with losses in 1983 of PTA 204 billion (about $1.6 billion in 1995 dollars), results improved steadily to a high point of profits of PTA 70 billion in 1989. After that, however, the trend headed downward, from bare profitability in 1990 to annual losses of PTA 79–175 billion in 1991–1994.[20] Burdened with a portfolio that included firms in such highly cyclical, employment-sensitive industries as steel, shipbuilding, and mining, during recessions the INI suffered disproportionately in comparison with the economy as a whole. Moreover, as long as INI firms continued to operate inefficiently and lose money, they could not attract private investors. The INI remained a prisoner of its Franco-era legacy, for many of its firms were still saddled with the operating practices of an earlier, protectionist era, yet their size and political importance did not permit failure or collapse.

In addition to INI reform, the other main component of the PSOE government's industrial-adjustment strategy was a broad effort to reconvert and reindustrialize targeted industrial sectors and regions. Socialist leaders, of course, were well aware of Spain's competitive handicap in having delayed industrial adjustment, and were determined to move quickly. According to the Industry and Energy Ministry official responsible for labor issues, "When

the Socialists came to power, most of the crisis sectors in other European countries had already been exposed to international competition and had taken
adjustment measures. In our case, industry had long been closed and protected, and managers had little experience with market competition. Thus
when adjustment finally became necessary, it was more intense—the labor
excess was greater, and the social impact was greater as well."[21]

At the outset, the government decided to address adjustment issues simultaneously across many sectors and within a period of about three years.
This plan imposed it own institutional logic. According to the official just
quoted, "We decided to adopt a common approach in all the crisis sectors,
even though the sectors had different characteristics. We had a limited but
comprehensive inventory of reconversion measures concerning financial, labor, and industrial-organizational issues that we adapted to each sector. This
was done so that the government wouldn't be overwhelmed by rivalry among
sectors. It was like a menu list in a restaurant; sectors had to devise their reconversion measures from that list. They couldn't go into the kitchen and ask
for something that wasn't on the list."[22]

In devising their menu, PSOE officials started not from scratch but from
the leftover recipes of their predecessors. From 1980 to 1982 the UCD governments of Suárez and Calvo-Sotelo had concluded industrial-adjustment agreements with employer representatives in eleven sectors, as well as in five individual firms. These agreements stipulated that the state would provide monetary concessions—including tax breaks, special-rate financing, and payments
to laid-off workers—to facilitate investment and reduction of unprofitable
capacity and labor.[23] Although lack of time and flawed execution meant that
these efforts bore little fruit,[24] they provided an institutional framework that
later guided the González government.

There were strong traces of this inherited framework in the two documents that defined the Socialists' reconversion strategy, a June 1983 white
paper and the July 1984 law.[25] Like the Socialists, the UCD government had
taken a broad, comprehensive approach that sought to adjust many sectors
simultaneously. Moreover, for specific sectors both governments emphasized
concertación (consensual, corporatist decision making) by state, employer, and
labor representatives—a reflection of the preference for *pactos sociales* employed
throughout the post-Franco transition.[26] Finally, there was considerable overlap in the sectors chosen; in several cases, the Socialists merely extended reconversion plans already under way.[27]

The sectors targeted by the Socialists formed a key component of Spanish
industry. Though representing less than 1 percent of all industrial firms, they
accounted for 6.6 percent of total production, 13.3 percent of exports, and 8.1

percent of employed workers.[28] They were an eclectic group that varied in many ways: in number of employees, in average firm size, in ownership composition (public versus private), and in degree of concentration. Two sectors, steel and shipbuilding, accounted for over half of the projected job cuts. In these two sectors the dominant firms were large, state-owned wards of the INI requiring reductions of over half their work forces. In other sectors, such as textiles and electronic components, the businesses tended to be privately owned and small scale. Some sectors needed relatively modest job cuts. The textile sector, for instance, lost less than 10 percent of its work force, while losses were less than 25 percent in, among other sectors, automotive electrical equipment, copper smelting, copper transformation, and heavy forging (see table 6.1).

Although the Socialists adopted much of their reconversion framework from previous UCD governments, they diverged from their predecessors in two ways. First, claiming that UCD labor policies had addressed only one side of the adjustment problem—income support for laid-off workers—the González government also emphasized retraining and reentry into the job market, chiefly through the creation of Fondos de Promoción de Empleo (FPEs), triparte sector-level agencies made up of representatives of firms and unions in the sector as well as government officials (from the National Employment Institute of the Labor and Social Security Ministry. The FPEs were charged not only with

Table 6.1   Spain: Industrial Reconversion—Work Force Reduction Targets

	Number of firms	Force Size (thous. of employees)	Reduction (thous. of employees)	Projected reduction (%)
Automotive electrical equipment	2	6.7	1.3	20
Electronic components	17	3.7	1.5	41
Fertilizers	11	9.4	3.4	37
Heavy forging	2	1.3	.3	24
Home appliances	18	23.9	12.6	53
Semi-transformation of copper	4	4.5	1.1	24
Shipbuilding (large firms)	2	21.9	11.9	54
Shipbuilding (small/medium firms)	27	15.4	7.4	48
Steel (integrated firms)	3	42.8	20.1	47
Steel (specialty firms)	11	13.7	8.7	64
Textiles	683	108.8	9.9	9
Other[a]	12	29.0	13.0	45
Total	792	281.1	91.2	32

Source: Ministerio de Industria y Energía, *Informe sobre la industria española 1989* (Madrid: MINER, 1990), 238
  a. Includes Alcatel Standard Eléctrica, Marconi Española, and Grupo Explosivos Río Tinto.

providing income support (normally 80 percent of a worker's most recent pay for up to three years), but also job training and placement.[29] To aid job placement, the FPEs, for example, offered businesses financial incentives to create jobs, especially in occupations "with a future."[30] FPEs were established for the four sectors considered to be the heart of the reconversion effort: shipbuilding, integrated steel, specialty steel, and home appliances.

A second PSOE innovation was the promotion of new industries, a goal for the most part ignored by previous reconversion plans. The favored tactic was the designation of Zonas de Urgente Reindustrialización (ZURs) in regions where crisis industries were concentrated. In each zone a management committee[31] sought to coordinate and stimulate new investment by offering direct subsidies (up to 30 percent of investment costs), preferential loan rates, and tax breaks. The ZURs were linked with the FPEs in that the former could only be established in regions where the latter existed; moreover, ZUR administrators could require firms receiving ZUR benefits to offer a specified percentage of new jobs to workers participating in the FPEs. By the end of 1985, eight regions had been declared ZURs.[32]

The reconversion process, spelled out in the July 1984 law, combined elements of state initiative and group consultation.[33] A sector's reconversion began with Spain's chief interministerial committee for economic affairs[34] appointing a group of civil servants (usually called the executive commission) to draw up a reconversion plan. After consulting with management, labor, and regional government representatives, the commission would draft a proposal covering labor reductions, capacity cutbacks, new investments, firm mergers and reorganizations, and other issues. The proposal would form the basis for negotiations by sectoral union and management representatives. Assuming the two sides reached agreement, the proposal, with any amendments, would be returned to the interministerial committee for review, approval, and submission to the prime minister and the cabinet *(consejo de ministros)*.[35] Final approval by the government would lead to a royal decree that, among other things, would establish a control and oversight commission to guide the reconversion process.[36]

Reconversion became a struggle for influence among several parties: the cabinet (which itself was sometimes divided), local and regional officials, employers and their associations, and labor unions. Although economic policy makers in the national government were united on the need for rapid adjustment, they were divided over measures. For example, Industry and Energy Minister Solchaga strongly pushed the comprehensive approach outlined in the June 1983 white paper, but Economics, Finance, and Commerce Minister Boyer opposed it, fearing that a formal law such as Solchaga proposed would commit the government to costly subsidies and tax breaks. Instead, Boyer advocated a firm-by-firm approach that would avoid the use of FPEs or other blanket instruments. Boyer, however, ultimately acceded to Solchaga's position.[37]

Predictably, in responding to reconversion efforts local and regional politicians acted as both defenders and promoters. On the one hand, they often tried to block, delay, or scale down plans to reduce jobs and production in local plants. This kind of opposition was to be expected in regions such as Galicia, the Basque Country, and Catalonia, where nationalist or conservative parties were influential in local government and unsympathetic to central authorities (especially Socialists). But local opposition was also found in such Socialist strongholds as Asturias and the southwestern city of Cádiz. In Asturias, according to the region's Socialist president during the 1980s, the regional government "always supported the unions because it felt that they were defending the interests of Asturias before the national government. The regional government here didn't want a direct confrontation with the central government because we're both Socialists, but we sought to have the national government's decisions move in our favor by taking advantage of the pressures generated by the unions."[38]

On the other hand, local and regional governments also figured prominently in industrial-promotion efforts, especially within the framework of the ZURs. Indeed, one of the main results of the ZURs was to shift control of the public funds intended for economic development from the central administration to local and regional governments. The ZURs, then, were a component, albeit a minor one, of a more general budgetary devolution from the center to the periphery.[39]

The main employers' association, the CEOE, as well as its sectoral federations, generally favored the government's reconversion plan and participated actively in the negotiation and oversight committees. The employers' only big complaint concerned the government financial instruments known as *créditos participativos* (participative loans), whose interest rates were linked to the profitability of the assisted firm and which were transformed into state-owned shares if the firm went bankrupt. The CEOE feared that such loans could easily lead to the "deceptive nationalization" of firms.[40] Once the 1984 law went into effect, however, the CEOE's fears were apparently allayed, for the organization became a strong supporter of the process.

Organized labor's response was highly diverse, varying not only across organizations but across different levels within organizations. Especially important were the metalworkers' federations in each of the two major confederations, the CCOO and the UGT, since much of the reconversion program targeted such basic industries as steel and shipbuilding. Of the two confederations, the Communist-leaning CCOO staunchly opposed the reconversion program from the outset. The nature of this opposition could be found in a comment by the head of the CCOO metalworkers' federation, Juan Ignacio Marín, who labeled the 1983 white paper a "deindustrialization plan" that manifested a "real obsession . . . to reduce employment."[41] A member of the CCOO's executive committee later viewed the PSOE's reconversion effort as "a reduction in the productive capacity of this nation's industrial structure. It wasn't exactly a reconversion—for example, planning the reconversion of obsolete sectors or regions and creating in parallel an alternative industrial tissue. In general terms, there hasn't been an active industrial policy but rather a cleaning up *(saneamiento)* to help enterprises become more competitive—in the case of public enterprises, to cut their losses. There was no strategy designed to reconstruct the industrial tissue, to search for more competitive sectors. That's been left to the initiative of the market." The main difference between the reconversion policies of the PSOE and UCD governments, he went on to say, was that "the Socialists carried out a much more rigorous, tougher policy, since the PSOE had a strong parliamentary majority and thus had the political strength to carry it through."[42]

The CCOO faulted the González government not only for its *fatalismo* but also for the procedures employed. In particular, the confederation protested mightily against two proposed measures. The first was the government's decision to exclude from the control and oversight commissions those unions that did not sign reconversion agreements. Because the CCOO refused to sign all such agreements, confederation officials denounced this measure as "a form of pressure and blackmail on the unions."[43] The second clash concerned the status of laid-off workers, namely whether the contracts of workers who joined the FPEs would be treated as canceled—as the government wished—or merely suspended, which the CCOO (as well as the UGT) favored. As we will see, this issue quickly became a flash point in dealings between the government and the unions, but was ultimately resolved in the unions' favor.

For the most part, government officials considered the CCOO an obstacle to be circumvented. According to one Industry and Energy Ministry official who worked closely with Solchaga, "the [CCOO] didn't want to be part of the dialogue and so they turned to confrontation in the streets."[44] Juan Ignacio Marín in particular came in for sharp criticism. In the opinion of a key negotiator for the Labor and Social Security Ministry, "Marín took a very intransigent position—he was very difficult."[45] Another official in the same ministry claimed that "with Marín it was impossible to agree on anything."[46] So difficult, in fact, that Marín's behavior became a point of contention, and Solchaga sought to have him excluded from the negotiations.[47]

Choosing an oppositional stance, the CCOO played its single card: mobilization of worker discontent in the targeted regions. Throughout 1983, 1984, and 1985 the confederation spearheaded countless strikes and demonstrations in cities in the Basque Country (Bilbao), Cantabria (Santander), Asturias (Gijón, Avilés, Oviedo), Galicia (El Ferrol, Vigo, Santiago de Compostelo), Andalusia (Cádiz), and Valencia (Sagunto). Whether this militancy translated into policy influence is unclear, however, for CCOO officials were mostly absent from the sectoral negotiations. But there is little doubt that the confederation's ability to pressure the government by bringing workers out into the streets made government officials wary of taking actions that would produce substantial economic dislocation.

With the CCOO in the streets, the UGT usually found itself alone on labor's side of the negotiating table.[48] As the PSOE's fraternal ally, the UGT initially supported the government's reconversion efforts, recognizing, in the words of its leader, Nicolas Redondo, that "sometimes unions have to negotiate sacrifices and not benefits."[49] This cooperative attitude encouraged government officials to consult UGT leaders throughout the formulation phase, from the issuance of the white paper in June 1983 to the passage of the final law in July 1984. During the implementation phase, the UGT signed agreements on labor issues for all of the affected sectors.

For all its support of the reconversion process, however, the UGT kept organizational self-interest ahead of blind loyalty to Socialist political leaders. According to Antonio Puerta, a top official of the UGT metalworkers' federation during this period (interviewed by the author in 1994),

> In those years the alternatives for the UGT were clear: either we entered into the process [of reconversion] or we didn't. If we didn't enter the process, the government would do it anyway. Then our only alternative would be to engage in direct, permanent confrontation with the government and hope for the best. Of course we didn't want this—we didn't believe in being the suicidal vanguard. If we had done this, we would have distanced ourselves from the rest of the workers in order to produce more political damage.[50]

In the opinion of government officials involved in the negotiations, the UGT was a vigorous partner-adversary, participating in the process but keeping its support conditional. Throughout the negotiations the UGT staunchly defended its interests, even to the point of withdrawing its support for the government on certain issues.[51] The most dramatic instance concerned the effect of FPEs on worker contracts. Although the UGT and the CCOO differed fundamentally on the need for reconversion, the two confederations jointly insisted that workers joining FPEs should be "suspended" from their previous

jobs rather than permanently laid off, as the government wanted.[52] In be-
hind-the-scenes negotiations with government officials, the UGT made this
issue a litmus test of its support for reconversion. With Industry and Energy
Minister Solchaga just as adamant in arguing for permanent layoffs, the dispute reached González himself, who had to mediate between the UGT and
one of his closest ministers. In the end, the UGT prevailed.[53]

This episode reveals much about both the power and the limits of organized labor during the initial reconversion phase. On the one hand, despite its
relatively low membership, the labor movement was able to launch an impressive series of strikes and demonstrations and to extract significant concessions
from the government. To be sure, most workers whose jobs were on the line
were easy to mobilize. Yet labor's efforts, both nationally and locally, played a
decisive role. From its headquarters in Madrid down to its local offices, the
CCOO constantly attacked the government's program. Also active at the local
level, albeit more sporadically and unevenly, were regional unions such as the
ELA-STV in the Basque Country. Even within the UGT, fierce resistance was
often found at the local level and among workers in certain companies, despite
the confederation's formal support. Indeed, whereas the CCOO and the UGT
were generally at odds at the national level, at the local level the two confederations' activists frequently worked in concert to resist or delay reconversion.

Complementing labor's street power was an equally important resource:
the UGT's access, via its fraternal ties to the Socialist party, to the highest levels
of the PSOE and the government. As a result, alongside labor's mass mobiliza-
tions were constant negotiations, many of them informal and confidential,
between UGT leaders and government ministers, including González, which
enabled UGT *jefes* such as Redondo and metalworkers' federation leader
Corcuera to wrest generous income-support measures from the government.

Labor's considerable influence, however, was insufficient to deter the government from its main goal of sharply cutting employment in the targeted
industries, and in the end the government achieved most of its job reduction
objectives. In this respect the government benefited crucially from the UGT's
broad support for reconversion. It can plausibly be argued that if the UGT had
formed a united opposition with the CCOO the outcome would have been
different. Worker opposition would certainly have been even more intense,
and the government would have lacked a workers' representative to deal with.
Under such circumstances, the government might well have been forced to
dramatically scale back its program, or perhaps even to shelve it.

After 1986, however, the government did abandon a central element of its
program, namely the attempt to restructure many sectors all at once. Rejecting
a global approach, government officials declared the beginning of a new phase

of "permanent adjustment" whereby reconversion would be carried out case by case. From 1987 to 1993, using most of the same labor adjustment measures adopted in 1983 and 1984, reconversion was undertaken principally in four sectors: integrated steel, specialty steel, shipbuilding, and household appliances.

This change in approach was part of a more general shift in industrial policy that became evident after the González government's first term (and coincided with Spain's entry into the EC). Industrial policy after 1986 featured greater emphasis on horizontal measures applying to all firms, as opposed to vertical measures focused on specific sectors. Emblematic of this changed emphasis was a celebrated statement by Solchaga's successor as industry and energy minister, Claudio Aranzadi that "the best industrial policy is one that doesn't exist."[54] Thus the government was much less inclined to intervene by way of broad sectoral programs, as it had in 1983–1984.

Moreover, industrial policy increasingly concentrated on technological promotion and innovation, not the downsizing of labor and productive capacity that had dominated the earlier period. The key agency in this new effort was the Center for Industrial Technological Development, which financed and administered a vast collection of projects that emphasized technology transfers, research and development, and scientific and industrial cooperation within the EU. Of great importance were programs to boost the design and fashion industries, environmental technologies, and industrial quality and safety.[55]

To account for this change in policy, in particular the adoption of a more ad hoc, case-by-case approach to reconversion, we must look to both economic and political factors. It is necessary to observe, first, that the 1983–1984 reconversion program had done much of the "dirty job" of adjustment. In addition, the economy's improvement in the late 1980s, which was accompanied by a flood of foreign investment and by rapid job creation, removed the sense of immediate crisis throughout the industrial sector. There was thus little perceived need for the kind of broad program launched in 1983–1984.

The government also abandoned the 1983–1984 approach because it was no longer politically feasible. With the breakup of the alliance between the UGT and Socialist leaders in mid-1985, and the UGT-CCOO rapprochement in opposition to government policy, the government after 1986 acted without support from organized labor. Such support was a precondition for any reconversion plan that would cut deeply into many industries at once. This logic was explained by Ignacio Fernández Toxo, Marín's successor as head of the CCOO's metalworkers' federation: "The political costs of the first phase of industrial reconversion beginning in 1983 were very high. These costs were lessened partly because the UGT supported the government's policies. But once the UGT and CCOO united against the government in 1986, the government tried to establish a new framework that would keep conflict with the unions from growing. This meant not adopting a policy of sectors in crisis that might give rise to union mobilization and opposition. It would have been much more difficult to repeat the 1983–1984 process, given the unity between these unions."[56]

During the post-1986 period, reconversion measures also changed, in particular expenditures for labor adjustment. Table 6.2, which presents labor adjustment costs by category and time period (1982–1988 and 1989–1992),[57] reveals two main trends. First, despite the more limited scope of reconversion in 1989–1992, in the sense of the number of sectors targeted, total labor costs (in nominal pesetas) exceeded those of 1982–1988. Although part of the difference was due to inflationary effects and the increase in budgetary resources linked to the economy's strong recovery in the late 1980s, another likely influence was the new configuration of alliances involving the government, the UGT, and the CCOO. Lacking labor support, the González government took a much softer approach to adjustment, which included the provision of benefits on a more generous scale.

This becomes even clearer when we consider a second trend in labor expenditures, namely the marked shifts in the proportions of the reconversion budget devoted to severance payments, preretirement pensions, and FPEs. Most striking was the pronounced decrease in reliance on severance payments, which was accompanied by a large increase in the use of FPEs. The chief difference between severance payments and FPE assistance was that the latter was geared toward worker retraining and job creation, whereas severance payments merely

Table 6.2   Spain: Labor Costs for Industrial Reconversion, 1982–1992 (in billions of pesetas)

	1982–1988	1989–1992	1982–1992
Lump-sum severance payments[a]	147.5	98.9	246.4
	(60.2%)	(31.6%)	(44.2%)
Preretirement pensions[b]	51.3	90.4	141.7
	(21.0%)	(28.9%)	(25.4%)
FPE expenditures	46.0	123.5	169.5
	(18.8%)	(39.5%)	(30.4%)
Total	244.8	312.8	557.6
	(100.0%)	(100.0%)	(100.0%)

Source: Labor and Social Security Ministry, personal communication.
  a. Workers less than 55 years old had the option of receiving a lump-sum severance payment in lieu of FPE benefits.
  b. For workers 55–59 years old, who were paid roughly 80% of former salary until entering the social security retirement system at age 60.

provided an income-support cushion. According to a former high-ranking INI official, by placing greater emphasis on FPEs, the government sought to offer displaced workers immediate alternatives to layoffs rather than, as was the case with severance payments, unemployment and an uncertain future. This shift can obviously be interpreted as an effort to mollify workers and dampen potential labor opposition.[58]

If there is evidence that the second phase of reconversion was designed with an eye to the dangers of labor mobilization, there is also evidence that the labor pacification strategy worked, for the second phase was marked by less labor conflict than the first. Paradoxically, the overall decline in worker opposition occurred against a backdrop of rising protests over the conduct of macroeconomic policy, which were spurred on by the UGT-PSOE divorce and the new UGT-CCOO alliance, and culminated in the December 1988 general strike. Labor peace was also assisted by a change in CCOO outlook in 1987, when the confederation underwent a bitter internal fight that in the end produced a new leadership more amenable to negotiation and bargaining with the government.[59] Especially important was the replacement of Juan Ignacio Marín as head of the CCOO metalworkers by Ignacio Fernández Toxo, who agreed to a reconversion plan for shipbuilding in 1988.[60] When asked why his union had endorsed this plan but not earlier ones, Toxo explained that in shipbuilding the fervent opposition of workers and unions during the previous decade had failed to stop massive job loss. It made no sense, he argued, to continue protesting for the sake of protesting. Rather, under these conditions it made more sense to negotiate. Toxo pointed proudly at the 1988 plan which, he said, "gave very good benefits to those workers leaving, and it provided significant investments in the industry, which would help those workers who remained."[61] Thus it appears that the government's change in reconversion strategy, combined with a more conciliatory stance on the part of the CCOO (at least vis-à-vis the major industrial sectors subject to reconversion, all of which were under the auspices of the metalworkers' federation), dampened worker mobilization during the second phase.

CONCLUSION

The PSOE government's industrial-adjustment policies left a mixed record. Efforts to make the INI more market driven produced impressive reductions in personnel, considerable privatization, and even, in the late 1980s, profits. Yet there was no miracle cure, and by the early 1990s the INI was again running huge deficits. Similarly, industrial reconversion reached most of its goals with respect to cutting capacity and jobs, but the cuts were not enough to ensure a solid return to competitiveness. Buoyed by the growth spurt of the late 1980s, many reconverted firms turned a profit, but dove into the red again with the onset of recession in the early 1990s.

Nevertheless, the González government could claim three accomplishments. The first was that it set a precedent: for the first time a Spanish government had carried out a sustained campaign to increase the competitive ability of the nation's industries. By seeking to make some of Spain's largest firms more efficient and to substantially reduce losses in the public industrial sector, PSOE leaders helped prepare Spain for full participation in the EC. If nothing else, industrial reconversion permanently changed expectations concerning the economic performance of public enterprises. It became difficult to imagine, for example, that the INI would return to its former role as a refuge for lame ducks.

Second, Socialist reconversion, at least before 1986, extended Spain's post-Franco pattern of *concertación*. Representatives of labor, management, and the central and regional governments were included in sectoral negotiations and as members of bodies such as the FPEs and the control and oversight committees. Although organized labor's engagement with reconversion was uneven—as, for example, in the CCOO's self-exclusion during the first phase versus its more cooperative stance after the 1987 change in leadership—at least one of the major confederations (the UGT) signed agreements for all of the reconverted sectors. Moreover, *concertación* continued even after the breakdown of the government's *política pactada* with labor over macroeconomic policy in 1986. Although it is difficult to judge the impact of the *concertación* process on Spain's quest to create a stable democracy, it is reasonable to assume that the impact was, on balance, salutary. Whether *concertación* was also economically beneficial is a more difficult judgment.[62]

Finally, the reconversion strategy worked in the sense of largely achieving the goals set for it. By 1990, as table 6.3 indicates, over 90 percent of the job cuts had been made. These cuts were far from superficial or painless. In the four largest sectors (integrated steel, specialty steel, shipbuilding, and home appliances), total employment plummeted from 118,000 in 1982 to 60,000 in 1990. Some of these job reductions would doubtless have occurred anyway, but the government could take credit for accelerating the process while providing income and other assistance for displaced workers.

Against these positive outcomes must be placed, of course, the fact that reconversion was no panacea for unprofitable operations. As was noted with respect to the INI, many firms that underwent restructuring remained vulnerable to boom-bust conditions, an indication that the emphasis on labor force reductions did not resolve all the problems of failing market performance. And Socialist industrial-adjustment strategy had only a slight, albeit positive,

Table 6.3   Spain: Industrial Reconversion—Work Force Reduction, 1982–1989

Sector	Projected (thous. of employees)	Actual Reduction[a] (thous. of employees)	Percentage of Target Achieved
Automotive electrical equipment	1.3	1.5	115.4
Electronic components	1.5	1.4	93.3
Fertilizers	3.4	2.5	73.6
Heavy forging	0.3	0.4	133.3
Home appliances	12.6	11.6	92.1
Semitransformation of copper	1.1	1.1	100.0
Shipbuilding (large firms)	11.9	11.7	98.3
Shipbuilding (small/medium-sized firms)	7.4	6.9	93.2
Steel (integrated firms)	20.1	18.7	93.0
Steel (specialty firms)	8.7	8.1	93.1
Textiles	9.9	9.9	100.0
Other[b]	13.0	10.0	76.9
All sectors	91.3	83.8	92.8

Source: Ministerio de Industria y Energía, Informe sobre la industria española 1989 (Madrid: MINER, 1990), 238.
   a. As of 31 December 1989.
   b. Includes Alcatel Standard Eléctrica, Marconi Española, and Grupo Explosivos Río Tinto.

effect on the nation's overall industrial structure. Especially in comparison with the economic performance of its European partners, years of reconversion did not greatly alter Spain's Achilles' heel, namely a production structure in which sectors with strongly growing demand contriubuted a relatively small proportion of valued added, whereas sectors with medium or weak demand contributed disproportionately to value added (see table 6.4).

Overall, industrial adjustment under the González government reflected a bias toward cushioning the shock of labor force reductions rather than a concerted effort to foster technological innovation. It will be recalled that the PSOE government's initial adjustment strategy paraded under the banner of reconversion *and* reindustrialization. Adopting instruments such as the FPEs and the ZURs to promote innovation, the government envisioned broad changes in technology and human capital that would link retirement of redundant workers and unneeded capacity to investment and job creation in industries "with a future." This vision of a coordinated movement of resources (labor and capital) out of obsolescent activities into dynamic ones went largely unrealized, for in practice most state aid went toward ensuring the success of reconversion, which overshadowed reindustrialization.[63]

Table 6.4   Spain: Changes in Industrial Structure, 1970–1990

	1970	1975	1980	1985	1990	EC Average, 1990
Sectors with strong demand[a]	11.2	11.7	12.2	12.9	13.3	26.8
Sectors with medium demand[b]	49.0	48.1	50.0	51.8	53.1	43.7
Sectors with weak demand[c]	39.8	40.2	37.8	35.3	33.6	29.5

Source: Javier de Quinto, *Política industrial en España: Un analysis multisectorial* (Madrid: Ediciones Pirámide, 1994), 28.
Note: Figures represent the percentage contribution to total value added of each type of sector.
  a. Includes aeronautics and aerospace, computers, electronics (consumer, defense, and communications), optics, and precision instruments.
  b. Includes rubber and plastics, automobiles, railway equipment, oil refining, electricity, paper, and food and drink products.
  c. Includes steel, aluminum, shipbuilding, mineral and metal transformation, wood and cork, textiles, leather products, and clothing.

The PSOE's labor measures during reconversion differed from those of most European nations in two ways. First, spending on displaced workers was relatively high. As a proportion of GDP, government spending on unemployment programs more than doubled in 1983–1993, with the increase being especially rapid after 1989. The available comparative data also indicate that during the early 1990s Spain's spending on such programs exceeded that of other EC nations.[64] Although this may appear unremarkable, given Spain's high level of unemployment, it must be remembered that Spanish government spending in general, and social spending in particular, was below the EC average.[65]

The second distinguishing trait of Spanish labor policy was an emphasis on passive income support as opposed to active measures such as retraining and job creation. Among EC nations in the late 1980s, for example, only Denmark devoted a lower proportion of its labor market spending to active measures.[66] As a result, the Socialists met with slight success in generating new jobs, as an examination of the seven ZURs, whose mission was to stimulate new investment and job creation in regions undergoing reconversion, indicates. Industry and Energy Ministry data indicate that from 1984 to mid-1991 the ZURs (and their successors)[67] created about 32,000 new jobs.[68] By 1991, on the other hand, reconversion programs had eliminated nearly 90,000 jobs— or almost three times as many as the ZURs created.[69] This is not surprising, given that the amount spent by the government on each job eliminated through reconversion was more than double the amount spent on each job created through ZUR-led reindustrialization.[70]

7
France

Nationalization
and
the Limits
of *Dirigisme*

Whereas the González government's industrial-adjustment strategy followed a deregulatory logic that sought to expose protected firms to market forces, the Mitterrand government's initial strategy embodied the opposite approach. The French Socialists' goal was to extend the state's directive powers into the private sector, in the process drawing some of the nation's largest businesses into the public domain. The centerpiece of this strategy was a sweeping nationalization program aimed at twelve industrial firms, thirty-six banks, and two finance companies, which entered the planning stage as soon as the Socialists gained power in June 1981 and was carried out in 1982.[1] It reshaped French industrial-ownership patterns,[2] giving France, after Austria, the largest public sector in Europe.[3]

This chapter examines the nature, fate, and impact of the 1982 nationalizations during the two periods of Socialist government (1981–1986 and 1988–1993) and asks three questions: Why did the French Left follow the path of nationalization? What became of the program? And what was the program's effect on industrial adjustment? The answers to these questions, however, are far from clear. For one thing, during the 1970s and early 1980s, when the Left was championing a broad nationalization program, the reasons for its endorsement of nationalization were diverse and even contradictory. Its attitudes toward nationalization were continually in flux, and even the Socialist government of 1981–1986 eventually abandoned its grandiose vision of a public sector that would serve as a kind of strike force against global economic competition. The subsequent Chirac government of 1986–1988 sought to undo the Socialists' work by reprivatizing the nationalized firms, an effort that was well under way until derailed by the October 1987 stock market crash and the Right's defeat in the 1988 elections. Mitterrand, on being reelected in 1988, proclaimed an end to both privatization and nationalization. But adhering to the status quo ultimately proved untenable as well, and cash-starved nationalized firms were able to pressure the government into allowing private capital to enter the public sector. By the time of the 1993 elections, some public-sector firms were being partially reprivatized (a trend that accelerated after the Right's return to power).

The ultimate impact of the nationalization program remains controversial and subject to widely divergent judgments by the Left and Right. This chapter will argue that nationalization brought about significant changes in the structure, operation, and performance of the affected firms. Most strikingly, it introduced fresh investment capital and made the firms more efficient. These achievements, however, bore little relationship to the original motivations for widespread nationalization, and the firms themselves, in their investment strategies, employment policies, and labor-management relations, more closely resembled their foreign capitalist competitors than anything remotely socialist. Asked in 1987 to identify the differences between the nationalized firms and private companies, an Industry Ministry official responsible for overseeing public industrial firms replied, "I can't tell you. I don't see any."[4] The fate of the 1982 nationalization program, in fact, signaled the demise of the Left's project of employing the *dirigiste* state to achieve its industrial and social goals.

RATIONALES AND RESULTS, 1981–1986

A chief reason why the 1982 nationalization program proved so controversial and impermanent was that its objectives were ambiguous and even contradictory. Such ambiguity, as in the case of another key Left concept of the 1970s, *autogestion,* helped build support for the Left before 1981 by attracting disparate constituencies. Once the Left came to power, however, unresolved conflicts about the purpose of nationalization could no longer be skirted. Before examining the results of nationalization during the 1981–1986 period of Socialist government, therefore, we need to analyze the objectives nationalization was designed to attain.

The original justification was, of course, to weaken capitalist power. As the 1972 Common Program of the Left stated, "In order to break the domination of big capital and to establish a new economic and social policy that departs from that carried out by big capital, the government will progressively transfer to the collectivity the most important means of production and financial instruments now in the hands of dominant capitalist groups."[5] Mainstream Left thinking of the early 1970s was influenced by the PCF's theory of state monopoly capitalism, which held that large private corporations had increasingly captured the state in their quest to restore declining profits.[6] And along with growing domination of the French state by large industrial concerns, the PCF contended, came widening social inequalities and deteriorating public services. Nationalizing these monopoly firms would ensure collective control at two levels—at the macrolevel by enabling public authorities to guide basic industrial and financial strategy, and at the microlevel by instituting new management structures in which employees would have a say in matters such as work organization and personnel management. In its eagerness to forge a left-wing identity and strike an electoral deal with the PCF, the PS accepted this view with few qualms.

During the late 1970s, however, the two parties increasingly diverged in their conceptions of the public sector. The PCF continued to promote nationalization as a battering ram against the capitalist fortress. According to the Communists, by expanding the public sector sufficiently a Left government could exert a controlling influence over private capital, thereby reducing and eventually eliminating its power. Although the Socialists did not entirely reject this rationale, they developed others as well.[7] In September 1981 the Socialist rationale for nationalization was put forward by Mitterrand during his first presidential press conference. He argued, first, that nationalization was "just and necessary" under certain conditions, namely when businesses "have become monopolies or are tending that way and . . . make products necessary to the nation. These firms should not have an economic and thus a political power that allows them to dominate decisions concerning the general interest. Neither should [such firms], having abolished all national competition beneath them, be masters of the market."[8] For Mitterrand and the Socialists, nationalization was a way of curbing the economic and political might of *les monopoles* by making them subject to the general interest.

Having genuflected to his left, Mitterrand, apparently sensing no contradiction, offered a second justification, not on the grounds that French capitalists were too strong but that they were too weak: "If we did not [nationalize these firms], they would be rapidly internationalized. I refuse an international division of labor and production that is decided from afar, obeying interests that are not ours. We are not a pawn on the chessboard of those stronger than we are. We must be clear about this: for us, nationalizations are a weapon for defending French production."[9] This rationale, first developed in *Le socialisme industrielle,* an influential work published in 1977 by Alain Boublil (who in 1981 became Mitterrand's leading industrial adviser), represented a return to traditional mercantilism, a reversion to a classic reflex of French political leaders of both the Left and the Right, namely distrust, not of the power of French capitalists, but of their lack of dynamism.[10] Corporate managers, Socialists claimed, had failed to invest in France, thus allowing foreign capital to capture large parts of the domestic market. Nationalization, it followed, was needed to defend the nation's industrial patrimony, or, in the favored phrase, "reconquer the domestic market." As one of Fabius's advisers later commented, "We went from the idea of breaking with capitalism to the very different idea of breaking with the failures of capitalism."[11]

The third and final rationale for nationalization put forward by Mitterrand at the press conference was the supposed economic success of France's existing public firms. "It is important to know," the president said, "that in France nationalizations work." Citing the automobile, oil, airline, helicopter, and banking industries, Mitterrand claimed that the French public sector, unlike those in other countries, "produces good results."[12]

Not surprisingly, given this congeries of justifications for nationalization, the firms nationalized in 1982 quickly became the focus of conflicting aims. An indication of the government's initial plans came in a February 1982 letter from Industry Minister Pierre Dreyfuss to the heads of the new public-sector firms, in which the minister outlined three goals: job creation, industrial modernization through increasing investment, and expansion of French industry both at home and internationally. According to Dreyfuss, the new public-sector firms were expected to stimulate industrial investment but also hire new workers and lead the fight against unemployment. They were to reorganize and rationalize their structures but also introduce new forms of employee participation in decision making. And they were to get their accounts out of the red but also step up research and development.[13] During the heady days of *relance,* when all seemed possible, few Socialist leaders asked whether these goals formed a coherent policy or were, in fact, an unwieldy wish list of unreconcilable objectives.

Nor did these leaders confront one obvious but unacknowledged contradiction in the Socialist conception of public enterprise. Although the nationalized firms presumably would serve the "collectivity" and thus help the government fulfill its industrial-policy objectives, they would also exercise, according to Dreyfuss, "complete autonomy." It was unclear, however, how such autonomy would be compatible with Dreyfuss's charge that they must also "respect the general orientations fixed by the State."[14] Could they, for example, help achieve the government's industrial-policy goals, especially those related to employment and investment, while functioning as autonomous market actors?

The answer to that question depended partly on the nature of the firms themselves—their industrial capacity—and partly on the state's ability to achieve its industrial-policy goals. As a group the firms shared four main traits: large size, international exposure, dependence on the state, and shaky finances. Although the first two traits made the nationalized firms important economic actors, the last two meant that they would be dubious weapons for reconquering the home market.

Because of their size, the nationalized firms gave the state a substantial stake in many industrial sectors.[15] Rhône-Poulenc, for example, was an important producer of synthetic fibers, basic chemicals, and pharmaceuticals. Thomson-Brandt specialized in consumer and professional electronics. Compagnie Générale d'Électricité (CGE) was a major producer of cables, computers, and electronics, and both CGE and Thomson had large stakes in telecommunications. Saint-Gobain-Pont-à-Musson's main area was glass products, but it also had an interest in computers through its shares in CII-Honeywell Bull and Olivetti. Péchiney's diverse metallurgical and chemical interests included aluminum, refined chemicals, and pharmaceuticals. The acquisition of Dassault-Breguet and MATRA allowed the state to dominate French aeronautics and weapons production. Finally, the nationalization of Usinor and Sacilor gave the state control of four-fifths of French steel production.

The nationalized firms were internationally active and exposed to foreign competition. An Industry Ministry official stated that the 1982 nationalizations represented "a fundamental change in the nature of the enlarged public sector: henceforth, international competition is the economic context of the public corporations."[16] Among the "Big Five" (Rhône-Poulenc, Thomson, CGE, Saint-Gobain, and Péchiney), foreign sales accounted for an average of 47 percent of total sales in 1980, and an average of 29 percent of the work force of those firms was assigned to foreign operations and subsidiaries. Whereas the public sector accounted for 12 percent of France's exports before nationalization began, after nationalization the figure rose to 31 percent, largely because of the acquisition of the Big Five. More important, the public sector's contribution to the trade balance was highly positive—a surplus of over Fr 70 billion in 1982, to which the Big Five and Renault contributed Fr 37 billion.[17]

Many of these firms, as national champions before 1982, had already become de facto public enterprises by virtue of their dependence on the state. Several relied heavily on state contracts. One-third of CGE's business, for instance, came from state institutions such as the Direction Générale des

Télécommunications (DGT), Electricité de France, the nationalized rail system, and the Paris metro. Thomson produced telecommunications equipment for the DGT as well as military guidance and communication systems.[18] Moreover, the firms nationalized in 1982 had already captured a large share of the grants, loans, and tax credits offered to industry by the state.[19] One result of this dependence on public subsidies was that the state, in return for extending loans and credits through its financial institutions, had acquired minority shareholder status in those firms. According to one estimate, by 1982 the main state credit agency, the Caisse des Dépôts, owned from 5.2 percent to 7.2 percent of each of the Big Five.[20]

But despite their size and importance, many of the firms nationalized in 1982 were performing poorly at the time of their acquisition by the state. Although firms such as Dassault, MATRA, CGE, and Saint-Gobain were flourishing, others were not, notably Péchiney, Thomson, Bull, Rhône-Poulenc, Compagnie Générale des Constructions Téléphoniques (CGCT), and the notoriously shaky steel companies, Usinor and Sacilor. The balance sheet for the new public industrial firms for 1981 and 1982 revealed an accumulated net loss of Fr 26.2 billion.[21]

Why were these firms losing so much money? A chief reason was the legacy of the Right's industrial policies. For example, the biggest losers, the two steel companies, owed much of their poor performance to several state-sponsored plans that mandated consolidation but allowed excess capacity and discouraged modernization (see chapter 8). Moreover, three of the Big Five, having diversified during the 1970s with the government's encouragement, now suffered from ill-conceived acquisitions. Although CGE and Saint-Gobain had invested in such profitable areas as advanced rail-transport equipment, telecommunications, and computers, the others had embarked on unprofitable ventures: Rhône-Poulenc in chemical and steel operations, Thomson in telecommunications, and Péchiney in fertilizers.[22]

The specific traits of the newly nationalized firms—their size, foreign exposure, dependence on the state, and weak financial condition—meant that the economic role of the public sector would change. First, the largest firms would be concerned mainly with attaining international commercial viability, not, as in the past, with providing public services such as electricity and public transportation. Given that these firms were crucial to France's trade balance, this meant that the state itself would assume the risks of international competition. Second, the financial weakness of these firms meant that the state's first priority would be to restore them to health, which posed the evident danger of deepening their dependence on the state. Finally, given the commercial and financial constraints under which both the firms and their state overseer would have to operate, it was uncertain whether the firms would be able to fulfill the "social" goals envisioned for them, including creating jobs and serving as social laboratories for new forms of management-employee relations.

The prospects for the newly enlarged public sector depended not only on the nature of the firms themselves but also on the state's capacity to mobilize the public sector as a central element of industrial policy. The question of the French state's strength has long fascinated observers, who have produced a massive though still inconclusive literature. Although many view France as the epitome of the "strong state"—a state with the internal cohesion and in-stitutional levers to define and achieve its own aims, even in the face of soci-etal opposition—others challenge this portrait.[23] In the sceptics' eyes, the French state is more internally divided, susceptible to societal influence, and inca-pable of achieving its goals than the conventional "strong state" depiction suggests.[24]

With respect to industrial policy, the sceptics argue that the state's vaunted efficacy has been eroded in two major ways. First, policy-making processes are increasingly characterized by intra-administrative division rather than cohe-sion, by fragmentation rather than coordination. Within the bureaucracy, conflicts among the various *corps*, divisions, and departments are endemic, with industrial policy itself being splintered among competing ministries, in-terdepartmental committees, funding organizations, and public and semipublic enterprises.[25]

It is claimed, moreover, that the state's capacity to oversee and direct the actions of large firms, both public and private, has declined. In oil, textiles, nuclear energy, steel, and other sectors, businesses have usually been able to initiate their own strategies and then convince state officials to approve what they propose. As a result, the state's sector-specific policies have often failed to achieve their goals. During the 1970s, for example, state efforts to rescue fail-ing industries (machine tools, shipbuilding, and basic chemicals) and to en-courage private firms to develop new products (computers and videocassette recorders) ended in failure. Even when the state has successfully undertaken direct production in "strategic" sectors—oil, telecommunications, nuclear energy, aviation, and aeronautics, among others—state officials have eventu-ally lost the power to decide industrial strategy, whereas the firms themselves have gained autonomy and the capacity to fend off external interference.[26]

Given these uncertainties surrounding the purposes, operations, and ca-pabilities of the newly nationalized firms, their success as an instrument of Socialist industrial policy was far from assured. To assess how they functioned and performed, we will examine three central issues: labor-management relations, state-management relations, and financial results. Labor-management relations can be examined by assessing two government actions that defined who would govern the nationalized firms. The first was the appointment of corporate directors. In selecting directors the government drew from the well that traditionally had supplied the leaders of large businesses—the *grande école–grand corps* network.[27] Throughout the public sector the Mitterrand government appointed directors (all of whom were men) who had already risen to the highest levels of management via this classic route. Competence, as classically defined by scholastic excellence and one's ability to maneuver within the *haute administration,* remained the major criterion for selecting the new public managers. In its appointments the government thus signaled its intention to maintain traditional patterns of elite recruitment.

The second action defining labor-management relations was the July 1983 Law on the Democratization of the Public Sector. Neither the 1972 Common Program nor the Socialists' 1980 manifesto, the Projet Socialiste, had provided a blueprint for the promised new management structures, and the final legislation emerged from consultations among ministries and union and management representatives from the nationalized firms. It was decided that each firm would have a board of directors representing the state, employees, and the public, with, in most firms, one-third of the directors being elected by the employees.[28]

The government's approach to the new boards of directors paralleled its earlier approach to employee participation in the private sector, as embodied in the 1982 Auroux laws.[29] In both cases, three principles guided the design of the new institutions: strengthening of the unions' legal-institutional presence, encouragement of negotiations between management and union representatives, and preservation of management's autonomy. To satisfy the first principle, the major unions were guaranteed a voice on the boards of directors. In general, the one-third of board seats reserved for employees could be filled only by employee candidates running on lists provided by the labor confederations designated "most representative" by the Labor Ministry. As for the second principle, the government left many aspects of union rights and labor-management relations to local negotiations, both within the boards of directors themselves and between unions and management. One key issue left for negotiation was the form and function of so-called workshop or office councils, which were intended to serve as consultative bodies for the boards of directors. Other questions to be negotiated firm by firm included union rights, the exercise of "freedom of expression of employees," and board member rights and privileges.[30]

Both the first and the second principles sought to institutionalize unions—

and employees more generally—as partners in defining company rules and regulations. The third principle, however, sharply circumscribed that role, for management's power to determine corporate strategy remained intact. Board members were to function strictly as consultants to management, with no veto over management's decisions in such strategic domains as employment and investment. According to the Industry Ministry official in charge of the nationalized sector at the time, the government, despite pressure from the CGT, rejected a formal charter that would codify the boards' duties and powers. Instead, the government relied on a less formal two-page circular sent by the prime minister to the relevant oversight ministries, outlining in general terms the boards' role.[31] This purposeful vagueness served to reinforce the position of each firm's CEO vis-à-vis its board of directors.

Let us now examine a second issue concerning the newly nationalized firms: state-firm relations. Every public enterprise was subject to the *tutelle* (oversight) of one of eighteen government ministries, whose goal was to ensure that the firm fulfilled its "public purpose." Although that purpose was easy to define for public utilities such as the national railway and the national electricity supplier, it was not so easy to define for companies that had to compete on the open market, given that market imperatives and "public purposes" could conflict.

The classic postwar solution to this problem of market competition was the "Renault model," whereby the state would grant a public company a generous degree of autonomy to allow it to optimize its market performance. During the time it was in opposition, the Left embraced the Renault model, but with an ambiguous qualification set out in the Common Program, which stated that public firms would have to "respect . . . the orientations" of a general economic plan approved by the government.[32] This ambiguity remained a feature of Socialist attitudes toward public firms after the PS came to power. All of the firms nationalized in 1982 were situated in highly competitive market environments and thus, at least at first glance, likely candidates for autonomy. Mitterrand's appointment of the Renault model's architect, former CEO Pierre Dreyfuss, as industry minister, reinforced the probability that the autonomy principle would predominate. But because several public firms were running huge losses, state rescue operations such as financial bailouts and sectoral reorganizations were, in the government's view, absolutely necessary. Indeed, restructuring the nationalized firms in order to rationalize their production activities absorbed much of the government's energies during the first two years after nationalization.[33] The notion that the public firms were part of a larger Left strategic vision was, moreover, suggested by the government's industrial *dirigisme* during its early years in power and by

Mitterrand's own public declarations. On one occasion, for example, after reaffirming that "the autonomy of decision and action of the nationalized firms must be total," Mitterrand stated, "I expect the public industrial enterprises to contribute to the objectives of national economic revival in terms of employment, investment, research, as well as the international presence *(rayonnement)* of France."[34]

How did Socialist oversight operate? We can examine this question by analyzing the Mitterrand government's use of *contrats de plan* (planning contracts), its major method for supervising public firms. These contracts, negotiated by eleven of the twelve nationalized industrial firms and their supervising ministries, covered corporate goals and strategies. Although contracts of this kind had been used sporadically by the Right, they had been limited mainly to financial questions,[35] whereas the Socialists sought to expand them to encompass industrial strategies, financial operations, and the national interest, and thereby link public-firm economic performance to the national planning process.[36] For the Socialists, planning contracts offered the best of all possible worlds: management autonomy, the encouragement of *concertation* to enable employees and unions to help shape the negotiations over the planning contract's provisions, and a guarantee that the nationalized firms' activities would be in accord with the government's economic and social objectives.

Although the groundwork for planning contracts had been laid while Dreyfuss was industry minister (June 1981–June 1982), the actual negotiations began under his successor, Chevènement, in July 1982. Chevènement conceived of *tutelle* as an exchange: the state would provide new operating capital, and in return the public firms would help the government meet its economic and social goals by maintaining or even increasing employment, engaging in research and development, negotiating and consulting with the unions, and contributing to a positive trade balance.[37] This conception, however, alarmed several of the public firms' presidents, including Jean Gandois, head of Rhône-Poulenc, who resigned, protesting that a public firm exposed to international competition could not also serve as an instrument of the government's industrial policy.[38]

From August 1982 until March 1983 the government orchestrated the first round of planning contracts in negotiations between the firms and the state, the latter represented by a new ten-person Industry Ministry body known as the Services des Entreprises Nationales.[39] The discussions proceeded smoothly, but Chevènement came under increasing fire for interfering with the firms' strategic decisions. Tensions between Chevènement and the corporate leaders climaxed at a January 1983 luncheon at the Élysée, at which the leaders of six firms complained bitterly to Mitterrand about Chevènement's heavy-handed actions. This meeting was a turning point in the government's *tutelle* policy. Three weeks after the luncheon, Mitterrand rebuked his industry minister in a Council of Ministers meeting by stating, "We can't have a coherent industrial policy if we have a meddling bureaucracy."[40] The disavowed Chevènement then submitted his resignation and was replaced by Mitterrand's protégé, Fabius, who clearly understood the president's desire for a less interventionist *tutelle*.

The changing of industry ministers coincided with France's major political and economic crisis of the early 1980s, the 1982–1983 U-turn in macroeconomic policy (discussed in chapter 4). Alongside this change to austerity was a marked change in relations between the state and the public firms, and in particular in the nature of planning contracts, for Fabius's treatment of the public firms was strongly influenced by the financial constraints of *rigueur*. From now on, the nationalized firms would have to start paying their own way. As Fabius later remarked, "If you think, as I do, that you must have a public sector, then it must perform well. That requires clear rules of the game— not to have profits as your sole objective, but not to neglect the profit element. What I saw of the public enterprises in 1983 was that if we continued in the same fashion, we would lose the practical and ideological battle of the nationalizations because all that would be drowned by massive deficits."[41]

To make his point, Fabius ordered all nationalized firms in the competitive sector (except the steel companies and CDF-Chimie) to break even within three years. In return, he promised the firms wide latitude, including the freedom to lay off unneeded workers. Fabius later explained his actions as follows: "What were the rules of the game? They were autonomy . . . that is to say, the minister of industry won't constantly be on the back of the directors of the nationalized firms. That took the form of the planning contracts where, after discussions, we set goals and then judged people on their work, but we left them free to manage. . . . Corporate managers didn't have to call up the minister to ask what to do."[42]

Under Fabius the planning contracts assumed a new goal. No longer were they meant to ensure that nationalized firms would help achieve the government's economic and social objectives. Now they became a "device for medium-term financial control,"[43] that is, for setting performance criteria that would return the firms to profitability. Accordingly, Fabius adopted a more flexible approach to the contracts. Whereas Chevènement had planned to renegotiate the existing contracts during the fall of 1983 and replace them with five-year contracts that would comply with the stipulations of France's proposed 1984–1988 national plan, Fabius notified the directors of the nationalized firms that the government would merely "update" the existing contracts year by year.[44] According to Fabius, the new approach meant that "the state only intervenes in big strategic decisions, and for the rest the public enterprises can operate in peace. They sign a contract with the state and we judge the results."[45]

One consequence of Fabius's decision was that the nationalized firms developed considerable financial independence from the state; in 1983, in fact, a creeping privatization of the public sector began. This *débudgetisation,* or financing of operations outside the state budget, took two main forms. First, after the passage of the so-called Delors Law in January 1983, public firms were allowed to solicit private capital by issuing nonvoting loan stock *(titres participatifs)* and preferred stock *(certificats d'investissement).* (The former gave a return based partly on the going bond rate; the latter's dividend was based on the financial performance of the issuing firm.) These mechanisms enabled the main public industrial firms to issue more than Fr 11 billion of stock in 1983–1985.[46] The nationalized firms also increasingly used their subsidiaries to pull in private capital, either by obtaining financing directly from subsidiaries that remained listed on the stock exchange (for example, Thomson's subsidiary Thomson-CSF and CGE's subsidiaries Alsthom and Alcatel), or, beginning in 1985, by newly listing wholly owned subsidiaries (such as the Saint-Gobain subsidiary Saint-Gobain-Emballage and the GCE subsidiary Gidadix). The latter method, which was, in effect, an illegal selling off of subsidiaries, was nevertheless allowed by the government, which favored the maneuver but wanted to avoid making it a matter of parliamentary debate during the period leading up to the March 1986 elections, by which time about seventy subsidiaries had been sold off.[47]

At this point we arrive at the question: So what? Did the French Socialists' nationalization program affect how these firms performed? Let us then assess this program from a third perspective, that of financial results. As table 7.1 demonstrates, the financial performance of the newly nationalized firms improved sharply from 1982 to 1985. Although three of the Big Five had been losing money when nationalized, by 1985 all were profitable enterprises. Of the other four fully nationalized firms, Bull managed a turnaround from near-bankruptcy to profitability, but in 1985 CGCT and the two steel companies were still deeply in the red (although their losses were down sharply from the previous year).

Of the other previously nationalized firms under Industry Ministry *tutelle,* three (EMC, ELF-Acquitaine, and CEA-Industrie) improved their balance sheets. Renault, once the pride of the public sector, incurred huge losses in 1984–1985, in part because of its failed joint venture with American Motors Corporation (see chapter 9). CDF-Chimie also lost money, although its situation was

Table 7.1   France: Public-Sector Net Operating Balances, 1981–1985 (in billions of francs)

	1981	1982	1983	1984	1985
Big Five					
CGE	586	638	662	797	1,185
Péchiney	-1,636	-3,008	-295	681	809
Rhône-Poulenc	-286	-787	129	2,026	2,429
Saint-Gobain	578	369	724	1,201	1,524
Thomson	-1686	-2,208	-1,251	-35	583
Subtotal	-926	-4,996	-31	4,670	6,530
Other Firms Nationalized in 1982					
Bull	-449	-1,351	-625	-489	110
CGCT	-29	-345	-555	-997	-382
Sacilor	-2,897	-3,737	-5,610	-8,141	-5,386
Usinor	-4,241	-4,604	-5,456	-7,399	-3,487
Subtotal	-7,616	-10,037	-12,246	-17,026	-9,145
Firms Nationalized Before 1982					
CDF-Chimie	-1,213	-834	-2,855	-930	-965
ELF-Acquitaine	4,493	4,330	4,559	7,655	6,362
CEA-Industrie	-8	-374	56	225	951
EMC	-120	-207	-160	25	87
Renault	-690	-1,281	-1,576	-12,555	-10,925
Subtotal	2,462	1,634	24	-5,580	-4,490
Total	-6,080	-13,399	-12,253	-17,961	-7,105

Source: *Le secteur public industriel en 1985* (Paris: Observatoire des Entreprises Nationales, Ministère de l'Industrie, des Postes et Télégraphes, et du Tourisme, 1986).
Note: Table provides information on the fourteen firms overseen by the Industry Ministry. Since this ministry does not oversee three of the firms nationalized in 1982—Dassault, MATRA, and Roussel-Uclaf—these are not included in the table.

special, for it had been forced by the state to take on the losing operations of Péchiney and Rhône-Poulenc during the 1983 reorganization of the chemicals sector. On balance, then, despite some persistant weaknesses, the public industrial sector's financial performance improved markedly during the first half of the 1980s.

Nationalization benefited the nationalized firms in two ways. First, the reorganizations that took place in 1982–1983 made those firms considerably more integrated and allowed them to focus more intensely on their traditional core activities. Although it can be argued that industrial rationalization was already taking place, nationalization facilitated this process.[48] Even the chief economist of the employers' organization, the Conseil National du Patronat Français (CNPF), readily conceded that the reorganizations were carried out more rapidly and efficiently than market forces would have allowed.[49] Second, the state pumped far more capital into these firms than they otherwise would have received. In 1982–1985, all companies in the public industrial sector received state subsidies totaling Fr 50.9 billion, of which Fr 15.6 billion went to the Big Five.[50] According to one estimate, the Fr 40 billion given to the *newly* nationalized firms (including Fr 20 billion for the steel companies) was twenty times the amount invested in those firms by private shareholders during the previous two decades.[51] Moreover, from 1981 to 1984 investment in the newly nationalized firms increased by 44 percent, but by only 26 percent in the industrial sector as a whole.[52] In purely financial terms, nationalization did not hurt the already profitable firms and greatly aided the sickly ones.

In two respects, however, the nationalization process disappointed its partisans. Among other things, the nationalized firms failed to hold the line against rising joblessness. Indeed, the 1983 turn toward autonomy and Fabius's decision that the nationalized firms must break even by 1985 almost guaranteed that they, like the private firms, would have to shed workers. From 1981 to 1985 the total number of workers employed by the twelve nationalized industrial firms declined by 11.4 percent, compared with a decline of 10.2 percent for the rest of the industrial sector.[53] Moreover, many of the newly nationalized firms, far from serving as potent weapons of national economic defense, turned out to be rubber swords. Rather than investing in and reconquering the domestic market, several were preoccupied with salvage and restoration operations. The Socialist theory that made public enterprise France's economic vanguard thus proved to be ill-suited to an industrial sector in sharp (and greater than expected) decline in a period of budget austerity.

Ultimately, the nationalizations of 1982–1986 must be judged on their impact on the economy as a whole, and in this respect the record is mixed. Although the director-general of the Industry Ministry claimed that nationalization "saved the furniture" by preventing many of the new public firms from going bankrupt,[54] others asserted that it merely rearranged the furniture, for example by reassigning the Big Five's failing operations to perpetual losers (CDF-Chimie, Sacilor, and Usinor) or winners (ELF-Acquitaine). According to one study, the nationalization and subsequent privatization of the twelve industrial firms produced a slight net profit for the state.[55] Yet this calculation neglects the fact that the twelve firms posted a cumulative operating loss for 1982–1985 of Fr 74.5 billion, even with state subsidies of over Fr 50 billion.

From a neoclassical perspective, it can be argued that the Mitterrand government merely socialized corporate losses and therefore wasted economic resources. That criticism, however, misses the key point that the nationalizations staved off even greater losses and, probably in several cases, bankruptcy. Without public intervention on a scale that only nationalization made possible, Thomson, Péchiney, Rhône-Poulenc, Bull, and other companies would have suffered greater losses than they did and might well have faced collapse. Politically and economically, the collapse of the nationalized firms—the equivalent for France of a Chrysler-size failure multiplied several-fold—would have been unacceptable.

FROM "NEITHER-NOR" TO "BOTH-AND": THE DEMISE OF *DIRIGISME*, 1988–1993

Having lost parliamentary control in March 1986, the Socialists regained it in June 1988 following Mitterrand's reelection and the new legislative elections he called. In the meantime, the public-sector landscape had changed dramatically, for Chirac's 1986–1988 government had launched a drive to privatize sixty-five companies, including the Big Five and the banks nationalized in 1982, whose total capitalization was about Fr 300 billion. Although this program was slowed dramatically by the October 1987 stock market crash, and brought to an end by the Right's legislative defeat eight months later, the Chirac government still managed to privatize four industrial groups (Saint-Gobain, CGE, CGCT, and MATRA), two investment banks (Paribas and Suez), two commercial banks (CCF and Société Générale), and four smaller banks. All told, the sell-offs brought Fr 73.7 billion into the state treasury.[56]

Although heralded as a rolling back of the state, these privatizations were, in fact, carried out in highly *dirigiste* fashion amidst secrecy, price fixing, and government selection of key shareholders. By reserving controlling interests for certain groups, the Chirac government created *noyaux durs* (hard cores) of institutional shareholders who were needed, the government argued, to provide necessary capital (given the stock exchange's relatively weak absorptive capacity), to maintain stability, and to discourage hostile takeovers, especially by foreign interests.[57] Critics charged that however laudable these goals, the *noyaux durs* were, in fact, dominated by Chirac's Gaullist political allies.[58]

Although observers disagree over whether the Chirac privatization strenthened the state's ability to achieve its economic goals,[59] all agree that the privatization began an important restructuring of French capital that continues to this day. Specifically, the creation of *noyaux durs* brought in, for the first time, institutional financial investors—the most important being the public and private banks and the insurance companies—as large shareholders of industrial capital.[60] Although core groups of investors were key shareholders in both financial and industrial enterprises before 1986, there was little overlap of ownership between the two domains. Banks and insurance companies tended to invest in other financial firms, and industrial firms likewise tended to invest in firms of their own type.[61] But privatization altered that pattern. The nationalized insurance company UAP, for example, became a shareholder in Saint-Gobain, CGE, and Havas (a travel agency), and was represented on their boards. The Banque Nationale de Paris, to offer another example, acquired shares in Saint-Gobain, Havas, and MATRA, and was also represented on their boards.[62]

The establishment of *noyaux durs* fostered complex ownership patterns in which the distinction between private and public capital on the one hand, and financial and industrial capital on the other, became increasingly blurred. The nationalized banks and insurance companies were part owners of the privatized firms, but the latter also owned shares in the nationalized banks and insurance companies. Suez and Saint-Gobain, for instance, each held shares in the other, as did CGE and Société Générale. As a result of reciprocal share ownership, French business structures began in some respects to resemble Germany's banking-industry partnerships and Japan's "affinity groups" of intertwined industries, banks, insurers, other service providers, and suppliers.

In his 1988 reelection campaign Mitterrand promised to halt privatization, yet also vowed not to undertake further nationalizations. "Neither privatization nor nationalization . . . let's stop the ballet," he urged.[63] He reasoned that with the establishment of the EC's Single Market less than five years away, French industry had to prepare itself for the new competitive environment. In an economic climate in which extranational competitiveness would be essential, the uncertainty created by large shifts in the public-private boundary, he argued, could only distract and weaken the nation's largest and most exposed firms.

As in many of his actions, Mitterrand made an economic virtue out of political necessity, for in fact by 1988 there was little public support for further expansion of the public sphere. Although nationalization had enjoyed widespread popular approval during the late 1970s and early 1980s, that support plummeted sharply with the policy U-turn of 1982–1983. Stathis Kalyvas plausibly argues that this "hegemonic breakdown" of the nationalization project resulted from a perception among much of the public that the nationalizations were actually one of the causes of the economic crisis.[64]

Mitterrand's *Ni-Ni* (Neither-Nor) policy, however, ultimately proved self-contradictory and therefore unworkable. On the one hand, the government expected all public firms in the competitive sector to turn a profit. Reaffirming its commitment to management autonomy, the government said that it would judge the firms only on "results." During the booming late 1980s, industrial dynamism depended on having sufficient investment capital, especially for foreign mergers and acquisitions. On the other hand, because of continued fiscal pressures—in particular, the need to dampen inflation and reduce the budget deficit—the state had diminishing financial resources to allocate to public firms. Moreover, the EC, led by Competition Commissioner Leon Brittan, was vigorously seeking to reduce state subsidies to business. These limitations forced nationalized firms to seek, and the government to allow, the growing presence of private capital in public enterprises.

Ni-Ni gave way in stages. The first breach came in April 1989 with the publication of the tenth five-year plan. In addition to allowing public firms to continue raising private capital by selling nonvoting shares and subsidiaries' shares on the stock market,[65] the plan permitted them to develop reciprocal shareholding alliances with French and other European firms. Usinor Sacilor (united since 1986) began negotiating the purchase of the German steel producer Saarstahl, a transaction that resulted in the latter becoming a minority shareholder in the former.[66]

By early 1990 the nationalized firms were pressuring the government to further relax its ban on privatization. A prime reason for this campaign was the rapid expansion abroad by nationalized companies, which needed extra cash for their acquisitions and government approval for their alliances with private firms.[67] Finally relenting in the face of a lobbying onslaught (including support from EC Commission president Jacques Delors),[68] the government abandoned *Ni-Ni* in February 1990, although without officially acknowledging a policy change. It did so by acceding to Renault's request for a reciprocal share ownership arrangement with Volvo, which, in effect, partially privatized Renault by giving Volvo a 25 percent ownership share (see chapter 9). The following month Rhône-Poulenc and Rorer Group, an American pharmaceutical firm, agreed to form a $3.15 billion joint venture in which the French firm would own 68 percent.[69]

By the end of the second Socialist government's first two years, nationalized firms had taken major steps to wean themselves from state financial aid—still without a formal change in policy but with full government encouragement.[70] This growing independence of public firms from government control was reinforced by a trend that began during the 1986–1988 privatization wave, namely the acquisition by banks and insurance companies of financial stakes in industrial companies. For example, the state gave the Banque Nationale de Paris and AGF (an insurance company) 17.5 percent of its shares in Péchiney in exchange for shares in the recipients. Such financial legerdemain boosted the capital resources of nationalized firms without taxing the state budget or raising the ire of Brussels.[71]

But even these maneuvers proved insufficient to give the nationalized firms the financial resources they required. Finally, in April 1991 the government officially dropped the *Ni-Ni* policy, although it stopped short of allowing full privatization. From then on, nationalized firms could sell up to 49.9 percent of their capital to private investors, provided the exchange formed part of a "strategic accord." The trigger for this change in policy was a financial crisis at Bull that required the state to craft a Fr 4 billion rescue package. By abolishing *Ni-Ni* the government signaled its unwillingness to undertake further bailouts. The government also, in the case of Bull, sought to persuade the Japanese electronics maker NEC to acquire a stake in the nationalized firm.[72] In the months following the Bull affair, the public firms ELF-Acquitaine, Credit Local de France, Total, and Rhône-Poulenc issued shares to private investors.

Thus within three years of Mitterrand's reelection, the president's attempt to stabilize the public-private boundary had to be abandoned. During the next two years, from spring 1991 to spring 1993, the government continued to permit partial privatizations of public firms, with most of the money gained from the sales going to fund unemployment programs and social security deficits. Providing a conceptual justification for a pragmatic adaptation, the Socialists labeled the new policy *Et-Et* (Both-And), indicating that both nationalization and privatization could be employed where needed. A PS position paper summarized the new policy as follows: "The State, in all cases, must exercise its role of stockholder flexibly and undogmatically."[73]

While moving far from their earlier conception of public firms as weapons for fighting monopoly capitalism or reconquering the domestic market, Socialist leaders stopped short of advocating a dismantling of the public sector. Instead, the new policy would be based on three principles. First, the state would retain control of industries "with a strong sovereignty content," which included not only defense firms but also public companies in strategic sectors such as electronic components, oil, nuclear energy, and computers. Second, the state would continue to intervene in financially risky sectors avoided by private capital, such as biotechnology and environmental management. Finally, any transfer of shares from the public to the private sector had to be justified as part of a coherent industrial strategy, and not merely serve as a way of funding budget deficits or job creation. Thus although the Socialists' acceptance of privatization brought them closer to the Right's more laissez-faire approach, the conceptual gap between the two camps remained considerable.

Despite the Socialists' refusal to surrender, at least in theory, the option of continued *dirigiste* intervention in the economy, in practice their influence over the public sector diminished steadily. Part of the reason stemmed from changes in the institutional environment such as privatization, financial deregulation, new EC rules on state subsidies and competition policy, and new capital structures. Another contributing factor was the state's policy of continuing to grant public firms almost total operational autonomy. A case in point was Industry Minister Roger Fauroux's creation of annually negotiated *contrats d'objectif* (goal-setting contracts) for public firms in competitive sectors. These contracts, the successors to the planning contracts employed by the first Socialist government, were the only instruments left to government officials to influence public-firm strategies. But according to an Industry Ministry official involved in the annual negotiations, the contracts were largely pro forma and even ignored by the firms themselves: "The goal-setting contracts weren't at all limiting or constraining. Once a year the firms' executives and state *tutelle* managers got together to discuss the firms' goals for the coming year. The firms themselves quickly saw what this meant. Some firms, one in particular, Usinor Sacilor, even refused to attend, saying that they didn't want to waste their time. And nobody within the administration or government opposed it. Other firms did it for a year or two, and then stopped. The only one that continued was Rhône-Poulenc, and it stopped in 1992 or 1993."[74]

CONCLUSION

Chapters 6 and 7 have revealed starkly different initial adjustment strategies on the part of French and Spanish Socialists. Unsurprisingly, these strategies reflected the assumptions and goals of macroeconomic policy. In the French case, adjustment focused on a dramatic expansion of the public sector. In part the fulfillment of an electoral pledge of long standing, in part a classic response *à la française* to a widely shared perception of industrial decline, the 1982 nationalization program embodied the Left's faith in *dirigiste* state action. No such belief existed among Spanish Socialists, for whom the public sector held little allure. Historically the preserve of an inward-looking, market-protected Francoist elite, Spain's public industrial sector, and especially the INI, was more a bureaucratic and fiscal albatross than an instrument of economic transformation.

The trajectories of the two countries' initial approaches also differed sharply. As with macroeconomic strategy, the story was essentially one of Spanish consistency and French inconsistency. The PSOE government adhered to a policy guided by the goals of efficiency and solidarity. Both INI reform and industrial-reconversion measures reflected a drive to reduce deficits and restore profitability while also cushioning the shocks of job displacement through generous income-support and other programs. By contrast, the Mitterrand government, having at first tapped the newly nationalized firms to be agents of job creation and reconquest of the domestic market, abruptly shifted its public-sector strategy in 1983, coincident with the U-turn in macroeconomic policy. Thereafter, nationalized firms were given increasing autonomy and a mandate to make money (or at least stop draining the state budget), whatever the cost in jobs.

Despite these initial differences, the French shift in 1983 signaled a growing convergence in approach between the two governments. With regard to public-sector management, both eventually adopted what PS leaders labeled a mixed-economy model that blended, albeit uneasily, neoliberal and *dirigiste* elements. All public-sector firms were expected to become more efficient by cutting operating costs (including the costs of labor) and improving the quality of output (products and services). Those firms exposed to market competition were expected to survive on their own without continued state financial support. In political terms, this shared emphasis on operational efficiency and market viability, pursued to the exclusion of other aims, marked the *banalisation* of public firms as potential instruments of social-democratic reform. Visions of such firms as social laboratories for new forms of employee participation and labor-management relations increasingly appeared to be whimsical daydreams at odds with market realities.

On the other hand, despite the disappearance of social reform as an aim of public-sector management, nationalized firms retained a role in foreign economic policy. Such firms were needed, both governments contended, to meet national production needs in strategic sectors such as energy and defense and for sectors such as advanced technologies that private investors refused to enter. In this way the *dirigiste* reflex remained alive, though much diminished. Socialists in both countries continued to view public industrial firms as the main agents of a muted brand of economic nationalism that would defend crucial aspects of the nation's economic security. Thus while admitting the need for private and public capital, to work together and even share ownership of businesses, both governments refused to sanction a wave of full privatizations, relying instead on selective, partial sell-offs in response to requests by individual firms. In all cases, they insisted on retaining strategic control of the firm in question, which for most officials meant at least a 20 percent ownership share.

However elaborate the justifications offered for continued state ownership of internationally exposed firms, the experience of public companies in the early 1990s underlined the eroding prospects for *dirigiste*-style state intervention.[75] People began to ask, if state-owned firms are required to compete in world markets, receive little or no state aid (because of EC regulations), and exercise almost complete operational autonomy, can they truly be distinguished from private firms? In the deregulating market and institutional framework in which European public firms were operating, the purpose of state ownership had become clouded, especially when, as in France and Spain, Socialist governments had jettisoned any pretense that such firms should play a transformative social or economic role.

8

Between Brussels and the Blast Furnace

Restructuring in the Steel Industry

No other economic issue in Socialist France and Spain provoked as much discord as restructuring in the steel industry. This was due to several factors, beginning with geography. In both countries, steel production was (and is) geographically concentrated. France's steel factories were located largely in the country's north (Nord–Pas de Calais) and northeast (Lorraine). In Spain, production was concentrated along the northern Atlantic coast (the Basque Country and Asturias) and, until the mid-1980s, in Valencia. Concentration made these regions heavily dependent on steel production and thus especially vulnerable to large-scale restructuring. Moreover, the scale, capital intensity, and product specialization of most steel plants meant that restructuring usually required relocating or closing unprofitable facilities and laying off hundreds or even thousands of workers. At the same time, strong local traditions of worker militancy, solidarity, and job defense meant that workers were likely to resist adjustment measures that threatened their livelihoods. This mix of economic dependency and worker mobilization made the steel regions unusually volatile.

Controversy also derived from the industry's politicization. By the early 1980s, the steel firms were largely nationalized, thereby ensuring that adjustment would be shaped by the visible hands of politicians as well as the market's less visible one. For workers threatened by a declining steel market, protesting against government restructuring plans was an eminently rational form of job defense. Adding impetus to workers' protests was their perception that the Socialists' actions constituted a political betrayal. Many steelworkers had voted for Socialist candidates in 1981 and 1982, in part out of the self-interested belief that a Left government would protect their jobs. For many steelworkers, then, the restructuring measures sponsored by Socialist leaders violated a basic trust.

This chapter looks at how the French and Spanish Socialist governments managed steel restructuring. It seeks to establish two conclusions. First, despite hundreds of strikes, "dead days," and demonstrations, Socialist governments in both countries ultimately carried out market-adapting measures that slashed productive capacity and labor forces by half while doubling productivity. Responding to the challenges of declining markets and EC regulation, both governments encouraged and even mandated sharp cuts in labor and production. At the same time, they sought to achieve "orderly" labor reductions by funding generous income-support programs for laid-off workers. In broad outline, these policies resembled the policies of other Western European governments that had to confront the problem of adjustment in the steel sector.

The second conclusion is that despite a common market-adapting approach, the restructuring processes of France and Spain differed in their trajectories, dynamics, and impact. In Spain, as we saw in chapter 6, the steel industry was foremost among the sectors initially targeted for reconversion. From the outset, PSOE government officials sought to stem the industry's substantial losses by retiring obsolete facilities and laying off workers. In France, by contrast, such consistency was missing. Early steel policy aimed to *increase* production, even in the face of a gathering market recession. With the 1983 U-turn in macroeconomic policy, however, came an abrupt shift in strategy, in which the government strove to restore financial viability to the industry, whatever the cost in jobs.

The dynamics of adjustment differed in that labor resistance was stronger in Spain than in France. Spanish workers were better mobilized and thereby able to exert stronger, more effective antirestructuring pressure on the government. As a result, by 1993 the French steel industry had outrun Spain's in achieving economic viability. In other words, even though French steel policy lacked the consistency of Spanish policy, restructuring in France was ultimately a greater success in market terms.

GLOBAL AND EUROPEAN STEEL: MARKETS IN DECLINE

To develop the conclusions outlined above, it is necessary to situate the French and Spanish cases in their global and European contexts, for steel adjustment in 1980s and early 1990s France and Spain cannot be examined apart from the powerful external constraints of the world steel market and EC regulation. The market for steel changed dramatically during the 1970s and 1980s under the influence of four related shifts. The most obvious was a flattening of growth in consumption and production compared with 1945–1973. After averaging 6.2 percent growth per annum during the 1950s and 5.5 percent during the 1960s, world crude steel production slumped to an average growth rate of 1.9 percent per annum during the 1970s and 0.7 percent during the 1980s. The downward trend continued into the early 1990s, when crude steel production contracted by an average of 2.0 percent per annum between 1990 and 1993.[1] Interestingly, this decline in growth rates has been accompanied by successive waves of technical innovation, including adoption of the basic oxygen furnace, the continuous caster, and, most recently, the scrap-fed electric-arc furnace (or minimill).[2]

Accompanying this slowdown in growth was a second shift, namely an increase in market volatility. After expanding steadily from 1945 to 1973, world production and consumption entered a two-decade period of volatility marked by three major contractions (1975–1977, 1980–1983, and 1990–1993) and two expansions (1978–1979 and 1984–1989). To protect themselves against these market shifts, producers resorted to or pressured politicians for import quotas, government subsidies, cartel-style market regulation of prices and production, and greater labor flexibility, among other things.

The third shift was the movement in production and consumption from the United States, Western Europe, and Japan to the NICs and the nonmarket economies of Eastern Europe, the former Soviet Union, and China. Contrary to popular belief, world steel production has not declined since the so-called golden age of the 1960s and early 1970s, for sharp drops in the advanced industrial states have been more than offset by the emergence of new producers elsewhere.[3]

The fourth shift was what might be called the internationalization of the steel trade, in which producers welcomed foreign investment and vigorously sought export markets for their products. Whereas in 1950 only 11 percent of world steel output was traded internationally, by 1988 that figure had risen to 26 percent, a result of more trade among the industrialized countries and rapid development of export capacity by NICs such as Brazil and South Korea.[4]

The transformations experienced by the industry posed difficult adjustment challenges for most EC steel companies. European steel production declined 30 percent from 1974 (the postwar record high) to 1983 (the postwar record low). A market resurgence in the late 1980s reduced that gap, but by 1992 EC production still remained over one-fifth below the 1974 level (see table 8.1). Even more dramatic was the human cost of this contraction, for the production increase in the late 1980s failed to reverse the sharp job losses that had begun after 1974. From 1974 to 1992, EC steel employment declined by nearly 60 percent.

Confronted with a market decline of this magnitude, European producers and the EC itself sought to manage the industry's contraction, a task complicated in the 1970s by the steel firms' tardy recognition of structural market changes. Throughout that decade many firms continued to add new production capacity, despite declining prices and sales. By the early 1980s capacity utilization had plummeted, yet producers and governments hesitated to close obsolete plants for fear of the social and political repercussions.[5] Further complications arose because of disputes among producers, owing mainly to differences in market position. These disputes, in turn, generated divisions among EC member states about the proper course of adjustment.[6]

The EC response was guided by the European Coal and Steel Community (ECSC), a regulatory body founded in 1951 to foster and coordinate economic growth. A supporter of steel industry expansion during its first twenty-five years, after 1974 the ECSC sought to orchestrate gradual reductions in steel capacity and production. A first attempt came in 1976 with the Simonet Plan, which attempted to limit production on a voluntary basis. Following the failure of producers to heed its guidelines, the ECSC adopted compulsory measures. Embodied in the 1977 Davignon Plan, those measures established mandatory minimum prices for certain steel products, investment controls (to closer ensure that increased capacity would be offset by reductions elsewhere), and

Table 8.1   European Steel: Production and Employment, 1974–1992

	Crude Steel Production (in millions of tons)			Employees (thousands)		
	1974	1992	Change (%)	1974	1992	Change (%)
Germany	53.2	39.7	-25.3	232.0	132.1	-43.1
France	27.0	18.0	-33.3	157.8	42.8	-72.9
Italy	23.8	24.8	4.2	95.7	49.9	-47.9
United Kingdom	22.4	16.2	-27.7	194.3	40.8	-79.0
Spain	11.5	12.3	6.5	89.4	33.3	-62.8
Other EC[a]	30.2	21.4	-29.1	115.4	57.0	-50.6
ALL EC[a]	168.1	132.4	-21.2	884.6	355.9	-59.8

Source: International Iron and Steel Institute, Steel Statistical Yearbook, various years; Eurostat, Iron and Steel Yearbook, various years.
   a. Includes Spain, Portugal, and Greece, even though not EC members in 1974.

control over imports (through negotiating "voluntary export restraints" with Third World producers).[7]

From 1977 to 1979 this plan worked well because the world economic recovery was helping to stimulate demand. The 1979 oil shock, however, triggered another brutal decline in the market. In 1980, amid increasing trade tensions and ruinous price discounting, the ECSC finally invoked article 58 of its founding treaty, which allowed it to declare a "manifest crisis" in the steel industry and set mandatory national production and capacity quotas for three main product lines. This was followed in June 1981 by binding measures to eliminate government subsidies to the industry.[8]

Initially intended to last only eight months, the article 58 regime survived nearly eight years (until August 1988). Although it forced companies to limit production and cut capacity, a major reason for its longevity was that it failed to restore prices and profitability, making further rounds of quotas and reductions necessary.[9] In addition, persistent losses drove some producers to seek extensions of government subsidy programs beyond their original termination dates, and such extensions were usually granted in exchange for capacity reductions.[10] All article 58 decisions, moreover, had to comply with the EC's unanimity rule, which meant that decisions on production quotas, capacity reductions, and government aid were all subject to intense bargaining that made the adjustment process lengthier and less thorough than a liberal market-driven process would have been.[11]

Beginning in the mid-1980s, several factors prompted a gradual return to a free market in steel, including a market upswing in 1986, the EC's new single-market project (encouraged by President Jacques Delors), and the failure of EC members to agree on plant closures, quotas, and subsidies.[12] By mid-1988 only about half of EC steel production remained under the quota regime. Finally, in July 1988, in a period of general market buoyancy, the Council of Ministers voted to abolish controls on steel.

The good times did not last long, however. Renewed recession in the early 1990s, coupled with rising imports from formerly Communist Eastern European producers, spurred further restructuring by the EC. In November 1992 the EC, rejecting a return to article 58, appointed a former European Commission official, Fernand Braun, to create a new plan. In addition to advocating a 20 percent cut in capacity, Braun proposed that the EC issue quarterly production "recommendations." His plan also contained an Ecu 450 million ($510 million) aid package from the EC to cover plant closures and associated labor costs.[13]

As in the past, however, producers disagreed on how capacity cuts should be shared. The crucial split was between subsidized and unsubsidized producers. The latter, notably British Steel, Usinor Sacilor, and several German firms, opposed the granting of subsidies in exchange for capacity reductions, whereas subsidized firms such as Spain's Corporación de la Siderurgia Integral (CSI), Italy's Ilva, and Germany's former Eastern producer Ekostahl favored the quid pro quo approach.[14] In December 1993, after a year of wrangling, the Council of Ministers agreed on a new restructuring plan, but continued opposition by unsubsidized producers, who judged it a giveaway to subsidized firms, threatened to undermine it.[15] Thus after nearly two decades of attempted market management, and despite impressive gains in technology and productivity, EU steel adjustment remained incomplete, in large measure because of deep divisions among producers and national governments over how the market should be regulated.

FRANCE: SOCIALIST MODERNIZATION

French steel, of course, did not remain immune to the crisis besetting European producers. Although the French steel industry, the backbone of early postwar modernization, quadrupled production between 1945 and 1960, by the mid-1960s it was plagued by overcapacity, obsolete technology, and low productivity. Despite three rationalization plans in 1966, 1977, and 1978, the key problems remained. Low productivity, in particular, made the French steel industry one of the least efficient steel industries in Europe and indeed the world, handicapped foreign trade, and led France to incur a growing trade deficit with the rest of the EC during the 1970s.[16] From 1974 to 1981, steel production dropped 21 percent (from 27.0 million metric tons [mmt] to 21.2 mmt) and employment in the steel sector declined nearly 40 percent (from 158,000 workers to 97,000).[17]

Of France's steel regions, the most affected was Lorraine, the industry's birthplace and site of many of the oldest and most obsolete installations. By the early 1970s, Lorraine's steel plants—undersized, plagued by poor transportation conditions and dwindling ore deposits, and producing badly adapted products—were uncompetitive. The most critical problem was their specialization in long products (beams, rails, wire rods, reinforcing bars, and the like), a market experiencing both declining demand and competition from new entrants (especially the minimills of Italy's Brescia region) whose production costs were lower. By contrast, other steel-producing regions—the Nord and, since 1973, the Fos-sur-Mer complex near Marseilles—had more modern facilities, which were geared toward the fast-growing market for flat products such as sheet and strip steel. In 1966–1974, while Lorraine producers were cutting back employment (from 91,000 workers to 81,000) Nord producers expanded their work force from 33,000 to 41,000. Lorraine's share of national steel production declined from 67 percent in 1959 to 44 percent in 1977.[18]

After 1945 the French steel industry's future became increasingly tied to the state—a link that was both a blessing and a curse. Although the state provided plentiful subsidies and credit, it also handicapped the industry. By periodically controlling steel prices in order to combat recurrent inflation, the state often forced the industry to sell below market value. Moreover, because of the small scale of the French stock market, the industry increasingly relied on state-supplied loans.[19] Although state aid offered financial protection, it also enabled steel producers to postpone restructuring and modernization. The long-term effect was to spawn excessive reliance on the state and a lack of market responsiveness.[20]

This weakness was of little concern during the industry expansion of the 1950s, but as demand declined in the 1960s steelmakers faced the problems of excess capacity and growing debt.[21] With its financial situation deteriorating, the industry approached the government in 1966 for the first of a series of rescue packages. In return for its help, the government demanded that the industry restructure and modernize. This plan, which was followed by two more in 1977 and 1978, marked the beginning of a fifteen-year effort by governments of the right to restructure the industry.

All three plans included industry reorganizations, which invariably led to growing unemployment and concentration of manufacturing. The most important industry consolidation occurred in 1966 with the merger of two large regional concerns: Usinor, based in the Nord, and Sacilor, based in Lorraine. All three plans also contained provisions for state loans for reorganization and investment, which moved the state ever closer to assuming financial responsibility for the industry's survival—state financial control increased in step with the industry's growing debility.[22] Finally, despite some attempts at cutbacks, all three plans failed to reduce production capacity, output, and manning levels to anywhere near the break-even point. Especially egregious was the 1968 decision, made in a period of declining demand, to build a huge seaside complex at Fos-sur-Mer. By the time of the last rescue package in 1978, industry debt had reached hopeless proportions: 112 percent of total annual sales, compared with about 20 percent in the United States and West Germany.[23] The 1978 plan converted the industry's debt into government-held debentures, giving the state a controlling equity interest in Usinor and Sacilor.[24]

When the Left assumed power in June 1981, it inherited an industry with an ambiguous legacy of opportunity and constraint. On the one hand, the state had a controlling interest in Usinor and Sacilor, which gave it nearly complete authority over investment, production, and employment decisions. The Left's promised nationalizations would only enhance that control. On the other hand, the regulatory and market spaces for exercising that control had shrunk radically since the early 1970s. Not only had the EC begun to set capacity and production quotas, but the industry's poor financial condition sharply curtailed the government's options. The Mitterrand government quickly had to address the question of whether its industrial ambitions were realistically matched with the limited maneuvering room it now had.

The Left and Steel: The 1982 and 1984 Plans

Steel had always figured prominently in the Left's economic and industrial platform. As noted in chapter 7, the 1972 Common Program of the Left targeted the two main steel firms as candidates for nationalization. Even as the industry faltered during the 1970s, Socialists continued to view it as "an indispensable link in the coherence of France's industrial tissue."[25] As a core industry that would provide essential semifinished goods to other industries, steel would play a key role in the Left's strategy of reconquering the domestic market. Far from endorsing the industry's contraction, presidential candidate Mitterrand pledged in 1979 to boost annual output from 23 million tons to 26 million tons.

Government leaders were under no illusions, however, that a public takeover would resolve the industry's problems. The nationalization measure itself, adopted in October 1981, was widely viewed as inevitable and hence generated little controversy. Because the Right's 1978 plan had, in effect, partially nationalized the industry, the door to state ownership already stood ajar. Moreover, full nationalization merely transformed state-held debt into state-owned shares, and was thus a financial maneuver rather than a shifting of control.[26] Beyond the nationalization measure of October 1981, however, the Socialists' plans for the industry remained vague.

Socialist restructuring strategy was ultimately embodied in plans announced in September 1982 and March 1984. As we will see, these plans were tightly linked to the government's broader adjustment measures, which in turn were shaped by the *relance* (described in chapter 4). Because of these linkages, steel restructuring underwent a shift parallel to that which occurred in macroeconomic policy.

The 1982 Plan

The 1982 plan emerged from negotiations among government, industry, and labor representatives.[27] Throughout the negotiations, the industry and labor camps fought each other and were also riven by internal divisions. The sharpest cleavage was a regional struggle for government support between Nord-based Usinor and Lorraine-based Sacilor.[28]

In formulating the plan, the government commissioned four studies, the most influential of which was prepared by Pierre Judet, an economics professor at the University of Grenoble. Judet sketched out three scenarios for the industry: a pessimistic scenario that foresaw output dropping to 20.2 million tons by 1986 (from 21.0 million tons in 1981), a less pessimistic scenario that foresaw a slight rise in output to 21.8 million tons, and an optimistic scenario that foresaw a rise to 24.0 million tons (a 14 percent increase).[29] In June 1982, after nearly a year of planning, the government adopted Judet's optimistic scenario as its 1986 target. The politically driven nature of this decision becomes obvious when we consider that French steel production had never attained such high levels of growth except in 1972–1974. To reach its goal, the government pledged that it would provide new investment capital of Fr 17.5 billion in 1982–1985—50 percent more than what the Giscard government had paid out during its last four years.[30] The government recognized, however, that even this substantial level of support would not reverse the downward trend in employment, for the steel industry was expected to lose 10,000 to 12,000 of its 100,000 jobs within two years.

As the government began implementing its ambitious plan—at a moment, it will be recalled, when it was reversing its macroeconomic policy—splits erupted within the industry. Not only did interfirm rivalry sharpen as Usinor and Sacilor vied for state funds, but intrafirm conflicts also flared. To offer an example of the latter, two of Sacilor's specialty steel producers, SAFE in Hagondange and SNAP in Pompey, competed against each other for government support after it was learned that the plan would force the closure of one of them. Such conflicts pitted plant against plant, even in the same region, and prevented the industry from devising a coordinated response to the plan.

Discord also flared up between the two major labor confederations and within the confederations themselves. Although both major confederations, the CGT and the CFDT, opposed the plan, they did so for different reasons. The CGT rejected all talk of job reductions, whereas the CFDT approved of the plan but accused management and the government of withholding information and failing to consult.[31] Both confederations, however, were reluctant to break openly with the government and therefore did not attempt nationwide protests. Within the confederations, old divisions resurfaced, especially within the CFDT, where national leaders as well as officials in the metal federation sympathetic to the principle of restructuring were opposed by local militants in Lorraine and elsewhere.[32] Local opposition to the plan was the impetus for many local demonstrations, but most failed to attract large crowds. In any event, because the projected job cuts were relatively slight and aimed at areas that had long experienced disinvestment and job loss, the demonstrations posed little political danger for the government.

Even as the plan was announced, however, its inadequacy became apparent. Customer orders for the second half of 1982 declined 20–30 percent over the previous year, and annual production was projected to drop 10 percent.[33] Government officials realized that achieving the production level envisioned by Judet's optimistic scenario would be impossible. The new industry minister, Chevènement, admitted that production would have to be cut 15 percent from the 1981 level.[34] In the end, the 1982 plan, far from resolving the industry's problems, merely postponed finding a solution to them.

The 1984 Plan

Steel's main problem in the early 1980s, from the government's point of view, was financial, for the state found itself in the odd position of boosting its aid to the industry even as the industry was racking up higher and higher deficits.[35] The government lacked the resources to cover the industry's losses and finance the industry's modernization at the same time. As we saw in chapter 4, by early 1983 the government had reached a crossroads in its retreat from *relance*, for the June 1982 measures—notably a four-month wage-price freeze, along with slower growth in government spending—had failed to halt the worsening trade and budget deficits. The government's response to this situation, the March 1983 Delors plan, sought, among other things, to cut public-sector corporate losses dramatically. Thus the steel industry's fate became increasingly tied to efforts to achieve budgetary *rigueur*, which implied that government subsidies to the industry would come under increasingly close scrutiny. Further adding to the fiscal pressure was the EC's looming deadline of 1 January 1986 for ending all public steel subsidies.

Despite these pressures, the government, fearing a social explosion and faced with a lack of consensus within the steel industry, sought to postpone its steel-related decisions for as long as possible. The focus of contention within the industry was Sacilor's proposal to build a universal rolling mill in the Lorraine town of Gandrange. According to Sacilor's president, the mill would enable his firm to consolidate long-product production in a state-of-the-art plant. Usinor's president, however, viewed this proposal as a threat to his firm and protested that the mill was not only too costly (it was expected to cost about Fr 2 billion), but would take market share away from Usinor's long-product plants in Valenciennes and Dunkirk.

The CGT and the CFDT were just as much at odds with each other. The CGT opposed any contraction of the steel industry, arguing that "it is absurd

to finance unemployment and not modernization."[36] The CFDT, having supported austerity since early 1983, was prepared to accept further cuts in capacity and employment if displaced workers were given income support and retraining. The CFDT also protested its exclusion from negotiations between
the government and industry representatives. A CFDT official with responsibility for Sacilor issues remarked: "For three months [Sacilor management]
hasn't told us anything. They assure us that discussions continue between the
two groups, but they inform us of nothing. We can barely follow through the
press the little war between Raymond Lévy and Claude Dollé [the presidents
of Usinor and Sacilor, respectively], where each one is trying to saddle the
other with the dying factories in Lorraine."[37] Aside from a few local demonstrations, however, union pressure was muted, for despite their dwindling
enthusiasm, the confederations continued, at least tacitly, to support the
government's economic policy.

By early 1984 it was clear that the 1982 plan had failed to reverse the
industry's decline, and the government decided it had to formulate a second,
more rigorous plan. In January it began new negotiations with management
and the unions, and by early March debate had coalesced around two alternative plans. As in 1982 and 1983, the main dispute was over Sacilor's proposed
universal rolling mill at Gandrange. On one side stood the mill's proponents,
who included all of the Sacilor unions.[38] The metalworkers' federations of the
CGT and CFDT also endorsed the mill, albeit cautiously, because building it
would require job cuts elsewhere. Others supporting the proposal included
political officials and business leaders from Gandrange's Orne Valley region.
Among government officials the mill's main backer was Industry Minister
Fabius, who at first had opposed its construction.[39] The mill's opponents included, not surprisingly, Usinor's management and unions, which claimed
that it would only worsen the glut in long-product production and jeopardize
existing plants in the Nord. Usinor presented its own plan, which was, of
course, more favorable to its own operations.[40] This plan was supported by
Prime Minister Mauroy, a Nord native who was not only prime minister but
also mayor of the Nord's largest city, Lille.

These divisions made achieving consensus within the government impossible. The final decision had to be made by Mitterrand himself, who had to
choose between his prime minister, Mauroy, and his protégé, Fabius. In a crucial meeting on 30 March 1984, Mitterrand, who had just returned from a
week's trip to the United States and who had not studied the issue, sided with
Mauroy. The mill, he decided, would not be built, meaning Lorraine would
suffer most of the steel industry's job cuts.[41]

The 1984 plan sought to rapidly phase out uneconomic operations while reinforcing operations that showed profit potential. In general, this meant promoting flat products such as the thin sheets used in automobile exteriors, for which demand remained relatively high, at the expense of long products such as rails and beams, for which demand had long been declining. Inefficient plants would be closed and their production shifted to the remaining plants, which would be modernized. Most new investment would be concentrated in the two modern facilities at Fos-sur-Mer and Dunkirk. Although the plan stopped short of merging Usinor and Sacilor, it combined their operations in two new joint subsidiaries, one specializing in long products (Unimétal) and the other in specialty steels (Asco-metal). Finally, at least 25,000 jobs, accounting for more than one-fourth of the industry's work force, would be eliminated.

Public reaction, as expected, was hostile in the regions targeted for closures and cutbacks. In the Lorraine region, for example, some workers erected road barricades of burning tires and strip metal (just as they had done in response to the 1978 and 1982 plans), and some local unions initiated "Operation Dead Region," a twenty-four-hour shutdown of businesses, transport, and communication lines. Yet such were the splits among the local unions and among organizations of local government officials that protests remained scattered.

At the national level, union reaction was similarly divided and largely ineffectual. The plan's harshest national labor critic, the CGT, opposed the cuts but could mobilize only limited demonstrations. The CFDT, which favored the steel industry's modernization, considered the cuts inevitable, but urged retraining and new regional investment to ease the plight of dislocated workers. The Force Ouvrière and the Confédération Française des Travailleurs Chrétiens opposed the plan but refused to organize protests against it. Another body, the Confédération Générale des Cadres, accepted the plan.[42]

The Communist Party was placed in a double bind, being both a part of the government and a self-proclaimed defender of workers' interests. In the weeks leading up to the plan's finalization, the PCF followed a strategy of participation without support by remaining in the government but criticizing its economic policy.[43] The PCF responded to the plan by publishing its own plan, which called for increasing production by nearly 25 percent within two years by building the Gandrange mill and maintaining production at Fos-sur-Mer, Longwy, and other sites.[44] Despite its break with the government's new policy, the PCF remained in the government for another three months, finally leaving in July when Fabius was appointed prime minister.

For different strategic reasons, then, the major organizations that might have been expected to contest the plan—the unions and the PCF—failed to mount an effective opposition.[45] Popular protest, though intense, remained fragmented and localized. Although the public's opposition created occasions for dramatic press photographs and temporarily hurt Mitterrand's popularity, it was not sufficient to force the government to rescind or substantially modify its plan.[46]

The New Steel Regime: Autonomy and Modernization

The March 1984 plan was a watershed in state management of the French steel industry. In the decade following its adoption the steel companies were given nearly complete operational autonomy. In all ways but one (to be discussed in a moment), they were expected to function as independent firms in competitive markets. This meant, above all, that they had to wean themselves from government subsidies (which were under pressure from budgetary constraints and EC regulations) and become financially solvent. Operational autonomy also meant that the firms were to decide questions of labor deployment according to market criteria. If existing job positions did not contribute to improving the firm's performance, management was expected to eliminate them.

Under this new regime, organized labor's institutional role was strictly limited to labor adjustment, especially to managing retraining and other programs for displaced workers. The CFDT in particular played an important role in designing and staffing worker retraining programs. Although this assistance was clearly important for displaced workers, it was well removed from strategic decisions about the industry, especially those concerning capital adjustment, from which unions continued to be excluded. The only body with capital adjustment powers over which the unions could hope to wield influence was Usinor Sacilor's board of directors, where, after the two steel giants were united in 1986, union representatives held six of the eighteen seats.[47] But even when all six union representatives acted in concert (a rare occurrence), organized labor obviously lacked the votes to have a decisive effect. The CFDT's board representative claimed that his strategy was to acquire information that would allow him to anticipate what management was about to do. Asked whether this strategy did not put his union in a largely reactive or defensive position, he said: "That's normal. We [the unions] are not the ones who are going to define industrial plans. Still, the idea is to make sure that management doesn't back us into a corner."[48]

Union influence remained limited for two other reasons: labor force changes and persistent interunion divisions. Restructuring not only eliminated more than half of all steel jobs between 1984 and 1994, it also increasingly reserved the remaining jobs for skilled and professional workers, who were less likely than unskilled workers to support unions. The result was a steady loss of union members in the steel industry, which sapped the mobilization capacity of the CGT and the CFDT. Those two confederations, moreover, remained deeply divided. The CFDT recognized that the industry was plagued by excess capacity and redundant labor and was willing to support reductions on the condition that income-support and retraining programs were established for laid-off workers. The CGT, on the other hand, continued to deny that the industry faced any real crisis, and refused to sanction any reductions in personnel or productive capacity.[49] Such strategic differences made cooperation between the confederations all but impossible.

Along with the industry's newfound autonomy came distinct changes in corporate strategy. In terms of market strategy, after 1984 the industry developed greater coherence in production and commercial operations. Key to this development was the Chirac government's 1986 decision to merge the two large firms into a single entity, Usinor Sacilor. According to Usinor Sacilor's chief economist, "This merger ended an absolutely idiotic competition between the two firms for new investments and installations. It also made medium- and long-range planning much more rational. We were also able to concentrate our sales forces. Finally, we developed an *esprit de groupe,* which was not always easy to do."[50]

After 1986, with Francis Mer heading what quickly became one of the world's largest and most profitable steel companies,[51] Usinor Sacilor pursued two objectives: a renewed focus on steel operations (as opposed to diversification) and internationalization. Usinor Sacilor refused to follow the path taken by USX, Nippon Steel, and Thyssen, which had branched out into energy production, computers, telecommunications, high-speed trains, and other activities unrelated to steelmaking. Concentrating on its traditional area of competence, however, meant remedying some long-standing weaknesses, such as its lack of attention to technological innovation. The firm decided to devote its research and development efforts to such areas as sandwich sheets (steel sheets with a middle layer of resin-plastic soundproofing material, used mainly in automobiles) and thin casting (a continuous casting process that allows the manufacturing process to move immediately from the steelmaking stage to the rolling of very thin sheets, thus eliminating formerly necessary intermediate steps).[52] This enabled Usinor Sacilor to become "a low-cost producer of increasingly higher value-added materials."[53] The firm also sought to develop its own commercial networks rather than continuing to rely on middlemen.

Usinor Sacilor also embarked on a campaign of vigorous foreign expansion, especially in Europe and the United States. For the most part, this took the form of acquisitions or joint ventures, especially in downstream activities such as steel transformation and distribution.[54] For example, during the late 1980s its foray into the U.S. market included a joint venture with Bethlehem Steel and purchases of a Chicago service center, two stainless-steel producers (J & L Specialty Products and Techalloy), and 50 percent of the wiremaker Georgetown.[55] Similar purchases and alliances were concluded in most EC countries.[56]

Strategic changes were also evident at the level of the firm, with work processes increasingly incorporating such concepts as multiskilling and "total quality." Integrative management methods that included various types of labor-management cooperation such as quality circles and expression groups also gained in popularity.[57] Accompanying these changes was a constant upgrading of the work force's education, training, and professional qualifications. The replacement of crude steel production by various forms of downstream transformation (hot and cold rolling, the production of specialty steels, and so forth) placed increased emphasis on the programming, operating, and maintaining of highly automated, computer-controlled equipment. As the CFDT representative on the Usinor Sacilor board of directors remarked in 1994, "When you visit a steel plant today, you have trouble finding a classic steelworker, the guy with the big biceps who taps steel. Now you have the guy in the control room who taps on his keyboard."[58] By the early 1990s, in fact, workers in direct production were in the minority.[59]

The goal of these changes in work organization and labor composition was, of course, to boost productivity. French steel's productivity, measured in terms of crude steel output per worker, more than doubled from 1983 to 1992, a performance that far exceeded the European average. By the early 1990s, France's steel productivity was second only to Italy's among the major EC producers.[60] By raising productivity, Usinor Sacilor returned to profitability in 1988 (as did most other European producers) and ceased receiving state subsidies. Its market performance was one of the strongest in the EC steel industry during the late 1980s and early 1990s.[61]

Socialist steel policy after 1984, for all its emphasis on market efficiency, also devoted close attention to the labor market consequences of adjustment. Insider accounts of the 1984 planning process reveal that Socialist leaders, like their conservative predecessors of the 1970s, feared the political fallout that would result from massive labor displacement, especially in Lorraine.[62] Accordingly, their labor market strategy was designed to limit the erosion in political support that was likely to follow.

In Lorraine, two measures were central to this strategy. The first was the April 1984 appointment of CFDT official Jacques Chérèque as the government's czar for steel adjustment in the region.[63] A Lorraine native and former steel-worker, Chérèque not only brought obvious bona fides to the task, but also a viewpoint compatible with the Socialists' new emphasis on modernization of the industry. Chérèque, for example, was a veteran advocate of programs to retrain displaced workers and attract new industrial investment. He had also worked for many years to make the unions equal partners with management and the state in steel-related decision making.

Chérèque's mission was to be both government ambassador and regional-development specialist. As ambassador, he was a visible demonstration of the government's concern for Lorraine, and could be expected to attract the support of many steelworkers, including CFDT members, for the government's strategy. As regional-development specialist, his task was to define and coordinate government strategy for reindustrializing Lorraine, which meant working closely with regional officials while presiding over at least three development agencies.[64] One focus was the redevelopment of abandoned industrial sites. Chérèque, for example, was instrumental in converting the site of his own firm, SNAP, into an industrial park for several light-manufacturing plants and office buildings. Another major project was the creation of the European Development Pole, a 1,200-acre industrial park at the intersection of the French, Belgian, and Luxembourgian borders. With funding from the EC Regional Development Fund and the three national governments, the European Development Pole aimed to create 8,000 new jobs.[65]

Vilified at first by most of his union colleagues for having sold out,[66] Chérèque eventually gained at least grudging respect for having stimulated investment and job creation. A typical response was that of a Longwy CFDT leader who had once protested against Chérèque by helping block a train carrying Chérèque to Longwy:

> Chérèque always went farther and faster, saying, for example, "The people of Lorraine have to get the blast furnace out of their heads." That was a provocation. We didn't understand how a CFDT militant could suddenly become a prefect. Personally I could never have done what he did. On the other hand, it's true that he was the man for the situation. At Longwy, some positive things have been done, such as the European Development Pole. Chérèque helped bring in a lot of industry. He has a media style and a style of personal contact that shook up people's habits.[67]

The second main element of the Socialists' reconversion strategy for Lorraine was to enlist the steel firms themselves in resolving problems arising from large-scale worker layoffs. The earlier restructuring plans of 1966, 1977, and 1978 had usually handled layoffs by giving the oldest workers early retirement or providing income support until they qualified for retirement benefits.[68] Although this approach avoided outright firings and the income insecurity that resulted, by the early 1980s many people had begun to understand that it not only created a distorted age structure in the work force but also ignored the need for worker retraining and job creation.[69]

Under the Socialists, therefore, the steel companies became the chief agents of efforts toward worker retraining and job creation, which were to be forwarded primarily through the Société pour le Développement de l'Industrie et de l'Emploi (SODIE), a subsidiary of Usinor Sacilor financed by the steelmaker and the state. Although companies such as SODIE had been formed for the steel industry and other restructuring industries since the early 1970s, their original purpose had simply been to redevelop abandoned manufacturing sites.[70] Under the Socialists, however, SODIE was given an expanded mission.[71] First, it was expected to stimulate investment in distressed steel regions by offering various kinds of assistance to investors, including below-market loans to cover land purchases, construction costs, market studies, technical support, legal and administrative counseling, and personnel recruitment. Second, SODIE was charged with helping retrain and find new jobs for laid-off workers.[72] Working individually with its clients, SODIE would pay for training courses and afterwards locate up to three new positions for each worker. In 1993 the Lorraine branch of SODIE created 1,200 new jobs through its investor inducements, while another 300 workers were retrained and placed in new positions. For all of France's steel regions from 1983 to 1993, SODIE claims that it created nearly 52,000 new jobs at a cost of Fr 2.7 billion (about $490 million), in addition to retraining and finding new jobs for almost 12,000 former steelworkers.

It would be wrong, however, to conclude that SODIE and the many other regional-developmental efforts succeeded in returning income and labor force activity in Lorraine and other steel-dependent localities to their former levels.[73] There is evidence, for example, that steelworkers' incomes dropped when they took new jobs outside the steel industry.[74] The job creation claims of SODIE and other development agencies must be treated with caution, since many projects, including a costly effort to launch a Smurf theme park on the site of a razed mill, were poorly conceived and administered.[75] On the other hand, it is incontestable that the combination of publicly sponsored measures—especially income support (through early retirement and preretirement schemes), job creation, and job retraining and placement—helped steel regions such as Lorraine adapt to fundamental shifts in economic structure. All things considered, the French Socialists' market-adapting approach to steel restructuring after 1984—a free hand for steel firms to adjust capital and labor to market conditions, coupled with extensive public intervention to cope with the employment and income consequences of that adjustment—was a fairly effective, albeit expensive,[76] strategy for balancing the twin imperatives of economic efficiency and social solidarity.

SPAIN: ADJUSTMENT AND RESISTANCE

Unlike their French counterparts, Spain's Socialists entertained no illusions that they could expand steel production, but instead sought to eliminate obsolete facilities, modernize potentially profitable operations, and establish more coherence among production units. These goals were, by and large, achieved. Yet despite Spain's consistency of purpose and execution, steel adjustment proved more difficult and met with more opposition than in France. In Spain, worker resistance and the legacy of earlier steel policies combined to force the government to delay and modify its original plans.

Earier steel policies constrained adjustment in four ways. First, the complex structure of the industry itself made crafting a single plan for steel impossible. Whereas by the early 1980s virtually all of the French steel industry was under the umbrella of Usinor and Sacilor, in Spain it was fragmented into three largely uncoordinated subsectors: integrated producers, producers of common steel, and producers of specialty steel (see table 8.2).[77] Differences among the subsectors with regard to ownership (public versus private), financial structures, product lines, and operating performance meant that each subsector had to be restructured separately, in negotiations involving over fifty firms. Each subsector's restructuring thus proceeded at a different speed, with varying results. In consequence, steel adjustment in Spain lacked the coherence that characterized the process in France after 1984.

A second barrier to adjustment was the steel industry's lack of international exposure. For all its weaknesses, French steel had long been exposed to foreign competition, whereas Spanish steel (and Spanish industry generally)

Table 8.2   Spain: Structure of the Steel Industry, ca. 1983

	Firms		Workers		Production	
	N	%	N	%	N[a]	%
Integrated steel	3	6	35,330	53	6.5	50
Common steel	31	61	13,770	21	4.8	37
Specialty steel	17	33	17,000	26	1.7	13
Total	51	100	66.707	100	13.0	100

Source: Ministerio de Industria of Energía (MINER), *Libro blanco de la reindustrialización* (Madrid: MINER, 1983), passim.
   a. In millions of metric tons.

had largely been sheltered from imports by prohibitive tariffs. Until the early 1960s, Spain produced nearly all the steel that it consumed, and even though imports rose during the late 1960s *apertura,* they remained fairly stable throughout the 1970s and early 1980s, never exceeding 30 percent of domestic production.[78] One result was that while most European producers were cutting output and capacity during the 1970s, Spanish firms, oblivious to world market signals, were increasing theirs. In the early 1980s, however, Spain's impending entry into the EC promised to subject the industry to competitive pressures within a new regulatory framework. Delayed exposure to competitive forces made the PSOE government's restructuring task all the more difficult.

Third, the legacy of government intervention itself handicapped adjustment efforts. The Spanish state's involvement with the steel industry dated back many years, but the nature of that involvement was not the same as France's. In 1950 the Franco government created the Asturias-based integrated steel producer Empresa Nacional Siderúrgica, Sociedad Anónima (ENSIDESA). The company's first purpose was to further national security by producing basic industrial goods with possible military applications. Its second purpose was to strengthen domestic competition by serving as an antimonopolistic counterweight to private steel firms. Both aims imparted to state steel policy a bias toward growth untempered by market considerations of profit and productivity. Francoist and post-Francoist governments alike were loath to cut production and lay off workers when the target was a public firm created to serve the national interest. With the stimulus of government support, ENSIDESA experienced continuous expansion into the early 1980s, despite its sharply declining performance throughout the 1970s. Reversing this trend would be a formidable task for the PSOE government.

A fourth reason why the Socialists faced a difficult challenge in trying to reform the steel industry had to do with the economic and political crises of the 1970s. As we saw in chapter 2, the world recession triggered by the 1973 oil shock coincided with the end of Franco's regime and the subsequent democratic transition. Anxious to avoid economic dislocations that could threaten political stability, both Francoist and post-Francoist officials sought to postpone or evade industrial adjustment, especially in basic industries employing large numbers of unionized workers.

Before the PSOE assumed power, adjustment in the steel industry took two main forms. The first was a mercantilist effort to expand exports while limiting imports. Whereas in 1974 Spain exported just 9 percent of its steel production, by 1982 that figure had jumped to 47 percent. Most exported steel was sold at below-market rates, leading to increased operating losses and accusations of dumping from Spain's European partners.[79] At the same time, high tariffs limited steel imports to less than 2 million tons per year, less than one-third the level of exports. The result was that steel production rose during the late 1970s and early 1980s, even though domestic consumption dropped well below the levels of the early 1970s.[80]

The second means of coping with the steel industry's problems amid political uncertainty in the late 1970s was, in classic INI fashion, the rescue of failing operations. For integrated producers, this meant aiding not only ENSIDESA[81] but also two private firms, Altos Hornos del Mediterráneo (AHM) and Altos Hornos de Vizcaya (AHV).[82] All three suffered from high debt, obsolete plants, high labor costs, poor transportation and distribution conditions, and badly integrated production structures.[83] By the late 1970s their financial losses forced the state to rescue them from collapse.[84] In the case of AHM, the state proceeded in two stages, first assuming the firm's vast debts, then nationalizing it in 1978. AHV avoided nationalization but also borrowed heavily from the state. The capstone of these rescue efforts was the UCD government's 1981 reorganization plan for the integrated subsector, which provided PTA 230 billion ($1.84 billion) for debt absorption, equipment modernization, and income support for laid-off workers. Unfortunately, the government's weakness prevented completion of this plan and its restructuring plans for other sectors.[85]

Nevertheless, government intervention allowed the steel firms to keep most of their workers on the job.[86] From 1974 to 1981, employment in the integrated subsector declined only 3.5 percent (from 41,406 workers to 39,949), whereas EC steel employment decreased 31 percent.[87] Although politically stabilizing in the short run, Spain's deferral of labor adjustment in the steel sector ultimately made the process more intractable. Productivity remained low by European standards, while labor costs increased alarmingly.[88]

Spanish Socialists and Steel: The "Battle of Sagunto"

When it came to power in 1982, the González government's situation vis-à-vis the steel industry, particularly the integrated producers, was similar to the situation the 1981 Mitterrand government had found itself in.[89] Although the government largely controlled the integrated subsector and thus had the power to direct restructuring, the financial weakness of the steel firms limited its options. This, however, did not stop Socialist leaders from moving early and decisively to restructure this key segment of the industry.

The focus of the government's efforts was the main AHM facility in Sagunto, about fifteen miles north of Valencia near the Mediterranean Sea. This plant was a logical candidate for restructuring for several reasons other than the fact that it was state owned. First, its three blast furnaces were obsolete, the most recent having been built in 1964 and the oldest in 1923. It also lacked a hot-strip mill, which meant that slabs produced by its blast furnaces had to be shipped elsewhere for transformation into coils before being returned for further treatment in AHM's cold-strip mill. This added to transportation and production costs and made Sagunto's products much more expensive than its competition's. AHM's production shortcomings made it by far the weakest performer of the three integrated firms. In 1981 it accounted for 22 percent of the integrated subsector's losses but employed only 4,500 workers, about 11 percent of the sector's 40,000 workers. AHM's restructuring thus held out the promise of a sizable financial payoff with relatively small personnel losses.

Politically, AHM was also a logical choice for restructuring, for Valencia's economy was less tied to steel than the economies of the other major steel-producing regions, Asturias and the Basque Country. The latter two regions depended heavily on both steel and public subsidies, and their displaced workers, facing few job alternatives, could be expected to mount strong resistance. There was also the danger that worker protests in Asturias and the Basque Country could snowball, because both regions were home to other industries targeted for restructuring, such as shipbuilding. Moreover, PSOE leaders were reluctant, at least initially, to focus on Asturias, a Socialist stronghold, or to stir up trouble in Bilbao, where AHV was based. Despite its failings, AHV remained a symbol of Basque industrial might, and layoffs in Bilbao could ignite nationalist opposition. Valencia, on the other hand, had not only the weakest labor movement of the three regions but also a diversified and flourishing economy. It seemed to the government, therefore, that closing Sagunto would not have an economically devastating effect on the Valencia region, for alternative employment was more readily at hand.[90]

At the beginning, however, the plan was not to close Sagunto, but to build the much-needed hot-strip mill. Since the 1970s, supporters of this idea had viewed a new mill as essential for Sagunto's future as a steel producer, much as the universal rolling mill had been seen as crucial for Sacilor's in Gandrange.[91] The problem, however, was that ENSIDESA and AHV also coveted new hot-strip mills to replace the ones they already had. Because the UCD government lacked the resources to build new mills for all three firms, the parties reached a standoff. Lacking the political strength to choose sides in this potentially explosive issue, the government simply avoided making a decision.

Within four months of taking office, however, the Socialists faced the issue head-on. In February 1983 Industry Minister Solchaga announced that the government would not build a hot-strip mill in Sagunto but would modernize existing ones in Avilés (ENSIDESA) and Ansio (AHV). The decision was a virtual death sentence for the Sagunto plant, whose cold-strip mill was to be upgraded but pressed into service as merely a processing facility for flat products. The decision, moreover, implied (although this remained unstated) that Sagunto's coke batteries, blast furnaces, and steel converters—in other words, its entire crude steel operation—would be shut down. All of this meant that within two years nearly half of Sagunto's work force would have to be eliminated.[92]

It is safe to say that the Socialists did not expect the firestorm that followed. During the next fourteen months the "Battle of Sagunto" mobilized the Valencia region in resistance against the government's plan. This protest was fueled by a sense of betrayal, for the decision went against the provisions of an earlier reconversion plan, established by the UCD government in May 1981, to keep the blast furnaces operating. From February 1983 on, there were almost daily actions to protest the Sagunto closures, including plant occupations, a general strike, and a huge demonstration that surrounded the regional government's offices and held regional legislators captive for several hours.[93] These actions forced the government to pull back temporarily. In early March Solchaga announced that he would give the control and oversight committee for the integrated subsector until 1 July to formulate its own restructuring plan, pending which no action would be taken.[94] Solchaga also vowed that if the committee failed to agree on a plan, the government would take action unilaterally.

Although momentarily thwarted, the government made Sagunto a test case of its overall adjustment strategy. According to a high-ranking Industry Ministry official,

> The government's industrial-reconversion program started with the decision to close the blast furnace at Sagunto. Although this decision affected relatively few workers and didn't greatly reduce our steel capacity, it sent a strong message that Spanish industry had to adjust. There were great demonstrations and protests against it, and Solchaga was under great pressure to cancel the decision. But González went on television and supported the process of industrial reconversion. That was the critical moment. If the government had backed down, it would have lost the possibility of carrying out adjustment.[95]

The four months of March through June 1983 witnessed continual protests throughout the Valencia region and even in Madrid. The protests were led by the CCOO, which, in addition to opposing the government's reconversion program in general, was also the majority union at the Sagunto works and thus spearheaded local action. The UGT, by contrast, was divided in its support for Sagunto. Whereas Sagunto's UGT activists naturally took a stance in defense of their plant, the UGT metalworkers' federation backed the government's plan. UGT locals at the other major steel sites in Asturias and the Basque Country supported the Sagunto workers perfunctorily at best. Thus the main opposition came from local CCOO and UGT activists, especially those on the AHM factory council.[96] Despite the localized nature of the opposition, the protesters were able to mount impressive actions that extended beyond the region, including a June rally by over 7,000 Sagunto workers at Industry Ministry offices in Madrid. The government, however, still refused to back down. A senior official in the Labor Ministry later recalled, "There was tremendous pressure on the government. I remember what happened here when we were deciding whether to close the Sagunto blast furnaces. There were thousands of people outside in front of the building. It was very dramatic, even traumatic. But we were convinced that if we didn't take such a step, the costs, not only in economic but also in political terms, would be much greater."[97]

Solchaga's four-month postponement failed to produce a solution to the controversy, for the control and oversight committee was unable to craft a plan by 1 July. As a result, the Council of Ministers proceeded to pass a decree law in early July embodying the government's intentions announced the previous February.[98] The decree law also incorporated the government's goals for the integrated subsector as a whole. New investments, especially for new steelmaking facilities, would be made in ENSIDESA and AHV. At the same time, capacity in the integrated subsector would be reduced to 7 million tons by 1990 (a 12.5 percent reduction from 1980's 8 million tons),[99] and the work force would be cut 27 percent. Although Sagunto would bear the greatest proportional job loss, ENSIDESA and AHV would lose more total jobs.[100] The cost of this restructuring plan, including labor adjustment, financial, and investment costs, was projected to be PTA 524 billion, or $4.2 billion.

In early September 1983, two months after the plan's announcement, AHM management ordered the closure of all of Sagunto's steelmaking operations. Management and government resolve to proceed with restructuring did little to dampen popular opposition, however. In fact, workers initially defied the order and continued to produce rails for the state railway, RENFE. Protests continued throughout the fall of 1983 and into the first months of 1984. By the time it was over, the Battle of Sagunto had sparked nine general strikes, twenty-four factory strikes, eleven demonstrations in Valencia, seven marches on Madrid, and an eighty-day period of defiance of management's orders to close parts of the plant.[101] Other incidents included hunger strikes, resignations of local Socialist officials and party leaders, and forcible confinements of AHM executives.

Although these protests failed to convince the government to rescind its plan, worker and community resistance succeeded in delaying the plan's implementation for well over a year by forcing the government to negotiate painstakingly with local unions, the factory council, Valencia officials, and the control and oversight committee. A final agreement was not reached and approved by Sagunto workers until April 1984. As one study remarks, "thirteen months of extraordinary political confrontation, punctuated by strikes, demonstrations and sporadic violence, had been required to reach an agreement on the retirement of approximately one million metric tons of the most obsolete raw steel production capacity."[102] Public pressure also compelled the government to provide more generous assistance for affected workers than originally intended. The original plan, in fact, had contained no provisions for alternative job creation. While remaining resolute in their aim of restructuring the industry, PSOE officials turned the focus of negotiations toward the consequences of adjustment by offering workers income support and new jobs. In the final labor accord, the government designated Sagunto a Zona de Preferentes Localización Industrial (Zone of Preferential Industrial Location), in which businesses would be granted tax incentives and subsidies to establish new operations. By the end of 1987, these efforts had led to the creation of nearly 2,400 new jobs, supported by government subsidies of PTA 4.76 billion (about $38.1 million)—nearly $16,000 for each job created.[103] The government also increased the number of workers eligible for income support through the FPEs.

After Sagunto: Contending with Workers, Contending with Brussels

Although the 1984 plan set a precedent as the first time a Spanish government had undertaken far-reaching adjustment in the steel industry, it failed to restore the industry to economic viability. By early 1986 government officials recognized that further restructuring would be necessary. Although the industry cut its real losses roughly in half from 1980 to 1986, it remained far from profitable.[104] Exports, usually subsidized, continued to provide an outlet for production that greatly exceeded consumption, while capacity remained much greater than production or consumption.[105] With Spain now in the EC and its steel industry increasingly subject to ECSC regulations, the industry needed to prepare for exposure to competitive conditions.[106]

In 1986, accordingly, the government declared a second reconversion, this time for the entire steel industry. With respect to the integrated subsector, attention now focused on AHV, whose performance was deteriorating much more rapidly than ENSIDESA's.[107] As in the Sagunto case, the new round of negotiations featured extensive talks among government officials, unions, and management, punctuated by periodic though more muted labor protests. But Spain was now part of the EC, and for this reason the plan had to be negotiated with Brussels as well. A final agreement was reached in April 1987 and provided PTA 223 billion ($1.8 billion) in aid for four firms—ENSIDESA, AHV, ACENOR (common steel), and FOARSA (specialty steel)—in return for elimination of 750,000 tons of capacity.[108] Spain pledged to decrease annual capacity to 17.25 million tons by 1989, a reduction of nearly 22 percent from the 1985 level.

As in the rest of Europe, the late 1980s brought an upswing in demand for steel, and after consecutive annual losses stretching back to the mid-1970s, both ENSIDESA and AHV turned a profit in 1989.[109] The resurgence was only temporary, however, and 1990 brought renewed recession, which plunged Spain's integrated producers, and most other European producers, back into the red.[110]

Thus despite six years of restructuring, costing an estimated PTA 750 billion ($6.0 billion), the Spanish steel industry still manifested fundamental weaknesses, especially with regard to costs and trade. Technological obsolescence, distribution inefficiencies, and high labor charges pushed Spanish costs as much as 30 percent higher than the European average.[111] Moreover, as Spain gradually entered the EC steel regime after 1985, its system of protected foreign trade dissolved; exports (no longer being dumped at below-market rates) declined, while imports (no longer subject to prohibitive tariffs) climbed. Between 1985 and 1989, Spain's sizable trade surplus in steel disappeared.[112] This deterioration was little noticed during the boom of the late 1980s, when domestic consumption increased substantially (by 80 percent in 1985–1989). The downturn that began in 1990 struck hard at domestic consumption, but did not greatly affect the structural shift in the trade balance. The result was a decline in steel demand without the escape valve of increased exports.[113]

In response, the government took two measures to reverse the industry's slide. First, it sponsored a 1991 reorganization plan that nationalized AHV and merged it and ENSIDESA into a single state-run entity known as the CSI (although AHV and ENSIDESA retained their corporate names and identities). The merger, like the Usinor-Sacilor merger of 1986, was designed to end the zero-sum conflict that pitted the firms (and their associated unions and local and regional governments) squarely against each other in struggles to avoid cuts and win new investment.[114] The goal was to coordinate investment projects and achieve greater coherence across product lines and production facilities.[115]

Although it created a more cohesive management structure, the merger did not settle the issue of how to pursue restructuring itself, a task made all the more necessary by EC pressure to slash capacity. The second government response to problems in the steel industry, accordingly, was to propose another major adjustment program, the third since 1982. Formulated by CSI management and backed by the government, the Competitiveness and Viability Plan called for the CSI to reduce capacity from 6 million tons to 4.5 million tons per year while eliminating nearly 10,000 jobs by 1998.[116] Capacity cuts would include shutting down the AHV-Ansio hot-strip mill and the blast furnaces at the ENSIDESA-Avilés and AHV-Sestao (Bilbao) works, leaving the ENSIDESA-Gijón plant as Spain's only integrated mill. The plan also included a controversial modernization component: the construction of a new electric-furnace minimill with an annual capacity of 900,000 tons, to be built on the site of the AHV-Sestao works. To cover the investment and labor costs, the plan projected a total expenditure of Ecu 4.5 billion ($5.5 billion).[117]

CSI's unions, predictably, viewed the proposed capacity and labor cuts as draconian. The integrated subsector, they argued, should maintain greater capacity (5.6 million tons) and build a bigger minimill (1.5 million tons) than the CSI proposed. The unions also demanded a more generous income-support package for layoffs.[118] To back their claims, the main unions, acting in concert, mounted strikes and demonstrations in both Asturias and the Basque Country. This campaign culminated in October 1992 with the "Iron March," a march by hundreds of Asturian and Basque Country steelworkers on Madrid.

Opposition to the CSI plan came not only from organized labor but also from Brussels. As a member of the EC, Spain had to submit its plan to the European Commission and the Council of Ministers for approval. But many commission and council members, as well as EC steel corporation executives, believed the plan had several flaws. Some viewed the minimill proposal as uneconomic, given the high cost of electricity and the scarcity of high-quality scrap metal in Spain.[119] Many believed the plan did not cut capacity deeply enough. The sharpest criticism came from Competition Commissioner Leon Brittan, who questioned the desirability of building the proposed minimill in light of Spain's and Europe's excess capacity. The European Commission demanded that Spain eliminate an additional 900,000 tons a year of capacity (although it did not explicitly bar the minimill). It also demanded a work force reduction of an additional 800 workers—a requirement the government termed "inadmissible and unjustified."[120] Finally, the plan's European opponents thought that its state subsidy provisions were too generous. One analyst, for example, referred to the plan as a $5 billion "political fix" to allow the government to pacify volatile regions such as the Basque Country.[121]

The government thus found itself caught between, on the one hand, mobilized Asturian and Basque interests that opposed the plan for being too rigorous and, on the other, the European Commission, which opposed it for being too lax. The government thus had to spend the latter half of 1992 and almost all of 1993 negotiating with the unions and then with Spain's EC partners. As in the past, the endgame in its negotiations with the unions focused on labor rather than industrial issues, especially income support for displaced workers. In return for the unions' tacit acceptance of the plan's industrial components, Industry Minister Aranzadi met most of the unions' demands regarding preretirement conditions and indemnities. A labor agreement was signed in January 1993.[122]

Reaching agreement with Brussels proved much more difficult because of the EC's strong bias against a continuation of government subsidies and the near-universal sentiment that Spain had not yet taken the harsh measures necessary for restructuring its steel industry. A breakthrough finally came in late 1993 when the Spanish suggested that the proposed Sestao minimill should be run not by the CSI but by a private financial consortium. Most EC officials and politicians involved in the negotiations agreed that this de facto privatization of new investment would sharply lessen the need for state subsidies and promote competition. After interminable wrangling and delays, the Council of Ministers approved Spain's revised plan in December 1993. In conjunction with a separate commitment to a more rapid closure of AHV's Ansio works, the new plan mandated that state subsidies totaling Ecu 2.88 billion ($3.28 billion) would be allowed, a considerable reduction from the Ecu 4.5 billion that the Spanish government originally proposed.[123]

CONCLUSION

Between Brussels and the blast furnace—between EC regulation and worker protests—Socialist leaders in France and Spain had only limited options in attempting to restructure the steel industry. On the one hand, the EC steel regime, although weakened by delays, exceptions, special pleading, and even deception on the part of some producers and their governments, was still able to restrict the leeway of firms and governments to determine policy with respect to capacity, production, prices, government aid, and other matters. On the other hand, efforts by public officials to carry out EC-mandated capacity and labor cuts often provoked collective resistance in the affected regions.

In the face of these constraints, both France and Spain adopted what this book has called a market-adapting approach. From the mid-1980s on, capital adjustment measures sought to establish a market-rational industry in which steel firms would exercise full operational autonomy, be exposed to market competition, and be weaned from public assistance in the form of subsidies and debt write-offs. This approach gave firms almost carte blanche to reduce capacity and labor in line with long-term declines in demand. It is important to underline the significance of this approach. Previous governments in both countries had attempted to rationalize the steel industry, but the result was the industry's complete dependence on state finance. The true innovation of Socialist steel policy in France and Spain was to move the industry away from this dependence and toward financial and operational autonomy.

At the same time, Socialist leaders took heed of the possible pitfalls of a rapid, brutal adjustment. They wanted to avoid the charge of betraying or abandoning workers whose jobs disappeared, and thus sought to guarantee affected workers a safety net in the form of income support or a new job. To achieve this orderly exit of labor, both governments used job buyouts, early retirement, local economic development, worker retraining, and other instruments. In their essentials, these programs resembled the programs used by other governments throughout Western Europe.[124]

Although the key development in French and Spanish steel industry restructuring was the two countries' convergence toward a market-adapting approach, there were also important national differences, particularly in terms of trajectories, dynamics, and outcomes. With respect to trajectories, we have noted the early French attempt to expand production versus the Spanish effort to cut capacity. Whereas the Mitterrand government pledged in 1982 to increase production by 14 percent, the early González government decided to restructure AHM-Sagunto practically out of existence. This difference in approach disappeared by the mid-1980s, however, after the French U-turn in macroeconomic policy dictated new criteria for public-sector management. France's 1982 and 1984 plans were thus strikingly different, with the latter mandating operational autonomy, market exposure, and financial solvency. By contrast, the PSOE government, having adopted a market-adapting approach at the outset, remained wedded to that approach throughout the following decade.

In terms of dynamics, steel restructuring gave rise to more opposition in Spain than in France. Although organized labor in both countries was unable to deter Socialist governments from following a market-adapting path, Spanish unions were able to mobilize more effectively and to extract more concessions. For all the protests in Lorraine and the Nord, there was no equivalent in France of the Sagunto resistance, in which 4,500 workers blocked a restructuring measure for well over a year and forced the government to establish generous severance and retraining programs. In comparison with Spanish labor, French steelworkers and their unions proved less able to mobilize and thus less influential in affecting the course of adjustment.

With respect to outcomes, we have observed that France's Socialists, despite their early *relance*-driven ambitions and subsequent policy reversal, were more successful than their Spanish counterparts in bringing the steel industry to operational and financial viability. "Success" can be measured by examining state aid patterns, productivity, and financial results before and after restructuring. Concerning state aid patterns, we have noted that by the late 1980s French producers were no longer receiving subsidies, but Spanish firms were. In the early 1990s, in fact, Usinor Sacilor (with French government support) was a strenuous antisubsidy advocate within the ECSC, pitting itself against subsidized firms such as CSI, which continued to lobby for state aid. By 1995, with profits again running strong after a downturn in the early 1990s, the Chirac-Juppé government decided that Usinor Sacilor was ready for the final step toward financial and operational independence—privatization— which was carried out successfully in July of that year.[125] Meanwhile, although CSI officials publicly vaunted the firm's market autonomy and even envisioned its ultimate privatization,[126] the Spanish firm remained dependent on state aid and had little immediate hope of finding private investors.[127]

Table 8.3 indicates that productivity throughout the EC increased by nearly 75 percent in 1982–1992. Productivity in the Spanish steel industry grew at an even greater rate, although by 1992 its still remained slightly below the EC average. France's productivity, which more than doubled during the same period, outshone both Spain and the EC as a whole. By 1992 French productivity was 13 percent higher than the EC average.

A final measure of success is financial performance. Given the above differences in state dependence and productivity improvement, it is hardly surprising that the French steel industry outperformed its Spanish counterpart. To consider one key financial measure, the net return on sales (net profits/ losses as a percentage of total sales), the French steel industry showed dramatic improvement in 1981–1992. During the difficult adjustment years of 1981–1986 the net return averaged -16.1 percent annually, but in 1987–1992 the annual average crossed the line from negative to positive and rose to 0.3 percent. The two main Spanish firms, ENSIDESA and AHV, had a combined

Table 8.3   Europe: Crude Steel Production per Worker, 1982–1992 (in tons)

	1982	1992	Change (%)
France	193	420	118
Spain	199	369	85
EC	217	372	71

Sources: Calculated from International Iron and Steel Institute, *Steel Statistical Yearbook,* various years.

average annual net return of –12.7 percent in 1981–1986, a figure that was actually somewhat better in market terms than Usinor Sacilor's during the same period. However, even though productivity rose sharply during the late 1980s, the net return for the two Spanish companies improved only slightly, to an average annual rate of –12.0 percent in 1987–1992.[128] By all three measures of success, then, the French steel industry responded to its adjustment crises more successfully than the Spanish industry.

How typical was steel as an example of restructuring? Did the patterns of convergence and difference identified in this chapter also hold for other sectors undergoing adjustment? To answer these questions, the next chapter considers a second important case, that of the automobile industry.

9

Just in Time?

Restructuring
in the
Automobile
Industry

In France, automobile industry restructuring followed the trajectory we are already familiar with: Socialist interventionism in 1981–1984 gave way, in tandem with the country's U-turn in macroeconomic policy, to progressive withdrawal from direct attempts to guide adjustment. By the mid-1990s, both of France's major automobile firms, Renault (nationalized) and Peugeot Société Anonyme (private), were formulating their strategies independently, in accordance with market factors rather than government directives.

Automobile industry restructuring in Spain, however, departed from the usual Spanish pattern of following a consistent trajectory. Throughout the 1980s the PSOE government sought, in line with its general market-adapting approach, to reduce its involvement in the industry. The most decisive step was the 1986 privatization of Sociedad Española de Automóviles de Turismo (SEAT), a company that had been established in the 1950s as part of Franco's plans for Spanish autarchy. In the early 1990s, however, the PSOE government reversed its strategy of reduced involvement, and public officials began to intervene in decisions concerning SEAT's fate.

French and Spanish automobile industry restructuring, therefore, followed exactly opposite trajectories: in France, failed interventionism followed by disengagement, and in Spain, failed disengagement followed by interventionism. We thus need to ask, what is the explanation for this contrast? In particular, how can we account for Spain's deviation from an adjustment strategy that otherwise favored market exposure over state intervention? And what light does automobile industry restructuring shed on industrial restructuring generally in Socialist France and Spain? These are the questions that form the basis for the rest of this chapter.

THE AUTOMOBILE INDUSTRY: THE GLOBAL CONTEXT

The automobile and steel industries were both mature industries in which markets were growing slowly or even declining, technologies were changing rapidly, and fresh sources of supply were being established by NICs. Both industries also developed many of the same problems, such as being weighed down by excess productive capacity and labor.[1] In two respects, however, the automobile industry's evolution was distinctive.

The first unique feature was the industry's globalization. Until the early 1970s the automobile industry was highly regionalized. National markets in each major region (North America, Japan, and Western Europe) were dominated by domestic firms. For example, although U.S. firms (especially Ford and General Motors) were allowed to establish branch plants in Western Europe, the markets of France, Britain, West Germany, and Italy remained for the most part the preserve of national firms.[2] Starting in the 1970s, however, regional concentration began to lessen as the largest firms increasingly globalized their production and sales. Unlike most steel firms, whose operations remained based primarily in their country of origin (despite a movement toward cross-national corporate alliances), the largest automobile MNCs devised complex strategies related to components sourcing, production, and distribution, with little regard for national boundaries.

The other distinctive feature of the automobile industry was what can only be termed the Japan factor. Not only did Japanese firms secure a significant share of the world auto market in a stunningly brief time (25 percent in barely a generation), they also pioneered innovative methods of lean production featuring just-in-time components delivery, multitasking, and long-term, cooperative relations with suppliers. These methods, with produced productivity rates often twice those of traditional Fordist manufacturers, revolutionized production practices throughout the industry.[3]

The Western European response to the Japanese challenge was two-fold. First, the EC began to regulate Japanese imports. Until the early 1990s, EC-wide regulation did not exist; instead, Western European nations established their own—widely varying—import policies.[4] As the EC prepared for the enactment of the Single Market Act by 1993, however, regulation tightened. Although the EC's 1992 liberalization project encouraged free trade in general, the prospect that Japanese automakers would have an open door to the European market scared producers such as Renault, Peugeot, Fiat, and Volkswagen—all high-volume firms operating in protected or quasi-protected markets. In 1991, after three years of negotiations, the EC and Japan reached a compromise that would give Japan full access to EC markets by the year 2000.[5] Yet the accord remains controversial, and it is likely that European producers, backed by the EU, will continue to resist the kind of Japanese market penetration that the United States experienced during the 1970s and 1980s.[6]

The second response to the Japanese challenge was the creation of a complex array of corporate alliances aimed at lowering design, production, and distribution costs and extending market presence. These alliances were of three main types: joint ventures for specific projects (such as were undertaken by Fiat and Saab, Mitsubishi and Volvo, General Motors and Isuzu, Honda and Rover, and Volkswagen and Suzuki); partial or full corporate acquisitions (including Saab by General Motors, Rover by BMW, Alfa Romeo by Fiat, Skoda by Volkswagen, SEAT by Volkswagen, Jaguar by Ford, Aston Martin by Ford, and American Motors by Renault); and cross-ownership arrangements and mergers (such as the failed Renault-Volvo partnership discussed below).

Accompanying this trend toward corporate restructuring was the familiar process of engaging in cost-reducing, productivity-boosting labor cuts, in which European firms downsized about as vigorously as their American counterparts. European producers eliminated nearly 300,000 jobs from 1978 to 1986 (see table 9.1). Only West Germany's firms, by far the most successful performers during the 1980s, were able to add rather than shed workers.[7]

Table 9.1   Automobile Industry Employment in Europe and the United States, 1978–1986 (in thousands of workers)

	1978	1986	Change (%)
Germany	602	772	28
France	494	370	-25
United Kingdom	485	265	-45
Italy	292	209	-28
Spain	160	122	-24
Total	2,033	1,738	-15
United States	1,005	843	-16

Source: James P. Womack and Daniel T. Jones, "European Automotive Policy: Past, Present, and Future," in Glennon J. Harrison, ed., Europe and the United States: Competition and Cooperation in the 1990s (Armonk, N.Y.: M. E. Sharpe, 1994), 208.

FRANCE: FROM INTERVENTION TO DISENGAGEMENT

As in the steel industry, French firms in the auto industry responded less successfully than their European competitors to the broad structural changes affecting their sector. Following the second oil shock in 1979, both Peugeot and Renault lost domestic and European market share to Volkswagen, Fiat, Ford, and General Motors, Europe's other high-volume producers.[8] This decline increasingly drew the French government into managing auto industry adjustment.

Both Peugeot and Renault were restructured during the 1980s. Peugeot's restructuring preceded Renault's and came about at the firm's initiative rather than the government's. Peugeot's adjustment was also more protracted and contentious than Renault's, for not only did the government have to negotiate with private rather than public managers, it also had to confront a more highly mobilized work force. For these reasons, the cases of Peugeot and Renault will be considered separately.

Peugeot: The Lessons of Talbot

Peugeot's restructuring occurred against a background of deteriorating finances and growing worker mobilization. Peugeot's financial problems, like those of France's steel companies, were caused by declining markets and strategic errors. Peugeot's most serious strategic errors were the acquisitions of Citroën in 1974 and Chrysler's European operations (renamed Talbot) in 1978.[9] In both cases, the automaker had difficulty absorbing plants and dealer networks, many of which were technologically outdated and inefficient. By mid-1980, in the aftermath of the previous year's oil shock, the company was forced to begin layoffs, most of which were handled through preretirement payments to or buyouts of immigrant workers (especially the North Africans who made up over half of Citroën's and Talbot's production force) to enable them to return home. About 24,000 jobs were eliminated by Peugeot in 1980 (compared with only 4,000 by Renault).[10]

The Left's election win in 1981 threatened to undermine an industrial relations environment at Peugeot that, especially in the Citroën and Talbot divisions, had long relied on a system of authoritarian work regulation enforced by a favored house union, the Confédération des Syndicats Libres (CSL).[11] Many workers, chafing under this system but previously powerless to change it, viewed the Left government as an ally in their quest for reform. André Sainjon, then head of the CGT's metalworkers' federation, later remarked, "You can't understand the conflicts of the early 1980s without understanding the workers' revolt against the management methods of Citroën and Talbot.

The big conflicts didn't start around questions of restructuring, but around a human problem: respect for human dignity. There was a strong demand by foreign workers to free themselves. Despite the cultural diversity in these plants, with seventeen different nationalities represented, workers were united in demanding respect for their human dignity."[12]

The Left's assumption of power also provided political cover for the CGT, which sought to increase its own influence by mobilizing this growing worker restiveness. Starting in the spring of 1982, the CGT initiated a wave of work stoppages that focused on two plants in the Paris region, the 6,500-worker Citroën plant in Aulnay-sous-Bois and the 17,000-worker Talbot plant in Poissy. Although the CGT presented predictable demands, such as for increased wages and a slower work pace, the real issue was union power. As a result, the CGT found itself opposed not only by management, which denounced it for "organizing violence and making its private law reign," but also by the CSL, which staged a large demonstration in front of the Labor Ministry accusing the CGT of blocking the "freedom to work."[13] In the Aulnay-sous-Bois conflict with Citroën, both labor-management and interunion relations were so acrimonious that negotiations had to be carried out by union and management representatives in eight different rooms linked by closed-circuit televisions.[14]

For both plants a government-appointed mediator made recommendations that were accepted by management and most of the affected unions and workers. But these settlements brought only a temporary truce and did little to restore calm in the plants or establish a new system of labor-management relations. The CGT and the CSL remained locked in low-intensity warfare, while Citroën and Talbot continued to decry CGT "terrorism."[15] For Socialist leaders these conflicts created growing tensions with the CGT and its ally, the Communists; although the government did not want to be seen as endorsing unions such as the CSL, neither did it want to see a major firm damaged by constant labor upheaval. This led, for instance, to Labor Minister Auroux's early 1983 accusation that the CGT was unable to control its members and was perpetuating violence, and to PS leader Jospin's condemnation of the CGT section at Aulnay-sous-Bois for acting irresponsibly.[16] Socialist leaders were careful, however, to keep their criticisms from creating an open break with the Communists.

By mid-1983 the combination of work disruptions and declining performance had produced a critical situation for Peugeot. During the past three years the firm had incurred operating losses totaling Fr 6 billion ($1.1 billion), while its debt had mounted to Fr 30 billion.[17] In July 1983 management responded by initiating a restructuring program that envisioned cutting 12,500 jobs. The program's first phase, aimed at Talbot, provided for the dismissal of nearly 3,000 workers, most of whom were production workers at the Poissy plant. The second phase, to be implemented later, was aimed at Citroën.

The announcement of the Talbot plan created a labor explosion that ultimately required intervention by the highest levels of the government and soured relations between the government and both the CGT and the CFDT. Because French labor law required government approval for mass layoffs, even by private firms, the plan became politicized and led to a situation in which government officials were negotiating with management and national union officials at the same time as local unions were seeking to mobilize workers against the job cuts. In what had become standard practice for handling controversial issues at Peugeot, the government appointed a so-called *sage* (wise man) to determine whether the firm's layoff request was economically justified. This allowed the government to buy time and test the degree of worker resistance to the proposed cuts. Meanwhile, the government began talks with union and management officials on a possible compromise. Leading the government's efforts was the Communist employment minister, Jack Ralite, whose apparent task was to contain the CGT by making it complicit in the negotiations.

The government's strategy was thus a delicate balancing act between economic and political imperatives. On the one hand, Socialist officials understood Peugeot's financial problems and its need to reduce labor costs. As Economy and Finance Minister Delors admitted, "Getting PSA [Peugeot] back on track will take the elimination of several thousand jobs."[18] Moreover, the adjustment plan, announced only four months after the government's economic policy reversal of March 1983, came at a moment when the government had begun emphasizing private-sector profitability, and thus Peugeot received a sympathetic hearing from the government. On the other hand, the government would have run political risks by approving mass layoffs. Not only was this the first time that such drastic cuts in the auto industry had been announced, but no other industry had yet envisioned job reductions of this scope, with the exception of the steel industry in 1982. And with popular support for the Left coalition apparently on the decline,[19] Socialist leaders wanted to maintain amicable public relations with their Communist allies in the government and labor movement. All of this gave the government an incentive to weaken or even nullify Peugeot's restructuring plan.

The Talbot layoff issue was equally risky for the Communists, who had to play two incompatible roles—government allies on the one hand and job defenders on the other. Caught in the middle were Employment Minister Ralite and CGT metalworkers' federation leader Sainjon (who was also a member of the PCF's Central Committee). Ralite and Sainjon were party moderates who had to negotiate a settlement acceptable to both Peugeot management and the affected workers. According to Sainjon, "The Communists in government were prisoners of a certain logic of governing. I'm sure that the Communist ministers were aware of the heavy industrial handicap that had been left by previous governments. At the same time, as members of the party, they wanted to have their voices heard, which meant not accepting restructuring passively, especially the social aspects."[20] Sainjon, who later broke with the PCF and resigned his party and union posts, also suspected party leaders of having ulterior motives: "I believe that Communist leaders sought to use conflicts in the automobile industry, especially the one at Talbot, to create a clash with the government so they could pull the Communist ministers out of the government. No one in the party discussed this with me at the time, but I have the feeling that party hard-liners wanted to sharpen a conflict that would enable them to say: blame the Socialists in government, and especially the president."[21]

Socialist and Communist officials, management, and the unions all had different goals for Talbot, and their failure to agree on what should be done resulted in a deadlock that lasted from July to November 1983.[22] Government negotiators wanted Peugeot to reduce the number of Talbot workers it intended to lay off and to improve its plans for retraining some workers and finding them new jobs as well as supporting other workers financially (while still allowing Peugeot to cut labor costs substantially). In late November, after Peugeot submitted a second worker-assistance proposal, the government informally consented to Peugeot's restructuring scheme and agreed that 3,000 Talbot workers could be fired. All that remained was for a Labor Ministry agency, the Inspection du Travail, to give official approval.[23] In early December, however, before approval was given, Talbot workers staged a show of defiance, occupying their plant and stopping production. The strikers, most of whom were immigrant workers, demanded that no workers be laid off and that management make a public commitment to maintaining both the Poissy plant and the Talbot line itself. The strike, whose beginnings were largely spontaneous, was quickly endorsed by CGT and CFDT local unions, which then competed for leadership. The government's attempt to set a precedent by negotiating mass firings with the major unions now lay in shambles and called into question the government's competence in handling crucial economic issues.

Surprised by the workers' revolt, government officials quickly retreated from their previous approval. Employment Minister Ralite, speaking before the National Assembly, criticized the Talbot plan for neglecting "the human and social aspects" of restructuring, even though he had approved the plan in November.[24] With the controversy now having escalated into a full-blown government crisis, Ralite, Prime Minister Mauroy, Economy and Finance Minister Delors, and Social Affairs Minister Bérégovoy tried to fashion a compromise by negotiating with labor confederation officials and management (but not with Talbot's local unions). After several days the parties, including Ralite and Sainjon, reached an agreement to reduce the number of Talbot workers to be fired from 2,905 to 1,905.

Unfortunately for the government, the Talbot workers, led by an intransigent CFDT local union, rejected the idea that anyone should be fired and refused to end their occupation of the plant. The CGT local union, trapped between striking workers on the one hand and its metalworkers' federation (which had approved the plan) on the other, was forced to disavow the metalworkers' federation and support the strike. With no negotiated resolution in sight, the government finally ordered riot police to remove the workers from the plant in early January 1984, which they did peacefully. The calm did not last long, however. When the plant was reopened several days later, vicious fights broke out between strikers and nonstrikers. Eventually, the workers returned and production resumed. Despite the opposition of local unions, the revised restructuring plan would be carried out.

The contending parties were quick to draw lessons from the Talbot affair. By far the most critical voice was that of the CFDT, which felt excluded from what it viewed as an agreement between Socialist ministers and the Communist movement (especially the CGT). Denouncing the government's "paternalist vision" and its "excess of statism," CFDT leaders harshly attacked Socialist officials for allegedly taking the place of unions in labor disputes.[25] General Secretary Edmond Maire declared: "What we are questioning in the Talbot conflict is the fact that [the government] wanted, in the most authoritarian manner possible, to impose on workers decisions that were taken without them, against them. We still consider [government leaders] to be incapable of understanding the situation, its difficulties. . . . In fact, the government wants to strengthen the authority of the PC [PCF] and the CGT to keep workers in their place."[26]

For the CGT as well, the Talbot conflict taught hard lessons about the dangers of complicity in restructuring decisions. Widely seen as a party to a plan that harmed worker interests, the CGT subsequently toughened its stance and increasingly opposed the government's more permissive stance toward mass layoffs proposed by management. The CGT's new approach was apparent, for instance, in April 1984, only three months after the end of the Talbot conflict, when Peugeot announced a restructuring plan for its Citroën division similar to the Talbot one.[27] Rather than negotiating with Peugeot as it had done in the Talbot case, the CGT led a week-long occupation of the Aulnay-sous-Bois plant.[28] For their part, Peugeot management also took a different tack toward the CGT, refusing to meet with its delegation in a June bargaining session that included all the other unions.[29]

Government leaders themselves, apparently taking the CFDT's criticisms to heart, changed their modus operandi after the Talbot affair. Where restructuring decisions were concerned, they now engaged in more consultation with unions and management. In the spring of 1984, for example, Industry Minister Fabius, who later claimed, "We learned the lessons of Talbot,"[30] approached the issue of steel industry restructuring by orchestrating extensive discussions between management, the unions, and the government.[31]

The Talbot conflict proved decisive for the government's industrial-adjustment strategy in two respects. First, it led to an estrangement, which ultimately became a divorce, between the government and both of the major labor confederations. Although the government continued to preach *concertation* with the CGT and the CFDT, the Talbot affair created a rupture that was never fully repaired. Within seven months of the conflict, the PCF had left the government, and its union ally, the CGT, had become a foe of the government's restructuring program.[32] As for the CFDT, although it remained more favorable toward restructuring and negotiations (as opposed to resistance and mobilization), it continued to regard the government warily and to guard its independence jealously.

Second, the Talbot conflict set a precedent for future adjustment, namely that layoffs on an enormous scale would be tolerated by the government. Within months of the conflict's end, the government approved restructuring plans for Citroën,[33] Renault, and the steel, coal, and shipbuilding industries, all of which entailed drastic labor reductions. Although the government might press management to increase layoff benefits, it would not stop management from restructuring as it saw fit.

Peugeot's adjustment measures of 1983–1984, which were soon followed by a market upswing, led to a return to profitability in 1985—the first year of profits after five years of losses totaling Fr 8 billion ($1.5 billion). Profit making continued into the early 1990s, as did restructuring (at a slower pace than before, but still relentlessly). The consequences for employment were predictable. By 1992 Peugeot employed roughly 157,000 people, down from 206,000 in 1983—a decrease of 24 percent.[34] Along with this reduction in jobs came a gradual adoption of Japanese-style practices stressing teamwork, skills upgrading, and cooperative union-management relations.[35]

As Peugeot's adjustment proceeded, the government maintained its largely noninterventionist stance. The events surrounding a seven-week conflict in 1989 over wages at Peugeot's main plants in Sochaux and Mulhouse provide one example of the government's approach. For several weeks Peugeot's CEO,

Jacques Calvet, refused to negotiate with labor, claiming that global competition made it impossible to increase his original wage offer. In response, unions, individual workers, and even several prominent Socialist leaders urged Prime Minister Rocard to intervene, if only to force Calvet to the bargaining table. But Rocard and other government officials were reluctant to pressure Calvet, and some were even publicly sympathetic to Calvet's plight. Industry Minister Fauroux declared, for example, "We must avoid a generalized wage explosion, and there will not be a new 'Grenelle.'[36] In this context it's up to M. Calvet, as with any CEO, to negotiate with his unions. It's not my job to intervene."[37] After five weeks of this standoff, Rocard appointed a mediator who was able to fashion a compromise that ended the strike, but government officials kept their distance throughout the conflict.[38] The Socialists' very different approach of only six years before, when Peugeot's request to lay off 3,000 workers had triggered energetic state involvement and provoked a government crisis, had become only a misty memory.

Renault: The Fall of the Workers' Fortress

Although Renault's restructuring, which began in 1985, came later than Peugeot's, the company's problems—a failure to control production costs, a pricing structure that provided inadequate margins, and an illusory sense of market dominance—were no less severe. Stéphane Doblin, Renault's director of planning during the mid-1980s (and the architect of its restructuring) later commented, "I think the firm had gone to sleep. Everybody said, 'We are the best, we know how to make small and midsize cars better than anyone.' This idea that Renault was great at producing small and midsize cars caused the firm to focus almost exclusively on the need and desire for growth. People believed that the firm could grow when others were contracting. It was an illusion."[39]

According to a high-ranking Industry Ministry official, these weaknesses grew out of an "enterprise culture" that prized Renault's role as a progressive firm that offered its workers secure, well-paying jobs: "Management felt itself loyal to an image, which was that Renault doesn't fire people, it doesn't close factories."[40] Underlying this image was, of course, the state safety net. Doblin said that Renault CEO Bernard Hanon "had always known the Renault approach where it was logical that there wouldn't be any profits. Since Renault's finances were part of the state budget, making profits served no purpose. It would just mean giving money to the state—thus it was better to redistribute the money among the employees. The most important consideration was to preserve social peace."[41]

Renault undertook an aggressive program of foreign expansion in the late

1970s, including an attempt to penetrate the American market by purchasing control of American Motors. The firm also invested heavily in new production technologies such as robotics.[42] When the world market downturn began in 1980, however, Renault's market share and financial performance dropped sharply. As was noted above, in 1980–1984 Renault's share of the European market declined more than any other producer's, while its domestic share also plummeted, from 40 percent to 31 percent.[43] Renault's American adventure turned sour as well, and the company eventually sold its stake in American Motors to Chrysler. From a modest profit position in 1979–1980, the firm's performance steadily worsened, culminating in a catastrophic 1984 loss of Fr 12.5 billion.

Renault's adjustment to its market decline was unusually slow. In addition to the problems mentioned above, Renault was, according to some observers, handicapped by its relationship with the new Mitterrand government. Although a publicly owned firm that received periodic state subsidies and was run by a CEO appointed by the government, Renault traditionally had enjoyed substantial operational autonomy.[44] Some observers claimed, however, that the firm was under pressure from the Mitterrand government to help fight unemployment by eschewing excessive layoffs, and thus that restructuring was delayed as long as possible. A Renault executive in personnel management recalled that "Hanon wasn't free to do as he wished. For political reasons, since he was CEO during the first years of the Left in power, Hanon wasn't allowed to lay off workers in response to the market. Thus to claim that Hanon let Renault lose millions isn't accurate, because the government was preventing him from making the necessary adjustments."[45]

By 1984, however, restructuring had become imperative for Renault, which was caught in the vise of escalating investment costs and declining markets. When spring arrived, Hanon, at Mauroy's urging, began consulting the unions about reductions in personnel.[46] At the same time, the firm hired Doblin as its new director of planning. Doblin, who had put together Fiat's 1980 restructuring effort (which had required 20,000 layoffs), was given the task of devising an adjustment strategy, which was drawn up during the summer, approved by Hanon, and presented to the unions for negotiation. Unlike Peugeot's approach, which had included mass layoffs, this plan sought to cut up to 10,000 jobs without layoffs, mainly through preretirement packages and other departure incentives (for example, to encourage immigrants to return home).[47]

Hanon apparently believed that his good relations with the CGT local union would enable him to gain union backing for his soft approach to labor adjustment. By late 1984, however, with the Communist Party now out of the government and staunchly opposing its economic policies, the local CGT refused to consent to any agreement, as did the local union of the CFDT (which was much smaller and less powerful than its CGT counterpart). According to Doblin, Hanon also encountered opposition from many of Renault's managers and executives. For these reasons, the plan to restructure Renault was still-born.

Hanon's failure to reverse Renault's slide led to his dismissal early in 1985. By then the government was firmly committed to reducing subsidies to public firms, Renault included. Happily for the government, a special commission report on the auto industry's decline, prepared in late 1984, gave it the political cover it needed to shake up Renault management.[48] In January 1985 Prime Minister Fabius replaced Hanon with Georges Besse, an engineer who had overseen restructuring at the newly nationalized firm Péchiney. Unlike the more conciliatory Hanon, Besse adopted a hard-line approach toward restructuring. According to Doblin, "Besse took a very 'nonsocial' position, meaning that he didn't see any particular role for the unions. For him it was his plan or nothing. Besse just said, 'It's going to be this way—there's no other solution.'"[49] Unlike the equally hard-line Calvet at Peugeot, however, Besse was low-key in his approach. Mostly ignoring or bypassing the unions and making decisions unilaterally, Besse did not unveil a grand plan, but instead carried out restructuring in incremental, unannounced steps.[50]

Not surprisingly, the CGT waged war against Besse from the outset. Tensions between the two culminated in an October 1985 strike focused on Renault's Le Mans and Boulogne-Billancourt plants. The CGT, however, failed to mobilize more than a quarter of the workers and finally had to call off the strike. Such was the CGT's isolation that three other labor confederations (the CFDT, the Force Ouvrière, and the Confédération Française des Travailleurs Chrétiens) organized a demonstration *against* the strike.[51] According to *Le Monde,* the CGT's defeat marked a turning point in Renault's history by dissolving the image of Renault as a workers' "fortress" in which the CGT shared power with management.[52]

By late 1985, then, Renault's course was set: the government expected management to turn a profit regardless of the impact on the work force. Unlike Hanon, Besse was virtually free of government pressure.[53] By the time of Besse's assassination by Action Directe terrorists in November 1986, he had cut Renault's work force by nearly 20,000 workers.[54] As in the steel industry, there were very few outright dismissals, for almost all the workers who were let go received retirement or severance benefits or retraining. As expected, these labor reductions improved Renault's financial and operational performance.[55] The same trend continued under Besse's successor, Raymond Lévy (1986–1992), who also worked with minimal government interference. As Lévy himself said, "I do essentially what I like. The government imposes nothing."[56] By 1987 Renault was in the black again, for the first time since 1980.

At the same time it was acquiring de facto operational autonomy, the firm was also proceeding slowly and haltingly toward de jure autonomy—that is, toward privatization. The initial move was made in late 1987 by the conservative Chirac government, which introduced a bill that would change Renault's legal status to allow the firm to go bankrupt if its liabilities exceeded its assets. The bill also permitted the entry of private capital into the firm's capital base,[57] and because Renault's debts exceeded its assets, provided a Fr 12 billion debt write-off to boost the firm's net worth into the black. The bill, however, was blocked by parliamentary maneuvering by the Communists and Mitterrand, and thus failed to gain approval before the 1988 elections that returned Mitterrand and the Socialists to power. Before leaving office, however, the Chirac government did gain the necessary EC consent for the proposals set out in the bill.

For Renault to be allowed to write off its debt, the firm's legal status had to be changed to that of a *société anonyme* (joint-stock company).[58] This was a step the reelected Mitterrand government was not prepared to take at first. It will be recalled from chapter 7 that Mitterrand's second term began with the *Ni-Ni* strategy—neither nationalization nor privatization—for public firms. In line with this approach, the government sought to separate the issues of state aid and legal status, and thus requested EC approval for a debt write-off without having to change Renault's legal status. But the EC was unwilling to agree to this, for as we saw in chapter 8 with respect to the steel industry, the EC's stance on state aid to public firms became increasingly stringent in the late 1980s in anticipation of the post-1992 Single Market.

The EC's opposition led to a two-year struggle with the French government over Renault. In the end the French blinked. Although the French government kept its no-nationalization pledge, it abandoned its stance against privatization, thus allowing Renault to privatize, albeit partially. The reason for this shift was that Renault and other internationally exposed state firms faced growing capital requirements. In addition to EC strictures on public subsidies, such firms had to face two challenges: first, a liberalizing business environment that, looking ahead to the new economic regime scheduled to arrive in 1992, placed a premium on corporate expansion throughout Europe and the world, and second, the French government's budgetary austerity, which sharply limited the amount of available state financial support.

Renault's response to this new business environment was to merge with Volvo in an alliance designed to marry Renault's low-end, high-volume product line (and strength in south European and Latin American markets) with the Swedish automaker's niche as a manufacturer of more expensive, higher-quality cars (and strength in northern European and North American markets). The union could not be consummated, however, without changing Renault's legal status to allow partial privatization, which the government finally did in April 1990, over the vigorous but futile objections of the Communist Party.[59] This action also paved the way for a compromise with Brussels over the state aid issue, and in the end, the EC allowed Renault to take about half of the Fr 12 billion debt write-off originally proposed.[60]

The Renault-Volvo alliance, however, was brought to an end in late 1993 by Swedish shareholders who feared Renault (and French government) domination.[61] But this failure did nothing to reverse the trend of French government disengagement from Renault. With the Right again in control of parliament after the 1993 elections, Prime Minister Balladur announced that the firm would be further privatized, and by July 1996 the state had become a minority shareholder with only 46 percent of Renault's stock.[62]

SPAIN: FROM DISENGAGEMENT TO INTERVENTION

As was mentioned in the introduction to this chapter, the PSOE government's handling of the Spanish auto industry did not display the consistency that usually characterized its restructuring efforts. The government at first tried to disengage itself from the auto industry but eventually reversed course by becoming closely involved in a major adjustment attempt in the 1990s. To understand this unusual trajectory, we must first examine the two-track policy legacy that the PSOE inherited from the Franco regime of the 1950s.

The first track had its origin in the Franco regime's drive for national economic self-sufficiency, which had prompted the regime to create for the auto industry, as it had for the steel industry, a company whose goal was to lessen Spain's dependence on imports by producing an essential product domestically. That company was SEAT, a state-controlled collaboration between the INI, private banks, and Fiat.[63] SEAT began mass producing cars under an arrangement with Fiat in 1957.[64] For the next two decades this partnership flourished, aided by the steady growth of demand for automobiles throughout the advanced industrial world. By 1960 SEAT was producing over 31,000 of its Model 600 cars a year—nearly 80 percent of the nation's auto production. A decade later, the main SEAT plant near Barcelona, which employed 20,000 workers, was turning out 280,000 cars a year, about 10 percent of which were exported.[65] Whereas in the beginning Fiat was chiefly responsible for product design and supplied most of the parts, SEAT increasingly developed its own network of local suppliers and a design and engineering capability.

SEAT also expanded its operations in Spain by acquiring a second main production facility, a plant in Landaben (near Pamplona) purchased from a British Leyland subsidiary in 1975.[66]

Expansion came to an end for SEAT, as it did for most auto firms, with the economic crisis of the 1970s. During the post-1973 recession the firm was hurt by poor sales and the rapid emergence of domestic competitors. SEAT's share of national production dropped from 62 percent in 1970 to 29 percent in 1980.[67] Moreover, growing trade liberalization in the post-Franco period brought a sharp rise in imports.[68] But the most critical development for SEAT was that Fiat itself began to experience severe problems in the late 1970s, which made it increasingly unwilling and unable to finance SEAT's losses.[69] The INI, which shared the responsibility for covering these losses, was understandably eager for Fiat to assume a larger ownership share.[70] After promising the Spanish government that it would do so, Fiat reversed course and by May 1981 had divested itself of all SEAT shares.

By the early 1980s, then, the INI had become the sole owner of a hemorrhaging and uncompetitive firm of its own creation. Two paths were followed to find a way out of this crisis. First, the INI looked for another major multinational auto firm as a replacement for Fiat. From 1979 to 1982, SEAT and INI officials held talks with almost every firm in that category, including Volkswagen, Renault, Peugeot, Toyota, and Nissan. Volkswagen expressed the most interest, and in September 1982, a month before the Socialists' election, SEAT and Volkswagen signed a commercial and production agreement.[71] Second, in 1981 SEAT management put forward a strategic plan to restore profitability, which included measures to lower costs and reduce the work force by 8,000 workers within two years. The plan failed to produce an instant turnaround, however, and the firm continued to lose heavily. In 1978–1983, losses totaled PTA 126 billion (about $1 billion).[72]

The second policy track inherited from the Franco era was the state policy of encouraging foreign firms to open branch plant operations in Spain. Realizing that SEAT could not by itself supply the domestic market and that branch plants could bring needed jobs and foreign capital, the Franco regime allowed Renault, Peugeot, Citroën, General Motors, Ford, Nissan, and other firms to build production facilities. Beginning in the 1950s and gaining momentum with the *apertura* of the 1960s, this open-door strategy generated a production boom. Whereas fewer than 9,000 vehicles were produced by foreign firms in 1960, by 1970 they were producing 170,000 a year. A decade later that figure reached 735,000, with about three-fourths of that output destined for export.[73] The Spanish auto industry, now producing over 1 million vehicles a year (SEAT included), had rapidly become Europe's fourth-largest producer after West Germany, France, and Italy.[74]

Socialist Strategy: Accommodating the Foreigners

In 1982 the González government inherited an industry of contrasts: on the one hand, a flourishing foreign sector attracted by low labor costs and tax and other incentives provided by a welcoming government, but on the other, a faltering state firm that had just found a potential corporate savior but whose future remained cloudy. In its essentials, the new government's strategy was simple and was shaped by the two-track approach inherited from the past: continued support for the investment and production efforts of foreign MNCs, and the pursuit of efforts to strengthen the flagship SEAT, principally by developing closer ties with SEAT's new partner, Volkswagen.

For the MNCs, the government's principal effort was a 1985 Industry Ministry "General Consolidation Plan" to stimulate investment. As was discussed in chapter 6, in 1985 the government was in the midst of implementing a sweeping industrial-reconversion program. The Socialists' willingness to aid firms in distress was not lost on Spain's auto producers, all of which (with the exception of Ford) were losing money. After a concerted lobbying campaign by these producers, the government agreed to give it aid as well. An Industry Ministry official who helped prepare the aid plan explained the decision this way:

> We decided to sign agreements with all the automotive MNCs operating in Spain in order to ensure large investments and a strong competitive position for their Spanish subsidiaries. Although this sector wasn't officially in the 1984 industrial-reconversion program, we employed the reconversion law, since one of its last paragraphs says that the administration can carry out any development or promotion programs it deems necessary. Thus we had an open door to take actions concerning financial aid (both to firms and to workers), even without a formal reconversion plan. We gave little money, but we studied specific ways in which we could help them, for example in terms of providng infrastructure, tax breaks, and special amortization programs. Our aim was to convince Ford, General Motors, and the other big automakers that Spain was a good place to invest.[75]

Aid agreements were signed with FASA-Renault (Renault's Spanish subsidiary), Citroën, Talbot, and Ford, which collectively pledged to invest PTA 200 billion ($1.6 billion) during the following decade, in return for the government incentives just mentioned.[76]

There is little question that this supportive environment helped multinational auto firms thrive, especially during the market rebound of the late 1980s. By 1991 Spain's annual output of 1.77 million vehicles made it Europe's third-largest producer after Germany and France (Italy was now fourth). Spain was also Europe's largest auto exporter, with 72 percent of production, or 1.28 million vehicles being shipped abroad.[77] The automotive sector (including trucks) was one of Spain's largest employers, with nearly 83,000 workers directly involved in production.[78]

As for the state's effort to secure SEAT's future through an alliance with Volkswagen, the record was decidedly mixed, for a promising beginning was followed by a severe market crisis in the early 1990s. The 1982 accord between the two firms failed to provide any immediate improvement in SEAT's declining performance.[79] Thus it is hardly surprising, given the PSOE government's emphasis on budget austerity and public-sector reform (notably reduction of operating losses), that Socialist leaders were anxious to reduce SEAT's fiscal burden. Because SEAT had a history of shared public-private ownership, state officials looked favorably on the notion of Volkswagen assuming an ownership share as a major way to lighten that burden. Despite its problems, then, SEAT's market viability, based on a respectable history of innovation, quality production, and commercialization, made it a potential candidate for partial or even total privatization.

At the same time, state officials were concerned about the conditions under which privatization would take place. SEAT was Spain's version of Renault: a state-sponsored national champion that historically had produced a popular consumer item while providing secure, well-paying jobs for its workers. Moreover, the firm's location in Barcelona made SEAT a potential pawn in any dispute between the central government and the fractious region of Catalonia. Socialist leaders, like Francoist and UCD leaders before them, had strong reasons for ensuring SEAT's survival, and were willing to pay a high price to do so.

Volkswagen's price turned out to be high indeed. After talks lasting over two years, the government and Volkswagen agreed in late 1985 on the conditions for a transfer of SEAT ownership and control from the INI to Volkswagen. The government consented, first of all, to pay off SEAT's accumulated debt of PTA 185 billion ($1.5 billion). In addition, the state would assume SEAT's losses for the next few years and provide other financial supports; by one estimate, the state eventually paid about PTA 400 billion (about $3.2 billion) to transfer SEAT to Volkswagen.[80] However exorbitant, this financial support ultimately enabled the government to attain its primary goal for SEAT: shifting ownership from the state to a MNC with deep pockets while ensuring the firm's survival as a corporate entity. As for Volkswagen, it immediately acquired a 51 percent ownership stake in SEAT, for which it paid the Spanish government DM 1.3 billion ($600 million). This share, the parties agreed, would rise to 75 percent by the end of 1986 and reach 100 percent not later than 1990. Volkswagen also pledged to invest at least DM 5 billion in SEAT, which would pay for, among other things, construction of a new plant in Martorell, about 40 kilometers from the main SEAT plant in the Zona Franca (free economic zone) near Barcelona.

For the next seven years, the transfer appeared to benefit all sides. Volkswagen fulfilled its pledges, becoming full owner of SEAT within the prescribed time. Volkswagen also carried out its investment program, the centerpiece of which was the Martorell plant, which was expected to cost PTA 220 billion, have a production capacity of 340,000 cars per year, and employ 6,000 workers.[81] In 1988, having been helped by the market rebound and its personnel-reduction measures, SEAT returned to modest profitability for the first time in a decade, and remained profitable for the next four years.[82] By the early 1990s, the state's agreement with Volkswagen seemed to have rescued SEAT from certain failure.

In reality, SEAT's future was anything but secure. SEAT's role in Volkswagen's global strategy was to fill a market niche, namely the production of small cars for southern Europe, in which SEAT would compete with Fiat, Renault, and Peugeot. Spain's advantage lay in its labor costs, which, despite the narrowing of the wage gap with the rest of Western Europe since Franco's time, remained below those of other European car-producing nations.[83] Exploiting this advantage meant emphasizing labor-intensive methods.[84] The new Martorell plant, therefore, was not highly automated but instead designed to operate in three shifts around the clock—the first time such an intensive production method had been employed in the European car industry. Moreover, the new plant was expected to rely heavily on imported Volkswagen components. Block and cylinder head assemblies, for example, would be brought in from Volkswagen plants outside Spain and then attached to locally produced fuel, exhaust, and ignition systems. The upshot was that parts designed or produced in Spain would account for less than 40 percent of the final product.

There were two long-term risks for SEAT in such a strategy. First, there was the possibility that SEAT could become Volkswagen's *maquiladora*—a labor-intensive assembly site for mostly imported parts. A technical analysis produced by a local business consulting firm offered the following observation: "Whereas in other European countries there is a clear correlation between the strength of the automobile industry and the strength of the parts-supplier industry, Spain has the anomaly of being an important car exporter while being a net importer of parts and equipment."[85] The danger in relying on imported parts lay in the potential for a diminution of Spain's competence in areas such as research and development, design, and machining. Moreover, heavy use of foreign auto parts would undoubtedly harm the network of parts suppliers that SEAT had fostered over the years.[86] The second risk was the prospect of large-scale personnel reductions, for the buildup of Martorell put in doubt the fate of SEAT's main works in the Zona Franca, which employed 16,000 of SEAT's 24,000 workers but were handicapped by obsolete facilities.[87] As Zona Franca workers realized from the start, leaner production inevitably meant a leaner work force.

Beyond these local considerations, SEAT also faced a threat arising from Volkswagen's strategic shift toward the former East Germany, and Eastern Europe in general, following the end of the Cold War. Though no one, least of all Volkswagen, had anticipated this shift at the time of SEAT's privatization, it was a logical strategy for Volkswagen after the fall of the Berlin Wall in late 1989. By 1992 Volkswagen had acquired the former East Germany's Trabant works and the Czechoslovakian automaker Skoda, had built a new factory in Mosel and was preparing to expand its sales activities throughout Eastern Europe. Naturally, SEAT's difficulties only reinforced Volkswagen's determination to shift operations eastward, and SEAT increasingly found itself losing a zero-sum game against low-wage competitors within the Volkswagen group itself. The only consolation, perhaps, was that SEAT was not alone, for the East's opening imperiled Spain's position as Europe's low-cost production site for all kinds of goods.[88]

In addition to these structural factors, SEAT's future also appeared doubtful because of its (and Volkswagen's) inability to overcome the threats posed by changing economic conditions, in particular the market's decline in the early 1990s. As we noted above, after 1988 SEAT and Volkswagen thrived in a buoyant market, but once demand began to fall in 1991, Volkswagen's performance plummeted. Although SEAT turned a profit in 1991, its performance deteriorated sharply the following year.[89] Thus the global recession of the early 1990s exposed the competitive weakness of both Volkswagen and SEAT, causing the two firms to drastically alter their strategy in 1993. The resulting crisis drew the Spanish government back in as a full—though unwilling—participant in efforts to salvage SEAT's survival as a Volkswagen subsidiary.

SEAT's 1992 reversal was not due to a fall in sales or productivity, both of which in fact increased or remained constant in comparison with the previous year, but to mounting debt payments, the negative effects of the peseta's 20 percent devaluation, the financial burden of launching the Martorell plant, and other factors.[90] By early 1993 SEAT had to contend with escalating losses and a total debt of nearly PTA 500 billion ($4.0 billion). In April, nevertheless, management and the unions signed an adjustment agreement that committed the firm to continued production of cars at the Zona Franca plant.[91] SEAT's financial condition, though alarming, did not appear catastrophic.

Attitudes changed abruptly in September 1993, when Ferdinand Piech, Volkswagen's president, called a board meeting to announce not only that SEAT's financial situation had deteriorated rapidly but that SEAT's management had misled Volkswagen about the gravity of the crisis.[92] Piech then fired SEAT president Juan Antonio Díaz Alvarez and declared that the Zona Franca facilities would be shut down in two years, resulting in a loss of 9,000 jobs. To cover SEAT's losses, Piech also threatened to acquire the Landaben plant from SEAT, which would transfer PTA 120 billion to SEAT but convert the facility into a Volkswagen assembly plant. He also threatened to abolish SEAT's autonomy by transferring all purchasing, financing, and design activity to Volkswagen's Wolfsburg headquarters.[93]

This threat to SEAT's survival inevitably triggered intervention by the Spanish and Catalonian governments. Volkswagen's apparent goal was to use government capitalization to partially renationalize SEAT—an unusual but shrewd strategy for a private firm.[94] Although both levels of government rejected this option, they differed on the path to take. The national government adopted a noninterventionist line, arguing that Volkswagen should resolve the crisis itself, whereas Catalonian president Jordi Pujol pressured for a 1984-style reconversion plan under which the national government would provide enormous amounts of aid.[95] Neither national nor Catalonia officials, however, opposed Volkswagen's plan to terminate production in the Zona Franca.

Predictably, the main labor confederations, the UGT and the CCOO, vigorously contested this plan. At the same time, they supported Volkswagen's call for SEAT's partial nationalization, on the condition that the state exercise more effective oversight over the firm's decisions.[96] Throughout the fall the two confederations cooperated in organizing a series of effective demonstrations and strikes, including a strike in which workers at Martorell refused to work overtime on Saturdays as an expression of support for Zona Franca workers.[97] These labor actions culminated in early November in a protest by 25,000 people that filled the downtown streets of Barcelona.[98]

Despite labor's mobilization, SEAT pushed ahead with its reorganization plan, which was finally approved by the Generalitat (the Catalonian government) in December 1993. Piech's direst threats were dropped: the SEAT name would continue to be used, and the proposals to transfer important functions to Volkswagen headquarters were quietly forgotten. Volkswagen, however, went ahead with the Landaben sale. More ominously for SEAT's long-term survival,

Volkswagen decided that Zona Franca production would be phased out. This would result in elimination of all 9,000 direct-production jobs (although there would be no outright firings), and the Zona Franca site would be converted into an industrial park housing parts suppliers. To aid the suppliers, SEAT pledged to boost the local (Spanish-made) content of its cars from the 1993 figure of 54 percent to 67 percent within three years.[99] The government, other than having to pay early retirement and other benefits to the laid-off workers, for the moment was able to avoid further financial commitments.

The first half of 1994, however, saw the government drawn into a rescue operation as SEAT's losses continued to grow. During the eighteen months leading up to May 1994 the company lost over PTA 200 billion ($1.6 billion). Volkswagen approached national and regional government leaders in May requesting PTA 50 billion ($400 million) for labor adjustment costs. Volkswagen's request contained an implied threat that without such aid it might absorb SEAT, ending the latter's existence as a firm with a Spanish identity.[100]

At first, the national government tried to resist Volkswagen's strong-arm approach. Industry Minister Juan Manuel Eguiagaray declared, "The Spanish government will not let itself be pressured. SEAT has already cost the state treasury too much money and, besides, the firm's situation is due to the poor management of German executives."[101] Ultimately, however, the government lacked the political leverage to ignore Volkswagen's demands. A critical factor in the political equation was the Catalonian government, whose leader, Pujol, could bring down the González government by instructing his party's representatives in the national legislature to withdraw their support for the PSOE.[102] Having already pledged PTA 8 billion in aid to Volkswagen, Pujol was not about to let it absorb or dissolve SEAT, the largest employer in Catalonia. Although conclusive proof is lacking, it is likely that Pujol made his continued parliamentary support of the Socialists contingent on the granting of national government aid.[103] Finally, in early July, officials from the Industry Ministry, Volkswagen, SEAT, and the Catalonian government agreed on an aid package of PTA 38 billion ($304 million)—PTA 30 billion from the national government and PTA 8 billion from the Generalitat—consisting primarily of low-interest loans for specific investment projects. In return, Volkswagen promised to invest PTA 206 billion ($1.65 billion) in SEAT in 1994–1997.[104]

Although Volkswagen also pledged that SEAT would continue to exist as a formal corporate entity, the latter's operational and strategic independence had been almost entirely eliminated. Moreover, despite Volkswagen's vow to increase local content in SEAT vehicles and maintain SEAT's research and development and design centers, other developments, particularly the sale of the Landaben plant, the closing of the Zona Franca facilities, and Volkswagen's growing emphasis on its Eastern European operations, indicated a downgrading of SEAT's status in Volkswagen's strategic plans. In the space of only a few years, SEAT had become a much-diminished presence with a doubtful future.[105]

The PSOE government's intervention during the 1993–1994 SEAT crisis was thus reactive and defensive, evidence of the state's weakness when pitted against Volkswagen rather than of the state's capacity to guide or influence industrial outcomes. The government's adjustment strategy for the automobile sector tended to strengthen the dominance of foreign MNCs at the expense of home-grown technological capacity. Continuing and reinforcing a long-standing policy of encouraging MNC branch plants, this strategy risked mortgaging the future by bolstering the *maquiladora* tendency noted earlier. Being primarily final-assembly operations, branch plants do not undertake core operations that have a high value-added content, such as research and development and design; these are usually reserved for MNC headquarters or other locations in the MNC's country of origin. In Spain, moreover, many of the components used for final assembly are not made by Spanish firms but are either built by MNC manufacturers in Spain or imported.

There are two main alternatives to such a pattern, both of which face daunting barriers to implementation. One is a nationalization of MNCs, in the sense of imposing local-content requirements on research and development, parts sourcing, and other activities with a high value-added content. The obvious problem is that Spain lacks leverage, and that any proposals along these lines would probably elicit threats by the MNCs to take their factories elsewhere. The second alternative would be to create a new national champion firm. However, not only would such a strategy be prohibitively costly, it would also require, as the creation of SEAT did, an alliance with another MNC, and the problem of technological dependence would remain.

From the perspective of the mid-1990s, then, Spain appeared wedded to its configuration of foreign-owned branch plant operations. Aside from the long-term technological disadvantages already discussed, it was also becoming clear, with the rise of the NICs and the opening of markets in Eastern Europe, that Spain was losing its historical labor cost advantage. The auto industry's long-term prospects, while hardly catastrophic, did not bode well for the nation's quest to boost itself into the middle range of Europe's industrial powers.

CONCLUSION

This analysis has revealed that the steel and automobile industries in France and Spain followed different restructuring paths, especially with regard to collective protest and political regulation. The auto industry experienced less worker resistance and public intervention, nationally and at the European level. Adjustment in the auto industry generated less controversy and opposition than did adjustment in the steel industry, for reasons to do with geography and the nature of the restructuring process itself. With both French and Spanish auto production facilities geographically dispersed, labor cutbacks were spread across many communities rather than concentrated in one or two regions. Although the workers whose livelihoods were at risk occasionally staged militant defenses of their jobs—at Talbot in late 1983 and at SEAT a decade later, for example—their protests did not spread beyond these localities to the extent seen in the steel industry.

As for the restructuring process itself, auto restructuring tended to be more gradual and incremental. Plants were rarely shut down or subject to sudden and extreme work force reductions, as happened in the steel industry. Adjustment typically proceeded in dribs and drabs, with some workers laid off and others retrained and reassigned. The climate of impending doom that surrounded steel industry adjustment was largely missing in the automobile industry.

Auto industry restructuring was also less subject to intervention by public authorities at the national or European levels. The predominance of private ownership and the industry's generally sound (albeit cyclical) financial performance kept strategic control in industrialists' hands and beyond the reach of EC policy makers. There was no equivalent in the auto industry of the steel industry's EC-orchestrated "manifest crisis" regime that led to regulation of production, capacity, and prices. As we have seen, where automobiles were concerned the EC was confined mainly to managing foreign trade, especially with Japan. In France and Spain, national governments exercised less direct control over automobiles than over steel. Until the early 1980s, France's major auto companies usually turned a profit and thus depended less on government aid than did the steel companies. Moreover, auto industry ownership was not entirely in public hands; although Renault was a nationalized firm, Peugeot was a family-held company that guarded its independence. In Spain, the entire auto industry was controlled by foreign multinationals after the sale of SEAT to Volkswagen in 1986.

These differences meant that governments and organized labor had less influence over auto restructuring than they did over steel restructuring, and at the same time, that auto manufacturers exercised greater power over restructuring than was the case in the steel industry. Moreover, because the EC was not involved in regulating auto production, external constraints on the auto industry came mainly from the market, not Brussels. For these reasons, there were more options for everyone involved in auto industry restructuring than was the case in the steel industry, and the restructuring process was less institutionalized. For the auto industry, government leaders, company officials, and unionists had to define not only the content of restructuring—including such matters as which plants and workers would be affected—but also the very process necessary for defining that content. New structures, patterns, and norms of decision making had to be created. In addition, because the French and Spanish governments exercised less control over auto firms than they did over steel firms, their ability to impose decisions on the auto sector was less sweeping, and the decisions themselves more ad hoc and less coherent.

Nevertheless, the story of auto industry restructuring in France and Spain supports this book's main arguments. By the mid-1980s both governments had adopted a market-adapting approach that sought to improve the market performance of corporate actors, both public and private. French and Spanish Socialists ultimately took measures to help the major auto firms compete more successfully in domestic and international markets. Most notably, with respect to all three of the main firms—Peugeot and Renault in France and SEAT in Spain—both governments approved the laying off of thousands of workers whose jobs could not be justified economically. At the same time, Socialists cushioned the shocks for these workers through preretirement benefits, severance payments, retraining, and other programs. As in the case of steel, this general approach had much in common with those followed by governments in Italy, the United Kingdom, and other West European countries whose nationally based auto firms faced adjustment crises during the 1970s and 1980s.[106]

It is important to emphasize that these policies were not based on a doctrinaire free-market philosophy in which the government would set the ground rules and then withdraw from the field to let the players compete. Not only did both governments provide generous benefits to affected workers, but in both cases the main goal was to foster a favorable market environment in which all companies could flourish. Both governments thus took steps to promote more efficient production operations, stimulate investment, and boost consumer demand. Cases in point include the Mitterrand government's replacement of Hanon in 1985 with the more rigorous Besse, the PSOE's government's restructuring plan in that same year to stimulate MNC investment, and the use of tax breaks by France and Spain to promote sales. Both governments, moreover, sought to protect state interests in the auto industry. The Mitterrand government, for instance, encouraged Renault's talks with Volvo concerning the French company's possible privatization and internationalization, but also defended Renault's status as a company in which the state was the majority shareholder. Likewise, the González government sought to ensure the survival of SEAT as a subsidiary of Volkswagen with a distinctive name and identity.

It is also necessary to recall that this book's basic argument identifies contrasts in trajectories, dynamics, and impacts. Here we return to the puzzle noted at the beginning of this chapter, namely that the trajectory of auto industry adjustment in France and Spain did not follow the usual pattern, for whereas the French scenario played out with typical inconsistency, the Spanish deviated from their usual consistency of approach. In France, the Mitterrand government initially intervened to influence the adjustment efforts of both Peugeot and Renault, mainly by seeking to mitigate or delay labor displacement. However, that approach changed in the mid-1980s, when the government began to move away from direct intervention, relying instead on measures to promote the industry's commercial interests as defined by the firms themselves. In Spain, by contrast, PSOE authorities, by privatizing SEAT, sought to remove the state from direct involvement in the industry. The SEAT crisis of the early 1990s, however, brought the state back in. Thus whereas French Socialist restructuring strategy shifted from intervention to withdrawal, Spanish Socialists moved in the opposite direction, from disengagement to intervention.

The question, then, is how do we explain the Spanish pattern? As the discussion in the preceding section made clear, the Spanish government's intervention in the SEAT crisis grew not out of reborn *dirigismo* or a growth in its ability to carry out its industrial goals but instead reflected the central state's weakness in the face of an alliance between a powerful multinational firm, the Catalonian provincial government, and organized labor. In fact, far from being a move away from a market-adapting strategy, the PSOE government's intervention of 1993–1994 was the very embodiment of such a strategy, in that its goal was to reinforce Volkswagen's and SEAT's financial positions. Spanish exceptionalism was therefore more apparent than real, for the government's goal—to restore or improve the profitability of all firms in the auto sector—remained consistent.

The dynamics of auto restructuring also followed the general pattern, for Spanish labor was more mobilized and influential than French labor in affecting the course of adjustment. Generally speaking, in both countries the labor factor was weaker in auto adjustment than in steel, as fewer workers were mobilized and their opposition was more sporadic. In Spain, although auto workers and their unions were largely quiescent throughout the 1980s and early 1990s, the labor movement played an important role during the 1993–1994 SEAT crisis, by pressuring the government to defend the Zona Franca site and save SEAT. The unions were also important allies of Pujol, the critical actor in this episode, who used his small but crucial Catalonian party as leverage to force the national government into preparing a rescue package for SEAT.

In France, unions were less consequential for adjustment. French labor, especially the CGT, was most active during the early adjustment period of 1981–1984. Talbot, Citroën, and Renault were all hit by antirestructuring strikes during this period, yet these strikes, even the most celebrated and notorious one at Talbot in late 1983, had little effect on the outcome of adjustment and failed to block the government's shift from active intervention to gradual disengagement. This shift also appears to have been a watershed event in the history of French union activism, for after 1985 labor was almost invisible as a collective actor in the auto sector, apart from the 1989 Peugeot strike, which had little to do with adjustment.

Finally, the impact of restructuring was different in France and Spain. In both steel and automobiles, France emerged by the mid-1990s in stronger financial and competitive shape than Spain. For both industries it is difficult to assess the impact of government policies on economic performance, and it would be unreasonable to impute all performance differences between the French and Spanish auto industries to those policies. Yet this book's analysis leads to the conclusion that Socialist restructuring in France reinforced the most positive qualities of Peugeot and Renault, namely their capacity for market autonomy and dynamism. This was accomplished mainly by a strategy of disengagement in which the state removed itself from direct intervention in corporate decisions. Even in Renault's case, state ownership was found to be completely compatible with managerial autonomy.

By contrast, the PSOE government's adjustment efforts tended to reinforce the most negative quality of the Spanish auto industry, namely its technological dependence on foreign capital, which led to a weakening of domestic industrial capacity. With options, Socialist leaders were unable to dislodge Spain from a restrictive economic niche in which its main advantage over other countries lay in its labor-intensive, low-wage assembly operations. After more than a decade of attentive Socialist support, foreign producers continued to call the tune, and Spanish political leaders dutifully continued to dance to it.

10
Conclusion

Industrial
Restructuring
and
Left
Coalitions

What choices do governments of advanced industrial nations have as they confront changes in the global economy, particularly long-term shifts in industrial structures? As was suggested in chapter 1, these governments face the dilemma of trying to promote adjustment and renewed growth while preserving social peace and political support. In confronting this dilemma, national leaders must play a two-level game. At the international level, they must seek to coordinate their policies with those of other nations while extracting maximum national advantage. At the domestic level, they must strive to build and maintain political support among various economic constituencies. As Robert Putnam argues, "At the national level, domestic groups pursue their interests by pressuring the government to adopt favorable policies, and politicians seek power by constructing coalitions among those groups. At the international level, national governments seek to maximize their own ability to satisfy domestic pressures, while minimizing the adverse consequences of foreign developments."[1]

The international level—that is, the global economy—is increasingly governed by norms combining collective regulation (as in the EU) and collective deregulation (as in NAFTA). Both kinds of regulation not only tend to limit the space for autonomous action by individual states, but also produce considerable labor market instability in the form of unemployment, precarious work, and rising wage inequality, thereby creating pressures for state intervention and protection. Pursuing global liberalization while maintaining domestic political support for intervention and protection—the two-level game—is the dilemma that governments in Europe and elsewhere have had to face.

Reconciling the demands of the two-level game is an especially acute problem for Left governments, for the constraints of international economic cooperation often have a dramatic impact on employment, a key concern of Left electoral coalitions. The Left faces the problem of reconciling two conflicting goals, social solidarity and economic efficiency. Ideologically bound to advance the economic interests of the disadvantaged, and even in some cases to transform capitalism itself, Left governments also face market pressures and even real-life capitalists who resist such aims. This problem, of course, has been a perennial one for European social democracy, which from its origins sought to reconcile capitalism and socialism through democratic participation and gradual reform. In this sense, the political challenges of the post-1973 global economy are the latest chapter in a long struggle over basic issues of resource distribution in capitalist societies. As in past economic crises, the question is: Who will bear the costs of capitalism's continual, ineluctable recomposition?

Changes in the world economy in the late twentieth century suggest, however, that the current crisis is not merely another oscillation of the economic cycle but part of a long-term transformation of capitalism itself. According to most observers, there has been a shift not only in economic structures but in the relative power of economic actors. Simply put, capitalist business interests have reinforced their leverage over labor and even over states. It is thus pertinent to ask whether Left governments can claim any distinctiveness of purpose or outcome compared with governments of the Center or Right. In the case of industrial restructuring, we may also ask whether Left governments are still able to fashion a distinctive approach, or are so constrained by the demands of competitive capitalism that their policies can only resemble those of non-Left governments.

One way of thinking about this question is to imagine the possible range of strategic approaches to industrial restructuring. Chapter 1 presented four ideal-type approaches: market-embracing, market-adapting, market-modifying, and market-resisting. It is obvious that the market-embracing approach, which emphasizes rapid market-led adjustment, is antithetical to conventional Left goals such as full employment, job protection, income redistribution, and collective control over investment decisions. The market-adapting approach is certainly more labor friendly than the market-embracing approach, in that it seeks to shield workers from labor market dislocations by relying on early retirement programs, income-support packages, and other measures. The market-adapting approach, however, grants primacy to market-driven adjustment and does not seek, to use the French Socialist phrase of the early 1980s, a "break with capitalism."

The market-modifying and market-resisting approaches, on the other hand, embody central Left themes, although each has potential drawbacks that require trade-offs among various goals. The market-modifying approach, like the market-adapting approach, accepts the basic capitalist framework, but seeks to modify that framework by enhancing organized labor's power within it. In return for labor's cooperation in carrying out adjustment programs, the market-modifying approach grants labor greater control over institutions that regulate labor and capital markets. An example of a market-modifying approach was the 1976 Meidner Plan in Sweden, which proposed a system of collective shareholding whereby workers would gradually gain power over corporate investment decisions.[2] Of the four approaches, however, the most classically Left is the market-resisting approach, which seeks to protect workers' jobs and incomes. But as the current wave of restructuring across Eastern Europe demonstrates, market-resisting job protection schemes that require the use of subsidies divert economic resources from elsewhere and may thus undermine a governing coalition's electoral and organizational cohesion. Moreover, by lowering productivity, the market-resisting approach risks retarding long-term economic growth.

Given the range of approaches to industrial restructuring, the question becomes: How likely is it that Left governments can still pursue strategies that embody goals such as full employment, job security, and enhanced institutional power for labor? An examination of the Socialist governments that recently held power in France and Spain is a promising avenue for addressing this question because both governments possessed three attributes that favored a leftist approach: a desire to reform their societies; a window for reform created by high public expectations at the beginning of their mandates; and longevity.

THE CENTRAL ARGUMENT: A RESTATEMENT

The central aim of this book has been to compare how the Socialist governments of France and Spain confronted the issue of industrial adjustment during the 1980s and early 1990s. The book's two key conclusions are by now familiar enough to need only a brief restatement.

Convergence: A Market-Adapting Approach

By the mid-1980s, Socialist restructuring strategies in France and Spain had converged toward a market-adapting approach. Despite differences in policy instruments and settings, both governments shared a core goal: restoring the market competitiveness of principal firms in key industries. This goal was consistent with a broader macroeconomic policy that sought to transfer income from workers and consumers to the private sector by slowing wage increases and inflation, reducing corporate taxes, and providing fiscal incentives for business investment. Crucial to this policy was the linking of monetary policy to the Exchange Rate Mechanism of the European Monetary System.

For industries facing long-term market shifts, the chief Socialist aim was industrial reconversion, that is, a program encompassing industrial and financial reorganization, technological modernization, and labor force reductions. In Spain, the main instrument for accomplishing this task was an ambitious program that sought to have state, employer, and worker representatives across a wide range of sectors enter into restructuring pacts. Industrial adjustment also meant a drive to improve the INI's performance. In France, the main measure was the 1982 nationalization program that vastly expanded the public industrial sector. In Spain throughout the period of Socialist government, and in France after 1983, state officials encouraged—and even ordered—targeted firms to cut losses, clean up their accounts, improve productivity, and produce profits. For public firms, this necessarily ushered in an era of expanded operational autonomy and privatization (though the latter was partial and selective).

In industries such as steel and automobiles, government-sponsored restructuring plans shared two main aims. First, for private firms such as Peugeot in France and the multinational auto firms in Spain, state officials sought to encourage favorable investment conditions. In France this led to the government's hands-off approach after the Talbot and Citroën affairs of 1983–1984, and in Spain to the government's 1985 investment inducement plan. Second, for public firms such as ENSIDESA, AHV, Usinor Sacilor, Renault, and SEAT, the goal was to break the long-established cycle of operating losses and state subsidies, even if, as in the case of SEAT, this meant privatization. For public firms other than SEAT, the state's requirement that they become profitable spurred efforts to regain domestic market share and expand abroad. Usinor Sacilor and Renault, for example, aggressively sought new markets and alliances in Europe and North America.

Reconversion in the steel, shipbuilding, coal, automobile, textile, and other industries inevitably led to substantial job losses. Not surprisingly, those whose jobs were at risk often resisted, sometimes violently. Yet in the face of worker protests, many led by disillusioned Socialist party members and voters, governments continued to encourage (and even require) firms to align their work forces with market conditions. Workers in restructured industries or firms were rarely fired, however; most were given some sort of income support (such as severance or preretirement payments) or job retraining (as in Usinor Sacilor's use of training-conversion contracts). In brief, Socialist industrial restructuring fostered labor force adjustment according to market-rational criteria while cushioning the impact of displacement on workers.

Compared with the industrial-adjustment approaches of predecessor governments in France and Spain, the approaches followed by the Socialist leaders of those two countries were unprecedented. Whereas the Giscardist and UCD governments of the late 1970s and early 1980s largely failed in their adjustment efforts, the Mitterrand and González governments took sustained, effective measures to strengthen industrial capacity. In a Left version of Nixon's visit to Peking, Socialist leaders sought to channel financial resources to private firms while stimulating investment and profit making—whatever the employment consequences. Earlier conservative governments had shied away from such measures for fear of negative political reaction. But if we turn our attention to the industrial-adjustment approaches being followed elsewhere in Western Europe in the 1980s and early 1990s, the French and Spanish approaches appear unexceptional. Most Western European governments used a similar mix of labor adjustment and worker compensation in their efforts to restore market performance while maintaining workers' living standards.[3]

This market-adapting approach is subject to critiques from both the right and the left. From a right-wing perspective, industrial adjustment in Western Europe (including Socialist France and Spain) was overly soft and lacked free-market rigor. U.S. trade representatives, for example, routinely denounced Western European restructuring as imposing insufficient labor cuts while providing overly generous compensation for workers. Left commentators could be critical as well, arguing that the Western European approach achieved nothing beyond relatively humane treatment for displaced workers. In their view, restructuring failed to challenge the fundamental tenets of a capitalist system based on profit making and perpetual creative destruction. All of these criticisms were justified, for the mainstream Western European approach to adjustment was neither liberal nor socialist, but sought to strike a balance between social solidarity and economic efficiency.

Divergence: Trajectory, Dynamics, Impact

Whereas the first branch of this book's argument emphasizes similarities—the convergence theme—the second branch emphasizes differences. With respect to the latter we find, first, that the trajectory of Spain's adjustment process was more coherent and consistent than France's. With the 1983 white paper serving as a master plan, the González government approached restructuring methodically and holistically, as a central aspect of macroeconomic strategy. In France, on the other hand, restructuring strategy shifted in tandem with the 1982–1983 U-turn in macroeconomic policy. At first, the Mitterrand government sought to stimulate growth *(relance)* and redistribute income while undertaking a state-led adjustment that featured the nationalization of several large industrial firms and nearly all of the banking sector. Conventional adjustment was downplayed or delayed, while expansion of production was encouraged. Abandonment of the *relance* strategy in 1983, however, gave rise to a new restructuring approach that sought to reduce excess capacity and improve productivity, all in the name of restoring international competitiveness.

In the second place, the dynamics of industrial adjustment in France and Spain differed in that the process was more conflictual in Spain. On the whole, Spanish workers resisted adjustment more vigorously than French workers did, and Spanish unions were more mobilized and influential than their French counterparts. Although neither country's labor movement was ultimately able to prevent political leaders from undertaking a market-adapting approach, Spanish labor more strongly shaped the course of decision making, including decisions on "social measures."

Finally, there were national differences in the impact of restructuring, for in conventional economic terms the Mitterrand government's adjustment process was more successful than the process undertaken by the González government. By the mid-1990s, core French industries such as steel and automobiles had become more competitive and less reliant on the state than those of Spain. Despite the fact that the French Socialists displayed less strategic coherence and consistency than was apparent in Spain, French policies facilitated a more thorough restructuring of basic industries.

EXPLAINING THE ARGUMENT

How, then, should we explain these similarities and differences? In attempting this task, we join a central debate in comparative political economy over the determinants of national economic policies. In answer to the question why national leaders adopt particular economic strategies, scholars have stressed many factors, including global economic constraints, state institutional structures, cultural values, political business cycles (the impact of elections on incumbents' fiscal and monetary policies), and the relative power of the main economic actors, business and labor.[4] The approach taken in this book is synthetic and multicausal. The explanatory issue at stake is not the absolute rightness or wrongness of particular variables, but the manner in which these variables combine in particular historical circumstances. As in any multicausal explanation, the question is, what does each variable contribute to the explanation?

This approach begins with the observation that economic policy is largely a function of three types of influences: possibility, will, and pressure. That is, leaders select policies based on what they *can* do, *desire* to do, and are *pressed* to do. As was first discussed in chapter 1, this observation leads us to posit four main explanatory variables: industrial capacity, state capacity, policy paradigm, and the nature of the governing coalition. Although all of these variables help explain the conclusions summarized above, this book has emphasized the role of pressure, particularly pressure emanating from the various elements of governing coalitions. Where the Mitterrand and González governments are concerned, the emphasis on pressure has in turn led to an emphasis on the two central elements of the leaders' governing coalitions, namely the Socialist parties and organized labor. Thus although this book has taken account of international constraints, state structures, key organizing ideas, and other considerations, it has focused most closely on governing coalitions, in particular the structures, resources, and goals of each coalition's constituent units.

This emphasis requires explanation. Public policies are never merely the result of such influences as the international system, institutional structures, and dominant ideologies, however important these may be. Although such factors define the policy space within which governments act, in the final analysis public policies are the product of collective design—the expression of the values and policy preferences of those who govern. These values and policy preferences emerge, in turn, from the internal politics of the governing coalition. The governing coalition, then, strongly influences political leaders' positions on basic issues such as economic and industrial policy. Moreover, a government's ability to carry out its programs depends on the governing coalition's ability to mobilize public support. As both policy shaper and public-opinion mobilizer, the governing coalition is a critical resource for political leaders.

In the French and Spanish cases, the character of the governing coalition was especially important because of the Socialist governments' reform aspirations. Taking office after decades of conservative rule, both French and Spanish Socialists faced strong resistance from individuals, organized groups, and institutions that wished to defend the status quo. In both cases, the nature of the governing coalition—its internal unity and mobilization potential—had a significant impact on the government's ability to execute its proposed reforms.

Explaining Convergence

How do the four variables mentioned above—industrial capacity, state capacity, policy paradigm, and the nature of the governing coalition—explain why

French and Spanish restructuring strategies converged toward a market-adapting approach? A first response to this question is to observe that in both countries a relatively weak industrial capacity limited the economic policy options available to Socialist leaders. As chapter 2 argued, industrial capacity had eroded noticeably by the early 1980s, and early adjustment measures—the Mitterrand government's industrial voluntarism and the González government's reconversion plan—failed to reverse the decline. Many French firms nationalized in 1982 were in dire financial condition, especially Usinor and Sacilor, and even national champions such as Renault were beginning to suffer losses. The condition of Spanish industry was, of course, even worse, because of the nation's legacy of backwardness and protectionism. Thus it is highly doubtful that either government could have sustained either a macroeconomic or an industrial strategy that departed significantly from the fiscally and monetarily restrictive approach favored by other Western European governments during the 1980s. The Mitterrand government's modest attempt to break free of the restrictive approach in 1981–1982 became a harsh lesson in the risks of swimming against the tide.

It is not enough, however, simply to explain why the French and Spanish followed the same path as other Western European governments. It is also necessary to understand how they were able to carry out fairly rigorous restructuring policies, even against often fierce opposition. That understanding draws on three of the variables mentioned above, namely state capacity, policy paradigm, and the nature of the governing coalition. First, both governments possessed significant capacity to act based on their institutional and political authority. In the institutional arena, both governments included powerful executive branches and highly centralized administrative structures that concentrated decision-making authority in the hands of the main economics ministries. In addition, because many of the firms targeted for restructuring were publicly owned, state officials were able to exercise direct control over the adjustment process. In the political arena, strong electoral majorities allowed government officials to gain parliamentary approval for most policy measures. This was clearest in the case of the PSOE's reconversion program, much of which had been attempted, without success, by the UCD. Similarly, the PS's dominance of the French political scene during its first term in office allowed it to reverse the course of its economic and industrial policy in 1982–1984. The PS and PSOE governments, then, had at their disposal only limited industrial-policy options, but had considerable power to execute those options.

The policy paradigm variable—ideas—also played an important role in adjustment. Both governments eventually adhered to the policy paradigm that the French labeled the mixed-economy society—that is, to an economic model that would reconcile market efficiency and an activist state. Central to this framework, as we have seen, was support for the aims and institutions of European integration, in particular the EMS. Although both governments shared the view that long-term national goals were best achieved through a union of European states, their reasons for holding that view differed. For most French leaders, solidarity with the EC flowed from a postwar foreign policy consensus among the major political parties (excluding, of course, the Communists) that construction of a European union was essential for promoting peace and economic growth. Specifically, a union was needed to respond to two external challenges: the possible rebirth of German expansionism and American economic hegemony. The EC, in their eyes, provided a regime for domesticating Germany's militaristic impulses while countering American industrial and financial competition. For Spanish leaders, on the other hand, solidarity with the EC offered the opportunity to fully join Europe after decades of isolation, dictatorship, and economic backwardness. Spanish Socialists believed that progressive change—especially the consolidation of democracy and the promotion of strong capitalist growth—could best be assured by formally associating Spain with its European partners.

Probably the most important variable in both countries, however, was the nature of the governing coalition. Both governing coalitions—PS and PSOE—were unwilling or unable to counteract the constraints of limited industrial capacity by mobilizing decisively in favor of an alternative to a market-adapting approach. For one thing, the parties themselves were unwilling to challenge prevailing orthodoxy. This unwillingness began at the top, where both parties were led by pragmatists, Mitterrand and González, whose commitment to opposing capitalist power was weak. Moreover, both parties rested on elitist membership and leadership structures dominated by middle-strata professionals, in which groups such as industrial workers, rural workers, and unskilled service workers were underrepresented. Missing from higher party structures, in other words, were some of the very groups most affected by restructuring. There was thus little inclination on the part of the two Socialist parties to press for adjustment measures that would depart radically from measures adopted elsewhere.

Moreover, other elements within the governing coalitions were also unable to support an alternative to a market-adapting strategy. Non-Socialist political parties, notably the Communists, were incapable of pressuring the Socialists from the left. In France the PCF was rapidly losing voters, its voter base having shrunk from more than 20 percent of the electorate during the late 1970s to about 10 percent by the mid-1980s. Although the PCF controlled four ministries from 1981 to 1984, it had little impact on economic policy, especially after June 1982. In Spain the PCE was, of course, never included in the governing coalition, and its political influence was negligible in any case. In the 1982 elections, it will be recalled, the PCE's share of the vote plummeted to 4 percent (from 11 percent in 1979), after which internal leadership struggles erupted and caused the party to splinter. The PCE's recomposition and reincarnation, in 1987, as the guiding force in Izquierda Unida helped reverse the Communists' electoral fortunes, but did little to boost their influence, since the PSOE continued, at least until 1993, to preserve its parliamentary majority.

More important, organized labor in both countries was hampered by weak structures, internal divisions, and tenuous relations with Socialist leaders, all of which harmed labor's ability to influence Socialist party and government officials. In France, union membership shrank during the period of Socialist rule to less than 10 percent of eligible workers, the lowest percentage in Western Europe. This was attributable in part to differences of opinion on adjustment strategy. In the cases of steel and automobiles, for example, the main labor confederations, the CGT and the CFDT, held different ideas about the nature of restructuring, and this limited their ability to mobilize workers. The confederations also lacked close ties to the PS, which meant that they had little clout at the upper levels of the party and the government. In Spain, the union movement did enjoy certain advantages over its French counterpart—particularly a stronger membership base, greater interconfederational unity, and stronger ties to the Socialist party—but these were insufficient to deflect the González government from carrying out its market-adapting strategy, despite growing opposition from the CCOO and the UGT.

Two caveats are necessary at this point. First, no claim is being made here that massive worker and union mobilization would have been sufficient to compel the French and Spanish governments to adopt alternative strategies. Even in Sweden, where organized labor's membership base, internal unity, mobilization capacity, and political ties to the government are all strong, the labor movement in recent years has lost influence over key aspects of economic policy. There is little doubt that external constraints, employer resistance, interunion and intraunion divisions, and the conservative tendencies of social-democratic politicians have blunted Swedish labor's reform potential, and the same general trend is visible elsewhere in Western Europe.[5] On the other hand, we can fairly conclude that in France and Spain strong, unified worker mobilization would have been necessary for any attempt at an alternative strategy. Nor should we conclude that organized labor's influence was inconsequential. As is argued below, the labor movements of France and Spain,

despite their weaknesses, did have sufficient mobilizational capacity and political influence to compel governments and employers to offer favorable concessions to workers affected by restructuring.

Explaining Divergence

Trajectory

To explain differences in trajectory, we must account for Spanish consistency
versus French inconsistency in restructuring. Although all four variables played
a role, the nature of the governing coalition in each country was especially
important. Considering, first, industrial capacity, we need to note that although
both countries' core industries displayed important structural weaknesses in
confronting international competition, French industry was stronger, and thus
international constraints weighed less heavily, at least initially, on French Socialists, who could exercise more latitude in managing adjustment. Spanish
Socialists, on the other hand, faced more limited adjustment options. This
difference helps explain the contrast in initial strategies, namely the Mitterrand
government's willingness to take a calculated risk with a policy of stimulation
and redistribution versus the González government's more moderate approach.

State capacity was also stronger in the French case. Through such instruments as public ownership of key firms, financial leverage, and centralized
administrative authority, the French state possessed the capacity both to intervene in and extract itself from various industrial sectors. The Spanish state,
however, did not have such powerful instruments at its disposal. In particular,
Spain's federal structure gave regional officials considerable resources to resist
and deflect decisions made at the center. This difference helps explain the
French state's decided *étatisme* at the outset as well as its ability to reverse
course successfully in 1982–1983. In this sense, French "inconsistency" can
be viewed as a manifestation of the French state's greater capacity.

Although the policy paradigms underlying French and Spanish industrial
restructuring came to resemble one another by the mid-1980s, the manner in
which they developed is important for explaining Spanish consistency and
French inconsistency. In both countries, Socialist Party endorsement of the
pro-European mixed-economy society paradigm came only after fierce internal struggles. The key difference was in the timing of those conflicts. In France
they reached a climax after the Socialists came to power, during the fateful
years 1982–1983; in other words, the French Socialist paradigm shift vis-à-vis
industrial restructuring accompanied a governmental shift in basic economic
strategy. Policy inconsistency, then, was partly the product of PS factional
conflicts that erupted during a period of economic crisis. In Spain, on the

other hand, internal PSOE disputes over the policy paradigm occurred before the party came to power, during the last years of Franco's rule and the period of democratic transition (1972–1979). By the time of the 1982 elections, González and the PSOE were firmly committed to a pro-European policy, which they did not waver from during their tenure.

We can see, then, that the industrial capacity, state capacity, and policy paradigm variables all contributed to trajectory differences. Nevertheless, the critical variable was the nature of the governing coalition. In Spain, the González government's consistency owed much to a governing coalition whose main party, the PSOE, was highly centralized and dominated by ideologically moderate leaders. This was also a party that exercised a strong influence over one of Spain's major labor confederations, the UGT, and rejected alliances with other political formations such as the PCE. For these reasons, the pragmatic González team had the benefit, from the start, of substantial political space to formulate and implement adjustment strategy. The Mitterrand government, however, initially lacked such latitude. As was discussed in chapter 4, its early strategy was strongly influenced by its left-leaning governing coalition, which was shaped by PS factionalism as well as by its PCF alliance strategy. The coalition endorsed a distinctly left-of-center policy paradigm that gave the first years of the Mitterrand government a reformist, even anticapitalist cast. Coalitional differences, we must therefore conclude, are crucial for explaining early differences in the economic and industrial policies of French and Spanish Socialists.

What, then, accounts for France's inconsistency in its approach toward macroeconomic policy and industrial adjustment, namely its 1982–1983 U-turn? The simple answer is: the left-leaning elements in the government coalition lost. This is not to conclude that government leaders simply yielded in the face of *relance*'s discouraging results. Although the choices open to the government became narrower and narrower during the Socialists' first two years in power, the possibility of alternative strategies remained. Socialist leaders weighed the costs and benefits of the alternatives and acted with an awareness of the likely consequences.[6] Yet the internal politics of the governing coalition were such that supporters of *l'autre politique*, notably the CERES, the PCF, and the CGT, became increasingly marginalized, while proponents of *rigueur*, notably Delors, Mauroy, and Fabius, grew in influence.

Dynamics

Spanish workers and unions, as we have learned, were more mobilized and more influential than their French counterparts. Spanish adjustment was distinctive in that it featured a considerable degree of worker opposition but also included the unions in some aspects of decision making. In France, conversely, restructuring was marked by lower levels of worker militancy and union political influence.

The variables of industrial capacity and state capacity help explain this difference. These variables were important because they partially determined the mode or form of restructuring, and therefore the opportunities available to organized labor. As was argued above, Spain's weak industrial and state capacity gave the González government an incentive to approach restructuring holistically and thus to launch a reconversion program that required strong union support. From the outset, unions were invited to participate with state and employer representatives in sectoral negotiations concerning labor-related issues such as work force reductions and compensation for displaced workers. But in France, where industrial and state capacity were stronger, the early Mitterrand government had more latitude in shaping a restructuring strategy. By focusing on *relance,* French Socialist leaders approached restructuring in a more ad hoc fashion, by way of corporate nationalizations and selective interventions. French unions were often consulted informally by the Mitterrand government, but there was no formal mechanism for giving them a place at the negotiating table. Union marginalization was thus virtually built into the French approach.

Reinforcing the variables of industrial capacity and state capacity was what this book has identified as the key variable—the nature of the governing coalition. Simply put, structural differences in Socialist party-union ties gave the Spanish labor movement a stronger mobilization capacity and more political influence than French labor had. Spanish labor, especially during the crucial 1983–1986 phase, made effective use of what can be called an inside-outside alignment. On the inside, the UGT, the PSOE's sister confederation, cooperated with government and employer representatives in the targeted sectors to ensure that there would be satisfactory compensation for affected workers. On the outside, the Communist-affiliated CCOO sponsored a vigorous campaign of grassroots resistance, which in many cases attracted local activists from other unions, including the UGT. Although the inside-outside alignment did not translate into sufficient labor influence to deter the government from adopting a market-adapting approach, it did enable organized labor to delay some restructuring plans (for Sagunto, the AHV works in Sestao, and other facilities) and obtain comparatively generous concessions for affected workers.

In France, by contrast, the labor movement lacked the organizational links and mobilizational capacity of the sort found in Spain. French labor was less integrated into the governing party and the government itself, and less able to mount effective opposition to adjustment measures. This is not to say that French labor was completely excluded from all aspects of restructuring, but as the course of restructuring in the steel industry indicated, organized labor's role was largely one of helping to administer labor adjustment programs such as worker retraining and placement schemes.

Impact

Finally, how do we explain differences in the impact of restructuring, specifically the Mitterrand government's greater success in carrying out its adjustment programs? Again, of the four variables, the nature of the governing coalition was especially important. In the French case, labor's relative weakness and lack of cohesion sapped its capacity to influence the impact of restructuring. Government policy makers thus faced relatively little pressure from their labor support base to move away from market-adapting measures. This, combined with the French state's stronger ability to intervene in and extract itself from particular industrial sectors, meant that the Mitterrand government was less susceptible than the González government to labor pressure.

In Spain, labor's insider influence (through the UGT) and street pressure (mainly from the CCOO) gave it more sway over the restructuring process, enabling it to delay some adjustment measures and to extract relatively generous compensation for laid-off workers. Although the PSOE was able to implement most of its restructuring program by the mid-1990s, many industries, including steel, coal, and shipbuilding, were still plagued by low productivity, excess labor, and operational losses, even after shedding tens of thousands of workers.

CONCLUSION: RESTRUCTURING AND THE MARGINALIZATION OF LABOR

A major lesson of this study—an inevitable one, perhaps, coming from a political scientist—is that economic change is a political as well as a market process. In the case of industrial restructuring, questions of how, when, and to what effect firms and whole industries adjust to shifts in their market environment are strongly affected by political considerations. Government industrial adjustment measures, too, feel the influence of politics. But what political factors matter most, and how do they matter?

Although it has attempted to demonstrate that international markets, industrial infrastructures, government institutions, policy paradigms, and other factors play a role in restructuring, this book has emphasized the importance of the governing coalition. The cases of France and Spain suggest that the mobilizational capacity of the governing coalition is especially critical, for that capacity shapes the nature of political support for or opposition to government policies, and thereby vitally affects the range of adjustment measures that are politically possible. Where Left governments are concerned, the governing coalition's ability to mobilize support or opposition strongly depends on the nature of relations between the dominant party and its allies within organized labor. Thus labor's own mobilizational capacity—its organizational strength as well as its structural ties to top party and government officials—is key to the governing coalition's ability to exert political influence. The labor movement thus stands in a strategic position to affect the course of industrial adjustment.

Having said that, we must also recognize the distinct and growing limits to organized labor's power. What was surprising about the French and Spanish cases was organized labor's increasing marginalization and even exclusion as restructuring progressed. This suggests that governing coalitions, like firms and industries, are the product of structuring actions by their leaders, and can be restructured as well.[7] Both Mitterrand and Gonzalez sought, from 1984–1985 on, to restructure their own governing coalitions so as to separate them from the main labor organizations and render labor increasingly peripheral as a political actor. This was a manifestly political choice, and probably a rational one as far as appealing to the electorate was concerned.

The present argument about labor power can be extended beyond France and Spain. As mentioned above, even in nations such as Sweden, where all-encompassing, centralized unions have cooperated closely with sympathetic social-democratic parties since the 1930s, the ability of organized labor to influence economic and industrial policy has clearly waned in recent years. This can be seen, for example, in the fate of an unambiguously market-modifying reform, the 1976 proposal by Sweden's leading blue-collar labor confederation, the Landsorganisationen (LO), to establish a system of collective shareholding through wage-earner funds (the Meidner Plan). It was hoped that the funds, which were legislatively authorized in 1983, would channel industrial investment in ways that would promote workers' interests, for instance by counteracting the tendency of Swedish multinationals to move production abroad. The funds, however, have fallen far short of their goal, in large measure because of resistance by private businesses and divisions between Social Democratic Party officials.[8] In Sweden and elsewhere, the political resurgence of private capital has tended to undermine Left party-labor ties. Increasingly, Left political leaders act in ways that reinforce their structural dependence on capital.[9]

This growing separation between organized labor and Left parties—a new version of "socialism without workers"—portends a fundamental shift in the historical relationship between these former allies. Clearly a major effect of industrial restructuring under Left auspices has been to make that relationship even more tenuous and problematic. If the immediate past is an accurate guide, the way ahead appears to lead to a future in which Left party-union ties will not be based on any sort of special relationship. Instead, Left parties will probably seek to maximize their space for independent action, while unions will have to rely on bargaining with governments, buttressed by periodic demonstrations of labor's mobilizational capacity. This is not to say that unions have become inconsequential to the ongoing reorganization of capitalism, but that their role is likely to be ever more defensive, their influence ever more contested and contingent on their ability to mobilize workers. The "dirty job" of industrial restructuring thus extends to the labor movement as well, as the movement seeks to restructure its own resources so that it can survive as a contender on increasingly forbidding terrain.

NOTES

INTRODUCTION

1. For an account of this plant closing, with an emphasis on how various members of the community experienced the end of a way of life, see Kathryn Marie Dudley, *The End of the Line: Lost Jobs, New Lives in Postindustrial America* (Chicago: University of Chicago Press, 1994).

2. This book uses the terms *restructuring* and *adjustment* interchangeably. They are defined more fully in chapter 1.

CHAPTER 1. DILEMMAS OF INDUSTRIAL RESTRUCTURING

1. The term "advanced industrial nations" is meant to encompass the members of the Organisation for Economic Co-operation and Development (OECD), of which there were twenty-four in 1993. These nations, some of which also belonged to the Group of Seven (G7) or to the European Union (EU), were the United States (G7), Japan (G7), Canada (G7), Germany (G7, EU), France (G7, EU), United Kingdom (G7, EU), Italy (G7, EU), Belgium (EU), Netherlands (EU), Luxembourg (EU), Ireland (EU), Denmark (EU), Greece (EU), Spain (EU), Portugal (EU), Austria, Finland, Iceland, Norway, Sweden, Switzerland, Turkey, Australia, and New Zealand. In 1994–1996, Mexico, the Czech Republic, Hungary, Poland, and the Republic of Korea also joined the OECD. In 1995, Austria, Sweden, and Switzerland joined the EU, bringing the EU's membership to fifteen nations.

A note on terminology: for clarity's sake, throughout this book the term *European Community (EC)* will generally be used instead of *European Union*. The official adoption of the latter term came in November 1993, upon ratification of the Treaty on European Union (better known as the Maastrict Treaty). Before that date, the official name was the European Communities (or, more simply, the European Community or EC), with three constituent parts: the European Economic Community, the European Coal and Steel Community, and the European Atomic Energy Community (EURATOM). Since most of the events discussed in this book predate 1993, we shall employ the name used concurrently with those events.

2. Consider the following indicators (figures are average annual percentages):

	1960–1973	1974–1995
Real GDP growth		
OECD	4.9	2.6
European Union	4.7	2.2
Consumer price increases		
OECD	3.9	7.8
European Union	4.6	7.9
Unemployment		
OECD	3.2	6.8
European Union	2.4	8.5

Sources: Loukas Tsoukalis, *The New European Economy,* 2nd ed. (New York: Oxford University Press, 1993), 24–26; Organisation for Economic Co-operation and Development, *Economic Outlook* 55 (June 1994) and 62 (December 1997).

3. Analyses of the new global economy, from highly academic to journalistic, are legion. A sampling of useful works includes Robert Gilpin, *The Political Economy of International Relations* (Princeton: Princeton University Press, 1987); Scott Lash and John Urry, *The End of Organized Capitalism* (Madison: University of Wisconsin Press, 1987); Robert Kuttner, *The End of Laissez-Faire: National Purpose and the Global Economy After the Cold War* (New York: Alfred A. Knopf, 1991); Lester Thurow, *Head to Head: The Coming Economic Battle Among Japan, Europe, and America* (New York: William Morrow and Company, 1992); Robert B. Reich, *The Work of Nations: Preparing Ourselves for 21st-Century Capitalism* (New York: Vintage Books, 1992); Martin Carnoy et al., *The New Global Economy in the Information Age: Reflections on Our Changing World* (University Park: Pennsylvania State University Press, 1993); Peter F. Cowhey and Jonathan D. Aronson, *Managing the World Economy: The Consequences of Corporate Alliances* (New York: Council on Foreign Relations, 1993); Richard J. Barnet and John Cavanagh, *Global Dreams: Imperial Corporations and the New World Order* (New York: Simon and Schuster, 1994); William Greider, *One World, Ready or Not: The Manic Logic of Global Capitalism* (New York: Simon and Schuster, 1997).

4. This has been happening for several decades. Among the OECD nations, employment in industrial manufacturing as a percentage of total civilian employment declined from 26 percent to 21 percent between 1960 and 1990, while the service sector's share rose from 43 percent to 63 percent. In terms of value added as a percentage of GDP, manufacturing's share dropped from 30 percent to 22 percent, whereas the service sector's share increased from 52 percent to 65 percent. These figures are based on Organisation for Economic Co-operation and Development, *Historical Statistics, 1960–1990* (Paris: OECD, 1992), 41, 62–63.

The locus classicus of the postindustrial thesis is, of course, Daniel Bell, *The Coming of Post-Industrial Society: A Venture in Social Forecasting* (New York: Basic Books, 1973). See also Reich, *The Work of Nations,* 174–80.

5. A clear statement of this perspective is found in Bruce Nussbaum, *The World After Oil: The Shifting Axis of Power and Wealth* (New York: Simon and Schuster, 1984).

6. See, for example, Michael J. Piore and Charles F. Sabel, *The Second Industrial Divide: Possibilities for Prosperity* (New York: Basic Books, 1984); Roger Boyer and Jean-Pierre Durand, *L'après-fordisme* (Paris: Syros, 1993); Ash Amin, *Post-Fordism: A Reader* (Oxford: Basil Blackwell, 1994).

7. The controversy has focused on three points:

(1) Whereas the postindustrial thesis suggests a zero-sum relationship between services and industrial manufacturing as the former replaces the latter, some commentators argue that manufacturing remains the core economic activity. Services will continue to depend on manufacturing, not only for obvious "downstream" services such as goods distribution, marketing, sales, and maintenance and repair, but also for "upstream" activities including design and engineering, finance and insurance, personnel recruitment and training, and payroll, inventory, and accounting services. Accordingly, "the key generator of wealth for the expanded and differentiated division of labor remains the mastery and control of production": Stephen S. Cohen and John Zysman, *Manufacturing Matters: The Myth of the Post-Industrial Economy* (New York: Basic Books, 1987), 260.

(2) The sunrise-sunset scenario posits the growing prominence of small firms vis-à-vis large ones. Harrison, however, argues that large firms remain more technologically innovative and generate more jobs than small firms because they have adapted their structures and practices to a more competitive environment. Through mergers and acquisitions, "strategic alliances," and adoption of "core-ring network" corporate structures, many large Fordist firms of two decades ago have successfully incorporated and refined post-Fordist practices. See Bennett Harrison, *Lean and Mean: The Changing Landscape of Corporate Power in the Age of Flexibility* (New York: Basic Books, 1994).

(3) The sunset-sunrise thesis often neglects the fact that although personnel and production levels in the older industrial sectors have indeed shrunk, in most cases this has happened *while* those sectors were adopting post-Fordist labor-saving technologies and flexible work processes. A typical example is the European steel industry, which has experienced sharp production and employment declines at the same time as it has raised productivity through the adoption of new technologies and forms of work organization (see chapter 8).

8. See, for example, "Who's in the Driving Seat? A Survey of the World Economy," *The Economist,* 7 October 1995. This is also the consensus of the works cited in note 3.

9. Miriam Golden and Jonas Pontusson, eds., *Bargaining for Change: Union Politics in North America and Europe* (Ithaca: Cornell University Press, 1992); Barnet and Cavanagh, *Global Dreams,* 310–38; Harley Shaiken, *Work Transformed: Automation and Labor in the Computer Age* (New York: Holt, Rinehart and Winston, 1984). For a comprehensive overview that documents a general decline in unionization rates, see Jelle Visser, "The Strength of Union Movements in Advanced Capitalism: Social and Organizational Variations," in Marino Regini, ed., *The Future of Labour Movements* (London: Sage, 1992), 17–52.

10. Frances Fox Piven, ed., *Labor Parties in Postindustrial Societies* (New York: Oxford University Press, 1992); Herbert Kitschelt, *The Transformation of European Social Democracy* (Cambridge: Cambridge University Press, 1994); Jonas Pontusson, "Explaining the Decline of European Social Democracy: The Role of Structural Economic Change," *World Politics* 47, no. 4 (July 1995): 495–533; Ronald Inglehart, *Culture Shift in Advanced Industrial Societies* (Princeton: Princeton University Press, 1990), ch. 8.

11. See Vincent Wright, "Conclusion: The State and Major Enterprises in Western Europe: Enduring Complexities," in Jack Hayward, ed., *Industrial Enterprise and European Integration: From National to International Champions in Western Europe* (Oxford: Oxford University Press, 1995), 335–40.

12. Edward N. Wolff, "International Comparisons of Personal Wealth Inequality," paper presented at the 23rd General Conference of the International Association for Research in Income and Wealth, St. Andrews, New Brunswick, Canada, 21–27 August 1994; Frank Levy and Richard Murnane, "Earnings Levels and Earnings Inequality," *Journal of Economic Literature* 30 (September 1992): 1331–81; Gordon Green, John Coder, and Paul Ryscavage, "International Comparisons of Earnings Inequality for Men in the 1980s," *Review of Income and Wealth* 38 (March 1992): 1–16; Bennett Harrison and Barry Bluestone, "Wage Polarization in the U.S. and the 'Flexibility' Debate," *Cambridge Journal of Economics* 14 (September 1990): 351–73.

13. See, for example, Gilpin, *The Political Economy of International Relations*. In reaction to new business patterns and the nation-state's decline, political officials at both the subnational (regional) and supranational levels have sought to extend economic regulatory authority in the public sphere.

14. See, for example, Wayne Sandholtz et al., *The Highest Stakes: The Economic Foundations of the Next Security System* (New York: Oxford University Press, 1992); Laura D. Tyson, *Who's Bashing Whom? Trade Conflict in High-Technology Industries* (Washington, D.C.: Institute for International Economics, 1992); Hayward, ed., *Industrial Enterprise and European Integration*.

15. Michael J. Trebilcock, Marsha A. Chandler, and Robert Howse, *Trade and Transitions: A Comparative Analysis of Adjustment Policies* (London: Routledge, 1990), 119–20.

16. In other words, parties commonly referred to as socialist, social-democratic, or labor parties.

17. As Scharpf comments, "Despite all the differences of interest among their constituents, [social-democratic governments] all remain committed to one priority above all other goals of economic and social policy: for them, the achievement and maintenance of full employment ranks first, above increasing real incomes or other distributional goals (and, of course, above the maintenance of price stability or of reducing the public sector deficit)": Fritz W. Scharpf, *Crisis and Choice in European Social Democracy* (Ithaca: Cornell University Press, 1991), 15.

18. Adam Przeworski, *Capitalism and Social Democracy* (Cambridge: Cambridge University Press, 1985).

19. Ibid., 29.

20. Mark Kesselman, "How Should One Study Economic Policy-Making? Four Characters in Search of an Object," *World Politics* 44, no. 4 (July 1992): 645.

21. A seminal contribution to this large literature is Francis G. Castles, ed., *The Impact of Parties: Politics and Policies in Democratic Capitalist States* (Beverly Hills: Sage, 1982).

22. See, for example, Douglas A. Hibbs, "Political Parties and Macroeconomic Policy," *American Political Science Review* 71, no. 4 (December 1977): 1467–87; Philippe C. Schmitter, "Interest Intermediation and Regime Governability in Contemporary Western Europe and North America," in Suzanne Berger, ed., *Organizing Interests in Western Europe: Pluralism, Corporatism, and the Transformation of Politics* (Cambridge: Cambridge University Press, 1981), 285–327; David R. Cameron, "Social Democracy, Corporatism, Labour Quiescence and the Representation of Economic Interest in Advanced Capitalist Society," in John H. Goldthorpe, ed., *Order and Conflict in Contemporary Capitalism* (Oxford: Clarendon Press, 1984), 143–78; James E. Alt,

"Political Parties, World Demand, and Unemployment: Domestic and International Sources of Economic Activity," *American Political Science Review* 79, no. 4 (December 1985): 1016–40; Peter J. Katzenstein, *Small States in World Markets: Industrial Policy in Europe* (Ithaca: Cornell University Press, 1985); Alexander Hicks, "Social Democratic Corporatism and Economic Growth," *Journal of Politics* 50, no. 3 (August 1988): 677–704; Geoffrey Garrett and Peter Lange, "Government Performance and Economic Performance: When and How Does 'Who Governs' Matter?" *Journal of Politics* 51, no. 3 (August 1989): 676–93. For a contrary view, see Robert W. Jackman, "The Politics of Economic Growth in the Industrial Democracies, 1974–80: Leftist Strength or North Sea Oil?" *Journal of Politics* 49, no. 1 (February 1987): 242–56.

23. Scharpf, *Crisis and Choice in European Social Democracy,* 9. A partial exception to the thesis of corporatism's decline is made by Crepaz, who argues that corporatist patterns still engender lower levels of inflation, unemployment, and work place conflict. In support of Scharpf, however, Crepaz finds that corporatism does not correlate with higher growth. See Markus M. L. Crepaz, "Corporatism in Decline? An Empirical Analysis of the Impact of Corporatism on Macroeconomic Performance and Industrial Disputes in 18 Industrialized Democracies," *Comparative Political Studies* 25, no. 2 (July 1992): 139–68.

24. Geoffrey Garrett and Peter Lange, "Political Responses to Interdependence: What's 'Left' for the Left?" *International Organization* 45, no. 4 (autumn 1991): 546–47.

25. An exception is Bo Strath, *The Politics of De-industrialization: The Contraction of the West European Shipbuilding Industry* (London: Croom Helm, 1987).

26. To be precise, this book's coverage extends from 1981 to 1993 for France and from 1982 to 1996 for Spain. In France, François Mitterrand was elected president in 1981, reelected in 1988, and served until May 1995. During the first twelve years of his presidency (through the 1993 legislative elections, which the Right won decisively), his Parti Socialiste (PS) controlled parliament in all but two years (1986–1988). In Spain, Felipe González and the Partido Socialista Obrero Español (PSOE) won four consecutive elections (1982, 1986, 1989, and 1993), albeit with steadily declining margins. In the March 1996 elections, the PSOE was defeated by the conservative Popular Party, after nearly fourteen years in office.

27. In France from 1971 to 1991, for example, manufacturing's share of the total wage-earning and salaried work force declined from 46 percent to 32 percent, while the service sector's share rose from 51 percent to 67 percent. In Spain during the same period, manufacturing employment as a proportion of total employment dropped from 49 percent to 38 percent, while the service sector saw a rise from 38 percent to 57 percent. In terms of absolute numbers, the size of the work force in both nations increased about 15 percent from 1971 to 1991, but the number of workers in manufacturing shrank by 19 percent in France and 17 percent in Spain. In the French service sector, however, the number of workers increased by 52 percent; in Spain the increase was 60 percent. See Organisation for Economic Co-operation and Development, *Labor Force Statistics, 1971–1991* (Paris: OECD, 1993), 226–27, 382–83.

28. John T. S. Keeler, "Opening the Window for Reform: Mandates, Crises, and Extraordinary Policy-Making," *Comparative Political Studies* 25, no. 4 (January 1993): 433–86.

29. As is the case with ideal types in general, the ones proposed here are not meant to be empirically descriptive of any particular government. In practice,

governments can be expected, first, to combine elements of these four approaches, and second, to vary over time in the weight they give to each.

30. See, for example, Daniel Singer, *Is Socialism Doomed? The Meaning of Mitterrand* (New York: Oxford University Press, 1988); James Petras, "Spanish Socialism: The Politics of Neoliberalism," in James Kurth and James Petras, eds., *Mediterranean Paradoxes: Politics and Social Structure in Southern Europe* (Providence: Berg Publishers, 1993), 95–127.

31. This is not to deny that in certain sectors, such as steel and coal, the French and Spanish governments frequently pressured their EC partners to permit the continued existence of subsidies and excess capacity, or at least to postpone their phasing out, in the name of "orderly reductions."

32. On France, see, for example, Howard Machin and Vincent Wright, eds., *Economic Policy and Policy-Making Under the Mitterrand Presidency* (New York: St. Martin's Press, 1985); John S. Ambler, ed., *The French Socialist Experiment* (Philadelphia: Institute for the Study of Human Issues, 1986); Peter A. Hall, *Governing the Economy: The Politics of State Intervention in Britain and France* (Oxford: Polity Press, 1986); George Ross et al., eds., *The Mitterrand Experiment: Continuity and Change in Modern France* (Oxford: Polity Press, 1987); Singer, *Is Socialism Doomed?;* Anthony Daley, ed., *The Mitterrand Era: Policy Alternatives and Political Mobilization in France* (New York: New York University Press, 1996); Vivien A. Schmidt, *From State to Market?: The Transformation of French Business and Government* (Cambridge: Cambridge University Press, 1996); Jonah Levy, *Tocqueville's Revenge: Dilemmas of Institutional Reform in Post-Dirigiste France* (Cambridge: Harvard University Press, forthcoming).

Among the few works on González's Spain are Donald Share, *Dilemmas of Social Democracy: The Spanish Socialist Workers Party in the 1980s* (New York: Greenwood Press, 1989); José María Maravall, "Politics and Policy: Economic Reforms in Southern Europe," in L. C. Bresser Pereira et al., *Economic Reforms in the New Democracies: A Social-Democratic Approach* (Cambridge: Cambridge University Press, 1993), 77–131; Petras, "Spanish Socialism."

33. See W. Rand Smith, "International Economy and State Strategies: Recent Work in Comparative Political Economy," *Comparative Politics* 25, no. 3 (April 1993): 351–72.

34. See, for example, Gabriel A. Almond, "Review Article: The International-National Connection," *British Journal of Political Science* 19, no. 2 (April 1989): 237–59; Peter A. Gourevitch, "The Second Image Reversed: The International Sources of Domestic Politics," *International Organization* 32 (autumn 1978): 881–911.

35. See, for example, Peter Gourevitch, *Politics in Hard Times: Comparative Responses to International Economic Crises* (Ithaca: Cornell University Press, 1986).

36. The seminal work on this issue is Peter J. Katzenstein, ed., *Between Power and Plenty: Foreign Economic Policies of Advanced Industrial States* (Madison: University of Wisconsin Press, 1978). Katzenstein's series, Cornell Studies in Political Economy, has published several important works in this vein, including John Zysman, *Governments, Markets, and Growth: Financial Systems and the Politics of Industrial Change* (Ithaca: Cornell University Press, 1983); Peter J. Katzenstein, *Small States in World Markets: Industrial Policy in Europe* (Ithaca: Cornell University Press, 1985); Gourevitch, *Politics in Hard Times*; G. John Ikenberry, *Reasons of State: Oil Politics and the Capacities of American Government* (Ithaca: Cornell University Press, 1988); Stephen Haggard,

Pathways from the Periphery: The Politics of Growth in the Newly Industrializing Countries (Ithaca: Cornell University Press, 1990); Jeffrey A. Hart, *Rival Capitalists: International Competitiveness in the United States, Japan, and Western Europe* (Ithaca: Cornell University Press, 1992). Other important studies include Hall, *Governing the Economy,* and Peter Evans, *Embedded Autonomy: States and Industrial Transformation* (Princeton: Princeton University Press, 1995).

37. Representatives of the statist approach include Eric A. Nordlinger, *On the Autonomy of the Democratic State* (Cambridge: Harvard University Press, 1981); Michael Mann, "The Autonomous Power of the State: Its Origins, Mechanisms, and Results," *Archives Européenes de Sociologie* 25 (1984): 185–213; Peter B. Evans, Dietrich Rueschemeyer, and Theda Skocpol, eds., *Bringing the State Back In* (Cambridge: Cambridge University Press, 1985). For critiques of this approach, see Gabriel A. Almond, "The Return to the State," *American Political Science Review* 82, no. 3 (September 1988): 853–74, and Paul Cammack, "Review Article: Bringing the State Back In?" *British Journal of Political Science* 19, no. 2 (April 1989): 261–90.

38. This literature is far too voluminous to cite here. Classic works in the pluralist-elitist dispute include Robert Dahl's early writings as well as the writings of C. Wright Mills, Floyd Hunter, and Nelson Polsby. The key debate within the Marxist tradition was that between Ralph Miliband and Nicos Poulantzas during the 1970s.

39. Jonas Pontusson, "From Comparative Public Policy to Political Economy: Putting Political Institutions in Their Place and Taking Interests Seriously," *Comparative Political Studies* 28, no. 1 (April 1995): 120. Pontusson's provocative essay is the source of the distinction between economic-structural and political-institutional variables.

40. This formulation is an expansion on Peter Hall's statement that "national economic policy is influenced most significantly, first, by what a government is *pressed* to do, and secondly, by what it *can* do in the economic sphere. To a large extent, the former defines what is possible": Hall, *Governing the Economy,* 232.

41. Glenn R. Fong, "State Strength, Industry Structure, and Industrial Policy: American and Japanese Experiences in Microelectronics," *Comparative Politics* 22, no. 3 (April 1990): 276.

42. This distinction is developed extensively in Katzenstein, ed., *Between Power and Plenty.*

43. It can be persuasively argued that there are other important possible sources of societal pressure, notably groups and interests lying *outside* the governing coalition. The argument is that such outside groups can influence the government as much or more than elements of the governing coalition, because the latter have nowhere else to go, whereas outsiders not only have another political home but may have the inclination and resources to create significant opposition if they are made to feel aggrieved. Applied to the study of social-democratic governments, this logic suggests that we should pay particular attention to governmental relations with organized business groups, especially employers' associations, whose relations with governments are often problematic. This book's response to that argument is simple: such an approach is perfectly justifiable, but it is not the one chosen here. This book focuses on intracoalitional relations because I am is interested in how social-democratic governments manage the tensions created by having to respond not only to market imperatives but also to demands coming from their base of political support-

ers. This is not to say that employers or employers' associations are ignored here, but simply that in the present analysis government-employer relations are less crucial than government-labor relations.

44. Peter A. Hall, "Policy Paradigms, Social Learning, and the State: The Case of Economic Policymaking in Britain," *Comparative Politics* 25, no. 3 (April 1993): 279.

45. See especially Hugh Heclo, *Modern Social Politics in Britain and Sweden* (New Haven: Yale University Press, 1974); Margaret Weir and Theda Skocpol, "State Structures and the Possibilities for 'Keynesian' Responses to the Great Depression in Sweden, Britain, and the United States," in Evans et al., eds., *Bringing the State Back In*, 107–68.

46. Although works in this tradition follow different paths, they are all concerned with the processes by which groups of people mobilize as collective actors through developing shared identities and modes of action. This research tradition is also concerned with the political and economic consequences of such mobilization. See Charles Tilly, *From Mobilization to Revolution* (Reading, Mass: Addison-Wesley, 1978); Garrett and Lange, "Government Performance and Economic Performance"; Walter Korpi, *The Democratic Class Struggle* (New York: Routledge, Chapman, and Hall, 1983); John D. Stephens, *The Transition from Capitalism to Socialism* (Urbana: University of Illinois Press, 1986); Sidney Tarrow, *Power in Movement: Social Movements, Collective Action and Politics* (Cambridge: Cambridge University Press, 1994), among other works.

CHAPTER 2. FAILING TO ADJUST

1. The best overall account of Franco's rule is Paul Preston, *Franco: A Biography* (New York: Basic Books, 1993). For a reliable analysis of the regime's autarchic economic policies, see Eduardo Merigó, "Spain," in Andrea Boltho, ed., *The European Economy: Growth and Crisis* (New York: Oxford University Press, 1982), 554–80.

2. From 1959 to 1973 the number of tourists visiting Spain each year increased from 4.2 million to 34.6 million. During the same period, over 1.5 million Spaniards left the country to work in France, Germany, Switzerland, and elsewhere. Direct foreign investment as a percentage of gross fixed-capital investment rose from 3.2 percent to 6.1 percent. Especially important was the growing presence of foreign multinational firms, which by 1974 had majority control over 120 of the nation's 500 largest industrial firms and some degree of investment in another 80 firms. Imports of goods and services increased from 7 percent to 19 percent of GDP, while exports rose from 10 percent to 14 percent of GDP. See Joseph Harrison, *The Spanish Economy in the Twentieth Century* (New York: St Martin's Press, 1985), 155 (on tourism); Richard Gunther, Giacomo Sani, and Goldie Shabad, *Spain After Franco: The Making of a Competitive Party System* (Berkeley: University of California Press, 1988), 27 (on labor emigration); Oscar Bajo and Angel Torres, "La integración española en la CE y sus effectos sobre el sector exterior," *Información comercial española* 708–09 (August–September 1992): 34 (on foreign investment); Charles W. McMillion, "International Integration and Intra-national Disintegration: The Case of Spain," *Comparative Politics* 13, no. 3 (April 1981): 296–98 (on foreign investment); Organisation for Economic Co-operation and Development, *Historical Statistics, 1960–1990* (Paris: OECD, 1992), 71–72 (on trade).

3. Consider, for example, the balance of payments of the following items (figures are annual averages, in millions of U.S. dollars):

	1960–62	1963–69	1970–73	1960–73
Trade	–287	–1,580	–2,333	–1,518
Travel (net)	348	1,016	2,131	1,191
Emigrants' remittances	109	312	652	366
Current balance	222	–328	516	31
Foreign investment (direct, portfolio, and real estate)	48	237	761	346

Source: Merigó, "Spain," 568.

4. Pere Escorsa, Federico Garriga, and Manuel Rajadell, "La especialización internacional de la industria española (1963–1988)," *Papeles de economía española* 56 (1993): 264.

5. Ramón Tamames, *Introducción a la economía española,* 20th ed. (Madrid: Alianza Editorial, 1992), 193.

6. According to Tamames, whereas most developed countries invested about 4 percent of their GDP in research and development, Spain invested only 0.7 percent: ibid., 196.

7. From 1960 to 1973 Spain's average annual GDP growth was 7.1 percent, compared with 4.8 percent for the OECD's European nations. Yet inflation was 6.8 percent, compared with 4.8 percent for the OECD's European nations. See Organisation for Economic Co-operation and Development, *Economic Outlook* 29 (July 1981).

8. For example, from 1960 to 1972 over 70 percent of all foreign investments went to the three regions mentioned. See McMillion, "International Integration and Intra-national Disintegration," 299–301.

9. José María Maravall, *The Transition to Democracy in Spain* (New York: St. Martin's Press, 1982), 123–24. See also Gunther, Sani, and Shabad, *Spain After Franco,* 26.

10. Maravall, *Transition to Democracy in Spain,* 127; Organisation for Economic Co-operation and Development, *Economic Outlook* 43 (June 1988): 183.

11. For example, as late as 1977 the average firm had only eleven employees, whereas in the early 1960s average firm size in such countries as West Germany (seventeen employees), the Netherlands (twenty-seven), and Belgium (twenty-seven) was already considerably higher. See Sama Lieberman, *The Contemporary Spanish Economy: A Historical Perspective* (London: George Allen & Unwin, 1982), 305.

12. José María Maravall, *Dictadura y disentimiento político* (Madrid: Alfaguara, 1978).

13. Paul Preston, *The Triumph of Democracy in Spain* (London: Methuen, 1986), 25–27.

14. Julio Segura and Arturo González Romero, "La industria española: Evolución y perspectivas," *Papeles de economía española* 50 (1992): 164.

15. Whereas direct foreign investment accounted for an annual average of 2.6 percent of gross fixed-capital formation during the 1965–1974 period, that figure declined to 1.8 percent in 1975–1979—at a time when domestic and foreign invest-ment was declining in real terms. And whereas Spain experienced net labor

emigration during the 1960s, after 1973 it witnessed a net annual immigration of over 40,000 individuals. Returning immigrants not only cut the volume of remittances (and thus aggravated the current accounts deficit), but also added to the domestic unemployment rolls. See Lieberman, *The Contemporary Spanish Economy,* 271, 319.

16. In the mid-1970s Spain depended on crude oil, virtually all of which was imported, for 72 percent of its primary energy consumption, whereas the EC average was 57 percent. Energy imports represented 13 percent of total imports in 1973, but by 1981 that percentage had risen to 42 percent. The cost of energy imports in 1981 was more than *seventeen* times as great as the cost in 1973. See ibid., 282–83; Harrison, *The Spanish Economy in the Twentieth Century,* 171.

17. Lively English-language accounts of this transitional period are found in Preston, *The Triumph of Democracy in Spain;* David Gilmour, *The Transformation of Spain: From Franco to the Constitutional Monarchy* (London: Quartet Books, 1985); Robert Graham, *Spain: A Nation Comes of Age* (New York: St. Martin's Press, 1984).

18. Lieberman, *The Contemporary Spanish Economy,* 275.

19. For example, 1978 wages and prices were to rise no more than 22 percent, versus an annualized rate of over 30 percent during the second half of 1977. For a general treatment of the pacts, see Angel Zaragoza, ed., *Pactos sociales, sindicatos, y patronal en España* (Madrid: Siglo Veintiuno Editores, 1988).

20. In 1980 the Interconfederal Framework Agreement was signed by the CEOE and the UGT. It was extended in 1981. In 1982 the National Agreement on Employment was signed by the government, the CEOE, UGT, and CCOO. For a description of these pacts, see Juan Ignacio Palacio Morena, "Relaciones laborales y ajuste industrial," in Jean Velarde et al., eds., *La industria española: Recuperación, estructura, y mercado de trabajo* (Madrid: Economistas Libros, 1990), 421–43.

21. Victor Pérez-Díaz, *The Return of Civil Society: The Emergence of Democratic Spain* (Cambridge: Harvard University Press, 1993), 224–25.

22. See Joe Foweraker, "Corporatist Strategies and the Transition to Democracy in Spain," *Comparative Politics* 20, no. 1 (October 1987): 57–72.

23. These trends are indicated by the following figures (annual percentage changes from previous year):

	1978	1979	1980	1981	1982
1. Consumer prices	19.8	5.7	15.6	14.6	14.4
2. Increase in contractual wages	20.6	4.1	15.3	13.3	12.0
(line 2/line 1)	(1.04)	(.90)	(.98)	(.91)	(.83)
3. Increase in actual wages (line 3/line 1)	25.4	2.5	16.1	15.4	14.0
	(1.28)	(1.43)	(1.03)	(1.05)	(.97)

Source: Organisation for Economic Co-operation and Development, *Economic Surveys: Spain,* various years.

24. Joaquín López Novo and P. L. Inso, "Social Pacts in Spain," unpublished paper, Instituto Juan March de Estudios Avanzados, Madrid, n.d., 4.

25. From 1974 to 1982, Spanish government expenditures (total government outlays as a percentage of GDP) increased from 23.1 percent to 37.5 percent, whereas

the average for OECD nations in Europe grew much less rapidly (from 40.4 percent to 49.1 percent). See Organisation for Economic Co-operation and Development, *Economic Outlook* 52 (December 1992): 215.

26. Pérez-Díaz, *The Return of Civil Society,* 224; Julio Alcaide Inchausti, "El gasto público en la democracia española: Los hechos," *Papeles de economía española* 37 (1988): 2–41.

27. Several factors have been viewed as responsible for French postwar growth, including:

(1) Physical determinants such as capital formation and the size and quality of the work force (for example, the availability of plentiful labor reserves from a large agricultural sector): see, among other studies, Jean-Jacques Carré et al., *Abrégé de la croissance française* (Paris: Seuil, 1973); François Caron, *An Economic History of Modern France* (New York: Columbia University Press, 1979).

(2) Changes in market conditions, in particular exposure to international competition and domestic deregulation, which sparked competition, investment, and growth: see William James Adams, *Restructuring the French Economy: Government and the Rise of Market Competition Since World War II* (Washington, D.C.: Brookings Institution, 1989).

(3) Cultural-attitudinal change, especially a new public consensus favoring innovation and growth: see Charles L. Kindleberger, "The Postwar Resurgence of the French Economy," in Stanley Hoffmann, ed., *In Search of France* (Cambridge: Harvard University Press, 1963), 118–58.

(4) New patterns of government economic regulation, including "indicative planning": see note 29 below.

28. John Zysman, *Political Strategies for Industrial Order: State, Market, and Industry in France* (Berkeley: University of California Press, 1977), 63.

29. The literature on planning is enormous. See, for example, Andrew Shonfield, *Modern Capitalism: The Changing Balance of Public and Private Power* (London: Oxford University Press, 1965); John A. MacArthur and Bruce R. Scott, *Industrial Planning in France* (Cambridge: Harvard Graduate School of Business Administration, 1969); Stephen S. Cohen, *Modern Capitalist Planning: The French Model* (Berkeley: University of California Press, 1977); Richard F. Kuisel, *Capitalism and the State in Modern France: Renovation and Economic Management in the Twentieth Century* (Cambridge: Cambridge University Press, 1981); Pierre Bauchet, *Le plan dans l'économie française* (Paris: Presses de la Fondation Nationale des Sciences Politiques & Economica, 1986); Henri Rousso, *De Monnet à Massé: Enjeux politiques et objectifs économiques dans le cadre des quartre premiers plans (1946–65)* (Paris: Editions du Centre Nationale de la Recherche Scientifique, 1986).

30. André Gauron, *Histoire économique et sociale de la Cinquième République,* vol. 1, *Le temps des modernistes* (Paris: La Découverte/Maspero, 1983), 85–94, 132–52; Suzanne Berger, "Lame Ducks and National Champions: Industrial Policy in the Fifth Republic," in William G. Andrews and Stanley Hoffman, eds., *The Fifth Republic at Twenty* (Albany: State University of New York Press, 1981), 295.

31. Bernard Soulage and S.-P. Thiery, "Quelles institutions pour une nouvelle politique industrielle?" *Revue d'économie industrielle* 23 (1983): 79–91; Peter A. Hall, *Governing the Economy: The Politics of State Intervention in Britain and France* (Oxford: Polity Press, 1986), 168; Ezra N. Suleiman, *Elites in French Society: The Politics of Survival* (Princeton: Princeton University Press, 1978), ch. 9.

32. Serge Berstein, *La France de l'expansion,* vol. 1, *La république gaullienne, 1958–1969* (Paris: Seuil, 1989), 271–72.

33. By one estimate, in the mid-1970s the majority of French MNCs—thirty-nine out of a sample of sixty-seven—were cutting back employment in France, and even those MNCs that were increasing employment in France were expanding employment abroad more rapidly: Julien Savary, *French Multinationals* (London: Pinter Publishers, 1984), 131. On the neglect of small firms, see Michel Delattre, "Les PME face aux grandes entreprises," *Économie et statistique* 148 (October 1982): 15.

34. Christian Stoffaës, "La France dans la compétition industrielle mondiale," in Michel Cicurel et al., *Une économie mondiale* (Paris: Pluriel, 1985), 276; Berger, "Lame Ducks and National Champions," 299; Gauron, *Histoire économique et sociale de la Cinquième République,* 1:141–44.

35. For example, according to a World Bank study, state financial assistance to the private sector—from targeted sectoral aid to funds for research and development, regional development, and export promotion—accounted for over *one-fifth* of private industrial investment in 1975. See Bernard Bobe, *Public Assistance to Industries and Trade Policy in France,* World Bank Staff Working Papers, no. 570 (Washington, D.C.: World Bank, 1983), 16.

36. Certainly one of the main reasons for the poor economic performance of many of the state-directed *grands projets* such as the Concorde and the Plan Calcul was that their *raison d'être* was rooted in *raison d'état* (especially strategic military or national prestige considerations) rather than market reasoning. See Berger, "Lame Ducks and National Champions," 294.

37. Consider the penetration ratios for the following sectors (figures are imports as a percentage of total domestic market in the corresponding sector; in 1970 prices):

	1959	1969	1979
Agriculture	12.9	12.4	14.7
Energy	16.3	17.7	18.8
Food products (IAA)	4.8	7.7	12.3
Industry	8.2	19.0	33.7
Services	7.1	6.8	6.9
All sectors	5.4	8.9	13.6

Source: B. Camus, *La crise du système productif* (Paris: Institut National de la Statistique et des Études Économiques, 1981), 173.

38. Interview with the author, March 10, 1987.

39. This Big Three deficit ballooned from Fr 15.9 billion in 1973 to Fr 55.0 billion in 1981. (Calculated on "CIF-FOB" basis, which, for imports, includes the cost of the goods, the costs of insuring them, and freight charges, and, for exports, the cost of the goods only. This method is commonly used in measuring international trade.) See Jacques Mazier, "Les impasses du redéploiement industriel," *Les cahiers français* 211 (May–June 1983): 25.

40. J. Nguyen Duy-Tan, *Le commerce extérieur de la France* (Paris: La Documentation Française, 1986), 22.

41. The following are the trade balances with selected countries and areas for the "consumer and household equipment goods" sector from 1973 to 1981 (figures are in billions of francs, calculated on CIF-FOB basis; see note 39):

	1973	1979	1980	1981
West Germany	1.0	–0.1	–0.2	–1.5
United States	0.4	–1.2	–2.9	–1.5
Japan	0.2	–0.9	–1.7	–2.9
OECD	1.7	–2.9	–5.3	–4.6
OPEC	1.1	3.1	4.4	5.7
Third World (excluding OPEC)	1.8	0.0	–1.0	–1.0
Total	4.2	–8.9	–12.6	–12.0

Source: Xavier Greffe, "Les entreprises publiques dans la politique de l'état," *Revue économique* 34, no. 3 (May 1983): 503 (based on figures published by the French customs authority).

42. Ibid., 503.

43. Mazier, "Les impasses du redéploiement industriel," 25.

44. Organisation for Economic Co-operation and Development, *Economic Surveys: France* (Paris: OECD, 1984), 38. The OECD's summary was based on an analysis by Michel Delattre, who defined "least competitive" products as those in which France's export/import ratio was less than 0.8, and "most competitive" as those in which the ratio exceeded 1.2.

45. See François de Combret, "Le redéploiement industriel," *Les cahiers français* 212 (July–September 1983): 8–12. De Combret was Giscard's technical adviser.

46. One obvious inconsistency arose from the different economic strategies followed by Giscard's two prime ministers, Jacques Chirac (1974–1976) and Raymond Barre (1976–1981). Whereas Chirac generally followed a stimulatory macroeconomic policy in the wake of the 1973 oil shock, Barre followed a much more restrictive approach. This analysis focuses on the Barre period.

47. Jonas Pontusson, "Apropos Mitterrand: State Power, Class Coalitions, and Electoral Politics in Postwar France," *Kapitalistate* 9 (1981): 131.

48. Diana Green, "Strategic Management and the State: France," in Kenneth Dyson and Stephen Wilks, eds., *Industrial Crisis: Comparative Study of the State and Industry* (Oxford: Martin Robertson, 1983), 167; J. Paul Horne, "France's Liberal Revolution—An Assessment," *European Report* (Paris: Smith, Barney, Harris, Upham, and Co., 1980).

49. Elie Cohen and Michel Bauer, *Les grandes manoeuvres industrielles* (Paris: Belfond, 1985), 265.

50. André Gauron, *Histoire économique et sociale de la Cinquième République,* vol. 2, *Années de rêves, années de crises (1970–1981)* (Paris: Editions la Découverte, 1988), 83.

51. Green, "Strategic Management and the State," 172.

52. The CIASI was created in 1974 to rescue firms that were basically efficient but experiencing temporary difficulties, especially lack of capital. See Elie Cohen, *L'État brancardier: Politiques du déclin industriel (1974–1984)* (Paris: Calmann-Lévy, 1989) and A. Burlaud et al., *Approche systematique des relations état-industrie: La relation d'aide* (Paris: Groupe École Supérieure de Commerce de Paris, 1984). The FSAI, created in 1978, sought to assist the redeployment process in regions severely affected by recession and plant closures. See Green, "Strategic Management and the State," 178–79. These committees represented a new type of structure that aimed to establish tighter industrial-policy coordination of such institutions as the national planning

commission (CGP), the regional economic planning agency (DATAR), the treasury, the Labor and Industry ministries, the Banque de France, and the prime minister's staff.

53. The committees declared, for example, that no more than 20 percent of any investment could come from public funds; the other portion had to be provided by private investors. See Berger, "Lame Ducks and National Champions," 305.

54. Green, "Strategic Management and the State," 177.

55. Berger, "Lame Ducks and National Champions," 292–310.

56. The two interministerial committees were the Comité Interministériel pour le Développement Industriel et le Soutien de l'Emploi (CIDISE), which provided risk capital for "dynamic" small and medium-sized companies, and the Comité Interministériel pour le Développement des Industries Stratégiques (CODIS), whose mission was to guide the "strategic" industries of the coming decades. The six priority sectors, to be financed through CODIS, were underwater exploration, automation of office procedures, consumer electronics, robots, bioindustry, and energy-saving equipment. CODIS attempted to identify firms capable of becoming world leaders, which were then encouraged to sign three- to four-year "development contracts" with CODIS specifying performance targets (such as for exports) in exchange for state aid. See Green, "Strategic Management and the State," 181.

57. Vincent Wright, "Socialism and the Interdependent Economy: Industrial Policy-making Under the Mitterrand Presidency," *Government and Opposition* 19 (1984): 292–93.

58. Green, "Strategic Management and the State," 169.

59. Organisation for Economic Co-operation and Development, *Economic Surveys: France* (Paris: OECD, 1984), 48.

60. M. Boeda, "Les comptes de la nation de l'année 1980," *Économie et statistique* 135 (July–August 1981): 48.

61. Investment rates (that is, investment as a percentage of value added) for 1973 and 1980 for the various industrial sectors were as follows:

	1973	1980
Intermediate goods	34.4	17.4
Capital goods	17.2	11.6
Land transport equipment	18.3	19.6
Consumer nondurables	12.7	8.9

Source: Pierre Muller, "La dégradation des comptes des entreprises industrielles depuis le premier choc pétrolier," *Économie et statistique* 165 (April 1984): 8.

62. Christian Stoffaës, "The Nationalizations, 1981–1984: An Initial Assessment," in Howard Machin and Vincent Wright, eds., *Economic Policy and Policymaking Under the Mitterrand Presidency, 1981–84* (New York: St Martin's Press, 1985), 152.

63. Average annual volume growth (at constant prices) in gross fixed-capital formation for the period 1976–1981 was as follows: France, 0.9 percent; West Germany, 3.0 percent; United States, 3.3 percent; Japan, 4.5 percent; Italy, 2.8 percent. See Organisation for Economic Co-operation and Development, *Economic Surveys: France* (Paris: OECD, 1984), 73.

64. The following figures represent employers' social security charges as a percentage of GDP:

	1973	1980	Change, 1973–1980
France	12.0	15.7	+3.7
United States	4.4	5.1	+0.7
Japan	2.7	4.2	+1.5
West Germany	7.7	8.8	+1.1
United Kingdom	3.6	5.1	+1.5
Italy	10.6	11.2	+0.6

Source: Jacques Mazier, Maurice Basle, and Jean-François Vidal, *Quand les crises durent . . .* (Paris: Economica, 1984), 258.

65. Christian Stoffaës, "La France dans la compétition industrielle mondiale," 273–74.

66. The most notable example of this strategy was a 1974 government-backed accord between the major unions and the employers' association granting workers who were laid off for "economic" reasons up to 90 percent of their pay for one year.

67. Jeffrey Sachs and Charles Wyplosz, "The Economic Consequences of President Mitterrand," *Economic Policy* 2 (1986): 269; Robert Boyer, "The Current Economic Crisis: Its Dynamics and Implications for France," in George Ross et al., eds., *The Mitterrand Experiment: Continuity and Change in Modern France* (Oxford: Polity Press, 1987), 37–38.

68. Gauron, *Histoire économique et sociale de la Cinquième République*, 2:52–61.

69. See especially Michael Loriaux, *France After Hegemony: International Change and Financial Reform* (Ithaca: Cornell University Press, 1991).

CHAPTER 3. BUILDING SOCIALIST COALITIONS

1. D. S. Bell and Byron Criddle, *The French Socialist Party: Resurgence and Victory* (Oxford: Clarendon Press, 1984), 29; Vincent Wright, *The Government and Politics of France,* 2nd ed. (New York: Holmes & Meier, 1983), 152–53.

2. Rebounding from near extinction (4 percent of the popular vote) in the 1956 elections, the Gaullists captured 20 percent of the vote in 1958, then 32 percent of the vote and 56 percent of the parliamentary seats in the 1962 elections. The Parti Communiste Français (PCF) and the Section Française de l'Internationale Ouvrière (SFIO) gained a combined total of only 35 percent of the popular vote in both the 1958 and 1962 elections, versus 41 percent in 1956.

3. Mitterrand, an eleven-time minister in the Fourth Republic (1946–1958), had long led small groups of loyalists such as the Union Démocratique et Socialiste de la Résistance and, after 1965, the Convention des Institutions Républicaines. Useful biographies of Mitterrand include Franz-Olivier Giesbert, *François Mitterrand ou la tentation de l'histoire* (Paris: Editions du Seuil, 1977); Denis MacShane, *François Mitterrand: A Political Odyssey* (London: Quartet Books, 1982); Wayne Northcutt, *Mitterrand: A Political Biography* (New York: Holmes and Meier, 1992; Alistair Cole, *François Mitterrand: A Study in Political Leadership* (London: Routledge, 1994). But see Catherine Nay, *Le noir et le rouge, ou l'histoire d'une ambition* (Paris: Editions Grasset et Fasquelle, 1984).

4. D. S. Bell and Byron Criddle, *The French Socialist Party: The Emergence of a Party of Government,* 2nd ed. (Oxford: Clarendon Press, 1988), 50.

5. The literature on the postwar non-Communist Left is vast. For a comprehensive

bibliography, see Alain Bergounioux and Gérard Grunberg, *Le long remords du pouvoir: Le parti socialiste français (1905–1992)* (Paris: Fayard, 1992), 531–48. Useful studies also include R. W. Johnson, *The Long March of the French Left* (London: Macmillan, 1981); Hugues Portelli, *Le socialisme français tel qu'il est* (Paris: Presses Universitaires de France, 1980); Olivier Duhamel, *La gauche et la Cinquième République* (Paris: Presses Universitaires de France, 1980); George A. Codding, Jr., and William Safran, *Ideology and Politics: The Socialist Party of France* (Boulder: Westview Press, 1979); Frank L. Wilson, *The French Democratic Left, 1963–1969: Toward a Modern Party System* (Stanford: Stanford University Press, 1971).

6. Frank L. Wilson, "The French Left in the Fifth Republic," in William G. Andrews and Stanley Hoffmann, eds., *The Fifth Republic at Twenty* (Albany: State University of New York Press, 1981), 186.

7. Michel Charzat et al., *Le C.E.R.E.S.: Un combat pour le socialisme* (Paris: Calmann-Levy, 1975); David Hanley, *Keeping Left? CERES and the French Socialist Party: A Contribution to the Study of Fractionalism in Political Parties* (Manchester: Manchester University Press, 1986).

8. Hervé Hamon and Patrick Rotman, *L'effet Rocard* (Paris: Stock, 1980).

9. So powerful was the exiled leadership that it even refused to give Socialists living in Spain a vote at the annual party congresses held in Toulouse. See José María Maravall, "From Opposition to Government: The Politics and Policies of the PSOE," in José María Maravall et al., *Socialist Parties in Europe* (Barcelona: Institut de Ciències Politiques I Socials, 1992), 7–8; David Gilmour, *The Transformation of Spain: From Franco to the Constitutional Monarchy* (London: Quartet Books, 1985), 90; Richard Gunther, "The Spanish Socialist Party: From Clandestine Opposition to Party of Government," in Stanley G. Payne, ed., *The Politics of Democratic Spain* (Chicago: Chicago Council on Foreign Relations, 1986), 11.

10. These events are described in detail in Richard Gillespie, *The Spanish Socialist Party: A History of Factionalism* (Oxford: Clarendon Press, 1989), 264–88. See also José María Maravall, *La política de la transición,* 2nd ed. (Madrid: Taurus, 1985), 169–72.

11. For useful bibliographical reviews, see two essays in *Sistema* 68–69 (November 1985): Andrés de Blas, "La transición democrática en España como objeto de estudio: Una nota bibliográfica," 141–48, and José Antonio Gómez Yañez, "Bibliografía básica sobre la transición democrática en España," 149–73. Historical overviews in English include Paul Preston, *The Triumph of Democracy in Spain* (London: Methuen, 1986); Donald Share, *The Making of Spanish Democracy* (New York: Praeger/Center for the Study of Democratic Institutions, 1986); José María Maravall, *The Transition to Democracy in Spain* (London: Croom Helm, 1982).

12. José Ramón Montero Gibert, "Partidos y participación política: Algunas notas sobre la afiliación política en la etapa inicial de la transición española," *Revista de estudios polítícos* 23 (September–October 1981): 44.

13. Within a year and a half of its surprisingly strong showing in the June 1977 elections, the PSOE's membership reached 100,000. Part of this increase derived from the absorption of several smaller parties such as Tierno Galván's Partido Socialista Popular and regional parties from Valencia, Aragon, Andalusia, Galicia, and Catalonia. See Richard Gunther, Giacomo Sani, and Goldie Shabad, *Spain After Franco: The Making of a Comparative Party System* (Berkeley: University of California Press, 1985), 160.

14. Ironically, this internal conflict resulted in part from the PSOE's own success,

for its rapid increase in membership—over twelvefold from January 1977 to January 1979—created problems of internal cohesion, discipline, and coordination. One result was that many rank-and-file members became critical of the "authoritarian" methods of Guerra and the central staff in imposing and maintaining control. See Gunther, "The Spanish Socialist Party," 18.

15. The struggle between the *críticos* and the *oficialistas* (as the González-Guerra supporters were called) began at the May 1979 party congress in which González proposed a renunciation of Marxism by the party, which had adopted Marxist principles in 1976. The critical sector defeated this resolution, whereupon González stunned the delegates by announcing his resignation as party chief. In an "extraordinary" congress the following September, however, he was unanimously reelected first secretary. The delegates also voted to renounce Marxism and to exclude all leaders of the critical sector from the executive commission and other key party posts.

There were two reasons for González's victory. First, despite his defeat on the Marxist question at the May congress, the delegates had approved delegate-selection rules that, at the September congress, gave the Andalusian contingent of his ally Guerra 25 percent of all delegates (delegates were required to vote en bloc). By contrast, the critical sector, which represented an estimated 40 percent of the rank-and-file, had just 10 percent of the delegates. Secondly, the critical sector failed to put forward a candidate for party leader and thus was unable to present a credible alternative to González. See Elizabeth Nash, "The Spanish Socialist Party Since Franco: From Clandestinity to Government, 1976–1982," in David S. Bell, ed., *Democratic Politics in Spain: Spanish Politics After Franco* (London: Frances Pinter, 1983), 57.

16. Maravall, "From Opposition to Government," 14.

17. At the September 1981 congress, for instance, attacks were launched by two dissident groups, the Izquierda Socialista and the Reflexiones Socialistas. See Nash, "The Spanish Socialist Party Since Franco," 56.

18. At the 1981 congress, only 29 percent of the delegates were veterans of the May 1979 congress, and most of the new delegates were González loyalists. See José Félix Tezanos, *Sociología del socialismo español* (Madrid: Tecnos, 1983), 140.

19. Hans-Jürgen Puhle, "El PSOE: Un partido predominante y heterogeneo," in Juan J. Linz and José Ramón Montero, eds., *Crisis y cambio: Electores y partidos en la España de los años ochenta* (Madrid: Centro de Estudios Constitucionales, 1986), 338; Gabriel Colomé and Lourdes Lopez Nieto, "The Selection of Party Leaders in Spain: Socialist Cohesion and Opposition Turmoil," *European Journal of Political Research* 24, no. 3 (October 1993): 349–50.

20. In 1982, one-half of the PSOE's 110,000 members were people who had joined since the 1977 elections. See Richard Gillespie, "Spanish Socialism in the 1980s," in Tom Gallagher and Allan M. Williams, eds., *Southern European Socialism: Parties, Elections, and the Challenge of Government* (Manchester: Manchester University Press, 1989), 61–62.

21. Under the arrangement that was eventually concluded, the PS and PCF agreed that in the first round of parliamentary elections they would each have candidates in all or nearly all of the country's 493 electoral districts. In districts where no one commanded a first-round majority—making a runoff election necessary—the PS and PCF would run just one candidate, who would be the PS or PCF candidate who had garnered the most votes in the first round.

22. Johnson, *The Long March of the French Left*, 141–42.

23. In runoff elections, PS candidates were supported by over 90 percent of first-round PCF voters, but PCF candidates attracted the support of only about two-thirds of first-round PS voters, because PS voters were much more likely than PCF voters to abstain or support conservative candidates. See Johnson, *The Long March of the French Left*, 223; Roland Cayrol, "Les attitudes des électorats de gauche: Changement social, liberté, alliances politiques," in SOFRES, *L'opinion française en 1977* (Paris: Presses de la Fondation Nationale des Sciences Politiques, 1978), 54.

24. The issue that ostensibly precipitated the break concerned the scope of prospective nationalizations, but the real issue was the power of each party in a future Left government. Mitterrand later claimed that "Common victory mattered less [to the Communists] than Socialist failure": quoted in François Mitterrand, *Ici et maintenant* (Paris: Fayard, 1980), 60. For an account of the deterioration in PS-PCF relations during 1977 and of the negotiations, see Johnson, *The Long March of the French Left*, 181–89.

25. Quoted in Roland Cayrol, "Le Parti Socialiste à l'entreprise," *Revue française de science politique* 28, no. 2 (April 1978): 296.

26. Chris Howell, *Regulating Labor: The State and Industrial Relations Reform in Postwar France* (Princeton: Princeton University Press, 1992); Henri Weber, *Le parti des patrons: Le CNPF (1946–1986)* (Paris: Editions du Seuil, 1986); Pierre Morville, *Les nouvelles politiques sociales du patronat* (Paris: Editions La Découverte, 1985).

27. The Force Ouvrière, whose anti-Communism remained one of its defining characteristics, was especially disheartened by the Socialists' attempts during the 1970s to forge an alliance with the Communists. The Force Ouvrière and the PS thus remained on distant terms throughout the 1970s and into the 1980s. See Bergounioux and Grunberg, *Le long remords du pouvoir*, 369.

28. The CFDT, with its early (1970) emphasis on *autogestion* and *planification démocratique*, clearly influenced the subsequent ideological evolution of the PS; however, relations between the two organizations were (and remain) complicated by factional divisions in the PS. For example, the Mitterrandiste faction long suspected the CFDT leadership of favoring Mitterrand's archrival, Rocard.

29. After the disappointing 1978 elections, the CFDT leadership concluded that the confederation had mistakenly subordinated labor-market activity to the failed political strategy of the Union of the Left. By "recentering" its action on the work place *(recentrage),* the confederation hoped to regain an autonomous voice and reenergize its activists. But the term *recentrage* immediately created confusion, as it also implied a possible political shift. For this reason, the leadership soon rebaptized the new strategy *resyndicalisation,* meaning reunionization. See Guy Groux and René Mouriaux, *La C.F.D.T.* (Paris: Economica, 1989), 206–13.

30. The CGT, founded in 1895, was taken over by a Communist majority in 1947. A minority hostile to Communism then left the confederation to form the CGT-Force Ouvrière (that is, the Force Ouvrière).

31. For excellent studies of the CGT, see George Ross, *Workers and Communists in France* (Berkeley: University of California Press, 1982), and René Mouriaux and Guy Groux, *La C.G.T.* (Paris: Economica, 1989).

32. PS delegates to the 1973 congress reported their labor organization member-ship as follows (figures are percentages that do not total 100 because of rounding):

FEN	24
CFDT	18
FO 10	
CGT	7
Other labor organizations	8
No labor organizations	32

Source: Roland Cayrol, "Les militants du Parti Socialiste: Contribution à une sociologie," *Projet* 88 (September–October 1974): 937.

33. In the mid-1980s, PS voters, local party activists, and congress delegates belonged to the following socioprofessional categories (figures are percentages):

	Voters	Activists	Delegates
Upper-level professionals			
(cadres supérieures)	9	28	42
Intermediate-level workers	22	39	37
Office workers *(employés)*	20	10	8
Nonoffice workers	23	10	2
Other	26	13	11

Source: Colette Ysmal, *Les partis politiques sous la Cinquième République* (Paris: Montchrestien, 1989), 197, reprinted in Henri Rey and François Subileau, *Les militants socialistes à l'épreuve du pouvoir* (Paris: FNSP, 1991), 76.

On the PS's organizational elitism, see Cayrol, "Les militants du Parti Socialiste," 929–40; Patrick Hardouin, "Les caractéristiques sociologiques du Parti Socialiste," *Revue française de science politique* 28, no. 2 (April 1978): 220–56; Paul Bacot, *Les dirigeants du Parti Socialiste* (Lyon: Presses Universitaires de Lyon, 1979); Portelli, *Le socialisme français tel qu'il est;* Roland Cayrol and Colette Ysmal, "Les militants du PS: Originalités et diversités," *Projet* 165 (May 1982), 572–86; Bell and Criddle, *The French Socialist Party: Resurgence and Victory;* Henri Rey and Francoise Subileau, "Les militants socialistes en 1985," *Projet* 198 (March-April 1986): 19–34.

34. Cayrol, "Le Parti Socialiste à l'entreprise," 297.

35. Ibid., 296–312.

36. Mark Kesselman, "Socialism Without the Workers: The Case of France," *Kapitalistate* 10–11 (1983): 11–41.

37. Ibid., 13.

38. Maravall, *La política de la transición,* 161–72.

39. Gunther, Sani, and Shabad, *Spain After Franco,* 66.

40. The CCOO, founded by Communists, independent socialists, Catholic worker activists, and even liberal members of the Falange, grew out of the Francoist industrial relations system that forbade free unionism but allowed limited forms of collective bargaining within the state-controlled Organización Sindical Española (OSE). The first *comisiones,* formed in the late 1950s, were ad hoc, firm-level committees that handled work place grievances. In the mid-1960s labor activists decided to create a national confederation of these committees (which the PCE came increasingly to dominate) and launch a "strategy of infiltration and occupation" of OSE work place institutions. In 1967 the CCOO was outlawed, but it continued to function and build grassroots opposition to the regime. See José María Maravall, *Dictadura y disentimiento político: Obreras y estudiantes bajo el franquismo* (Madrid:

Ediciones Alfaguara, 1978), 60; Gunther, Sani, and Shabad, *Spain After Franco,* 204–05.

41. Thus when the PCE sought in July 1974 to coordinate the anti-Franco opposition by establishing the Junta Democrática—a coalition that included the CCOO, Galván's Partido Socialista Popular, and smaller groups—the PSOE countered by founding the Plataforma de Convergencia Democrática, which criticized the Junta's "bourgeois" tendencies.

42. Maravall, *La política de la transición,* 176.

43. Gillespie notes that although the early PSOE was influenced intellectually by French Marxists such as Guesde and Lafargue, its founders—who went on to establish the UGT in 1888—did not share Guesde's disdain for organized labor. Party-union relations were thus closer in Spain than in France not only in the 1980s, but a century earlier. See Gillespie, *The Spanish Socialist Party,* 9.

44. Despite the UGT membership requirement, only 59 percent of PSOE members in 1981 actually belonged to the confederation. In 1982 that figure dropped to 52 percent. See Puhle, "El PSOE," 331.

45. Victor M. Pérez-Díaz, *Clase obrera, partidos, y sindicatos* (Madrid: Fundación del INI, 1980), 109; Peter McDonough, Antonio López Pina, and Samuel H. Barnes, "The Spanish Public in Political Transition," *British Journal of Political Science* 11, no. 1 (January 1981): 76.

46. In the words of one Socialist deputy, "The UGT is walking along the same road as we are. They are an extension of the party. We want them to attract new members to the party, and we in turn want to strengthen the UGT": quoted in Gunther, Sani, and Shabad, *Spain After Franco,* 209.

47. A study by Robert M. Fishman of work place leaders in Madrid and Barcelona in the early 1980s found evidence of PSOE influence over the UGT but also evidence of union autonomy. About 10 percent of UGT work place leaders characterized PSOE-UGT relations as "control by the party over the union," 40 percent as "influence by the party over the union without reaching total control," and most of the rest as "mutual influence between party and union but with autonomy for each of them." See Robert M. Fishman, *Working-Class Organization and the Return to Democracy in Spain* (Ithaca: Cornell University Press, 1990), 177.

48. The PSOE also enjoyed considerable support among members of other unions. A national survey found that more CCOO members voted for the PSOE than for the PCE in the 1979 elections (45 percent versus 39 percent). See Pérez-Díaz, *Clase obrera, partidos, y sindicatos,* 109.

49. The UGT's rise can be measured by its candidates' performance in elections to the *comités de empresa,* workers' committees that are required by law every two years in firms with over fifty employees. Following are the results for the three voting periods in 1978–1982 (figures are vote percentages obtained by candidates with the corresponding affiliation):

	1978	1980	1982
UGT	21.7	29.3	36.7
CCOO	34.4	30.9	33.4
Union Sindical Obrera	3.9	8.7	4.6
Regional unions	1.0	3.4	4.5
Other	20.9	11.9	8.7
No union affiliation	18.1	15.8 ·	12.1

Source: Modesto Escobar, "Works or Union Councils? The Representative System in Medium and Large Sized Spanish Firms," Working Paper 1993/43 (Madrid: Instituto Juan March de Estudios e Investicaciones, February 1993), 25.

50. F. Miguélez, "Las organizaciones sindicales," in Faustino Miguélez and Carlos Prieto, eds., *Las relaciones laborales en España* (Madrid: Siglo Veintiuno, 1991), 217.

51. In Fishman's survey of unionized and nonunionized Madrid and Barcelona work places, less than 10 percent of work place leaders belonged to the PSOE. Moreover, the PSOE presence was strongly related to firm size. In large firms (1,000 or more employees), 17 percent of work place leaders were PSOE members, whereas the figure was only 2 percent in small firms (50–249 employees). See Fishman, *Working-Class Organization and the Return to Democracy in Spain,* 171.

52. Gunther, Sani, and Shabad, *Spain After Franco,* 210; Fishman, *Working-Class Organization and the Return to Democracy in Spain,* 168.

53. The following table, adapted from a study undertaken in the early 1990s, indicates the highest educational level attained by PSOE voters, members, and leaders (figures are percentages). The pattern was much the same in the late 1970s.

	Voters	*Members*	*Leaders*
Primary school or less	74	74	8
Vocational training	3	6	2
Secondary school	12	9	11
Postsecondary study	5	5	20
University	6	6	69

Source: Adapted from Maravall, "From Opposition to Government," 29. *Note:* Figures in the last column are the mean for three groups of leaders (the parliamentary group, the federal committee, and the executive commission).

54. Maravall, "From Opposition to Government," 12.

55. George Ross and Jane Jenson, "Strategy and Contradiction in the Victory of French Socialism," in Ralph Miliband and John Saville, eds., *The Socialist Register 1981* (London: Merlin, 1981), 93.

56. This division of labor was evident during the creation of the 1972 Common Program of the Left, when the CERES negotiated and helped draft the sweeping economic provisions (which included plans for large-scale nationalizations), while Mitterrand outlined the much more moderate foreign policy and constitutional proposals. See Portelli, *Le socialisme français tel qu'il est,* 110.

57. This catch-all quality can be seen in the party's identification of its targeted electoral base, the class front *(front de classe),* which it defined as those "who have been dispossessed of their means of work and have become dependent on monopolistic firms": quoted in Paul Bacot, "Le Front de classe," *Revue française de science politique* 28, no. 2 (April 1978): 282. Though expressed in a *marxisant* vocabulary, the class front concept encompassed not only industrial workers but also wage and salary earners in general, and even farmers, artisans, and other groups. See Hughes Portelli, "Nouvelles classes moyennes et nouveau Parti Socialiste," in Georges Lavau, ed., *L'univers politique des classes moyennes* (Paris: Presses de la Fondation Nationale des Sciences Politiques, 1983), 271.

58. Bernard E. Brown, *Socialism of a Different Kind: Reshaping the Left in France* (Westport: Greenwood Press, 1982), 70.

59. The PSOE claimed that "the economic subjugation of the proletariat is the primary cause of enslavement in all forms of social misery, intellectual degradation and political dependence": PSOE, *XXVII congreso del PSOE* (Barcelona: Avance, 1977), 115–16, quoted in Gunther, "The Spanish Socialist Party," 16.

60. José María Maravall, "La alternativa socialista: La política y el apoyo electoral del PSOE," *Sistema* 35 (March 1980): 9–11.

61. This concept, obviously borrowed from the French Left (and Yugoslavian theorists before it), promised, as we have seen, the empowerment of workers and citizens in firms and local public institutions such as schools and town councils. The career of *autogestión* within the PSOE was even more ephemeral and fraught with ambiguity than it was in the PS. See Santos Juliá, "The Ideological Conversion of the Leaders of the PSOE, 1976–1979," in Frances Lannon and Paul Preston, eds., *Elites and Power in Twentieth-Century Spain* (Oxford: Clarendon Press, 1990), 271–75; Gillespie, *The Spanish Socialist Party,* 322–23.

62. See the proposals outlined in the PSOE-published book by Equipo Jaime Vera entitled *La alternativa socialista de P.S.O.E. (algunas contribuciones)* (Madrid: Editorial Cuadernos para el Diálogo, 1977). See also Gunther, "The Spanish Socialist Party," 16–17.

63. Quoted in Gillespie, *The Spanish Socialist Party,* 323.

64. Montero Gibert, "Partidos y participación política," 44.

65. Debate has focused on whether González was "truly" a *marxisant* leftist from 1974 to 1976, or merely adopted a Marxist framework to advance his own standing. No doubt there is some truth in both interpretations: adopting a Marxist stance assisted González's rise within the party, yet it is likely that González was also comfortable with such a position, at least until late 1976. See Donald Share, *Dilemmas of Social Democracy: The Spanish Workers Party in the 1980s* (New York: Greenwood Press, 1989), 41; Gunther, "The Spanish Socialist Party," 13–14.

66. Juliá, "The Ideological Conversion of the Leaders of the PSOE," 273–74.

67. Gillespie, *The Spanish Socialist Party,* 303–04.

68. Maravall, "From Opposition to Government," 11.

69. Donald Share, "Two Transitions: Democratisation and the Evolution of the Spanish Socialist Left," *West European Politics* 8, no. 1 (January 1985): 82–103.

70. In 1977 González and Guerra declared, "Today the concept of working class is updated by including in it all salaried persons who, occupying an indirect place in the productive process, have been brought into the fight to build a more just and equal society for everyone. Thus, office workers, physicians, lawyers, writers, and engineers today find themselves in a process of becoming salaried employees *(un proceso de asalarización)* which puts them together with manual workers": Felipe González and Alfonso Guerra, *Partido Socialista Obrero Español* (Bilbao: Ediciones Albia, 1977), 24.

71. Preston, *The Triumph of Democracy in Spain,* 154.

72. Donald Share, "Spain: Socialists as Neoliberals," *Socialist Review* 18 (January–March 1988): 56.

73. Samuel H. Barnes, Peter McDonough, and Antonio López Pina, "The Development of Partisanship in New Democracies: The Case of Spain," *American Journal of Political Science* 29, no. 4 (November 1985): 716; Peter McDonough, Samuel H. Barnes, and Antonio López Pina, "Authority and Association: Spanish Democracy in Comparative Perspective," *Journal of Politics* 46, no. 3 (August 1984): 680.

74. José María Maravall and Julián Santamaría, "Crisis del Franquismo, transición política, y consolidación de la democracia en España," *Sistema* 68–69 (November 1985): 117.

75. McDonough, López Pina, and Barnes, "The Spanish Public in Political Transition," 76; José María Maravall, "Politics and Policy: Economic Reforms in Southern Europe," in Luis Carlos Bresser Pereira, José María Maravall, and Adam Przeworkski, eds., *Economic Reforms in New Democracies: A Social-Democratic Approach* (Cambridge: Cambridge University Press, 1993), 90–91; Rafael López Pintor, "El estado de la opinión pública española y la transción a la democracia," *Revista española de investigaciónes sociológicas* 13 (January–March 1981): 20–21.

76. Mitterrand made a star appearance at the PSOE's 1974 Suresnes congress (which elected González as first secretary) but treated the new leader and his Sevillian entourage coldly, following which González met SPD leader Willy Brandt and began a warm friendship. Gillespie suggests that Mitterrand cultivated friendly relations with the PCE in order to highlight the PCE's "Eurocommunism" compared with the PCF's Stalinist tendencies, while at the same time deflecting claims that he was intrinsically anti-Communist. See Gillespie, *The Spanish Socialist Party*, 373–76.

77. The PSOE's adoption of the concept of *autogestión* is a case in point. Indeed, Gillespie notes that "The key doctrinal texts of the PSOE founders came from the pens of Guesde, his colleague Gabriel Deville, and Lafargue": Gillespie, *The Spanish Socialist Party*, 8.

78. Charles T. Powell, "La dimensión exterior de la transición española," *Revista CIDOB afers internacionals* 26 (1994): 54–57.

79. Bell and Criddle, *The French Socialist Party: Resurgence and Victory*, 195; Tony Judt, *Marxism and the French Left* (Oxford: Clarendon Press, 1986), 265–66.

80. The economic groups that traditionally supported the Right, such as small farmers, artisans, and shopkeepers, were the ones declining most rapidly, whereas rapidly increasing middle-strata groups such as lawyers, teachers, and engineers tended to favor the Left. Moreover, the decline of religious practice in France (the proportion of regularly practicing Catholics decreased from 35 percent–40 percent of the population in the mid-1950s to 17 percent in 1977) worked to the Left's benefit, given the strong link between church attendance and conservative voting. See Johnson, *The Long March of the French Left*, 110.

81. Puhle, "El PSOE," 297.

82. Barnes, McDonough, and López Pina, "The Development of Partisanship in New Democracies," 712–13.

83. Puhle, "El PSOE," 341.

84. For example, Jacques Chirac, the Gaullist leader, former prime minister, and defeated presidential candidate, refused to back Giscard in the runoff against Mitterrand. Giscard received only 73 percent of Chirac's first-round supporters; the rest either voted for Mitterrand (16 percent) or abstained (11 percent). See Jerôme Jaffré, "De Valéry Giscard d'Estaing à François Mitterrand: France de gauche, vote à gauche," *Pouvoirs* 20 (1981): 13–15.

85. Quoted in *Le Monde*, 23–24 August 1981.

86. Rafael López-Pintor, "The October 1982 General Election and the Evolution of the Spanish Party System," in H. R. Penniman and E. Mujal-León, eds., *Spain at the Polls, 1977, 1979, and 1982* (Durham: Duke University Press, 1985), 301–03.

87. Ibid., 309.

88. Barnes, McDonough, and López Pina, "The Development of Partisanship in New Democracies," 702–03.

89. Puhle, "El PSOE," 295.

90. Ibid.

91. Surveys indicate that the percentage of the electorate declaring a partisan tie leaped from 37 percent in 1980 to 60 percent in 1984. The percentage of the electorate declaring an affiliation with the PSOE more than doubled, from 15 percent to 34 percent. See Barnes, McDonough, and López Pina, "The Development of Partisanship in New Democracies," 703.

92. López-Pintor, "The October 1982 General Election and the Evolution of the Spanish Party System," 311.

93. Peter McDonough, Samuel H. Barnes, and Antonio López Pina, "Economic Policy and Public Opinion in Spain," *American Journal of Political Science* 30, no. 2 (May 1986): 448.

PART III. MACROECONOMIC POLICY IN THE NEW EUROPE

1. Obviously the line between macroeconomic policy and industrial policy is difficult to draw. In this book *macroeconomic policy* means measures that attempt to influence the operation of the economy as a whole, not just particular aspects or sectors, and includes fiscal and monetary policy and such matters as financial, trade, and labor regulation.

2. The notion of goals, instruments/techniques, and settings is taken from Peter A. Hall, "Policy Paradigms, Social Learning, and the State: The Case of Economic Policymaking in Britain," *Comparative Politics* 25, no. 3 (April 1993): 278.

CHAPTER 4. FRANCE: GOOD THINGS FIRST, BAD THINGS AFTER

1. For basic information on many of the government reforms mentioned in this and the following chapters I have relied on the compilation by J. Paul Horne, *French Government Measures, June 1981–March 1986* (Paris: Smith Barney, Harris Upham and Co., 1986).

2. The typical *contrat de solidarité*, signed by an employer, one or more local unions, and a government representative, called for the employer to offer voluntary early retirement to workers over age fifty-six and to replace them with young workers. The government would pay retirement benefits to the departing workers.

3. Alain Fonteneau and Pierre-Alain Muet, *La gauche face à la crise* (Paris: Presses de la Fondation Nationale des Sciences Politiques, 1985), 114.

4. *Le Monde,* 3 December 1981.

5. Elie Cohen, "Les socialistes en l'économie: De l'age des mythes au déminage," in Elisabeth Dupoirier and Gérard Grunberg, eds., *Mars 1986: La drôle de défaite de la gauche* (Paris: Presses Universitaires de France, 1986), 78; Frank L. Wilson, "Socialism in France: A Failure of Politics, Not of Policy," *Parliamentary Affairs* 38, no. 2 (spring 1985): 163–79.

6. Interview with the author, 25 March 1987.

7. This was a sore point with the Socialists, for most forecasters, including the

OECD, had predicted (wrongly) that GDP throughout the industrialized nations would rise 2 percent during 1982. The Socialists thus wagered (wrongly) that their reflation would coincide with an expanding world economy. In the end, French GDP expanded from 1.2 percent in 1981 to 2.5 percent in 1982, whereas GDP growth among the OECD nations dropped from 1.6 percent in 1981 to zero in 1982.

8. In the eleven days following Mitterrand's election, the Banque de France had to spend $5 billion, or about one-fifth of total foreign reserves, to support the franc, and several advisers were pressing Mitterrand to unilaterally devalue the franc by as much as 20 percent. According to his new prime minister, Pierre Mauroy, Mitterrand revealed his decision on inauguration day as the two were riding in an open car down the Champs Élysées. Savoring the cheers of the crowd, Mitterrand said, "One doesn't devalue on a day like this": Pierre Mauroy, C'est ici le chemin (Paris: Flammarion, 1982), 19.

9. Econometric studies for 1981–1983 indicate that without the relance GDP would have grown only 1.3 percent instead of 3.0 percent; investment would have fallen 9.5 percent instead of only 4.7 percent; and the French economy would have lost an additional 320,000 jobs. See Fonteneau and Muet, La gauche face à la crise, 127.

10. French consumer price increases, which roughly matched the EC average in 1980 (an annual rate of 13.6 percent versus the EC's 13.7 percent), exceeded the EC average in 1981 (13.4 percent versus 12.4 percent) and 1982 (11.8 percent versus 10.9 percent). See Organisation for Economic Co-operation and Development, Economic Outlook 54 (December 1993): 140.

11. The number of unemployed, for example, rose 260,000 between June 1981 and June 1982, compared with an increase of 365,000 for the twelve months before June 1981. See Organisation for Economic Co-operation and Development, Economic Surveys: France (Paris: OECD, 1983), 12.

12. Ibid., 19.

13. The following table shows percentage increases in unit labor costs over the preceding year for France and the OECD European nations in 1980–1983.

	1980	1981	1982	1983
France	13.2	12.0	10.5	8.7
OECD-EUROPE	12.5	10.8	8.9	6.8

Source: Organisation for Economic Co-operation and Development, Economic Outlook 54 (December 1993): 137.

The employers' association, the Conseil National du Patronat Français (CNPF), claimed that the wages, taxes, and social charges paid by businesses increased by Fr 100 billion in 1982. See Le Monde bilan économique et social, 1982 (Paris: Le Monde, 1982), 56.

14. The following are the percentage changes over the preceding year in France's gross fixed-capital formation: 1980, 2.6; 1981, –1.9; 1982, –1.4; 1983, –3.6; 1984, –2.6. See Organisation for Economic Co-operation and Development, Economic Outlook 54 (December 1993): 130.

15. Within the EMS the franc was devalued 3.0 percent and the mark was revalued 5.5 percent—in effect, an 8.5 percent devaluation of the franc against the mark. See Fonteneau and Muet, La gauche face à la crise, 192–93.

16. For example, during one week in March 1982 the Banque de France had to

spend Fr 10 billion ($1.8 billion) to support the currency. Foreign exchange reserves, excluding gold, fell 60 percent between the time of Mitterrand's election and early June 1982. To cover the trade deficit and defend the franc, French central bankers dramatically increased foreign borrowing. Net government-authorized borrowing increased from $6.2 billion in 1981 to $9.2 billion the following year. See Pierre Favier and Michel Martin-Roland, *La décennie Mitterrand,* vol. 1, *Les ruptures* (Paris: Seuil, 1990), 414; Volkmar Lauber, *The Political Economy of France: From Pompidou to Mitterrand* (New York: Praeger, 1983), 184; Organisation for Economic Co-operation and Development, *Economic Surveys: France* (Paris: OECD, 1983), 30.

Throughout this book, dollar equivalents of values given in French francs are estimated by using a conversion ratio of $1 = Fr 5.5, or approximately the dollar-franc exchange rate between 1980 and 1995.

17. Interview with the author, 3 December 1987.

18. Ibid.

19. Within the EMS the franc was devalued 5.75 percent and the mark was revalued 4.25 percent, which translated into a 10 percent devaluation of the franc against the mark.

20. *Le Monde,* 15 June 1982.

21. The only strong partisans for rigor at this time were Mauroy, Finance Minister Delors, and Planning Minister Rocard. Other top officials such as Budget Minister Fabius, Industry Minister Chevènement, and Pierre Bérégovoy (secretary general of the Élysée) continued to advocate reflation, even if that meant resorting to some forms of protectionism.

22. Interview with the author, 10 March 1987.

23. *Témoinage Chrétien,* 8 July 1983.

24. According to one estimate, only one-quarter of the 2 percent net fiscal stimulus of GDP in 1981 was due to the new Left government; the rest resulted from the Giscard-Barre reflation. See David R. Cameron, "The Colors of a Rose: On the Ambiguous Record of French Socialism," Working Paper #12, Center for European Studies, Harvard University, 1988, 33.

25. The 1981 budget deficit represented less than 2 percent of GDP, and the 1982 budget called for the deficit to increase to 2.6 percent of predicted GDP. These were comparatively modest figures, given that deficits on the order of 5 percent of GDP were common throughout the EC. See P. Petit, "Full-Employment Policies in Stagnation: France in the 1980s," *Cambridge Journal of Economics* 10, no. 4 (December 1986): 306.

26. Fonteneau and Muet, *La gauche face à la crise,* 123, 131.

27. The accumulated trade deficit for 1981–1982 was about Fr 155 billion, of which Fr 59 billion was due to rising energy prices and Fr 39 billion to the dollar's surge (about two-fifths of France's imports were dollar denominated). Thus nearly two-thirds of the trade deficit during this period resulted from changes in these two external factors: ibid., 81.

28. Ibid., 202.

29. Quoted in *Business Week,* 10 January 1983.

30. Chris Howell, *Regulating Labor: The State and Industrial Relations Reform in Postwar France* (Princeton: Princeton University Press, 1992), 157; Organisation for Economic Co-operation and Development, *Economic Surveys: France* (Paris: OECD, 1984), 17.

31. *Le Monde*, 31 December 1982.

32. Observers familiar with the continuities underlying France's economic policy making will not be surprised to learn that this statement was first employed by Giscard's industry minister, André Giraud, in 1978. See *Le Monde*, 15 September 1978.

33. See Organisation for Economic Co-operation and Development, *Economic Surveys: France* (Paris: OECD, 1983), 51.

34. The *filière* concept contrasted with the *créneau* or niche approach followed by Giscard and Barre, which sought to promote internationally competitive firms in particular market segments. The niche approach, the Socialists argued, produced few spin-offs to other firms or to the country's industry as a whole.

35. Elie Cohen, "L'état socialiste en industrie: Volontarisme politique et changement socio-économique," in Pierre Birnbaum, ed., *Les élites socialistes au pouvoir: Les dirigeants socialistes face à l'état, 1981–1985* (Paris: Presses Universitaires de France, 1985), 228.

36. Christian Stoffaës, *Politique industrielle* (Paris: Institut d'Études Politiques, 1984), 159.

37. Renault, Thomson, and nine other nationalized companies in internationally competitive sectors lost a total of Fr 12.5 billion in 1981, while the noncompetitive public sector (electricity, gas, railroads, and so on) fared even worse, losing over Fr 20 billion. See *Le Monde*, 4 February 1983.

38. Organisation for Economic Co-operation and Development, *Economic Surveys: France* (Paris: OECD, 1984), 9, 22.

39. In 1982 foreign exchange reserves were reduced from Fr 33 billion in August to less than Fr 12 billion in December. In September this deterioration forced the government to negotiate a standby line of credit of $4 billion with a consortium of European and American banks. According to the U.S. treasury representative in France, James Fall, negotiations for this line of credit were tense, for the French government negotiators initially refused to agree to any measures to increase domestic austerity. French officials, he claimed, were surprised at how strongly foreign creditors opposed the Mitterrand government's economic policy. They learned from this episode that the international financial community would no longer finance France's public debt unless macroeconomic policy changes were made. Interview with the author, 26 February 1987.

40. See *Le socialisme et la France* (Paris: Le Sycomore, 1983), a book published by the CERES under the pseudonym Jacques Mandrin.

41. Philippe Bauchard, *La guerre des deux roses: Du rêve à la réalité* (Paris: Grasset, 1986), 143.

42. Essential sources for this struggle include: Bauchard, *La guerre des deux roses;* Favier and Martin-Roland, *La décennie Mitterrand;* Serge July, *Les années Mitterrand: Histoire baroque d'une normalisation inachevée* (Paris: Grasset, 1986); Thierry Pfister, *La vie quotidienne à Matignon au temps de l'Union de la Gauche* (Paris: Hachette, 1986).

43. Michel Camdessus, the director of the treasury, argued that "the other policy," by requiring France to leave the EMS, would precipitate a devaluation of the franc of at least 20 percent against the mark. Because France's foreign reserves were already depleted, the treasury would, he continued, quickly have to defend the franc by raising interest rates from 14 percent to 20 percent. Leaving the EMS would thus

eventually require even greater austerity than the measures Delors proposed. See Favier and Martin-Roland, *La décennie Mitterrand,* 471.

44. Despite his growing unpopularity, Mauroy offered several advantages, the most obvious being policy continuity. Rigor would remain, and so would its promoter. In addition, Mauroy maintained good relations not only with PS leaders outside parliament and the government but also with the PCF and the two major Left labor confederations, the CGT and CFDT. Finally, Mauroy's potential replacement, Delors, badly alienated Mitterrand and his top advisers during a luncheon on 22 March. That evening, Mauroy brought his resignation to Mitterrand, but Mitterrand asked him to stay on as prime minister. The new Mauroy government was announced to the press two days later.

45. Peter A. Hall, "The Evolution of Economic Policy under Mitterrand," in George Ross et al., eds. *The Mitterrand Experiment: Continuity and Change in Modern France* (Oxford: Polity Press, 1987), 57.

46. Tax measures included a 1 percent surcharge on taxable 1982 income (later modified to exempt low-income and large families); a forced loan from those who paid over Fr 5,000 in taxes in 1982, equal to 10 percent of the tax paid; an 8 percent rise in gas and electricity charges; and increased taxes on alcohol and tobacco. Program cuts and subsidy limits aimed at public-sector firms were put in place to reduce the budget deficit below 3 percent of GDP. Because the forecasted 1983 budget deficit was already at that level, the new policy meant no net fiscal stimulus through 1984.

47. Louis Gallois, "L'industrie, affaire nationale," *Politique industrielle* 1 (fall 1985): 13.

48. The FIM replaced the CODIS, Giscard's 1979 version of a fund for industrial modernization. The main differences were, first, that the FIM was funded mainly by the new public savings account, whereas the CODIS was funded by the treasury, and second, that the FIM was placed under the control of the Industry and Research Ministry, whereas the CODIS was managed by the Finance Ministry. Otherwise, the aims, types of financial instruments and incentives used, and procedures were quite similar. See *Journal Officiel,* 29 July 1983.

49. Agence National de Valorisation de la Recherche, *Réflexions sur un premier bilan du FIM* (Paris: Agence National de Valorisation de la Recherche, 1986), 31.

50. *Le Monde,* 29 April, 15 September 1983.

51. The newly nationalized companies lost Fr 16.5 billion in 1982 and over Fr 12 billion in 1983. See *L'Express,* 27 April 1984.

52. Quoted in *Libération,* 19 March 1984.

53. Quoted in ibid., 10 May 1984.

54. Interview with the author, 3 December 1987.

55. Organisation for Economic Co-operation and Development, *Economic Surveys: France* (Paris: OECD, 1985), 19.

56. Ibid., 21, 25.

57. *L'Express,* 7 December 1984.

58. *Le Monde,* 17 January 1984.

59. Interview with Pierre Héritier, 24 April 1987.

60. *New York Times,* 15 July 1984.

61. In 1973, 56 percent of PS congress delegates said that "Construction of

socialism based on self-management *(socialisme autogestionnaire)"* was "very important"; however, in 1983 only 17 percent held this opinion. Two long-time party
analysts commented: "This is a sign of a party that, in power, is constrained to
manage [the economic crisis] to the point that most of its activists no longer seek to
promote a model of social organization." See Colette Ysmal and Roland Cayrol,
"Militants socialistes: Le pouvoir use," *Projet* 191 (January–February 1985): 28.

62. *L'Express,* 30 December 1983.

63. The PS gained only 21 percent of the vote, and Left candidates as a whole
captured just 38 percent. Especially apparent were defections by erstwhile Left
supporters: only 77 percent of 1981 Left voters who voted in 1984 continued to
support Left candidates, whereas 95 percent of 1981 Right voters who voted in 1984
remained loyal to Right candidates. This election also witnessed the sudden emergence of Jean-Marie Le Pen's National Front, which gained 11 percent of the vote. See
Elisabeth Dupoirier, "Chassés-croisés électoraux," in Dupoirier and Grunberg, eds.,
Mars 1986, 170.

64. For an excellent analysis of Socialist-Communist relations in 1981–1984, see
George Ross and Jane Jenson, "Pluralism and the Decline of Left Hegemony: The
French Left in Power," *Politics & Society* 14, no. 2 (1985): 147–83.

65. Personal income taxes were cut 5 percent, the "progressive surtax" levied in
March 1983 was repealed, and business taxes were reduced by Fr 10 billion. To
compensate for the loss in revenue, the government increased less visible taxes on
telephones and gasoline. See *Le Monde,* 14 September 1984.

66. Organisation for Economic Co-operation and Development, *Economic Surveys:
France* (Paris: OECD, 1987), 14.

67. The financial reforms were of three types:

(1) Creation of one large financial market for borrowing and lending money,
which was open to the state, banks, and businesses. Previously, French financial
markets had been partitioned *(cloisonnés),* that is, divided into short-, medium-, and
long-term markets, as well as into specialized markets for mortgages and other
transactions. Managed individually by the state, they had made open-market bank
intervention impossible.

The government also included in its reform package the creation of a futures
market (MATIF).

(2) Reduction of preferential-rate *(prêts bonifiés)* loans, to allow state financial
lenders (Crédit Immobilier, Crédit Nationale, and others) to offer low rates of interest
for certain types of investments. Although it gave the state substantial say over how
credit would be allocated, this reform also proved costly (because it attracted a large
volume of loans at below-market rates) and administratively cumbersome.

(3) Changes in monetary regulation. The main reform was to abolish credit
ceilings *(encadrement du crédit),* which had allowed the state to set the amount of
credit available to the banks. Henceforth banks would no longer be limited by these
ceilings and could increase lending by placing additional reserves with the Banque de
France.

The above information is derived from author interviews of Jean-Charles Naouri,
Bérégovoy's cabinet director, on 5 May, 6 June, and 2 July 1987, and from *Livre blanc
sur la réforme du financement de l'économie* (Paris: Ministère de L'Economie, des
Finances et du Budget, 1986).

68. For example, the Labor, Employment, and Professional Training Ministry instituted a youth employment program, Les Travaux d'Utilité Publique, as well as a "reconversion leave" for workers laid off for economic reasons, which provided these workers income support while they underwent new job training. The ministry also increased funds for on-the-job professional training and for facilitating the hiring of workers on fixed-length contracts. See *Le Monde dossiers et documents: Bilan du septennat, 1981–1988*, 61.

69. Olivier Jean Blanchard and Pierre Alain Muet, "Competitiveness Through Disinflation: An Assessment of the French Macroeconomic Strategy," *Economic Policy* 16 (August 1993): 12–56.

70. *L'année politique, économomique, et sociale 1989* (Paris: Éditions Évènements et Tendances, 1990), 512–13.

71. In 1988–1990, when growth in France averaged 3.7 percent annually, unemployment dropped only about 1 percent, from 10.0 percent to 8.9 percent. For the EC as a whole, growth averaged 3.6 percent annually, while unemployment dropped from 9.9 percent to 8.4 percent. See Organisation for Economic Co-operation and Development, *Economic Outlook* 54 (December 1993). Several studies documented a growing inequality in income distribution as well as an increase in "precarious" forms of work (part-time work, fixed-length contracts, and so forth). See, for example, Centre d'Étude des Revenus et des Couts, *Constat de l'évolution recente des revenus en France, 1986–89* (Paris: Centre d'Étude des Revenus et des Couts, 1990).

72. For example, at every *rentrée sociale*—the September "reentry" after the summer vacation—the Rocard government announced an employment plan to increase job training and hiring. In 1988 the government created the Revenu Minimum d'Insertion, a program that provided a guaranteed income to people who had long been unemployed, on the condition that they would cooperate with government agencies in seeking jobs or job training. By the end of 1991, over 580,000 people were receiving an average of Fr 1,850 ($336) per month. To finance this program, a "solidarity tax" was levied on the very rich. See Margaret Maruani and Emmanuèle Reynaud, *Sociologie de l'emploi* (Paris: Éditions La Découverte, 1993), 90–92.

73. Sandholtz argues that French enthusiasm for European collaborative projects grew out of the failure of *dirigiste*-style national champion projects such as the 1982 *filière électronique* plan. See Wayne Sandholtz, *High-Tech Europe: The Politics of International Cooperation* (Berkeley: University of California Press, 1992), 146–52.

74. From 1989 to 1991, consumer price increases in France averaged 3.4 percent annually, versus an average of 5.3 percent among the OECD's European members. French government balances as a percentage of GDP decreased by an average of 1.6 percent annually, versus OECD-Europe's average annual decrease of 3.5 percent. France's GDP growth averaged 2.5 percent annually, versus OECD-Europe's 2.7 percent.

75. The trade deficits for industrial products (excluding military products) in 1987–1989 were as follows: 1987, Fr 36.8 billion; 1988, Fr 66.6 billion; 1989, Fr 83.3 billion. See *L'année politique, économique, et sociale 1989*, 556.

76. Criticism from the CERES was especially harsh: *Le Monde*, 10 December 1990. For a critical assessment of the Rocard government's social policy, see Chris Howell, "The Fetishism of Small Difference: French Socialism Enters the Nineties," *French Politics and Society* 9, no. 1 (winter 1991): 26–39.

77. Alain Gélédan, *Le bilan économique des années Mitterrand, 1981–1993* (Paris: Le Monde-Editions, 1993), 138–47.

78. *L'année politique, économique, et sociale 1992* (Paris: Éditions Évènements, 1993), 516.

79. After referenda in which the Danes rejected the Maastricht Treaty and the Irish narrowly approved it, Mitterrand decided to submit the adoption question directly to the French electorate in September 1992. (An alternative would have been to have it approved by the National Assembly.) In the run-up to this referendum, opponents of monetary union mobilized effectively and put the government on the defensive. The result, an unconvincing 51–49 percent vote in favor of the treaty, fell short of the resounding approval Mitterrand expected. Having misjudged the public mood, Mitterrand was widely criticized for being politically inept and out of touch.

80. *Financial Times,* 20 November 1992.

81. GDP growth in France in 1988–93 averaged 2.1 percent annually, versus the EU average of 2.2 percent.

82. Blanchard and Muet, "Competitiveness Through Disinflation," 31.

CHAPTER 5. SPAIN: THE PRICE OF EUROPEAN MEMBERSHIP

1. Quoted in the *New York Times,* 12 August 1985.

2. Interview conducted by Donald Share, quoted in his "Spain: Socialists as Neoliberals," *Socialist Review* 18 (January–March 1988): 44.

3. Interview in *Tiempo,* 15–21 August 1988, quoted in José María Maravall, "Politics and Policy: Economic Reforms in Southern Europe," in Luiz Carlos Bresser Pereira et al., *Economic Reforms in New Democracies: A Social-Democratic Approach* (Cambridge: Cambridge University Press, 1993), 95.

4. Interview with the author, 11 November 1993.

5. Antonio García Santesmases, "Evolución ideológica del socialismo en la España actual," *Sistema* 68–69 (November 1985): 61–78.

6. In 1980 Spain's CPI increased 15.6 percent. The EC average was 13.7 percent. By 1982, even though Spain's rate had dropped to 14.4 percent, the EC average had declined even more, to 10.9 percent.

7. Organisation for Economic Co-operation and Development, *Economic Surveys: Spain* (Paris: OECD, 1984), 25.

8. Augusto López-Claros, *The Search for Efficiency in the Adjustment Process: Spain in the 1980s,* International Monetary Fund Occasional Paper no. 57 (Washington, D.C.: International Monetary Fund, 1988), 11–12.

9. The UGT was the only labor confederation to sign the Economic and Social Accord. The CCOO claimed that the agreement did not adequately protect workers' buying power. For a summary of the two accords' provisions, see Carlos Alonso Zaldívar and Manuel Castells, *España fin de siglo* (Madrid: Alianza Editorial, 1992), 307. See also Justo Domínguez, "Diez años de relaciones industriales en España," in Angel Zaragoza, ed., *Pactos sociales, sindicatos, y patronal en España* (Madrid: Siglo Veintiuno Editores, 1990), 75–105.

10. López-Claros, *The Search for Efficiency in the Adjustment Process,* 14. Unlike the French Socialists, who initially delayed devaluing the franc for several months, the PSOE government devalued the peseta by 8 percent within weeks of taking office.

Spanish leaders viewed devaluation as way to improve the country's competitive position, whereas French leaders saw it as an admission of national weakness.

11. *New York Times*, 25 February 1983; *Financial Times*, 6 March 1985.

12. Real unit labor costs in industry (1975=100) dropped from 114.9 in 1982 to 102.2 in 1985. See López-Claros, *The Search for Efficiency in the Adjustment Process*, 24.

13. For example, in 1983–1984 merchandise exports increased an annual average of 12.1 percent, whereas imports other than oil increased only 5.6 percent. See ibid., 16.

14. Foreign direct investment in 1986 was 43 percent greater than the previous year, with much of the increase coming from Spain's new EC partners. See ibid., 28.

15. Organisation for Economic Co-operation and Development, *Economic Surveys: Spain* (Paris: OECD, 1986), 60–62.

16. According to OECD figures, the annual increase in gross fixed-capital investment averaged 12.9 percent for 1986–1989, versus the EC average of 6.5 percent.

17. Spain's entry as a full-fledged member into the EC was not immediate. Although quotas on imports from other EC members were removed and EC companies were now free to invest in the country, other aspects of EC integration, such as the elimination of customs duties, alignment with the Common Agricultural Program, and participation in the EMS, were to be phased in over seven years. See Eric Solsten and Sandra W. Meditz, eds., *Spain: A Country Study* (Washington, D.C.: Federal Research Division, Library of Congress, 1990), 203.

18. The percentage of Spain's exports going to EC nations increased from 52 percent in 1985 to 64 percent in 1987. During the same period, EC imports as a proportion of all Spanish imports increased from 37 percent to 55 percent. See Organisation for Economic Co-operation and Development, *Economic Surveys: Spain* (Paris: OECD, 1989), 27.

19. Oscar Bajo and Angel Torres, "La integración española en la CE y sus effectos sobre el sector exterior," *Información comercial española* 708–09 (August–September 1992): 36.

20. Ludolfo Paramio, "Las relaciones entre partido y sindicato: El amor y la conveniencia," *Claridad* 12 (March-April 1986): 5–17; Richard Gillespie, "The Breakup of the 'Socialist Family': Party-Union Relations in Spain, 1982–89," *West European Politics* 13, no. 1 (January 1990): 47–62.

21. Pensions rose by 40 percent in real terms from 1977 to 1985, while employer and worker contributions fell from 95 percent to 77 percent of total revenue. This led to an increasing reliance on the state budget to make up the shortfall. At the same time, the ratio of contributors to beneficiaries was also shifting to the economy's detriment, from 3:1 in 1977 to 2:1 in 1985, with 1.5:1 projected for 1993. Responding to this unsustainable balance, the government sought to increase the number of contributors, reduce the number of beneficiaries, and decrease the average pension amount. See López-Claros, *The Search for Efficiency in the Adjustment Process*, 27.

22. Temporary workers as a proportion of all wage earners increased from 15.6 percent in 1987 to 26.6 percent in 1989. The 1989 figure was by far the highest among Western European countries that year. See Organisation for Economic Co-operation and Development, *Economic Surveys: Spain* (Paris: OECD, 1994), 104.

23. Worker-delegate election results were as follows (figures are percentages):

	1982	1986
UGT	36.7	40.9
CCOO	33.4	34.5
Union Sindical Obrera	4.6	3.9
Region unions	4.5	4.0
Other unions	8.7	9.9
No labor affiliation	12.1	7.6

Sources: Jesús Albarracín, "La política de los sindicatos y la dinámica del movimiento obrero," in Miren Etxezarreta, ed., *La reestructuración del capitalismo en España, 1970–1990* (Barcelona: Icaria, 1991), 417–18; Modesto Escobar, "Works or Union Councils? The Representative System in Medium and Large Sized Spanish Firms," Working Papers 1993/43 (February 1993), Madrid Institutio Juan March de Estudios e Investigaciones, 25.

24. Interview with the author, 27 October 1993.

25. Interview with the author, 23 July 1994.

26. A wave of student strikes and demonstrations in early 1987 contested government reforms that students perceived as harming their interests in a time of economic insecurity. See Cyrus Ernesto Zirakzadeh, "Traditions of Protest and the High-School Student Movements in Spain and France in 1986–87," *West European Politics* 12, no. 3 (July 1989): 220–37.

27. Interview with the author, 5 June 1992.

28. Quoted in the *Financial Times,* 24 February 1989.

29. After four years of robust growth, unemployment had been reduced by only about 4 percent (from 20.8 percent in 1986 to 16.9 percent in 1989). Inflation resurfaced in 1989, increasing to 6.8 percent from 4.8 percent the previous year. Finally, current balances, after being in a positive position in 1984–1987, plunged into a deficit position in 1988 (at 1.1 percent of GDP) and 1989 (at 2.9 percent of GDP).

30. According to OECD figures, per capita GDP increased from $8,681 in 1987 to $11,738 in 1990.

31. *El País,* 16 November 1992.

32. The broad band permitted the peseta's value to vary up to 6 percent around the weighted average of all EC currencies, whereas the narrow band would have allowed only 2.25 percent.

33. Organisation for Economic Co-operation and Development, *Economic Survey: Spain* (Paris: OECD, 1993), 35.

34. The following indicators demonstrate the sharp growth in both the budget deficit and government spending (figures are percentages of GDP):

	1989	1990	1991	1992	1993
Government financial balances	-2.8	-3.9	-5.0	-4.5	-7.2
Government spending	40.9	41.8	43.3	44.5	46.9

Source: Organisation for Economic Co-operation and Development. *Note:* Negative figures indicate budget deficit.

35. *Financial Times,* 14 May 1993.

36. According to José Folgado Blanco, economic director of the employers' association, the CEOE, the government's economic policies in 1989–1993 were "absolutely antibusiness." Interview with the author, 7 July 1994.

37. The criteria were (1) the inflation rate could not exceed by more than 1.5 percentage points the average rate of the three EC nations with the lowest inflation rates; (2) long-term interest rates could not exceed by more than 2 percentage points the average rate of the three EC nations with the highest long-term interest rates; (3) the budget deficit had to be less than 3 percent of GDP; (4) public debt could not exceed 60 percent of GDP; and (5) for two years prior to convergence, the currency could not be devalued and had to remain within the ERM's narrow band. By the end of 1991, Spain had met only the fourth criterion. See *The Economist,* 25 April 1992.

38. On the unions' views, see *El País,* 10 April 1992. The CEOE's position was outlined by the organization's economic director in an interview with the author, 7 July 1994.

39. Deputy party leader Alfonso Guerra, having been forced out as deputy prime minister in January 1991 over charges of abuse of influence, led a steady barrage against Solchaga.

40. For a convincing analysis of this issue as it affected France, see Michael Loriaux, *France After Hegemony: International Change and Financial Reform* (Ithaca: Cornell University Press, 1991).

41. A key initiative driving this increase in government spending was the political and administrative decentralization that gave regional governments (the "autonomous communities") a significant budgetary role. For a discussion of the impact of regionalization on public finances, see Organisation for Economic Co-operation and Development, *Economic Surveys: Spain* (Paris: OECD, 1993), 58–80.

42. For example, of twenty-one OECD nations in 1991, France ranked sixth in social protection spending as a percentage of GDP. Although that percentage dipped slightly from 1983 to 1989, it began increasing again after 1989. See Organisation for Economic Co-operation and Development, *Economic Surveys: France* (Paris: OECD, 1994), 60.

43. For example, in 1991 social protection spending in Spain accounted for only about 20 percent of GDP, as against more than 27 percent in France and an average of slightly over 21 percent throughout the OECD. Yet from 1980 to 1991, Spain's rate of growth in real social protection spending was fourth highest among the twelve EC nations. See ibid., 60–61.

44. The following analysis uses strike rates as a rough measure of labor's political opposition. Although strike activity does not necessarily reflect worker opposition to government economic policy, one can argue that the politicized nature of the labor movement and industrial relations in both France and Spain, especially during a period in which Socialist governments were widely expected to favor labor's interests, makes strike rates a useful indicator of labor opposition.

45. In a national survey carried out in October–November 1984 (after two years of PSOE rule), voters evidenced a broad populist and statist tendency in their views on social equality and the proper role of the state in such matters as economic planning and the provision of social services. These opinions, however, were not polarized along class, religious, or party-identification lines. Public opinion on economic issues demonstrated considerable incoherence and vagueness, which the authors of one

scholarly analysis call a reflection of "the heterogeneous, interclass composition of the government's constituencies." See Peter McDonough, Samuel H. Barnes, and Antonio López Pina, "Economic Policy and Public Opinion in Spain," *American Journal of Political Science* 30, no. 2 (May 1986): 475.

46. François Platone, "Les communistes au gouvernement: Une expérience complexe et contradictoire," *Revue politique et parlementaire* 914 (January–February 1985): 28–49.

47. According to European Commission strike data for 1986–1990 reported in *The Economist,* 25 April 1992, France's annual average of 75 working days lost per 1,000 employees ranked it seventh-highest out of eleven EC nations (excluding Belgium). By comparison, Spain's average of 647 days lost put it in second place.

48. First becoming evident in the late 1970s, the decline of unionism persisted throughout the 1980s and into the 1990s. By one estimate, membership declined from 30 percent of all eligible workers in the mid-1970s to 14 percent in 1991: Dominique Labbé, "Trade Unionism in France Since the Second World War," *West European Politics* 17, no. 1 (January 1994): 148. Especially severe was the erosion of the CGT, which had been an almost hegemonic force since 1945 and played a leading role in the tumultuous events of May–June 1968. For statistical data on the decline of workers' confidence in unionism, see *Le Nouvel Observateur,* 20–26 December 1985.

Plant-level elections for *comités d'entreprise* revealed (1) a sharp decline in CGT influence, from 49 percent of workers' votes in 1966–1967 to 23 percent in 1990–1991; (2) stable support for the CFDT at about 20–23 percent; (3) a slow but steady rise in the influence of the third-largest confederation, the Force Ouvrière, from 8 percent in 1966–1967 to 12 percent in 1990–1991; (4) an increase in support for nonunion candidates, from 15 percent in 1966–1967 to 29 percent in 1990–1991; (5) a small decline in voter turnout, from over 70 percent in the late 1960s to about 65 percent in the early 1990s. For a succinct summary of these trends, see Dominique Labbé, "Les élections des comités d'entreprise," *Revue française de science politique* 43, no. 2 (April 1993): 317–26.

49. Chris Howell, *Regulating Labor: The State and Industrial Relations Reform in Postwar France* (Princeton: Princeton University Press, 1992), esp. ch. 7.

50. Representatives of the many studies of the Auroux laws are Michel Coffineau, *Les lois Auroux, dix ans après février 1993: Rapport au premier ministre* (Paris: La Documentation Française, 1993); Frank L. Wilson, "Democracy in the Workplace: The French Experience," *Politics & Society* 19, no. 4 (December 1991): 439–62; Bernard E. Brown, "Worker Democracy in France: Are You Serious?" *French Politics and Society* 8, no. 2 (spring 1990): 13–23; Bernard H. Moss, "Industrial Law Reform in an Era of Retreat: The Auroux Laws in France," *Work, Employment & Society* 2, no. 3 (September 1988): 317–34; W. Rand Smith, "Toward *Autogestion* in Socialist France? The Impact of Industrial Relations Reform," *West European Politics* 10, no. 1 (January 1987): 46–62.

51. The chronological structure of table 5.3 follows the three main phases of European economic activity during the 1980s and early 1990s, namely recession and slow recovery in 1981–1985, brisk expansion in 1986–1990, and renewed recession in 1991–1993. For the sake of economy of presentation, it does not provide separate figures for 1986–1988, the years in which Mitterrand was forced to "cohabit" (as the French called it) with a conservative prime minister and legislature.

52. France's growth rate was slightly higher than the European average during the *relance* years of 1981–1982, but below average in 1983–1985.

53. Organisation for Economic Co-operation and Development, *Economic Surveys: Spain* (Paris: OECD, 1992), 72.

54. Organisation for Economic Co-operation and Development, *Economic Surveys: Spain* (Paris: OECD, 1994), 68–83.

55. In one of Europe's most dramatic job loss/job creation performances, Spain lost nearly 2 million jobs in 1975–1985, but created almost as many new ones in 1985–1990. During the latter period, Spain's rate of job creation was three times the OECD-Europe average. Unfortunately, as we saw earlier, much of the increase was in part-time and temporary jobs. See Alvaro Espina, *Empleo, democracia, y relaciones industriales en España* (Madrid: Ministerio de Trabajo y Seguridad Social, 1991), 363–64.

56. Whereas the employed labor force population increased by 579,000 in the decade 1975–1985, it increased by 1,445,000 in 1985–1990. This increase resulted not only from a baby boom that took place in the 1960s and 1970s but also from the entry of a much higher proportion of females into the labor force. See ibid., 365–67.

57. Organisation for Economic Co-operation and Development, *Economic Surveys: Spain* (Paris: OECD, 1994), 73.

58. The problem of long-term unemployment was, of course, a general one throughout the EC. In Spain, the problem arose rapidly with the massive job losses of 1975–1985. Whereas in 1975 only 17 percent of unemployed workers had been jobless for at least one year, by 1985 that percentage had increased to 57 percent: López-Claros, *The Search for Efficiency in the Adjustment Process,* 22. In 1992 Spain ranked fourth among ten EC nations in its proportion of long-term unemployed in the unemployed population (47.4 percent). It also had the highest unemployment rate among people aged sixteen to twenty-four (34.4 percent): Gérard Cornilleau, "Données de base sur le chômage en Europe," in Pierre-Alain Muet, *Le chômage persistant en Europe* (Paris: Presses de la Fondation Nationale des Sciences Politiques, 1994), 48.

59. For example, in 1989 the unemployment rate among French young people (sixteen to twenty-four years old) was 19.6 percent, versus the EC average of 17.6 percent, despite the fact that a smaller proportion of French young people were in the active labor force (41.3 percent versus the EC average of 50.4 percent). See Organisation for Economic Co-operation and Development, *Economic Surveys: France* (Paris: OECD, 1992), 67.

CHAPTER 6. SPAIN: PUBLIC SECTOR REFORM AND INDUSTRIAL RECON- VERSION

1. In an April 1980 poll, 40 percent of a national sample favored nationalizations of the kind the Left was proposing, 38 percent opposed them, and 22 percent were undecided: Elisabeth Dupoirier and Muriel Humbertjean, "Privatisations," in SOFRES, *L'état de l'opinion: Clés pour 1988* (Paris: Seuil, 1988), 30. Much of the public's enthusiasm arose from the expectation that the new public firms would generate well-paying, secure jobs. See Jack Hayward, *The State and the Market Economy: Industrial Patriotism and Economic Intervention in France* (London: Wheatsheaf, 1986), 228.

2. See, for example, Monique Dagnaud and Dominique Mehl, *L'élite rose: Qui*

gouverne? (Paris: Editions Ramsey, 1982); Pierre Birnbaum, ed., *Les élites socialistes au pouvoir 1981–1985* (Paris: Presses Universitaires de France, 1985).

3. Richard Gillespie, *The Spanish Socialist Party: A History of Factionalism* (Oxford: Clarendon Press, 1989), 408–09.

4. Nancy Bermeo, "The Politics of Public Enterprise in Portugal, Spain, and Greece," in Ezra N. Suleiman and John Waterbury, eds., *The Political Economy of Public Sector Reform and Privatization* (Boulder: Westview, 1990), 144.

5. Ibid., 148–49.

6. The following discussion is based on interviews with the INI's chief historian, Francisco Comín Comín (8 June 1992 and 21 July 1994), and his book (coauthored with Pablo Martín Aceña), *INI, 50 años de industrialización en España* (Paris: Espasa Calpe, 1991). See also Pedro Schwartz and Manuel-Jesús González, *Una historia del Instituto Nacional de Industria (1941–1976)* (Madrid: Editorial Tecnos, 1978).

7. Martín Aceña and Comín Comín, *INI,* 321.

8. Ibid., 508, 521. Note: Estimates of dollar equivalents of values given in pesetas use a conversion ratio of $1 = PTA 125. This is approximately the average dollar-peseta exchange rate during the 1980–1995 period.

9. Organisation for Economic Co-operation and Development, *Economic Surveys: Spain* (Paris: OECD, 1984), 44. It should be noted that the INI encompassed only part, albeit the major part, of the public-enterprise sector. INI losses accounted for nearly two-thirds of public-sector losses in 1977–1982. Other institutions with responsibility for the public sector included the Instituto Nacional de Hidrocarburos, created in 1981 mainly by reorganizing the INI's energy-related firms; the Dirección General del Patrimonio, which included the telecommunications giant Telefónica, the news agency EFE, and several banks; and state companies such as Spanish Railways (RENFE) and Spanish Radio and Television (RTVE). For a description of these institutions, see Peter J. Donaghy and Michael T. Newton, *Spain: A Guide to Political and Economic Institutions* (Cambridge: Cambridge University Press, 1987), 136–50.

10. As was mentioned in chapter 5, Rumasa, Spain's largest holding company, was an exception. With Rumasa facing bankruptcy in 1983, the government nationalized the company, but then reorganized and completely reprivatized it over the next two years. See *Financial Times,* 6 March 1985.

11. Quoted in *El País,* 28 July 1983.

12. Martín Aceña and Comín Comín, *INI,* 651; *El País,* 26 March 1994.

13. Oscar Fanjul and Luis Mañas, "Privatization in Spain: The Absence of a Policy," in Vincent Wright, ed., *Privatisation in Western Europe: Pressures, Problems, and Paradoxes* (London: Frances Pinter, 1994), 147.

14. Martín Aceña and Comín Comín, *INI,* 550–51; *El País,* 18 March 1990.

15. Interview with the author, 8 July 1994.

16. Quoted in *El País,* 31 August 1992.

17. Under the 1985 Single Market Act, all such subsidies were to cease on 1 January 1993. Spain, however, received a partial exemption because of its relatively recent entry into the EC, the size of its work force, and the politically sensitive nature of the affected sectors. The quid pro quo for this exemption was the structural reorganization of 1992, which was intended to make the granting of state subsidies as transparent as possible. Only INI firms were permitted to receive state aid; Teneo firms were excluded.

18. *The Economist,* 29 October 1994.

19. Author interview with, Javier Blanco, the INI's director of communications, 25 October 1993.

20. See the INI's annual reports.

21. Author interview with Alvaro Espina, 26 October 1993.

22. Ibid.

23. Miquel Navarro, *Política de reconversión: Balance crítico* (Madrid: Eudema, 1990), 72–114. The sectors were home appliances ("white goods"), specialty steel, common steel, integrated steel, textiles, automotive electrical equipment, shipbuilding, semitransformation of copper, electronic components, footwear, and heavy forging. The firms were Asturiana de Zinc, General Eléctrica Española, Westinghouse, Standard Eléctrica, and Automóviles Talbot.

24. Most of the sectoral plans were drawn up between June 1981 and June 1982, and thus by the time of the October 1982 elections the plans had had, at most, only a little over a year to operate. The UCD government, its attention diverted by internal political problems, exercised little oversight in the execution of these plans and failed to promote programs of reindustrialization and worker retraining. One result was that nearly all moneys were spent on early retirement schemes, not job creation. See ibid., 105–07.

25. Ministerio de Industria y Energía, *Libro blanco de la reindustrialización* (Madrid: Ministerio de Industria y Energía, 1983); *Ley 27/1984 de 26 de julio, sobre reconversión y reindustrialización* (Madrid: Boletín Oficial del Estado, 28 July 1984).

26. Victor Pérez-Díaz, *El retorno de la sociedad civil* (Madrid: Instituto de Estudios Económicos, 1987), 45–123.

27. In four sectors (automotive electrical equipment, semitransformation of copper, electronic components, and heavy forging), the PSOE carried through to completion reconversion plans begun under the UCD. In six sectors (home appliances, specialty steel, common steel, integrated steel, textiles, and shipbuilding), reconversion had been begun and abandoned by the UCD but was reactivated by the PSOE. One sector, footwear, and the five firms targeted for reconversion in 1980–1982 (see note 23 above) were excluded from the Socialists' plans. However, several new sectors (notably fertilizers) and firms (such as Explosivos Río Tinto and Grupo ITT) were added to the list.

28. Ministerio de Industria y Energía, *Libro blanco de la reindustrialización,* 44–45.

29. Ibid., 228.

30. According to ibid., 245, the FPEs would be "an important instrument for channeling human and financial resources from sectors in decline toward lines of production with a future, both in the industrial sector and in services."

31. Each ZUR management committee included representatives of the central government, the region, and the FPEs (including employers and the unions). "Region" is used here as a shorthand for the seventeen *comunidades autónomas* established under the 1978 constitution.

32. These were Asturias, Barcelona, Cádiz, Galicia-Ferrol, Galicia-Vigo, Madrid, Nervión (the Basque Country), and Sagunto (Valencia). Sagunto, the site of a very controversial steel plant closing in 1983–1984 (see chapter 8), was specially designated a Zone of Preferential Industrial Location, but its administration was almost identical to that of the other zones. See Alberto Lafuente Félez and Ramón Pérez Simarro,

"Balance y perspectivas de las ZUR," *Papeles de economía española* 35 (1988): 221.

33. The following discussion is based on the procedure outlined in article 2 of the reconversion law.

34. This committee, officially called the Comisón Delegada del Gobierno para Asuntos Económicos (Delegated Government Commission for Economic Affairs) included the undersecretary of state for the economy and the ministers of economics, finance, and commerce; public works; labor and social security; industry and energy; agriculture; and transport and tourism.

35. If the two sides did not agree, the executive commission submitted a report and recommendation to the interministerial committee, which then made its own recommendation to the government.

36. In keeping with the practice of political pact making, this commission (Comisión de Control y Seguimiento) would include representatives of the central government, the regional government, management, and labor. PSOE officials, seeking not only to encourage "cooperative" union behavior but also to favor the UGT at the CCOO's expense, insisted that only unions which had signed reconversion agreements could sit on control and oversight commissions. Because the CCOO (as well as several smaller unions in the Basque Country, Galicia, and Catalonia) refused to sign such agreements, this stipulation was viewed by many as a thinly disguised attempt to circumvent labor opposition. Even the UGT joined the other unions in protesting against the stipulation, but to no avail.

37. The Boyer-Solchaga struggle began in June 1983 after the white paper's publication and lasted until the government's issuance of a royal decree law on reconversion and reindustrialization in November (RDL 8/1983), which served as a temporary framework for reconversion until the main law was passed in July 1984. Boyer and Solchaga put aside their differences in order to fight the UGT on the status of workers' contracts under reconversion. See José Antonio Sánchez and Robert Santos, *La conjura del zar* (Madrid: Ediciones Temas de Hoy, 1990), 341–45.

38. Author interview with Pedro de Silva, 8 November 1993.

39. Spain's regionalization process, codified in the 1978 constitution and begun in 1980 with the passage of the Law for the Financing of Autonomous Regions, shifted much of the responsibility for social programs and economic development from the central government to the regions. With the regions' increase in authority also came a greatly expanded budgetary role. Regional government spending as a proportion of all government spending went from zero in 1980 to 25 percent in 1992. (Local government spending remained roughly constant at about 10 percent, while the central government's proportion dropped from 90 percent to 65 percent.) Even more impressive was the rise in the regional governments' proportion of spending on public-investment projects—from zero in 1980 to over 40 percent in 1992. See Organisation for Economic Co-operation and Development, *Economic Surveys: Spain* (Paris: OECD, 1993), 67, 70.

40. This was a constant CEOE theme during the months between the publication of the white paper in June 1983 and the passage of the reconversion law in July 1984. See, for example, *El País*, 16 June, 19 June, 28 July 1983.

41. *El País*, 23 June 1983.

42. Author interview with Julian Ariza, 27 October 1993.

43. Quoted in *El País*, 28 November 1983.

44. Author interview with Fernando Maravall, 27 June 1994.

45. Author interview with Carlos Navarro, 8 July 1994.

46. Author interview with José Fernando Sánchez-Junco, 24 July 1994.

47. In October 1983, in the midst of negotiations between the government and the unions to define reconversion procedures and measures, Marín and his staff launched a protest by locking themselves in the offices of the Industry and Energy Ministry for twenty-four hours. Police had to be called in to remove them. The following week, Industry and Energy Minister Solchaga refused to meet with Marín and demanded that the CCOO send another representative. From that time on, the CCOO was absent from the *concertación* process. See *El País*, 5 November 1983.

48. This remark does not take into account the smaller labor confederations such as the Unión Sindical Obrera and the Basque ELA-STV.

49. *El País*, 17 October 1983. For a statement of the UGT's position, see Unión General de Trabajadores, *Qué es la reconversión industrial* (Madrid: UGT, 1983), esp. 207–43.

50. Interview with the author, 23 July 1994.

51. As we saw in the previous chapter, such a break came in mid-1985. According to several government officials interviewed by the author, although it did cause tensions between the government and the UGT in 1983–1984, the reconversion program itself did not play a role in precipitating the break.

52. For both unions the issue was less one of holding out hope for a return to the status quo ante (in which "suspended" workers, unlike those whose contracts were canceled, could return to their old jobs if circumstances permitted) than of preserving a protected legal status for workers. Under the Franco regime, the notion that workers held their jobs as of right was written into law, in large measure as an effort to legitimate authoritarian rule. The notion continued after his death, especially among public-sector workers. Because the largest firms in steel and shipbuilding, the core of the reconversion program, were all state run, their workers considered themselves virtual civil servants with lifetime tenure. For a union in these sectors to have countenanced permanent layoffs would have been considered an act of betrayal.

53. This bitter controversy raged behind the scenes for months in late 1983 and early 1984. The first piece of legislation on reconversion, a royal decree law passed by the Cortes in early December, included the phrase *rescisión de contratos,* implying permanent termination. The UGT raised an uproar. After several meetings with government officials, including González, UGT leaders extracted a promise that subsequent regulations, including the final reconversion law, would not mention termination *or* suspension, and that the contract details of each reconversion would be managed on a case-by-case basis.

In January 1984, in a major reconversion effort involving Aceriales, a specialty steel firm in the Basque Country, Solchaga insisted on contract terminations. Feeling betrayed, UGT leaders made their disagreement public by joining with the CCOO and the Basque ELA-STV in supporting mass demonstrations against the Aceriales plan. After discussions that involved González, the government moved in the UGT's direction, agreeing to suspend rather than terminate the contracts of the affected workers. González's final effort in this episode was to persuade Solchaga not to resign, for the industry and energy minister emerged from the battle feeling defeated and believing that he had been abandoned by his government. For an account of these events, see Sánchez and Santos, *La conjura del zar,* 342–52.

54. Aranzadi repeated this phrase in an interview with the author, 19 September 1994.

55. One indicator of the shift in emphasis from reconversion to technological promotion and innovation was the fact that the Industry and Energy Ministry's 1990 annual report devoted only four pages to reconversion, whereas projects relating to technological promotion and innovation took up twenty pages. See Ministerio de Industria y Energía, *Informe sobre la industria española 1990* (Madrid: Ministerio de Industria y Energía, 1991).

56. Interview with the author, 15 June 1994. This analysis was confirmed in several other interviews with unionists and government officials.

57. Figures are not available for individual years. Therefore, 1989–1992 must serve as an approximation for the post-1986 period.

58. Author interview with Federico de Loro, the former director general of the INI, 15 March 1995.

59. The CCOO's internal struggles were a reflection of the larger crises affecting Spanish Communism during the 1980s, when factions within the splintered Communist movement vied for control of the CCOO. Although long-time party leader Santiago Carrillo resigned as head of the PCE in 1982 (and quit the party in 1985 to form his own party), his supporters, including metalworkers' confederation leader Juan Ignacio Marín, remained in high-level CCOO positions. During 1987 opposition to the *Carrillistas* grew, and in November Marín was defeated as confederation leader by a supporter of Gerardo Iglesias, the head of the PCE. With the retirement that same month of the CCOO's general secretary, Marcelino Camacho, the *Gerardistas* were able to replace him with one of their supporters, Antonio Gutiérrez. The election of Gutiérrez as general secretary brought a new generation of leaders to power in the CCOO, a generation that, compared with its predecessors, was less ideological and more open to dialogue with employers and the government: author interview with Ignacio Fernádez Toxo, CCOO metalworkers' secretary, 15 June 1994; Roger G. McElrath, *Trade Unions and the Industrial Relations Climate in Spain* (Philadelphia: Wharton School Industrial Research Unit, University of Pennsylvania, 1989), 114–15.

60. Author interview with José Fernando Sánchez-Junco, the Industry and Energy Ministry official responsible for reconversion negotiations in the metallurgy sector, 24 July 1994.

61. Interview with the author, 15 June 1994.

62. In the interviews conducted for this book, several government officials argued that organized labor had too much influence over the reconversion process and that the government should have spent less time talking and more time doing the work of reconversion. As Fernando Maravall, a high official in the Industry and Energy Ministry, said, "I think there was too much negotiation with the unions. Things could have been done with more force. . . . There were also other sectors that should have been slated for reconversion but were not, for political reasons. Mining, Hunosa [the state coal mining firm], wasn't part of the reconversion, for example. The measures for reducing capacity were insufficient." He went on to suggest that part of the reason for the government's solicitousness toward labor was González's desire to retain the support of both the UGT and the PSOE's left wing, and for that reason González did not back Solchaga as strongly as he could have. Interview with the author, 27 June 1994.

63. This was the opinion of all the government, management, and labor officials interviewed by the author.

64. Government spending on unemployment as a percentage of GDP averaged 2.22 percent annually in 1983–1985 and 4.21 percent annually in 1991–1993. Comparable data for 1990–1991 indicate that Spain's percentage exceeded that of all other European nations. In 1991 the Spanish figure was 3.78 percent, whereas figures for the other eleven EC members ranged from 0.25 percent (Luxembourg) to 3.48 percent (Denmark). See *La Vanguardia,* 10 October 1993 (using OECD data).

65. According to the OECD, in 1993 Spain's general governmental outlays equaled 47.6 percent of GDP, versus an EC average, excluding Spain and Luxembourg, of 52.4 percent.

66. Alvaro Espina, *Empleo, democracia, y relaciones industriales en España* (Madrid: Ministerio de Trabajo y Seguridad Social, 1991), 475.

67. Although the ZURs, created in 1984, continued to operate into the 1990s, their functions were largely taken over after 1988 by a new agency managing what were called Zonas de Declive Industrial (Zones of Industrial Decline, or ZIDs). The data reported here refer to the results of both the ZURs and the ZIDs.

68. Ministerio de Industria y Energía, *Informe sobre la industria española 1990* (Madrid: Ministerio de Industria y Energía, 1991), 271–72.

69. According to Industry and Energy Ministry figures, reconversion had eliminated 88,388 jobs by December 1990: ibid., 228.

70. At an exchange rate of PTA 125 to the dollar, the government spent $45,243 for each job eliminated and $22,923 for each job created through the ZURs and the ZIDs. These figures were calculated by the author as follows: (1) Labor costs per job eliminated as of 31 December 1993: labor costs totaling PTA 557.654 billion (table 6.2) divided by 98,605 jobs eliminated (figures supplied to the author by the Labor and Social Security Ministry); (2) Subsidies per job created as of 15 May 1991: ZUR/ ZID subsidies totaling PTA 92.268 billion divided by 32,200 jobs created (figures from Ministerio de Industria y Energía, *Informe sobre la industria española 1990,* 271–72).

CHAPTER 7. FRANCE: NATIONALIZATION AND THE LIMITS OF *DIRIGISME*

1. Within days of the June 1981 legislative elections, work teams in the Élysée and Matignon began writing the nationalization bill, planning how to compensate shareholders, and drawing up management guidelines. In September the Council of Ministers adopted the *projet de loi,* which then went to the National Assembly for debate. After vigorous opposition from the Right—which proposed nearly 3,000 amendments—the bill passed in mid-December. In January 1982, however, the Constitutional Council found the bill's compensation provisions too low. After the government proposed generous increases, bringing the sum to be spent on buying out private investors to nearly Fr 50 billion, the revised bill was voted into law on 11 February 1982. For a summary of these events, see Lionel Zinsou, *Le fer de lance: Essai sur les nationalisations* (Paris: Olivier Orban, 1985), 71–80.

2. The twelve industrial firms included (1) five large multinational corporations that were fully nationalized (Thomson-Brandt, Compagnie Générale d'Électricité, Péchiney-Ugine-Kuhlmann, Saint-Gobain-Pont-à-Mousson, and Rhône-Poulenc); (2) two heavily indebted steel firms that were fully nationalized (Usinor and Sacilor); (3)

two privately held, defense-related companies that were nationalized at 51 percent (Dassault-Breguet and MATRA); and (4) three industrial groups that were under the full or partial control of foreign multinational corporations (CII-Honeywell Bull, Compagnie Générale des Constructions Téléphoniques, and Roussel-Uclaf). In the case of the last three, all fully nationalized, the government concluded its nationalization agreements with the multinational parent corporations. It is also to be noted that the nationalization of the two steel firms, Usinor and Sacilor, was carried out in October 1981, several months before the rest of the nationalizations. This was because the steel industry's dire condition and its extreme financial reliance on the state made its nationalization largely a technical matter that could be handled quickly and separately from the other targeted firms (see chapter 8).

The impact of the Socialist nationalizations on industrial ownership patterns can be seen in the figures for sales, employment, and investment. In 1981, before the nationizations, public-sector companies accounted for 17.2 percent of French industrial sales, but for 29.4 percent after nationalization. Their share of the French work force jumped from 11.0 percent to 22.2 percent, and their contribution to of French industrial investment (excluding the energy sector) from 12.1 percent to 25.9 percent. See Organisation for Economic Co-operation and Development, *Economic Surveys: France* (Paris: OECD, 1983), 50.

3. In 1983 Armand Bizaguet sought to assess the economic weight of the public sector in Western European countries by taking the mean average of the following three indicators: public-sector employees as a percentage of all employees, public-sector value added as a percentage of total value added, and public-sector gross fixed-capital formation as a percentage of total gross fixed-capital formation. In the period immediately following the 1982 nationalizations in France, the numbers were as follows: Austria, 25.0 percent; France, 22.4 percent; Italy, 20.0 percent; United Kingdom, 18.7 percent; West Germany, 13.2 percent; Ireland, 13.0 percent; Benelux, 9.6 percent. Bizaguet also estimated that the French nationalizations added 661,000 employees to public-sector payrolls, giving France a total of nearly 2.3 million public-sector employees, the largest public-sector work force in Europe. In absolute numbers of employees, the next largest public sector was the United Kingdom's, which employed 2.1 million people. See Armand Bizaguet, "L'importance des entreprises publiques dans l'économie française et européenne après les nationalisations de 1982," *Revue économique* 34, no. 3 (May 1983): 462–63.

4. Author interview with Liliane Sardais, 15 May 1987.

5. *Programme commun de gouvernement du Parti Communiste et du Parti Socialiste* (Paris: Editions Sociales, 1972), 113.

6. Parti Communiste Français, *Traité d'économie politique: Le capitalisme monopoliste d'état*, 2 vols. (Paris: Editions Sociales, 1971–1972).

7. See Jocelyn Barreau, et al., *L'état entrepreneur: Nationalisations, gestion du secteur public concurrentiel, construction européenne (1982–1993)* (Paris: L'Harmattan, 1990), 17–19, 38–46.

8. Quoted in *Le Monde*, 25 September 1981.

9. Ibid.

10. Alain Boublil, *Le socialisme industrielle* (Paris: Presses Universitaires de France, 1977).

11. Zinsou, *Le fer de lance*, 61.

12. *Le Monde,* 25 September 1981.

13. Letter dated 17 February 1982, reprinted in "Nationalisations industrielles et bancaires," *Les cahiers français* 214 (January–February 1984): 12.

14. Ibid.

15. This is indicated by the following figures, which represent public-firm sales as a percentage of total sales in the corresponding sector immediately before and immediately after the 1982 nationalizations:

	Before	After
Aeronautic construction	50	84
Steel	1	79
Armaments	58	75
Synthetic fibers	0	75
Metallurgy (nonferrous metals)	13	63
Basic chemicals	23	54
Consumer electronics	1	44
Office automation and computers	0	36
Glass	0	35
Pharmaceuticals	9	28
Electrical equipment	0	26
Household appliances	0	25
All of above sectors	18	32

Source: Adapted from André G. Delion and Michel Derupty, *Les nationalisations 1982* (Paris: Economica, 1982), 191.

16. Christian Stoffaës, "The Nationalizations, 1981–1984: An Initial Assessment," in Howard Machin and Vincent Wright, eds., *Economic Policy and Policy-Making Under the Mitterrand Presidency, 1981–1984* (New York: St Martin's Press, 1985), 146.

17. *Le Monde: Bilan économique et sociale 1981* (Paris: Le Monde, 1981), 30–31; Philippe Barret, "Une voie de passage obligée: Les nationalisations," *Politique aujourd'hui* 5 (July–August 1984): 33–41; Stoffaës, "The Nationalizations," 147.

18. Delion and Derupty, *Les nationalisations 1982,* 44.

19. For example, the 1976 Hannoun Report revealed that Thomson, CGE, CII-Honeywell Bull, Alsthom-Atlantique, Empain, Dassault, and Aerospatiale received nearly 50 percent of all industrial subsidies. Others firms receiving sizable subsidies included the main steel and chemical companies and Saint-Gobain. See Jacques Mazier, "Les limites de la stratégie de redéploiement," *Les cahiers français* 212 (July–September 1983): 16.

20. Jack Hayward, *The State and the Market Economy: Industrial Patriotism and Economic Intervention in France* (London: Wheatsheaf, 1986), 226–27.

21. "Nationalisations industrielles et bancaires," 23–24.

22. Zinsou, *Le fer de lance,* 27.

23. Representative works in the statist tradition include Andrew Schonfield, *Modern Capitalism: The Changing Balance of Public and Private Power* (New York: Oxford University Press, 1965); Frank L. Wilson, *Interest-Group Politics in France* (Cambridge: Cambridge University Press, 1988); David Wilsford, "Tactical Advantages Versus Administrative Heterogeneity: The Strengths and Limits of the French State," *Comparative Political Studies* 21, no. 1 (April 1988): 126–68; John Zysman, *Govern-*

ments, Markets, and Growth: Financial Systems and the Politics of Industrial Change (Ithaca: Cornell University Press, 1983), ch. 3; Stephen S. Cohen, *Modern Capitalist Planning: The French Model* (Berkeley: University of California Press, 1977).

24. For an excellent review of scholarly analyses of the French state, see Jonah Levy, *Tocqueville's Revenge: Dilemmas of Institutional Reform in Post-Dirigiste France* (Cambridge: Harvard University Press, forthcoming), esp. chs. 1–2.

25. Jean-Claude Thoenig, *L'ere des technocrats: Le cas des Ponts et Chausées* (Paris: Editions d'Organisation, 1973); Ezra N. Suleiman, *Politics, Power, and Bureaucracy in France* (Princeton: Princeton University Press, 1974); Hayward, *The State and the Market Economy;* Howard Machin and Vincent Wright, "Economic Policy Under the Mitterand Presidency, 1981–1984: An Introduction," in Machin and Wright, eds., *Economic Policy and Policy-Making Under the Mitterand Presidency, 1981–1984,* 9–17.

26. See, for example, Harvey B. Feigenbaum, *The Politics of Public Enterprise: Oil and the French State* (Princeton: Princeton University Press, 1985); Elie Cohen and Michel Bauer, *Les grandes manoeuvres industrielles* (Paris: Belfond, 1985); Helen V. Milner, *Resisting Protectionism: Global Industries and the Politics of International Trade* (Princeton: Princeton University Press, 1988), ch. 8.

27. All the Big Five CEOs fit this pattern. Jean Gandois of Rhône-Poulenc was a Polytechnique graduate and a member of the Corps des Ponts et Chaussées. Roger Fauroux of Saint-Gobain was a graduate of the École Nationale d'Administration and a member of the Inspection des Finances. Jean-Pierre Brunet of CGE had served as a diplomat, was a member of the board of the public firms Air France and ERAP, and was general counsel for the Banque de France. Georges Besse of Péchiney was a Polytechnique graduate and a member of the Corps des Mines. Alain Gomez of Thomson was a graduate of the Harvard Business School and the École Nationale d'Administration and a member of the Inspection des Finances.

28. The law provided that the workers in any nationalized firm with at least two hundred employees had the right to elect representatives to the board of directors. The same provision applied to subsidiaries of the nationalized firms in which the state had a 50–90 percent ownership share. The boards included not only employee members but also representatives of the state, the public at large, and even shareholders. The number of representatives from each group was a function of company size and the degree of state ownership. For a fuller description, see Richard Holton, "Industrial Politics in France: Nationalisation Under Mitterrand," *West European Politics* 9, no. 1 (January 1986): 77–78.

29. W. Rand Smith, "Towards *Autogestion* in Socialist France? The Impact of Industrial Relations Reform," *West European Politics* 10, no. 1 (January 1987): 38–54.

30. Jean-François Amadieu, "Le développement du syndicalisme d'entreprise" (thèse de doctorat, Université de Paris IX–Dauphine, 1986), 140–43.

31. Author interview with Thierry Le Roy, 25 June 1987.

32. *Programme commun de gouvernement du Parti Communiste et du Parti Socialiste,* 113.

33. There were four major restructurings.

(1) In the chemicals sector, the government decided to make CDF-Chimie (specializing in fertilizers and organic chemicals), ELF-Acquitaine (petrochemicals), and Rhône-Poulenc (fine chemicals) the foci of activity. To accomplish this, the government reassigned production responsibilities among the three firms (Rhône-Poulenc's fertilizer works, for instance, went to CDF-Chimie, and its petrochemicals

manufacturing division was shifted to ELF-Acquitaine). In addition, Péchiney's sizable chemicals division was divided up and handed over to the three firms so that Péchiney could focus on nonferrous metals.

(2) In the steel sector, Sacilor and Usinor became the two dominant manufacturers, absorbing the steel operations of Péchiney, Creusot-Loire, and several other smaller producers.

(3) In the computers sector, Bull was made the dominant producer and Saint-Gobain was forced to sell its one-third share in Olivetti.

(4) In the telecommunications sector, CGE was designated the main supplier, which required Thomson to cede its telecommunications operations to CGE.

34. Statement to the Council of Ministers, 17 February 1982, quoted in Elisabeth Vessillier, "Aspects financiers des nationalisations," *Revue économique* 34, no. 3 (May 1983): 481.

35. The origin of the planning contract was the so-called Nora Report of 1967, which sought to codify relations between the public firms and the state to ensure managerial autonomy. There were two short-lived precedents for the Left's attempt to revive such contracts: the 1970–1971 *contrats de programme* (program contracts) with the electricity, railroad, and radio-television companies, and the 1977 *contrats d'entreprise* (enterprise contracts) with Air France, Charbonnages de France, and the nationalized shipping company. See Jean-Pierre Anastassopoulas, "State-Owned Enterprises Between Autonomy and Dependency," *Journal of Public Policy* 5, no. 4 (1986): 536–37.

36. The Left presided over two plans between 1981 and 1986, the 1982–1983 Interim Plan (which replaced the plan created by the previous government) and the Ninth Plan (1984–1988). The Socialists gave planning considerable lip service but little political support, as could be seen in Mitterrand's appointment of a party foe, Michel Rocard, as the first planning minister.

37. Barret, "Une voie de passage obligée," 37.

38. See Gandois's interview in *Le Monde*, 7 August 1982.

39. The following is based largely on the author's interview with Thierry Le Roy, the head of the Services des Entreprises Nationales between 1982 and 1984, 25 June 1987. See also Barreau, et al., *L'état entrepreneur,* 56–68.

40. Quoted in *Le Monde,* 4 February 1983.

41. Interview with the author, 9 December 1987.

42. Ibid.

43. Saul Estrin and Peter Holmes, "How Far Is Mitterrand from Barre?" *Challenge* (November–December 1983): 49.

44. Barret, "Une voie de passage obligée," 38.

45. Interview with the author, 9 December 1987.

46. Maurice Blin, "Nationalisations: La fin d'une idéologie," *Politique industrielle* 3 (spring 1986): 73.

47. Author interview with Laurent Fabius, 9 December 1987; Amadieu, "Le développement du syndicalisme d'entreprise," 124; Vivien A. Schmidt, "Industrial Management Under the Socialists in France: Decentralized *Dirigisme* at the National and Local Levels," *Comparative Politics* 21, no. 1 (October 1988): 61.

48. See, for example, the analyses of restructuring in the chemicals and electronics industries in Zinsou, *Le fer de lance,* chs. 5–6.

49. Author interview with Armand Lepas, 17 March 1987. This sentiment was echoed by the CEOs of several large firms, both public and private. See Vivien A. Schmidt, *From State to Market? The Transformation of French Business and Government* (Cambridge: Cambridge University Press, 1996), ch. 4.

50. Blin, "Nationalisations," 70.

51. David R. Cameron, *The Colors of a Rose: On the Ambiguous Record of French Socialism* (Cambridge: Center for European Studies, Harvard University, 1987), 29.

52. Organisation for Economic Co-operation and Development, *Economic Surveys: France* (Paris: OECD, 1987), 33.

53. These figures are the author's calculations and are based on *Le secteur public industriel en 1985* (Paris: Observatoire des Entreprises Nationales, Ministère de l'Industrie, des Postes et des Télécommunications, et du Tourisme, 1986), passim; Organisation for Economic Co-operation and Development, *Labor Force Statistics, 1966–1986* (Paris: OECD, 1988), 223.

54. Author interview with Louis Gallois, 11 May 1987.

55. This study, produced by the Cours des Comptes in 1990, indicated that the initial buyout (including associated expenditures) cost the state slightly less than the Fr 56.1 billion in privatization revenues that flowed to the state in 1986–1988. In other words, the total profitability of the nationalization effort was less than 1 percent. See *L'année politique, économique, et sociale 1990* (Paris: Editions Événements et Tendances, 1991), 473.

56. Michel Derupty, *Les privatisations* (Paris: Documentation Française, 1988); Michel Bauer, "The Politics of State-Directed Privatisation: The Case of France, 1986–88," *West European Politics* 11, no. 4 (October 1988): 49–60; Ezra N. Suleiman, "The Politics of Privatization in Britain and France," in Ezra N. Suleiman and John Waterbury, eds., *The Political Economy of Public Sector Reform and Privatization* (Boulder: Westview, 1990), 113–36; Schmidt, *From State to Market?*, ch. 5.

57. In general, shares were divided as follows: at least 10 percent for company employees, up to 20 percent for sale on international security markets, 15–30 percent for the *noyaux durs,* and the rest offered for sale to the public. See Wladimir Andreff, "French Privatisation Techniques and Experiences: A Model for Central Europe," in Fernandino Targetti, ed., *Privatisation in Europe: West and East Experiences* (Aldershot: Dartmouth, 1992), 145.

58. Pierre Joxe, president of the Socialists' parliamentary group, accused Finance Minister Balladur of creating an "economic counterpower" of a few leaders "linked to the same party": quoted in *Les Echos,* 28 October 1987. See also Olivier Drouin and Patrice Piquard, "Quand privatisation rime avec restauration," *L'évènement du jeudi,* 17 September 1987; *Le Monde,* 17 September 1987.

59. For example, Bauer in "The Politics of State-Directed Privatisation," 60, claims that privatization "bolstered up a traditional system of 'establishment solidarity' structured around an all-powerful Minister of Finance." Levy, *Tocqueville's Revenge,* ch. 1, argues that it served to dilute state power.

60. This and the following paragraph are based largely on the excellent summary in Schmidt, *From State to Market?*, ch. 12.

61. The main exceptions were the business investment banks Paribas and Suez, which maintained extensive industrial interests.

62. Ironically, the presence of nationalized banks and insurance firms as share-

holders in newly privatized companies meant that the latter remained tied indirectly to the state.

63. François Mitterrand, "Lettre à tous les français" (presidential campaign platform, 1988).

64. According to a study by Kalyvas that draws on data from French opinion surveys, the percentage of the French population with a favorable attitude toward nationalization dropped from 49 percent in August 1981 to 33 percent in February 1984 (in the same period, the percentage of the population registering an unfavorable attitude rose from 33 percent to 48 percent). This dislike of nationalization persisted at least until mid-1987. Kalyvas concludes that "The abruptness of the shift [in attitude], combined with the absence of an alternative ideological project by the Right [at the time of the shift], indicates that people came to believe that there is something inherently wrong with nationalization. Economic crisis thus became equated to an excess of state intervention." See Stathis N. Kalyvas, "Hegemony Breakdown: The Collapse of Nationalization in Britain and France," *Politics & Society* 22, no. 3 (September 1994): 316–48 (statistics at 324; quotation at 333).

65. Péchiney, for example, created a subsidiary, Péchiney International, which then sold 25 percent of its shares to finance the acquisition of a U.S. firm, American Can. See *New York Times,* 9 May 1989.

66. *Le Monde,* 5 April 1989.

67. In 1985 French firms invested Fr 900 million less in other EC nations than those nations' firms invested in France. By 1988, however, the investment balance had shifted greatly in France's favor to Fr 27 billion. During the same period, France's investment balance with the United States ballooned from Fr 1.2 billion in France's favor to Fr 41.2 billion in France's favor. On a global scale, the balance was Fr 1.1 billion against France in 1985 but Fr 63 billion in France's favor in 1988. See *Tribune de l'Expansion,* 23 January 1990.

68. Even the head of the Haut Conseil du Secteur Public, Michel Charzat, a close ally of CERES leader Jean-Pierre Chevènement, came out in favor of privatizing up to 49 percent of nationalized firms. See *Libération,* 25 January 1990.

69. *Wall Street Journal,* 13 March 1990.

70. In 1988–1990, public enterprises received financing of Fr 183.5 billion, of which less than 8 percent (Fr 13.8 billion) was in the form of direct capital contributions from the government *(dotations en capital).* By contrast, about 19 percent (Fr 34.4 billion) came from capital markets and 47 percent (Fr 85.7 billion) from reinvested profits. See *Tribune de l'Expansion,* 9 May 1990.

71. *Le Monde,* 29 September 1990.

72. *Financial Times,* 6 April 1991.

73. The *Et-Et* policy was officially adopted in May 1992 by the PS's *comité directeur* in its "Contrat de législature 1993–98," a preelectoral party position paper. See *Le Monde,* 26 May 1992.

74. Author interview with Jean-François Carallo, 12 October 1994. See also Barreau, et al., *L'état entrepreneur,* 65–68; Schmidt, *From State to Market?,* ch. 7.

75. See Schmidt, *From State to Market?,* ch. 8.

CHAPTER 8. RESTRUCTURING IN THE STEEL INDUSTRY

1. International Iron and Steel Institute, *Steel Statistical Yearbook* (Brussels: International Iron and Steel Institute, 1993), 1; *World Steel in Figures, 1994* (Brussels: International Iron and Steel Institute, 1994), 1.

2. The following table indicates the share of world steel output produced by various processes (figures are percentages):

	1974	1992
Basic oxygen furnace	52	59
Open hearth	30	12
Electric-arc furnace	17	29

Source: Calculated from International Iron and Steel Institute, *Steel Statistical Yearbook,* 1978 and 1993.

3. The following production figures (in millions of tons) demonstrate these shifts:

	1973	1992	Change (%)
United States	137	84	−39
Western Europe	179	157	−12
Japan	119	98	−18
Centrally planned economies	207	235	14
Rest of world	54	149	176
World	696	723	4

Source: International Iron and Steel Institute, *Steel Statistical Yearbook,* various years. *Note:* Centrally planned economies include USSR (CIS), Eastern Europe, China, North Korea.

4. William T. Hogan, *Global Steel in the 1990s: Growth or Decline?* (Lexington, Mass.: Lexington Books, 1991), 143–44.

5. In 1974–1980, EC production declined 19 percent (from 156 tons to 127 tons), whereas capacity increased 13 percent (from 179 tons to 202 tons). As a result, capacity utilization slipped from 87 percent to 63 percent. See the Eurostat figures reported in Susan N. Houseman, *Industrial Restructuring with Job Security: The Case of European Steel* (Cambridge: Harvard University Press, 1991), 12.

6. During the 1970s, German, Dutch, and Luxembourgian producers remained relatively competitive and thus opposed EC intervention, favoring instead a largely voluntary approach within a producers' cartel. On the other hand, French, Belgian, British, and Italian producers, all facing sizable losses, lobbied for EC intervention, including compulsory production quotas and protection from external competition: ibid., 14–15. For a comprehensive overview of the European steel industry and its regulation during the 1970s and early 1980s, see Yves Mény and Vincent Wright, "State and Steel in Western Europe," in Mény and Wright, eds., *The Politics of Steel: Western Europe and the Steel Industry* (Berlin: Walter de Gruyter, 1986), 1–110.

7. Thomas Howell et al., *Steel and the State: Government Intervention and Steel's Structural Crisis* (Boulder: Westview, 1988), 78.

8. Article 4.C. of the ECSC's founding treaty prohibits state subsidies to the industry; however, article 95 allows the European Commission to grant exceptions for

research and development aid, regional investment aid, income support and retrain-ing for laid-off workers, and other measures. In practice, subsidies to cover operating losses were also allowed. Under the article 58 regime, operating subsidies were to cease by 1985, while subsidies for new investments were to end by 1986. Neither of these deadlines was met. See *Le Monde*, 26 June 1981.

9. For example, in August 1982 the Council of Ministers gave the EC three years to reduce steel production by 32 million tons (from the 1980 level). That target was reached in August 1985, at a cost of 200,000 jobs. However, because of continued market decline, there still remained excess capacity of 20–25 million tons. See *Le Monde*, 2 August 1985.

10. According to an EC official involved in making decisions concerning the steel industry, a rough quid pro quo applied in negotiating subsidy/capacity trade-offs in the early 1990s. At that time, the EC allowed governments to spend about Ecu 1 billion ($1.1 billion) in subsidies for every 750,000 tons of annual productive capacity eliminated. Author interview with Julian Foley, 13 October 1994.

11. There is, of course, a socioeconomic side to this issue. Houseman, for example, argues that "slower productivity growth and other possible adverse effects arising from strong worker rights to job security [in the EC] may be viewed, in part, as a price paid for greater employment and community stability and for a more equitable distribution of the costs and risks of economic change." See Houseman, *Industrial Restructuring with Job Security*, 127–28.

12. In 1987, for instance, the largest integrated producers resisted capacity cuts, especially where the increasingly profitable production of hot-rolled metal strips was concerned. Around the same time, British Steel, which had just regained profitability after a drastic Thatcher-imposed restructuring, was registering its opposition to continued production quotas, while Germany, whose steel industry remained unprofitable, insisted on maintaining them. Another issue that continued to divide profitable and unprofitable producers in 1987 was subsidies. See *The Economist*, 28 September 1987; *Financial Times*, 28 September 1987.

13. *Financial Times*, 15 February 1993.

14. See *Wall Street Journal*, 8 July 1993; *Financial Times*, 30 September 1993; *La Tribune Desfosses*, 18 November 1993.

15. Under the plan, the EC's state-owned steel companies were entitled, in total, to Ecu 6.8 billion ($7.5 billion) from the national governments, on the condition that capacity in the EC steel sector would be reduced by more than 5 million tons. See *Financial Times*, 15 February 1994.

16. In 1976, annual steel output per worker in France was 150 tons, far behind that of West Germany (200), the United States (236), Italy (241), and Japan (335). Within the EC, only Britain had a lower figure (123). See Stephen Woolcock, "The International Politics of Trade and Production in the Steel Industry," in John Pinder, ed., *National Industrial Strategies and the World Economy* (Totowa, N.J.: Allanheld, Osman, 1982), 59. On France's growing trade deficit in steel within the EC, see Pierre Judet, *L'évolution des débouchés de la sidérurgie française: Perspectives à moyen terme* (Paris: Ministère de l'Industrie, 1982), 73.

17. Organisation for Economic Co-operation and Development, *World Steel Trade Developments, 1960–1983* (Paris: OECD, 1985).

18. Vincent Hoffmann-Martinot and Pierre Sadran, "The Local Implementation of

France's National Strategy," in Mény and Wright, eds., *The Politics of Steel,* 538.

19. Raymond Lévy, "Industrial Policy and the Steel Industry," in William J. Adams and Christian Stoffaës, eds., *French Industrial Policy* (Washington, D.C.: Brookings Institution, 1986), 65.

20. Arezki Dahani, "La sidérurgie: Le poids de l'assistance permanente," in Bertrand Bellon and Jean-Marie Chevalier, eds., *L'industrie en France* (Paris: Flammarion, 1983), 121–56; Michel Freyssenet, *La sidérurgie française, 1945–1979: L'histoire d'une faillite, les solutions qui s'affrontent* (Paris: Savelli, 1979); Diana Green, *Managing Industrial Change? French Policies to Promote Industrial Adjustment* (London: Department of Industry, 1981); Jack Hayward, *The State and the Market Economy: Industrial Patriotism and Economic Intervention in France* (London: Wheatsheaf, 1986); Jean G. Padioleau, *Quand la France s'enferre* (Paris: Presses Universitaires de France, 1981); André Signora, "La restructuration de la sidérurgie française," *Revue d'économie politique* 90, no. 6 (1980): 917–27; Christian Stoffaës, "Le dysfonctionnement du système acier," *Revue d'économie industrielle* 8, no. 2 (May 1979): 114–23; Philippe Zarifian, "La politique industrielle dans la sidérurgie française de 1977 à 1983: Le jeu de l'échec," *Cahiers du CRMSI* 9 (August–September 1984): 5–107.

21. John A. MacArthur and Bruce R. Scott, *Industrial Planning in France* (Cambridge: Harvard Graduate School of Business, 1969), 370–71.

22. Victoria Marklew, *Cash, Crisis, and Corporate Governance: The Role of National Financial Systems in Industrial Restructuring* (Ann Arbor: University of Michigan Press, 1995), 85–112.

23. Zarifian, "La politique industrielle dans la sidérurgie," 9–10.

24. Over Fr 18 billion of steel company debt owed to the government (especially the Fonds de Développement Économique et Social) and to private and public banks was converted into "special participatory loans" that bore interest at a token rate of 0.1 percent. Debt was thus converted into assets to be added to the firms' capital. Through this and other measures, about two-thirds of the industry's equity came under state control. See Green, *Managing Industrial Change?,* 28.

25. Parti Socialiste, *Projet socialiste pour la France des années 80* (Paris: Club Socialiste du Livre, 1980), 194.

26. *Le Monde,* 10 October 1981.

27. Key government personnel included Mitterrand, Prime Minister Mauroy, Finance Minister Delors, Budget Minister Fabius, and Industry Minister Dreyfuss. Also important for framing the options were their executive staffs *(cabinets ministeriels)* and industrial specialists. Less central to the negotiations—but still influential—were parliamentarians, mayors, prefects, and other political officials from the steel regions. The industry itself was represented primarily by Usinor and Sacilor management. The CGT, CFDT, and their sectoral and territorial subunits spoke for labor.

28. Predictably, each firm lobbied to protect its own plants and garner new investment funds. One result of their competition for state aid was that the amounts sought were pushed higher and higher and eventually exceeded available state resources. In June 1982, for example, the vice-president of a committee charged with coordinating the two firms' proposals claimed that the Economic and Social Council of Lorraine had requested Fr 13 billion in state subsidies for Lorraine steel, even though the steel industry as a whole was slated to receive only Fr 4–5 billion, and all nationalized industries only Fr 9 billion: *Le Nouveau Journal,* 9 June 1982. The

competition between the two firms for government money would become a major reason for merging them in 1986.

29. Judet, *L'évolution des débouchés de la sidérurgie française.*

30. In line with EC strictures on government aid, the plan also required the major firms to break even by the beginning of 1986. See *Le Monde,* 10 June 1982.

31. Claude Durand et al., "Les syndicats et la politique industrielle du plan acier," *Cahiers du CRMSI* 7 (April–May 1984): 57–58; *Le Matin,* 28 June 1982.

32. These cleavages had been especially sharp during the formulation of the 1979 plan. See Anthony Daley, *Steel, State, and Labor: Mobilization and Adjustment in France* (Pittsburgh: University of Pittsburgh Press, 1996), 140–42.

33. *Le Monde,* 26–27 September 1982.

34. *Libération,* 29 September 1982.

35. Operating losses mounted steadily from Fr 7 billion in 1981 to Fr 11 billion in 1983.

36. Institut Syndical d'Études Recherches Économiques Sociales, *Rapport annuel sur la situation économique et sociale de la France* (Paris: CGT, 1983), 203–04.

37. *Le Matin,* 14 April 1983.

38. In a rare show of unanimity, the unions placed a full-page open letter to Mitterrand in *Le Monde* arguing that the mill, by allowing Lorraine steel to modernize and consolidate, would help restore the region's economic health. See *Le Monde,* 19 March 1984.

39. According to a leading Industry Ministry official at the time, Fabius's steel advisers had opposed the mill on economic grounds, but Fabius himself supported it because he believed France's industry minister should be an advocate for modernization. Author interview with Louis Gallois, general director of industry, 1982–1986, 11 May 1987.

40. Usinor proposed to consolidate production of one type of long product, large beams, at its Valenciennes plant (which would be modernized), and to execute similar consolidation-modernization programs for other long products (rails, small beams, and wire rods) at other existing plants.

41. For a vivid account of this struggle, see Pierre Favier and Michel Martin-Roland, *La décennie Mitterrand,* vol. 2, *Les épreuves* (Paris: Seuil, 1991), 43–70.

42. *Le Matin,* 1 April 1984.

43. *Libération,* 2 April 1984.

44. *L'Humanité,* 13 April 1984.

45. The only serious protest within the PS came from four Lorraine legislators who quit the party's parliamentary group. See *Le Monde,* 2 April 1984.

46. *Le Point,* 9 April 1984.

47. This level of representation was in accordance with the 1983 law on the democratization of the public sector, which stipulated that in all companies of more than 200 employees in which the state held at least 50 percent ownership, the employees would elect one-third of the board of directors. Candidates had to come from lists presented by the major recognized unions.

48. Author interview with Pierre Carémiaux, 17 October 1994.

49. One of the CGT's two representatives on the Usinor Sacilor board of directors said the following in 1994:

All the strategic orientations of the government and steel industry imply that

we suffer from excess production. But when one identifies the social needs of this nation and social needs at the world level, we [the CGT] say it's not possible to conclude that there is excess production. Steel equals social progress. . . . In France, if you look at the state of housing, infrastructure, consumption of intermediate goods, there are so many needs. To say there's too much steel and therefore we have to reduce capacity is like saying, "There's too much milk, we have to kill the cows." But when you have people on the planet dying of hunger, it would be unacceptable to kill cows in France. We can't accept the principle of going along with the dismantling of the steel industry."
Author interview with Pierre Loparelli, 21 October 1994.

50. Author interview with André Signora, 16 September 1994.

51. In 1988 Usinor Sacilor produced 19.5 million tons, making it the second-largest producer in the world after Nippon Steel (28.3 million tons). In 1988 and 1989 Usinor Sacilor led all other steel companies in the world in net profits. See "Usinor-Sacilor: Champion du monde," *L'expansion,* 24 January 1990, 78.

52. See ibid., 76–83; "Lorraine, moral d'acier," *L'express,* 22 June 1990, 72–74.

53. Daley, *Steel, State, and Labor,* 153.

54. *Le Figaro,* 8 March 1993.

55. "France Is Quietly Forging a Steel Empire," *Business Week,* 30 April 1990, 90–91.

56. See, for example, the extensive list in the *Financial Times,* 6 December 1989.

57. Daley, *Steel, State, and Labor,* 156–66; Guy Groux and Catherine Lévy, "Mobilisation collective et productivité économique: Le cas des 'cercles de qualité' dans la sidérurgie," *Revue française de sociologie* 26, no. 1 (January–March 1985): 70–85.

58. Author interview with Pierre Carémiaux, 17 October 1994.

59. The following table traces changes in the work force representation of nonproduction employees (engineers, managers, technicians, and office workers) and direct-production employees (skilled, semiskilled, and unskilled production workers) in the steel industry (figures are percentages):

	1976	1980	1984	1988	1992
Non-production employees	33	37	43	49	57
Direct production employees	67	63	57	51	43

Source: Fédération Française de l'Acier, *Bulletin statisque acier,* various years.

60. In 1983 crude steel output per worker in France was 193.8 tons; the EC national average was 228.6 tons. In 1992 the figures were as follows: EC national average, 371.9 tons; France, 419.6 tons; Italy, 497.6 tons. Figures calculated from International Iron and Steel Institute, *Steel Statistical Yearbook,* various years.

61. The only exception to this positive portrait was Usinor Sacilor's relatively high level of debt. A major criticism of Francis Mer's strategy was that with the return of profits in the late 1980s, the firm focused on expansion abroad rather than on retiring its debt. The firm's debt/capital ratio, which dipped below 1.0 in 1989, afterwards consistently exceeded that figure. See *La Tribune Desfosses,* 15 November 1993.

62. See, for example, Favier and Martin-Roland, *La décennie Mitterrand,* 2:43–70; Jacques Attali, *Verbatim,* vol. 1, *Chronique des années 1981–1986* (Paris: Fayard, 1992), 568–617.

63. Chérèque's official title was préfet délégué de la Lorraine. He remained in that

position until 1988, when he was named junior minister for regional management and reconversion, a post he held until 1991.

64. For example, Chérèque created a regional commission comprising the presidents of Usinor and Sacilor, central government administrators, heads of redevelopment companies (discussed later in this chapter), and Banque de France representatives. This group met monthly to evaluate the progress of income-support and job creation programs. Author interview with Chérèque, 18 October 1994.

65. As of March 1994, the European Development Pole had created nearly 3,000 jobs, with another 4,200 "negotiated": European Development Pole administrative office, personal communication, October 21, 1994.

66. A former CFDT regional official told the following story: "I invited Chérèque to our congress in 1985. I was the only one in the CFDT who agreed to go meet him at the train station—nobody else would do it. There were people in the CFDT who wanted to turn their card in, it was a scandal, there was a kind of riot. The CGT people were also saying to us, 'Ah, Chérèque the prefect is closing factories with the CFDT's approval.' It was very difficult." Author interview with François Introvigne, 18 October 1994.

67. Author interview with Robert Giovanardi, 21 October 1994.

68. Since 1967 several conventions had been signed between management and the unions to regulate departure conditions for workers. Until the 1984 convention, the main emphasis was on age-related measures, particularly the lowering of the retirement age and the age for "preretirement" benefits. There were no provisions for retraining workers or seeking to stimulate new job-creating investment.

69. Because of the focus on eliminating the oldest workers and hiring few young workers, the employee age profile was becoming tightly bunched in the 40–50 year old bracket.

70. Hoffmann-Martinot and Sadran, "The Local Implementation of France's National Strategy," 556–57.

71. The following comments are largely based on interviews with Jacques Stevens, a member of Usinor Sacilor's Social Affairs Department (29 September 1994), and Jean-François De Guillaume, the director of SODIE's Lorraine office (21 October 1994).

72. The main instrument in this effort was the *contrat-formation-conversion* (training-conversion contract) signed by the individual worker and SODIE. Among the labor confederations, the CFDT played a particularly active role in helping to administer the contract program.

73. For a comprehensive list of programs focusing on reconversion aid, including important programs financed by the EU, see Conseil Économique et Social, *L'evaluation de la politique d'aides à la localisation des activités dans les zones de conversion* (Paris: Direction des Journaux Officiels, 1994), 15–19.

74. According to a national survey of SODIE-sponsored workers who had been retrained and had found new jobs, 65 percent claimed that their monthly income was lower than what they had received at Usinor Sacilor. See Cabinet Européen pour le Développement et la Recherche Économique et Sociale, "Perception de l'action de SODIE par les salariés d'Usinor-Sacilor reclassés hors-sidérurgie" (private report, June 1994).

75. For an excellent critique of the government's regional-development efforts, see Daley, *Steel, State, and Labor,* 190–95.

76. A full financial analysis of steel reconversion aid is beyond the scope of this book. We can establish a rough estimate for Lorraine in 1982–1992, however, by noting that aid policies (new investment incentives, worker retraining, and so on) triggered an expenditure of Fr 21 billion (Conseil Économique et Social, *L'evaluation de la politique d'aides*, 492). Income support (early retirement and preretirement) absorbed Fr 5.3 billion (that is, Fr 1 million per worker for 5,300 workers). The total aid package, then, was Fr 26.3 billion, or about $4.8 billion.

77. The largest of these subsectors, comprising the integrated producers, converted iron ore and coke into semifinished or finished steel products using coke ovens, blast furnaces, steelmaking converters, rolling mills, and other equipment. In the early 1980s this subsector consisted of three firms—two nationalized and one private— located in Asturias, the Basque Country, and Valencia. The second subsector, which manufactured what the Spanish called common steel (*acero común*), transformed scrap iron and scrap steel in small electric-arc furnaces (minimills) to produce steel suitable for long products such as reinforcing bars and wire rods. This sector encompassed about thirty firms (mainly private) scattered throughout the country. The specialty steel subsector produced stainless steel and steel alloys. In the early 1980s this subsector included seventeen private firms, located mainly in the Basque Country.

78. Ramón Tamames, *Estructura económica de España*, 19th ed. (Madrid: Alianza Universidad Textos, 1990), 322–23.

79. Howell et al., *Steel and the State*, 374–76; *El País*, 29 November 1980.

80. Tamames, *Estructura económica de España*, 326.

81. In 1973 ENSIDESA absorbed UNINSA, another failing Asturian integrated producer. The UNINSA plant was located near Gijón, ten miles from ENSIDESA's main plant in Avilés.

82. The two private firms had an intertwined history. AHV was established in 1901 with the merger of several smaller firms in the Basque Country. AHM, founded as the independent firm Siderúrgica de Mediterráneo in Valencia in the early 1920s, was bought by AHV in 1940. Thirty-two years later, in 1972, AHV brought in several partners, including U.S. Steel and a number of banks, to participate in a reorganiza- tion of Siderúrgica de Mediterráneo, which was renamed AHM.

83. Luis Albentosa and José Zaragoza, "Estructura y política siderúrgica," *Información comercial española* 591 (November 1982): 75–84.

84. ENSIDESA, the least unsuccessful of the three, had average annual losses of 12.3 percent (based on sales) in 1977–1981, when AHM and AHV posted losses of 39.7 percent and 15.3 percent, respectively: Mikel Navarro Arancegui, *Crisis y reconversión de la siderúrgia española, 1978–1988* (Madrid: Junta del Puerto de Pasajes/ Ministerio de Obras Públicas y Urbanismo, 1989), 16.

85. Tamames, *Estructura económica de España*, 331.

86. It will be recalled that Francoist labor laws, most of which were carried over into the post-Franco democratic system, also gave workers unusually strong job protection.

87. Tamames, *Estructura económica de España*, 16; Eurostat, *Iron and Steel Yearbook 1984* (Brussels: Eurostat, 1985), 14.

88. For example, EC productivity in 1981 was 230 tons per worker, versus Spain's 168. Moreover, Spanish personnel costs (as a percentage of total sales) nearly doubled from 16.4 percent in 1974 to 31.6 percent in 1981. These figures are calculated from

Eurostat, *Iron and Steel Yearbook 1984;* International Iron and Steel Institute, *Steel Statistical Yearbook,* 1983; Navarro Arancegui, *Crisis y reconversión de la siderúrgia española,* 16.

89. The following account focuses mainly on the integrated sector.

90. Navarro Arancegui, *Crisis y reconversión de siderúrgia española,* 92.

91. Mill advocates also pointed to a 1982 technical report by the Kawasaki Steel Corporation which justified a new mill on economic grounds. See *Informaciones,* 3 September 1982.

92. *El País,* 26 February 1983.

93. Miguel Olmos, *La batalla de A.H.M.: Breve historia de la siderúrgia saguntina* (Valencia: Fernando Torres, 1984), 105.

94. As will be recalled from chapter 6, control and oversight committees consisting of government, management, and labor representatives were formed for each of the industrial sectors targeted for reconversion.

95. Author interview with José Fernando Sánchez-Junco, 11 November 1993.

96. Author interview with Adolfo Alonso, general secretary of the UGT Basque Country metalworkers' federation, 4 November 1993. See also "Altos Hornos del Mediterráneo: Las enseñanzas de una lucha," *El metalúrgico* 22 (May 1984): 12.

97. Author interview with Carlos Navarro, 8 July 1994.

98. This decree law then went to the Cortes for final approval. As mentioned in Chapter 6, it was finally approved in November 1983.

99. Oscar Fanjul and Fernando Maravall, "¿A qué ritmo avanza la reconversión industrial en España?" *Papeles de economía española* 21 (1984): 312.

100. The following were the projected job cuts for 1984–1990:

	Workers (N)	Jobs Cut (N)	Reduction (%)
ENSIDESA	21,255	5,755	27.1
AHV	10,676	1,350	20.8
AHM	3,767	1,895	46.6
All three firms	35,698	9,629	27.3

Source: Navarro Arancegui, *Crisis y reconversión de la siderúrgia española,* 96. *Note:* Number of workers as of 31 December 1983.

101. "Altos Hornos de Mediterráneo," 11.

102. Howell et al., *Steel and the State,* 383.

103. Calculated from Alberto Lafuente Félez and Ramón Pérez Simarro, "Balance y perspectivas de las ZUR," *Papeles de economía española* 35 (1988): 221–22.

104. The industry's losses were reduced from PTA 34.3 billion ($274 million) in 1980 to PTA 18.0 billion (about $144 million) in 1986. See Navarro Arancegui, *Crisis y reconversión de la siderúrgia española,* 128.

105. In 1985 production totaled 14.2 million tons, of which 7.8 million (55 percent) was exported, whereas consumption was only 6.1 million tons. Total capacity was about 22 million tons per year, meaning that capacity utilization (production/ capacity) was only 64 percent. See *El País,* 13 April 1987; Tamames, *Estructura económica de España,* 326.

106. In its EC membership treaty, Spain negotiated a three-year exemption (to January 1989) from ECSC strictures, during which time the country could subsidize its

steel industry, although the subsidies had to be negotiated with and approved by the ECSC.

107. An October 1986 report by the McKinsey Group projected that if no further modifications were made to the 1984 plan, AHV would lose PTA 19.8 billion ($158 million) by 1989, versus ENSIDESA's losses of PTA 4.1 billion. See *El País*, 9 December 1986.

108. *Cinco Días*, 24 April 1987.

109. ENSIDESA earned PTA 9.0 billion, while AHV earned PTA 4.4 billion (a total of PTA 13.4 billion, or $107 million, for the two companies). In 1988 they had lost PTA 6.9 billion and PTA 4.6 billion, respectively. See *La Gaceta*, 14–15 October 1989; *El País*, 20, 28 February 1990.

110. Total losses in the integrated subsector were as follows: 1990, PTA 4 billion; 1991, PTA 58 billion; 1992, PTA 84 billion. These figures are from annual reports published by ENSIDESA and AHV.

111. In 1991, for example, it cost AHV $380 and ENSIDESA $350 to produce one ton of hot-rolled strip steel, compared with the European average of $290 per ton. See *El País*, 4 January 1992.

112. In 1985 the surplus was 6.36 million tons; by 1989 it had shrunk to 0.41 million tons: Tamames, *Estructura económica de España*, 326.

113. *Cinco Días*, 22 June 1993.

114. According to the Socialist former president of Asturias, "economic rationality" would have favored concentrating investment in Asturias, but the Basques were "obsessive about keeping that blast furnace [at Sestao]—it's part of their tradition, it's important symbolically." In his view, this "polemic" between the two regions has hindered adjustment in both since the early 1980s. Author interview with Pedro de Silva, 8 November 1993.

115. *Cinco Días*, 9 August 1990.

116. Another part of the plan called for restructuring in the specialty steel subsector at a cost of Ecu 505 million (about $653 million).

117. Corporación de la Siderurgia Integral, "Plan de competitividad de AHV-ENSIDESA," Madrid, April 1992; *Wall Street Journal*, 11 November 1992.

118. Because almost all layoffs would be handled through preretirement packages, the unions focused on the length of time before formal retirement that workers could hold this status, and on what percentage of past income would be used in determining benefits. The unions wanted to preserve the status quo ante that had originated in the restructuring wave of 1984–1990, when the preretirement period was deemed to extend from ages 52 to 65 and the benefit level was set at 80 percent of final salary. CSI management proposed a preretirement period of ages 52 to 60 and a 77.5 percent benefit. Management's plan would have cost an estimated PTA 600 billion ($4.8 billion), whereas the unions' version would have cost PTA 800 billion ($6.4 billion). See Federación de Metal-Vizcaya, "Alternativa de UGT al plan de competitividad de la CSI para A.H.V" (1992); *La Voz de Asturias*, 27 August 1992; *La Vanguardia*, 25 November 1992.

119. *Wall Street Journal*, 20 October 1992.

120. *El País*, 15, 16 October 1992.

121. *Wall Street Journal*, 11 November 1992.

122. See "Acuerdo sobre cobertura socio laboral para los trabajadores excedentes del

plan de competitividad de la Corporación de la Siderurgia Integral," 19 January 1993. This agreement was signed by the UGT, the Unión Sindical Obrera, and the Confederación de Cuadros (a union for managers and executives), but not by the CCOO.

123. *La Vanguardia,* 18 December 1993.

124. Houseman, *Industrial Restructuring with Job Security,* 27–45.

125. *Le Monde,* 8 July 1995.

126. Author interview with Acacio Rodríguez García, the chief operating officer of the CSI, 1 July 1994.

127. As a postscript, CSI's situation had changed by mid-1997. Following the PSOE's defeat in the March 1996 elections, the new government led by Prime Minister José María Aznar encouraged CSI to find a "strategic foreign investor," and in August 1997 CSI completed a share swap and merger arrangement with the private Belgian producer, Arbed—an arrangement that partially privatized CSI. Henceforth, the new Arbed-CSI group could boast of the second largest combined output in Europe after British Steel. See *Financial Times,* August 1, 1997.

128. All figures in this paragraph were calculated from company annual reports.

CHAPTER 9. RESTRUCTURING IN THE AUTOMOBILE INDUSTRY

1. The industry defines automobiles to include coupes, sedans, station wagons, minivans, sport-utility vehicles, and light trucks. Automobiles account for the bulk of motor vehicle production.

2. Peter F. Cowhey and Jonathan D. Aronson, *Managing the World Economy: The Consequences of Corporate Alliances* (New York: Council on Foreign Relations Press, 1993), 93.

3. See, for example, James P. Womack, Daniel T. Jones, and Daniel Roos, *The Machine That Changed the World* (New York: Rawson Associates, 1990); Davis Dyer, Malcolm S. Salter, and Alan M. Webber, *Changing Alliances* (Boston: Harvard Business School Press, 1987); Michael A. Cusumano, *The Japanese Automobile Industry* (Cambridge: Harvard University Press, 1985); David Halberstam, *The Reckoning* (New York: William Morrow, 1986); Harry C. Katz and Charles F. Sabel, "Industrial Relations and Industrial Adjustment in the Car Industry," *Industrial Relations* 24, no. 3 (fall 1985): 295–315.

4. Some European nations gave the Japanese fairly open access to their markets and allowed them to acquire a sizable market share. *Le Monde,* 21 March 1989, reported that the following shares of national auto sales went to Japanese firms in 1988: Ireland, 42 percent; Greece, 35 percent; Denmark, 33 percent; the Netherlands, 26 percent; Belgium, 21 percent. Nations that sharply limited Japanese access included Spain (0.1 percent), Italy (0.7 percent), France (3 percent), and Portugal (8 percent).

5. Japan's market share would be permitted to rise from 11 percent in 1991 to 16 percent by 2000, with most of the increase coming from Japanese plants operating in EC countries. See *Le Monde,* 28–29 July 1991; Jean-Pierre Lehmann, "France, Japan, Europe, and Industrial Competition: The Automotive Case," *International Affairs* 68, no. 1 (January 1992): 47–49.

6. According to two leading authorities writing in 1994, "quite literally no one in either Japan or Europe believes" that Japanese imports will flow freely into Europe after 1999. See James P. Womack and Daniel T. Jones, "European Automotive Policy: Past, Present, and Future," in Glennon J. Harrison, ed., *Europe and the United States:*

Competition and Cooperation in the 1990s (Armonk: M. E. Sharpe, 1994), 209.

7. On the German industry's performance, see Wolfgang Streeck, "Successful Adjustment to Turbulent Markets: The Automobile Industry," in Peter J. Katzenstein, ed., *Industry and Politics in West Germany: Towards the Third Republic* (Ithaca: Cornell University Press, 1989), 113–56.

8. The following were the European market shares of the six main European producers in 1980 and 1984 (figures are percentages):

	1980	1984	1980–84
Renault	14.7	10.9	–3.8
Peugeot	14.6	11.5	–3.1
Volkswagen	12.0	12.0	0.0
Fiat	11.8	12.7	0.9
Ford	11.0	12.8	1.8
General Motors	8.4	11.0	3.6
Other	27.4	29.1	1.7

Source: New York Times, 2 June 1985.

9. These acquisitions led to the creation of a new corporate entity, Peugeot Société Anonyme (PSA), which had two main divisions. The first, Automobiles Peugeot, included the original Peugeot firm and Talbot. The second was Automobiles Citroën. As was the case at General Motors, both divisions were under a single CEO and management board.

10. *Le Monde,* 21–22 December 1980.

11. For a participant-observer view of work inside a Citroën plant, see Robert Linhart, *The Assembly Line* (Amherst: University of Massachusetts Press, 1981).

12. Interview with the author, 18 December 1990.

13. *Le Monde,* 12, 14 May 1982.

14. Local unions involved in these negotiations included, in addition to the CGT and the CSL, the CFDT, the FO, the CFTC, and the CGC.

15. *Le Figaro,* 8 September 1982.

16. *Le Monde,* 18, 25 February 1983.

17. *Le Monde,* 14 July 1983.

18. Quoted in *Le Figaro,* 16–17 July 1983.

19. As readers will recall, the Left had performed poorly in the March 1983 municipal elections.

20. Interview with the author, 18 December 1990.

21. Ibid.

22. In October, however, the government did approve that part of Peugeot's restructuring plan that involved moving 4,300 Talbot workers to preretirement status.

23. The Inspection du Travail had to approve all plans for mass layoffs.

24. *Le Monde,* 14 December 1983.

25. Author interview with Pierre Héritier, head of the CFDT's Economic Section, 24 April 1987. See also the strike analysis prepared by the CFDT's Talbot Section, *L'effet Talbot ou les raisons profondes d'un conflit* (Poissy, 1984).

26. Quoted in *Le Point,* 16 January 1984. In more colorful language, the head of the CFDT metalworkers' federation said: "All it takes today is for a government minister to say that shit tastes like jam, and everybody says it's jam. The CFDT says

no. Shit is always shit. The government thinks that because it is a government of the Left it knows what is good for the workers. And when workers don't understand they're stupid (*cons*)." Quoted in *Libération*, 7 January 1984.

27. The Citroën plan would cut 6,000 jobs, 2,937 by layoffs. Most of the layoffs would occur at the Aulnay-sous-Bois plant.

28. For the CGT perspective, see the interview with metalworkers' federation leader André Sainjon in *Révolution*, 18 May 1984.

29. *Les Echos*, 7 June 1984.

30. Interview with the author, 9 December 1987.

31. As chapter 8 noted, the second steel restructuring plan was formulated in March 1984.

32. Metalworkers' federation leader Sainjon, however, remained in contact with the government, even though General Secretary Krasucki and most of the CGT leadership were hostile to further dealings with the government. Sainjon remarked that his penchant for compromise and negotiation led PCF "hard-liners" in the CGT to condemn him as "reformist." Interview with the author, 18 December 1990.

33. As had happened with Talbot, the number of layoffs originally requested by Citroën was reduced by about a thousand, from 2,937 to 1,909. See *Le Monde*, 25 August 1984.

34. *La Tribune Desfosses*, 4 February 1993.

35. *Tribune de l'Expansion*, 27 July 1990.

36. This refers to the negotiations between employers, unions, and the government held at the Labor Ministry's Rue de Grenelle offices in May 1968, which resulted in a large rise in real wages.

37. Quoted in *Le Monde*, 17–18 September 1989.

38. Pierre Mathiot and René Mouriaux, *Conflictualité en France depuis 1986: Le cas de Peugeot-Sochaux* (Paris: CEVIPOF, 1992).

39. Interview with the author, 17 December 1990.

40. Author interview with Christian Stoffaës, 30 November 1990.

41. Interview with the author, 17 December 1990.

42. For example, despite a loss of Fr 2 billion in 1981–1982, Renault devoted the enormous sum of Fr 17 billion to investment in new production technologies during those two years. Peugeot spent only about half as much on new production technologies during that period. See *Le Monde*, 27 May 1982.

43. Ahmed Bounfour, *L'avenir de l'industrie automobile mondiale: Quelles stratégies?* (Paris: Documentation Française, 1987), 129.

44. See, for example, Carl Cavanagh Hodge, "The Future of Four Wheels: Government and the Automobile Industry in France and West Germany, 1971–1985," *Governance* 4, no. 1 (January 1991): 42–66; Ben Dankbaar, "Sectoral Governance in the Automobile Industries of Germany, Great Britain, and France," in J. Rogers Hollingsworth et al., eds., *Governing Capitalist Economies: Performance and Control of Economic Sectors* (New York: Oxford University Press, 1994), 156–82; Pierre Naville et al., *L'état entrepreneur: Le cas de la Régie Renault* (Paris: Editions Anthropos, 1971).

45. Author interview with Christian Morel, 13 December 1990.

46. As was mentioned earlier, following the Talbot conflict in January 1984 the government sought to avoid further labor explosions by becoming much more amenable to consultation.

47. *Le Monde*, 25 September, 17 October 1984; *Financial Times*, 3 October 1984.

48. Author interview with Pierre Amouyel, Renault's chief economist, 30 September 1994. For a summary of the work of this commission, which was headed by L'Oréal president and Mitterrand friend François Dalle, see "L'industrie automobile française," *Liaison Sociales*, 24 October 1984.

49. Interview with the author, 17 December 1990.

50. *Le Matin*, 10 May 1985.

51. *Les Echos*, 15 October 1985.

52. *Le Monde*, 17 October 1985.

53. Interviews with Renault executives elicited several anecdotes attesting to Besse's autonomy, such as one relating to an official trip to the USSR by Mitterrand, who brought along Besse and several other CEOs. At one point, Mitterrand asked Besse to build a plant in the USSR. According to Pierre Amouyel, "Besse just said no, and that was the end of it." Interview with the author, 30 September 1994.

54. *Le Monde*, 9 November 1990.

55. Although losses continued under Besse, they shrank from Fr 10.9 billion in 1985 to Fr 5.5 billion in 1986, according to Renault's annual reports. Worker productivity jumped 26 percent during that period: *Financial Times*, 1 October 1986.

56. *Business Week*, 21 August 1989.

57. The proposed change in status was from *régie* to *société anonyme*. Renault's *régie* status, established when the firm was nationalized in 1945, shielded it from bankruptcy.

58. *Wall Street Journal*, 30 March 1988.

59. *Le Monde*, 29–30 April 1990.

60. *Tribune de l'Expansion*, 23 May 1990.

61. In a move that stunned Swedish and French officials, Volvo stockholders revolted against the merger. This was followed in early December 1993 by the Volvo board's rejection of the merger, whereupon the board's chairman, Pehr Gyllenhammar, "architect of the deal and ardent supporter of Swedish integration into the European Community," resigned. See *New York Times*, 19 December 1993.

62. *The Financial Times*, 18 July 1996.

63. SEAT was not the first such venture. In 1946 the Franco government established a truck-building firm, Empresa Nacional de Autocamiones, S.A. (ENASA), through collaboration with the private firm Hispano Suiza. On SEAT's early history, see Pablo Martín Aceña and Francisco Comín Comín, *INI, 50 años de industrialización en España* (Madrid: Espasa Calpe, 1991), 228–29; Ramón Tamames, *Estructura económica de España*, 19th ed. (Madrid: Alianza Universidad Textos, 1990), 345–46; Eulàlia Solé, *SEAT 1950–1993* (Barcelona: Ediciones de la Tempestad, 1994), 20–26.

64. Initially, SEAT's capital structure was as follows: INI, 51 percent; six Spanish banks (notably Banco Urquijo), 42 percent; Fiat, 7 percent.

65. Tamames, *Estructura económica de España*, 345; *El País*, 26 September 1993.

66. Solé, *SEAT*, 59–60.

67. Tamames, *Estructura económica de España*, 345.

68. Imports jumped from 7,700 units in 1978 to 36,000 units in 1980. See Solé, *SEAT*, 76.

69. SEAT lost PTA 45.6 billion (about $365 million) in 1978–1980, the first substantial losses in the firm's history: ibid., 74, 81.

70. Fiat had already increased its ownership share in SEAT to 36 percent in 1967 (at which time the INI's share dropped to 35 percent).

71. According to this agreement, Volkswagen would sell SEAT cars through its European sales network and produce 120,000 cars a year using SEAT facilities.

72. *El País,* 2 January 1985.

73. In 1980 the main non-Spanish producers were as follows (figures are units produced):

FASA-Renault	324,680
Ford	260,005
Citroën	84,836
Peugeot-Talbot	65,756
Total	735,277

Source: Tamames, *Estructura económica de España,* 345.
Note: General Motors did not begin production until 1982.

74. Manuel Castells et al., *Neuvas tecnologías, economía, y sociedad en España* (Madrid: Alianza Editorial, 1986), 2:576.

75. Author interview with José Fernando Sánchez-Junco, 11 November 1993.

76. José Fernando Sánchez-Junco, "La política de reconversión industrial" (text of press conference remarks), 12 December 1987; *El País,* 3 October 1985.

77. *Cinco Días,* 1 June 1992.

78. *Le Monde,* 13 June 1992; *El País,* 15 October 1993.

79. From 1984 through 1986, the firm's annual losses varied from PTA 28 billion to PTA 36 billion. Its cumulative losses for 1984–1986 were PTA 101 billion ($808 million). See *La Gaceta de los Negocios,* 25 May 1989.

80. *El País,* 14 February 1993.

81. The Martorell plant came on line in early 1993. See *El País,* 23 February 1993.

82. In 1988–1991, SEAT earned PTA 23.2 billion ($186 million), which can be compared with its loss of PTA 104.5 billion ($836 million) in 1984–1987.

83. Taking the labor costs (gross hourly wage and social costs) of the Spanish motor vehicle industry in 1988 as 100, motor vehicle industry labor costs in other countries were as follows: West Germany, 176; Italy, 127; France, 113; United Kingdom, 103. Calculated from figures in the *Financial Times,* 22 February 1989.

84. SEAT's president remarked, "We have to keep clear that the costs of capital in Spain are double, but the costs of labor are half the German level": ibid.

85. Societat de Gestió Comarcal, *Crisis SEAT: Crisis componentes automoción* (Sant Just Desvern, Spain: Societat de Gestió Comarcal, 1993), 41.

86. In 1994 an estimated 50,000 to 70,000 workers were employed by SEAT's parts suppliers. Author interview with José Antonio Estudillo, the UGT official responsible for SEAT affairs in Barcelona and the Zona Franca, 13 July 1994; *El País,* 5 January 1994.

87. For example, in SEAT's "strategic and industrial plan" for 1989–1998, the Zona Franca was to receive only PTA 142 billion, compared with PTA 220 billion for Martorell. Moreover, only PTA 28 billion of the Zona Franca's sum was set aside for the years 1993–1998, whereas Martorell would receive PTA 74 billion during that period. See *El País,* 10 November 1988.

88. The authors of MIT's International Motor Vehicle Program study declared, "We expect that Eastern Europe will replace Spain as the production locale for the most

inexpensive, basic cars and trucks": Womack et al., *The Machine That Changed the World*, 267.

89. Volkswagen's faltering performance—it suffered losses of DM 700 million ($320 million) in 1991—was attributable to several factors, especially high German labor costs and the firm's strategic failures, including its collapse in the North American market. In 1990 it sold only 70,000 cars in the United States, whereas in the early 1970s it had sold over 500,000 annually. As for SEAT, after turning a profit of PTA 8.5 billion in 1991, it piled up losses of PTA 12.8 billion in 1992. See *El País*, 27 September 1991.

90. Most of the costs were linked to investment loans for the Martorell facility, many of which came from German banks and even from Volkswagen itself, and thus were denominated in deutsche marks. Moreover, imported parts from Volkswagen were also charged to SEAT in transfer prices counted in marks. All of these costs ballooned when the peseta was devalued. To a large extent, therefore, SEAT's debts and operating losses in 1992 and 1993 were the result of its ties to Volkswagen. See *Wall Street Journal*, 15 September 1993.

91. "Acuerdo: Expediente regulación de empleo," Generalitat de Catalunya, Barcelona, 20 April 1993.

92. SEAT president Juan Antonio Díaz Alvarez predicted in June that 1993 losses would be about PTA 12 billion, but by September it was clear that they would exceed PTA 100 billion. See *El País*, 20 September 1993.

93. *El País*, 3 October 1993.

94. According to a CCOO official involved in the management of the SEAT crisis, Volkswagen favored SEAT's partial nationalization because that was one of the few legal ways SEAT could receive state aid and still comply with EU competition policy. At the same time, Volkswagen would lose none of its technological or commercial control over SEAT, even if the government held part of SEAT's capital. Author interview with Simón Rosaldo, 14 July 1994.

95. *El País*, 12 October 1993.

96. Author interviews with UGT and CCOO officials at SEAT's Barcelona headquarters, 13 July 1994.

97. *El País*, 3 November 1993.

98. *El País*, 10 November 1993.

99. All of the points mentioned in this paragraph are contained in the agreement approved by the regional government. See Generalitat de Catalunya, Departament de Treball, Direció General de Relacions Laborals, "Expediente de regulación de empleo," Barcelona, 15 December 1993.

100. *Cinco Días*, 11 May 1994; *El Mundo*, 20 May 1994.

101. Quoted in *El País*, 1 June 1994.

102. After the 1993 elections, in which the PSOE gained only 159 of 350 legislative seats, González formed a coalition with Pujol's 17-seat party, Convergència i Unió. Pujol's support was thus critical for the government's survival.

103. *ABC*, 27 June 1994; *Wall Street Journal*, 11 July 1994.

104. "Acuerdo entre Volkswagen A.G., SEAT S.A., el Ministerio de Industria y Energía, y la Generalitat de Catalunya," Madrid, 11 July 1994.

105. In 1990–1994 SEAT's work force shrank by 42 percent (from 21,592 to 12,553 workers) while production dropped 37 percent (from 500,000 to 313,000 units annually. See *El País*, 10 July 1995.

106. For case studies of auto industry adjustment in several Western European nations, see (in addition to sources cited in note 3) James Laux, *The European Automobile Industry* (New York: Twayne, 1992); Lowell Turner, *Democracy at Work: Changing World Markets and the Future of Labor Unions* (Ithaca: Cornell University Press, 1991); Victoria Marklew, *Cash, Crisis, and Corporate Governance: The Role of National Financial Systems in Industrial Restructuring* (Ann Arbor: University of Michigan Press, 1995); Miriam A. Golden, *Heroic Defeats: The Politics of Job Loss* (Cambridge: Cambridge University Press, 1997), ch. 3.

CHAPTER 10. CONCLUSION

1. Robert D. Putnam, "Diplomacy and Domestic Politics: The Logic of Two-Level Games," *International Organization* 42, no. 3 (summer 1988): 434.

2. For an interesting discussion of the fate of this plan, see Jonas Pontusson, *The Limits of Social Democracy: Investment Politics in Sweden* (Ithaca: Cornell University Press, 1992), esp. ch. 7.

3. See Susan N. Houseman, *Industrial Restructuring with Job Security: The Case of European Steel* (Cambridge: Harvard University Press, 1991); Bo Strath, *The Politics of De-industrialization: The Contraction of the West European Shipbuilding Industry* (London: Croom Helm, 1987).

4. See, for example, the sources cited in chapter 1, note 36.

5. See, for example, Pontusson, *The Limits of Social Democracy;* Sven Steinmo, "Social Democracy vs. Socialism: Goal Adaptation in Social Democratic Sweden," *Politics & Society* 16, no. 4 (1988): 403–46; Peter Swenson, "Bringing Capital Back In, or Social Democracy Reconsidered: Employer Power, Cross-class Alliances, and Centralization of Industrial Relations in Denmark and Sweden," *World Politics* 43, no. 4 (July 1991): 513–44.

6. David R. Cameron, "Exchange Rate Politics in France, 1981–1983: The Regime-Defining Choices of the Mitterrand Presidency," in Anthony Daley, ed., *The Mitterrand Era: Policy Alternatives and Political Mobilization in France* (New York: New York University Press, 1996), 58.

7. For an extensive comparative analysis of political restructuring by European social-democratic parties, see Herbert Kitschelt, *The Transformation of European Social Democracy* (Cambridge: Cambridge University Press, 1994). See also Thomas A. Koelble's analysis of union-party relations in social-democratic movements, "Recasting Social Democracy in Europe: A Nested Games Explanation of Strategic Adjustment in Political Parties," *Politics & Society* 20, no. 1 (March 1992): 51–70.

8. Pontusson, *The Limits of Social Democracy,* ch. 7.

9. This is convincingly demonstrated for the British Labour Party by Mark Wickham-Jones's study of the party's attempt to regain the political favor of business interests during its time in opposition. See "Anticipating Social Democracy, Preempting Expectations: Economic Policy-Making in the British Labour Party, 1987–1992," *Politics & Society* 23, no. 4 (December 1995): 465–94.

INDEX